Communications in Computer and Information Science 1556

More information about this series at https://link.springer.com/bookseries/7899

Raian Ali · Hermann Kaindl ·
Leszek A. Maciaszek (Eds.)

Evaluation of Novel Approaches to Software Engineering

16th International Conference, ENASE 2021
Virtual Event, April 26–27, 2021
Revised Selected Papers

Editors
Raian Ali
Hamad bin Khalifa University
Doha, Qatar

Hermann Kaindl
TU Wien
Vienna, Austria

Leszek A. Maciaszek
Wrocław University of Economics
Wrocław, Poland

Macquarie University
Sydney, Australia

ISSN 1865-0929 ISSN 1865-0937 (electronic)
Communications in Computer and Information Science
ISBN 978-3-030-96647-8 ISBN 978-3-030-96648-5 (eBook)
https://doi.org/10.1007/978-3-030-96648-5

This Springer imprint is published by the registered company Springer Nature Switzerland AG
The registered company address is: Gewerbestrasse 11, 6330 Cham, Switzerland

Preface

The present book includes extended and revised versions of a set of selected papers from the 16th International Conference on Evaluation of Novel Approaches to Software Engineering (ENASE 2021), held as an online event during April 26–27, 2021.

ENASE 2021 received 96 paper submissions from authors in 30 countries, of which 16% are finally included in this book as extended versions. These papers were selected by the event chairs and their selection is based on a number of criteria that include the classifications and comments provided by the Program Committee members, the session chairs' assessment, and also the program chairs' global view of all papers included in the technical program. The authors of selected papers were then invited to submit revised and extended versions of their papers having at least 30% innovative material.

The mission of ENASE is to be a prime international forum to discuss and publish research findings and IT industry experiences with relation to novel approaches to software engineering. The conference acknowledges evolution in systems and software thinking due to contemporary shifts of computing paradigm to e-services, cloud computing, mobile connectivity, business processes, and societal participation. By publishing the latest research on novel approaches to software engineering and by evaluating them against systems and software quality criteria, ENASE conferences advance knowledge and research in software engineering, including and emphasizing service-oriented, business-process driven, and ubiquitous mobile computing. ENASE aims at identifying most hopeful trends and proposing new directions for consideration by researchers and practitioners involved in large-scale systems and software development, integration, deployment, delivery, maintenance, and evolution.

The papers included in this book contribute to the understanding of relevant trends of current research on novel approaches to software engineering for the development and maintenance of systems and applications, specifically with relation to software for social media, (end-)user-centered design, user interfaces, software engineering education, enterprise information systems, business process engineering, requirements engineering, development process, software architecture, and code mining.

We would like to thank all the authors for their contributions and the reviewers for ensuring the quality of this publication.

April 2021

Raian Ali
Hermann Kaindl
Leszek Maciaszek

Preface

Organization

Conference Chair

Leszek Maciaszek	Wroclaw University of Economics and Business, Poland, and Macquarie University, Australia

Program Co-chairs

Raian Ali	Hamad Bin Khalifa University, Qatar
Hermann Kaindl	TU Wien, Austria

Program Committee

Wasif Afzal	MDH, Sweden
Issa Atoum	World Islamic Sciences and Education University, Jordan
Marco Autili	University of L'Aquila, Italy
Richard Banach	University of Manchester, UK
Ellen Barbosa	University of São Paulo, Brazil
Jan Blech	Aalto University, Finland
Iuliana Bocicor	Babes-Bolyai University, Romania
Ugo Buy	University of Illinois at Chicago, USA
Ahmet Cakir	ERGONOMIC Institut, Germany
Serban Camelia	Babes-Bolyai University, Romania
Glauco Carneiro	Universidade Salvador (UNIFACS), Brazil
Anis Charfi	Carnegie Mellon University, Qatar
Guglielmo De Angelis	IASI-CNR, Italy
Fatma Dhaou	University of Tunis El Manar, Tunisia
Mahmoud EL Hamlaoui	University of Mohammed V in Rabat, Morocco
Anna Fasolino	Università degli Studi di Napoli Federico II, Italy
Maria Ferreira	Universidade Portucalense, Portugal
Massimo Ficco	University of Campania Luigi Vanvitelli, Italy
Stéphane Galland	Université de Technologie de Belfort Montbéliard, France
José Garcia-Alonso	Universidad de Extremadura, Spain
Nicolas Gold	University College London, UK
John Grundy	Monash University, Australia

Lukasz Radlinski	West Pomeranian University of Technology in Szczecin, Poland
Philippe Roose	IUT de Bayonne et du Pays Basque, France
Gunter Saake	Institute of Technical and Business Information Systems, Germany
Gwen Salaün	Grenoble INP and Inria, France
Richa Sharma	Lock Haven University, USA
Josep Silva	Universitat Politècnica de València, Spain
Riccardo Sisto	Polytechnic University of Turin, Italy
Michal Smialek	Warsaw University of Technology, Poland
Ioana Sora	Politehnica University of Timisoara, Romania
Andreas Speck	Christian-Albrechts-Universität zu Kiel, Germany
Maria Spichkova	RMIT University, Australia
Witold Staniszkis	Rodan Development, Poland
Chang-ai Sun	University of Science and Technology Beijing, China
Jakub Swacha	University of Szczecin, Poland
Stephanie Teufel	University of Fribourg, Switzerland
Francesco Tiezzi	University of Camerino, Italy
Porfirio Tramontana	University of Naples Federico II, Italy
Hanh Nhi Tran	University of Toulouse, France
Christos Troussas	University of West Attica, Greece
Andreea Vescan	Babes-Bolyai University, Romania
Bernhard Westfechtel	University of Bayreuth, Germany
Martin Wirsing	Ludwig-Maximilians-Universität München, Germany
Igor Wojnicki	AGH University of Science and Technology, Poland
Sebastian Wrede	Bielefeld University, Germany
Dinghao Wu	Pennsylvania State University, USA
Jifeng Xuan	Wuhan University, China
Nina Yevtushenko	Ivannikov Institute for System Programming of the Russian Academy of Sciences, Russia
Alfred Zimmermann	Reutlingen University, Germany

Additional Reviewers

Mohammad Aldabbas	University of Fribourg, Switzerland
Peter Alexander	RWTH Aachen University, Germany
Selin Aydin	RWTH Aachen University, Germany
Daniele Bringhenti	Politecnico di Torino, Italy
Maxime Labonne	Airbus Defence and Space, France
Erick Petersen	Institut Polytechnique de Paris, France

Christian Plewnia	RWTH Aachen University, Germany
Alex Sabau	RWTH Aachen University, Germany
Nils Wild	RWTH Aachen University, Germany

Invited Speakers

Stefan Kramer	Johannes Gutenberg-Universität Mainz, Germany
Panos Markopoulos	Eindhoven University of Technology, The Netherlands
John Grundy	Monash University, Australia

Contents

Theory and Practice of Systems and Applications Development

Validating *HyDe*: Intelligent Method for Inferring Software Architectures from Mobile Codebase 3
Dragoş Dobrean and Laura Dioşan

Considerations for Indigenous Cultural Aspects in Software Development: A Case Study 29
Philemon Yalamu, Abdullah Al Mahmud, and Caslon Chua

Modelling Age of End-Users Using Wire-Frames 44
Hourieh Khalajzadeh, Tanjila Kanij, Aria YukFan Jim, Hyun Shim, Jue Wang, Lionel Richie Wijaya, Rongbin Xu, and John Grundy

A Framework for Privacy and Security Requirements Analysis and Conflict Resolution for Supporting GDPR Compliance Through Privacy-by-Design 67
Duaa Alkubaisy, Luca Piras, Mohammed Ghazi Al-Obeidallah, Karl Cox, and Haralambos Mouratidis

The Relevance of Privacy Concerns, Trust, and Risk for Hybrid Social Media 88
Angela Borchert, Aidmar Wainakh, Nicole Krämer, Max Mühlhäuser, and Maritta Heisel

From Business Process Textual Description to BPEL Models 112
Wiem Khlif, Nadia Aloui, and Nourchène Elleuch Ben Ayed

XtraLibD: Detecting Irrelevant Third-Party Libraries in Java and Python Applications 132
Ritu Kapur, Poojith U. Rao, Agrim Dewam, and Balwinder Sodhi

Automation of the Software Development Process from ReLEL Using the Praxeme Approach 156
Rapatsalahy Miary Andrianjaka, Mahatody Thomas, Livaniaina Razanakolona, Ilie Mihaela, Razafimahatratra Hajarisena, Ilie Sorin, and Razafindrakoto Nicolas Raft

Stakeholder-Centric Clustering Methods for Conflict Resolution in the Requirements Engineering Process 183
Ishaya Gambo and Kuldar Taveter

Challenges and Novel Approaches to Systems and Software Engineering (SSE)

CitrusGenome: Applying User Centered Design for Evaluating the Usability of Genomic User Interfaces 213
Alberto García S., Carlos Iñiguez-Jarrín, Oscar Pastor Lopez, Daniel Gonzalez-Ibea, Estela Pérez-Román, Carles Borredà, Javier Terol, Victoria Ibanez, and Manuel Talón

Addressing the Influence of End User Human Aspects on Software Engineering 241
John Grundy, Ingo Mueller, Anuradha Madugalla, Hourieh Khalajzadeh, Humphrey O. Obie, Jennifer McIntosh, and Tanjila Kanij

Gender Classification Models and Feature Impact for Social Media Author Profiling 265
Paloma Piot-Perez-Abadin, Patricia Martin-Rodilla, and Javier Parapar

Agile Mindset Adoption in Student Team Projects 288
Simona Motogna, Dan Mircea Suciu, and Arthur-Jozsef Molnar

Systems and Software Quality

Ontology-Based Natural Language Processing for Process Compliance Management 309
Muhammad Atif Javed, Faiz Ul Muram, and Samina Kanwal

UI-Test: A Model-Based Framework for Visual UI Testing– Qualitative and Quantitative Evaluation 328
Bryan Alba, Maria Fernanda Granda, and Otto Parra

Author Index 357

Theory and Practice of Systems and Applications Development

Validating *HyDe*: Intelligent Method for Inferring Software Architectures from Mobile Codebase

Dragoş Dobrean(✉) and Laura Dioşan

Computer Science Department, Babes Bolyai University, Cluj Napoca, Romania
{dobreand,lauras}@cs.ubbcluj.ro

Abstract. Interacting with businesses, searching for information, or accessing news and entertainment sources all have a common feature, they are predominately accessed nowadays from mobile applications. The software architecture used in building those kinds of products represents a major factor in their lifecycle, costs, and roadmap, as it affects their maintainability and extensibility. In this study, our novel approach designed for detecting MVC architectural layers from mobile codebases (that use SDK for building their UI interrfaces) is validated and analysed from various perspectives (Artificial Intelligence, architectural rules, empiric evaluation). Our proposal is validated on eight different-sized iOS codebases corresponding to different mobile applications that have different scopes (both open and closed source). The performance of the detection quality is measured by the accuracy of the system, as we compared to a manually constructed ground truth, achieving an average accuracy of **85%** on all the analyzed codebases. Our hybrid approach for detecting architectural layers achieves good results by combining the accuracy of the deterministic methods with the flexibility for being used on other architectural patterns and platforms via the non-deterministic step. We also validate the workflow of the proposal from an empirical point of view through an interview with two mobile application developers.

Keywords: Mobile applications software architecture analyser · Automatic analysis of software architectures · Structural and lexical information · Software clustering · Hybrid approach

1 Introduction and Context

With over two-thirds of the world's population using them [21], smartphones have become our most personal device. We use these devices for communicating with others, entertainment, analyzing our health, ordering food, exercising, finding a date, and so much more. Slowly they have even started to be a replacement for wallets, as they allow us to make payments, store digital tickets, and validate the identity of the owner.

In the beginning, mobile applications were simple pieces of software that most often handled a small number of states and displayed data obtained from a server. Later, this kind of software became quite complex, and nowadays mobile apps do a lot of processing on the device itself, they run Artificial Intelligence algorithms, manipulate and

R. Ali et al. (Eds.): ENASE 2021, CCIS 1556, pp. 3–28, 2022.
https://doi.org/10.1007/978-3-030-96648-5_1

store databases, handle and process information from all kinds of sensors (gyroscope, LiDar, GPS, accelerometer, etc.) and do heavy, high-performance computer graphics processing. With the increased complexity of the apps, rapid hardware advancements, and huge market demand for new and exciting features, software architecture has come to play a major role in the lifecycle of mobile products.

With this study, we are furthering our work [12] towards creating an autonomous system for improving the architectural health of those projects since a large number of the mobile codebases do not have a well defined architectural pattern in place, or even if they do, it is not consistently implemented all over the codebase [11]. In [16] we have presented our hybrid approach for solving the problem of inferring architectural layers from mobile codebases, we called it *HyDe*. With *HyDe* we continue our pursuit in developing new and novel ways for automatically detecting the architectural layers (and their composition) of mobile codebases. Our hybrid approach takes advantage of the software development kits (SDKs) used in building those kinds of applications. By using the information from those SDKs insightful data can be extracted regarding the types of the components in the codebase and the architectural layer they should reside in. In addition to the usage of information from SDKs, Machine Learning (ML) techniques are also involved in some of the introduced approaches for aiding the process of categorizing the components of a mobile codebase in architectural layers.

With this study, we pave the way for building a system capable of identifying architectural issues early, in the development phase, or Continuous Integration (CI)/Continuous Delivery (CD) pipelines, and to lay a strong foundation of knowledge that could also be applied to other platforms. Such a system would benefit both developers as well as managers as it could provide insightful information regarding the architectural health of a codebase, and would also be capable of showing the progress as is being made in long refactoring periods. An architecture checker system would also benefit beginner developers or new developers on a project, as it would allow them to spot architectural issues while they are developing new features. More experienced developers could also use it when reviewing the code submitted by others.

Mobile startups are another area where such a system would be valuable, as it could help them implement a certain software architecture in their minimum viable products that would later be able to support the full product.

Education is another area where such a system would be useful, as architectural issues are very common in the code written by students. By having a system that highlights the architectural issues in the projects they develop, they would grow to be much more experienced from an architectural point of view and would implement systems that are flexible, testable, and maintainable.

In [13] we have presented our purely deterministic approach for automatically detecting architectural layers, in [15] we have furthered that research by solving the same problem using Machine Learning techniques. Our newest proposal is a hybrid one in which our two previous approaches (the deterministic and non-deterministic ones) are combined. By using a hybrid approach, we try to obtain the accuracy of the deterministic methods while taking advantage of the flexibility of the non-deterministic approach and to pave the way for more specialized architecture detection (such as MVVM, MVP, VIPER, etc.), we call this approach *HyDe* (Hybrid Detection).

The purpose of this study is to find a viable way of combining the deterministic methods (such as SDK inheritance) with non-deterministic ones into a hybrid approach capable of analyzing mobile codebases and flexible enough to support enhancements for the analysis of other non-mobile codebases or more specialized architectures.

Research Challenges. The main challenges of these research topics are:

- architecture detection using a combined approach (deterministic + non-deterministic);
- a clustering process that works while combined with the information obtained from the deterministic process;
- automatically inferring the architectural layers of an MVC codebase that uses an SDK for building the user interfaces—as those SDKs usually contain more types of items than web SDKs.

Contributions. The main contributions of this study are listed below:

- a new workflow for automatic detection of architectural layers using a hybrid system;
- a novel approach at combining a deterministic method that uses SDK and lexical information for detecting architectural layers in a codebase with a non-deterministic one that uses a wide range of features extracted from the codebase (such as the number of common methods and properties and components name similarities) for solving the same problem;
- an innovative way of leveraging the information from the deterministic step to aid the non-deterministic one to increase the accuracy;
- gaining more insights regarding the functionality of our proposal in an industrial context;
- learn more about the features which are important for developers when using a software architecture checker system.

This is an extended study of our previously published work [16]; with this new work, our focus in on the validation of the proposal, and we present new evaluation metrics and data. The numerical evaluation step was enriched with 2 new research questions which examine our proposed approach by analyzing the topological structure of the analyzed codebases and the dependencies between the components for getting insights on the extensibility and maintainability of the analyzed codebases. In addition to this, we've also conducted an empiric evaluation study, where the workflow of our approaches is analyzed in real-world scenarios, and interviews were conducted with 2 mobile developers, for getting insights on the practicality of our approaches. Furthermore, we've also added details about the comparison of the features of our approach with other related work from literature.

The paper is structed as follows. The next section introduces the formalisation of the scientific problem and presents details about other related work. Section 3 introduces our approach *HyDe*. The numerical experiments and analysis of the method are presented in Sect. 4 and 5. Section presents the empirical evaluation of our study while the end of the paper is presents our conclusions and some directions for further work in Sect. 7.

2 Scientific Problem

A mobile codebase is made of components (classes, structures, protocols, and extensions); we represent a codebase in a formal matter by using the following notation $A = \{a_1, a_2, \ldots, a_n\}$ where a_i, $i \in \{1, 2, \ldots, n\}$ denotes a component.

The purpose of this study is to find a way for splitting the codebase into architectural layers. An architectural layer is represented by a partition P of the components $P = \{P_1, P_2, \ldots, P_m\}$ in the codebase that satisfies the following conditions:

- $1 \leq m \leq n$;
- P_j is a non-empty subset of A, $\forall j \in \{1, 2, \ldots, m\}$;
- $A = \cup_{j=1}^{m} P_j$, $P_{j_1} \cap P_{j_2} = \emptyset, \forall j_1, j_2 \in \{1, 2, \ldots, m\}$ with $j_1 \neq j_2$.

In this formulation, a P_j ($j \in \{1, 2, \ldots, m\}$) subset of A represents an architectural layer.

Since we are using a hybrid approach, the detected architectural layers (partitions) P_1, P_2, ... P_m are determined by applying a set of deterministic rules and a clusterization process on some of the output partitions.

In order to apply a clustering algorithm, each component a_i ($i \in \{1, 2, \ldots, n\}$) has to be represented by one or more features or characteristics. We suppose to have k features and we denote them by $F(a_i) = [F_i^1, F_i^2, \ldots, F_i^k]$.

The purpose of the hybrid approach is to output partitions of components that match as best as possible the ground truth (the partitions provided by human experts).

The **Model View Controller** is one of the most widespread presentational architectural patterns. It is used extensively in all sorts of client applications, web, desktop and mobile. It provides a simple separation of concerns between the components of a codebase in 3 layers:

- Model—responsible for business logic.
- View—responsible for the user's input and the output of the application.
- Controller—keeps the state of the application, acts like a mediator between the Model and the View layer.

There are many flavours of MVC in which the data-flow is different, but they all share the same model of separation. MVC is also the precursor of more specialised presentational architectural patterns such as Model View View Model (MVVM) or Model View Presenter (MVP) [9, 14].

In this study, the focus is on analyzing MVC architectures, therefore, the number of partitions $m = 3$. For a better understanding of the concepts, we are going to substitute the notation of partitions $P = \{P_1, P_2, P_3\}$, with $P = \{M, V, C\}$, as this notation better reflects the partition and the output layers we are interested in finding, M representing the Model layer, V representing the View layer, and C being the Controller layer. For the rest of the paper, this notation will be used to refer to the partitions for architectural layers.

Other studies have focused on architecture recovery by clusterization. For instance, Mancoridi [27], Mitchell [28] or Lutellier [26] from a structural point of view, Anquetil [1] or Corazza [8] from a lexical point of view and Garcia [18] or Rathee [33] from a structural and lexical point of view. However, none of those approaches specifically focused on mobile codebase or codebases that use SDKs for building their UI interfaces.

HyDe combines our previous work, regarding splitting a mobile codebase into architectural layers, a deterministic approach where information from the mobile SDKs is being used for detecting the architectural layers for a certain component using a set of rules [13] with a non-deterministic one for which we previously paved the way with a study where we have applied Machine Learning techniques for solving the same problem [15].

3 *HyDe*: A Two-Stage Automatic Detection of Architectural Layers in Mobile Codebases

In the vast majority of cases, mobile applications are clients – they use presentational software architectures, and one of the most commonly used architectural patterns for developing these kinds of products is MVC [40]. *HyDe* combines our two previous approaches (the deterministic approach – *MaCS* [13] and the non-deterministic one – *CARL* [15]) for solving the problem of inferring the architectural layers from a mobile codebase. Just like with *MaCS* and *CARL*, our initial study focuses on inferring the architectural layers and their composition from MVC codebases.

With *HyDe* we want to leverage the performance of the deterministic approach (*MaCS*) and increase its flexibility (suited for more complex architectural patterns) by using techniques from the non-deterministic step (*CARL*). This new approach statically analyses the components of the codebase and uses the definition of the components, their methods signatures as well as the properties of those components, moreover, it leverages the information from the mobile SDKs for improving the categorization process. *HyDe* applies serially *MaCS* and *CARL* since the two approaches are combined into a single one, the input and the way *CARL* works it's slightly different than the one presented in our initial non-deterministic approach study [15]). In addition to this, our new proposal is also characterized by two important features: unsupervised – which means there is no prior knowledge needed before analyzing a codebase – and autonomous – no developer involvement needed.

3.1 Pre-processing

The preprocessing step is identical to what we did on our two previous approaches: the examined codebase is statically analyzed and information regarding the components is being extracted (a comprehensive presentation of the pre-processing particularities can be found in [13]). As an outcome of this step, we have the set of components $A = \{a_1, a_2, \ldots, a_n\}$ where every a_i, $i \in \{1, 2, \ldots, n\}$ is characterised by:

- name
- type (class, struct, protocol)
- path
- inherited types
- all the private, static, and non-static methods and properties.

3.2 Deterministic Step

In this part of the process, *MaCS* [12] is applied: the codebase is split into architectural layers based on the set of heuristics and the involvement of the SDK entities after its topological structure has been defined.

Extraction. After the preprocessing step, a directed graph (topological structure) is being created for the extracted components. The nodes represent codebase components (classes, structs, enums, protocols) while the links between nodes are represented by dependencies between the components. Unlike a typical topological structure, in this one we could have one or multiple links between a pair of components; for instance, if component A has 3 properties of type B, then the graph will contain 3 directed links between the node A and B.

Categorization. The categorization part is where the deterministic step places the components in architectural layers. Since our focus was on MVC architectures, the output of this step is represented by 3 sets of components each corresponding to one of the MVC architectural layers (Model, View, Controller).

When we have developed *MaCS* we have come up with 2 different flavors, one which worked well on small-sized codebases – SimpleCateg. [12]) – and another one – CoordCateg. [12] – which is better suited for medium and large-sized codebases. Since one of the cornerstones of *HyDe* is to be an inference method capable of analyzing more complex architectural patterns and codebases we have decided for the categorization process to use the CoordCateg. approach as it is better suited.

The architectural layers are being defined in a deterministic manner by using the CoordCateg. approach heuristics:

- All Controller layer items should inherit from Controller classes defined in the used SDK;
- All View layer items should inherit from UI classes defined in the used SDK;
- All the remaining items are treated as Model layer items;
- All the components which have properties or methods that manipulate Controller components (including other Coordinating Controller components, also) are marked as Coordinating Controllers.

The Coordinating Controllers are simple plain objects that manipulate the flows and states of the application; together with the components which inherit from an SDK-defined Controller component they form the Controller layer of the analyzed codebase.

The output of *MaCS* represents a partition $P = \{M, V, C\}$, where the M, V, and C subsets are constructed by applying the above rules over all the codebase's components $A = \{a_1, a_2, \ldots, a_n\}$. To be able to formalize these decision rules, we involve the concept of a predicate as follows: a predicate of type X over two components as $pred_X(el_1, el_2)$ is True if we can apply the action X over el_1 and we obtain el_2. The proposed checker system defines the following predicates:

- $pred_{instanceOf}(component_a, Type) = True$ when $component_a$ is a variable of type $Type$;
- $pred_{inheritance}(component_a, component_b) = True$ when $component_a$ inherits from $component_b$;
- $pred_{using}(component_a, component_b) = True$ when $component_a$ has a property or a method that takes as a parameter a value of type $component_b$;
- $pred_{using}(component_a, listComponent_b) = True$ when $component_a$ has a property or a method that takes as a parameter a value of a type present in the $listComponent_b$ list;
- $pred_{inheritance}(component_a, listComponent_b) = True$ when $component_a$ has a inherits from a type present in the $listComponent_b$ list;

With these definitions in place we can represent the layers using the above-stated rules as sets:

$$\begin{aligned} C_{simple} = \{a_i | pred_X(a_i, \text{SDK's Controller}) = True, \\ \text{where } X \in \{instanceOf, inheritance\}, a_i \in A\} \end{aligned} \tag{1}$$

$$\begin{aligned} Coordinators = \{a_i | a_i \in A, \exists v \in a_i.properties \text{ and} \\ c \in C \text{ such as } pred_{instanceOf}(v, c) = True \text{ or} \\ \exists m \in a_i.methods \text{ and } c \in C \text{ such as} \\ pred_{using}(m, c) = True\} \end{aligned} \tag{2}$$

$$C = C_{simple} \cup Coordinators \tag{3}$$

$$\begin{aligned} V = \{a_i | pred_X(a_i, \text{SDK's View}) = True, \\ \text{where } X \in \{instanceOf, inheritance\}, a_i \in A\} \end{aligned} \tag{4}$$

$$M = A \backslash (V \cup C) \tag{5}$$

The output of the categorization process represents the initial assignment of components into architectural layers – this categorization is identical to what we would have obtained from applying *MaCS*. This initial categorization has a high accuracy for the View layer due to the heuristics used. The Controller layer is also being detected with good accuracy, and this information will be used later in the non-deterministic step.

While the results obtained from this initial deterministic step are very promising, in the case of more complex architectural patterns this method can not be applied successfully due to the heuristics used. In addition to this, the performance for the Coordinating Controllers and Model layer could be further improved even in the case of MVC.

3.3 Non-deterministic Step

With the non-deterministic step, of *HyDe* we have tried to improve the performance of the approach but more importantly to pave the way for more specialized architectures and custom architecture support. Our previous approach *CARL* [15] – in which we have used only Machine Learning techniques (clustering) for solving the problem of splitting codebases into architectural layers had increased flexibility over *MaCS* but it lacked the performance. With those ideas in mind, we've decided to pursue a hybrid approach in which the output of *MaCS* is used as input for *CARL*. In order for this new approach to work, the feature selection had to be changed; even if the algorithm involved in the clusterization process is the same as in the case of *CARL*, the input and feature detection is completely different.

As we have previously stated, the output of the deterministic step is an initial distribution of components into architectural layers. This initial split has a very high accuracy for the View layer that's why this is marked as the final View layer and its components are not feed to the non-deterministic step. With this non-deterministic step, we want to achieve a better separation of components from the Model and Controller layers (M and C partitions) which was not possible with the help of heuristics; that is why the clustering algorithm works only with the components from the Model and Controller layer – as they were received from the deterministic step. The purpose of the clustering process is to find particularities in the data which were less obvious to us or for which we couldn't come up with a good enough heuristic. The View layer (V) is ignored as the detection precision for this layer is 100% (see Table 3).

Therefore the set of analysed elements is represented by $E = M \cup C = \{a_{i_1}, a_{i_2}, \ldots, a_{i_k}\}$, where a_{i_j} is a component from set A (see problem definition) and denotes a component that was identified as either as a Model or Controller element by the Deterministic step, and k represents the number of components in E.

Feature Extraction. The feature extraction part is one of the most important steps in a clustering algorithm as based on its selection the clustering algorithm could yield good or not so good results. We could have 2 different sets of features extracted from the same data collection which yield completely different results after the clustering process was applied.

For every component analyzed by the non-deterministic step, we have 2 sets of information, the one obtained from the preprocessing stage and the one obtained from the deterministic step (in which layer it was placed the Model or Controller layer).

To come up with a good selection of features, we have applied *HyDe*, with different feature selections on a mid-sized codebase (E-Commerce) that had the ground truth previously constructed by 2 senior developers. We have tried multiple features such as:

- Levenshtein distance between the components name;
- Whether a component inherits from a Model component (from the output of the deterministic step);
- Whether a component is using a Controller or Model component (it has properties or methods that use Controller or Model items from the deterministic step output);
- Whether a component is using a Controller component (it has properties or methods that use Controller items from the deterministic step output);
- Whether a component is a class or another type of programming language structure (such as structs, protocols, extensions);
- Whether a component is included in the Controller components (from the output of the deterministic step);

- Number of common methods between the analyzed components;
- Number of common properties between the analyzed components.

By using a trial and error approach of various combinations of features from the ones above we have found out the configuration that yields the best results on our benchmark application.

Two features take into account the already obtained assignments in the first step of our proposed system:

- Whether a component is included in the set of Controller components (from the output of the deterministic step). We associate a score θ if the component is included in the Controller layer and 0 otherwise. The score value has no influence over the detection process because, by normalization, a Boolean feature is created.

$$F_1(a_i) = \begin{cases} \theta, & \text{if } a_i \in C \\ 0, & \text{otherwise;} \end{cases} \tag{6}$$

- Whether a component is using a Controller component (it has properties or methods that used Controller items from the deterministic step output). We associate a score of 1 if the component uses another component from the Controller layer and 0 otherwise.

$$F_2(a_i) = \begin{cases} 1, & \text{if } pred_{using}(a_i, C) = \text{True} \\ 0, & \text{otherwise.} \end{cases} \tag{7}$$

In addition to those two rules, for every pair of components from the analyzed set (E) we compute the following values for the feature set of a component:

- a feature that emphasizes the similarity of two components' names

$$F_3(a_i) = [NameDist(a_i, a_{i_1}), NameDist(a_i, a_{i_2}), \ldots, NameDist(a_i, a_{i_k})] \tag{8}$$

  where $NameDist(a_{i_1}, a_{i_2})$ is the Levenshtein distance [25] between the names of component a_{i_1} and component a_{i_2};
- a feature based on how many properties two components have in common

$$F_4(a_i) = [CommProp(a_i, a_{i_1}), CommProp(a_i, a_{i_2}), \ldots, CommProp(a_i, a_{i_k})] \tag{9}$$

  where $CommProp(a_{i_1}, a_{i_2})$ is the number of common properties (name ant type) of component a_{i_1} and component a_{i_2};
- a feature based on how many methods two components have in common

$$F_5(a_i) = [CommMeth(a_i, a_{i_1}), CommMeth(a_i, a_{i_2}), \ldots, CommMeth(a_i, a_{i_k})] \tag{10}$$

  where $CommProp(a_{i_1}, a_{i_2})$ is the number of common methods (signature, name, and parameters) of component a_{i_1} and component a_{i_2}.

The output of this feature extraction phase is represented by the matrix that encodes all five feature sets, $M = F_1 \cup F_2 \cup F_3 \cup F_4 \cup F_5$. In fact, a $(3 \times k + 2) \times k$ matrix, that contains the feature set for every component in the codebase is constructed.

Clusterization. As a clusterization algorithm, we have used the same one as on *CARL* – Agglomerative Clustering [31] – a hierarchical, bottom-up approach, as using a trial and error approach, we have discovered that this works best for the type of problem we want to solve. Unlike *CARL*, *HyDe* only applies the clusterization process to the Model and Controller components obtained from the deterministic step and has only two output clusters that correspond to the remaining architectural layers from MVC (the Model and Controller). For measuring the similarity between clusters, we have used a well-known, highly used approach – the Euclidian distance [20].

After the clusterization process has finished, we need to assign semantics to the output clusters – which one corresponds to the Model and which one to the Controller layer. To accomplish this, we've leveraged the information from the SDK and marked it as the Controller layer, the output cluster which has the highest number of components that inherit from an SDK-defined Controller element.

If this process is applied to more complex architectural patterns – where more architectural layers should be discovered by the clusterization process, a set of architecture-specific heuristics should be used for assigning architectural layers to the output clusters.

Once this final step has been completed, the entire *HyDe* process is finished and we have 3 sets of components corresponding to the three architectural layers from MVC. The View layer is determined by the deterministic step, while the other two layers are detected by applying the non-deterministic step. A sketch of our system is depicted on Fig. 1.

We have conducted a literature study where we have compared our proposals with other methods from the literature. Unlike any other method to our knowledge, our proposals are the only ones that use the information from the SDKs for enhancing their detection mechanism. Other methods from literature rely only on structural and lexical information from the codebases. Moreover, to our knowledge *HyDe* is the only approach that uses a combination of heuristics together with clustering for inferring the architectural layers, the other methods use only one of the three possibilities present in literature (static analysis, heuristics, or clustering).

The vast majority of other methods from literature work at a package or module level, all our proposals, including *HyDe*, work at a class level as our long-term plan is to detect architectural issues at a component level. By analyzing either the modules or the packages only the macro-structure of the codebase could be analyzed and we are particularly interested in what happens at a micro-structure level, as the vast majority of precursor steps towards an architectural drift start here. Since *HyDe* works at the smallest level of architectural elements (classes) that makes this proposal is a well-suited candidate for highlighting architectural issues more accurately and early, in the development phase.

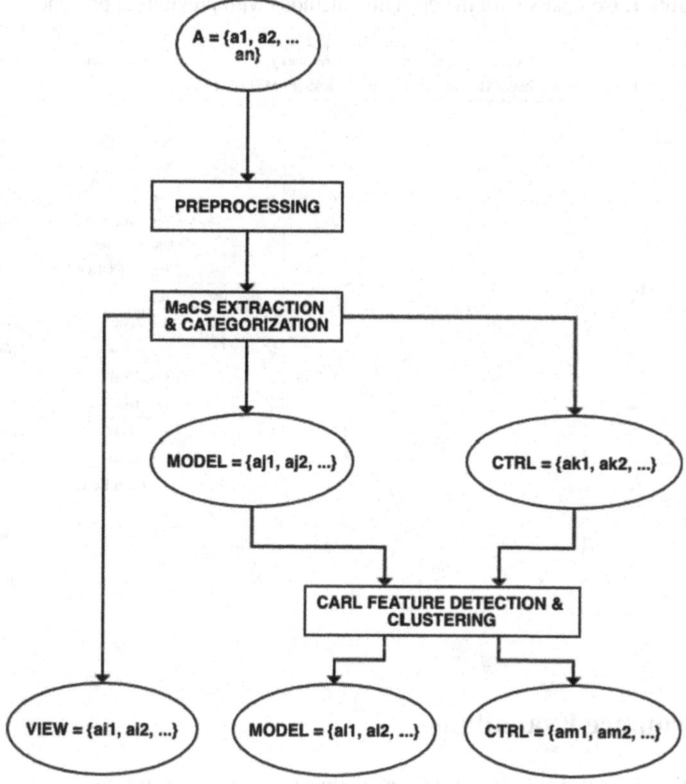

Fig. 1. Overview of the *HyDe* workflow [16].

Our proposals works with multiple programming languages and unlike other approaches from literature they are not bound to a single language. The only constraint of *HyDe* in respect to the programming languages it can be applied to is the fact they need to be Object-Oriented ones. Other approaches such as [30] or [36] for on non-Object-Oriented languages, but only take advantage of the structural information and work at a module level.

Another feature that makes our proposals stand out among the other work done in this space, is the fact they are platform-agnostic, which means *HyDe* as well as *MaCS* and *CARL* work on multiple platforms, not only mobile ones. The only constrain is that those platforms should use SDKs for building out their user interfaces. To the best of our knowledge, no other method from literature is platform-agnostic, there are indeed other approaches developed specifically for mobile applications, but even those are focusing on the Android platform, and they are not transferable to iOS, or other mobile platforms (Table 1).

Table 1. Comparison of the detection methods with previous approaches.

Approach	Information			Analysis			Granularity			Language dependent	Platform
	Structural	Lexical	SDK	Static	Heuristics	Clustering	Package	Module	Class		
[4]	✓	✓	–	–	✓	–	✓	–	–	No	Not mobile
[5]	✓	✓	–	–	✓	–	✓	–	–	No	Not mobile
[6]	✓	✓	–	–	✓	–	✓	–	–	No	Not mobile
[17]	✓	–	–	–	✓	–	✓	–	–	No	Not mobile
[23]	✓	–	–	–	✓	–	✓	–	–	Yes (Java, C#, C++ and Smalltalk)	Not Mobile
[30]	✓	–	–	✓	–	–	–	✓	–	Yes (C, COBOL)	Not mobile
[33]	✓	✓	–	–	–	✓	–	–	✓	Yes (Java)	Not mobile
[35]	✓	–	–	✓	–	–	–	–	✓	Yes (Java)	Not mobile
[36]	✓	–	–	–	–	✓	–	✓	–	Yes (C/C++)	Not Mobile
[37]	✓	✓	–	–	–	✓	–	✓	–	Yes (Java)	Not mobile
[38]	✓	–	–	–	✓	–	–	✓	–	Yes (Java)	Not mobile
[42]	✓	–	–	–	✓	–	–	–	✓	Yes (Java)	not mobile
[7]	✓	✓	–	✓	–	–	–	–	✓	Yes (Java)	Android
[9]	✓	✓	–	–	✓	–	–	–	✓	Yes (Java/Kotlin)	Android
MaCS [13]	✓	–	✓	–	✓	–	–	–	✓	No	Platform agnostic
CARL [15]	✓	✓	✓	–	–	✓	–	–	✓	No	Platform agnostic
HyDe	✓	✓	✓	–	✓	✓	–	–	✓	No	Platform agnostic

4 Performance Evaluation

Our evaluation is two-folded: validation of the categorization process and analysis of how the architectural rules are respected or not. With both approaches, we were interested in the same metrics. The evaluation methodology was inspired by [32] which was used as a starting point in our study.

In the **validation** stage, to measure the effectiveness of the categorization, we compare the results from manual inspection (that acts as ground truth) to those of our methods. To validate the performance of our approach, we are using the following metrics for analyzing the result of the *HyDe* against a ground truth obtained by manually inspecting the codebase by two senior developers (with a development experience of over five years):

- accuracy: $Acc = \frac{N^{AllLayers}_{DetectedCorrectly}}{N_{allComponents}}$,
- precision for the layer X: $P_X = \frac{N^X_{DetectedCorrectly}}{N^X_{TotalDetected}}$,
- recall for the layer X: $R_X = \frac{N^X_{DetectedCorrectly}}{N^X_{GroundTruth}}$,

where:

- $N^X_{DetectedCorrectly}$ is the number of component detected by the system which belong to the X layer and are found in the ground truth for that layer;
- $N^X_{TotalDetected}$ is the number of component detected by the system as belonging to the X layer;

- $N^{X}_{GroundTruth}$ is the number of component which belong to the X layer in the ground truth.

In addition to those metrics, we are also interested in the performance of the process not only from a software engineering point of view but also from a Machine Learning perspective. To analyze the ML performance of our approach we have used the following metrics:

- Silhouette Coefficient score [34] and
- Davies-Bouldin Index [10].

The Silhouette Coefficient measures how similar is a component of a cluster compared to the other elements which reside in the same cluster compared to the other clusters. The range of values for this score is $[-1; 1]$ where a high value means that the component is well matched in its own cluster and dissimilar when compared to other clusters. We have computed the mean Silhouette Coefficient score over all components of each codebase.

Davies-Bouldin Index is defined as the average similarity measure of each cluster with its most similar cluster. The similarity is represented by the ratio of within-cluster distances to between-cluster distances. The Davies-Bouldin Index indicates how well was the clustering performed; the minimum value for this metric is **0**, the lower the value the better.

Both of these metrics provide insightful information regarding the clustering performance: the Silhouette Coefficient score indicates how well are the components placed, while the Davies-Bouldin Index expresses whether or not the clusters were correctly constructed.

The Machine Learning perspective was applied to the output data obtained from the entire *HyDe* process, when computing these metrics we looked at the final result, and we've viewed the output architectural layers as clusters, even some of them might come from a deterministic step (View layer in our particular case). By computing these metrics, we can also understand the structural health of the codebase, how related are the components between them, and how high is the degree of differences between architectural layers.

In the **analysis** stage we are interested in the topological structure of the analyzed codebases. Furthermore, the architectural dependencies are studied to serve as a basis for an informed discussion about how the codebase respects the architectural rules and about how well-suited the system is for expected changes.

We were interested in the number of external dependencies (*#ExtDepends*) of a layer. *#ExtDepends* represent the links between the components of a layer and components which reside within the other two layers of MVC. Moreover, the *#CompleteExtDepends* include the external links relative to MVC layers and the links with other SDKs and third-party libraries defined types, as well as Swift predefined types (such as String, Int) or codebase defined types (such as closures).

Another important metric is the number of different external links (*#DiffExtDepend*)—the number of different codebase components on which a certain component depends. The components with a large amount of different dependent items which violate the architectural rules are problematic and represent architectural pressure points in the analyzed codebase.

Besides these metrics, we also have two ones oriented for evaluating how well-suited the system is for expected changes: Cumulative Component Dependency (CCD) and Average Component Dependency (ACD) [19,22].

- *The CCD is the sum, over all the components in a subsystem, of the number of components needed in order to test each component incrementally* [22].
- The ACD is defined as the ration between the CCD of the subsystem and the number of components of the analysed subsystem [22]. $ACD = \frac{CCD(Subsystem)}{\#Components}$.

The CCD indicates the cost of developing, testing, and maintaining a subsystem. When developing a new feature or modifying an already existing one in a large number of cases the changes will impact more components of the subsystem, that is why the cost is better reflected by using the ACD metric. Note that architectural change metrics (e.g. architecture-to-architecture, MoJoFM, cluster-to-cluster [24]) can not be used to establish which rules are violated since the conceptual/intended architectures of the analyzed systems are unknown.

5 Numerical Evaluation

Our analysis focuses on MVC, a widely used architectural pattern [40] for mobile development. Our experiments are run on the iOS platform; however, they can be replicated on other platforms that use SDKs for building their user interfaces.

For validating our proposal, we have compiled a list of questions for which we search answers with our experiments:

- **RQ1** - How can the deterministic approach and the non-deterministic one be combined?
- **RQ2** - How effective and performant is the *HyDe* approach?
- **RQ3** - What are the downsides of using a hybrid approach for architectural layers detection?
- **RQ4** - What is the topological structure of the codebase after applying *HyDe*?
- **RQ5** - What is the extensibility and maintainability of the codebases by using *HyDe* for inferring architectural layers?

5.1 Analysed Codebases

We have conducted experiments on eight different codebases, both open-source and private, of different sizes:

- Firefox - the public mobile Web browser [29],
- Wikipedia - the public information application [41],
- Trust - the public cryptocurrency wallet [39],
- E-Commerce - a private application,

- Game - a private multiplayer game.
- Stock - a private trading application,
- Education - a private education application for parents,
- Demo - the Apple's example for AR/VR [3].

We were interested in MVC codebases, as this is one of the most popular software architecture used on client applications. iOS applications implement the MVC pattern more consistently than Android, as Apple encourages developers to use it through examples and documentation [2]. To our knowledge, there is not a selection of repositories used for analyzing iOS applications, that is why we have manually selected the codebases. The selection was performed to include small, medium, and large codebases. In addition, we have included both private source and open source codebases as there might be differences in how a development company and the community write code. Companies respect internal coding standards and styles that might not work or are different than the ones used by open-source projects.

Table 2. Short description of investigated applications [16].

Application	Blank	Comment	Code	No. of components
Firefox	23392	18648	100111	514
Wikipedia	6933	1473	35640	253
Trust	4772	3809	23919	403
E-Commerce	7861	3169	20525	433
Game	839	331	2113	37
Stock	1539	751	5502	96
Education	1868	922	4764	105
Demo	785	424	3364	27

Table 2 presents the sizes of the codebase, blank – refers to empty lines, comment – represents comments in the code, code states the number of code lines, while the number of components represents the total number of components in the codebase.

5.2 Validation - Stage

After the experiments were conducted on all of the codebases, we have analyzed the results based on the 3 questions which represent the base for this study.

RQ1 - How Can the Deterministic Approach and the Non-deterministic One Be Combined? For constructing a system that would yield good results and involve a hybrid approach, it is clear that the only way to do it is to apply the non-deterministic approach after the deterministic one. These approaches can work well together if we leverage the best parts from both of them and try to improve the methods where they lacked.

From [13] it is clear that the deterministic approach works really well for the layers for which there are rules strong enough to determine the components with high accuracy. In the case of the current study, *MaCS* was able to identify with high accuracy the View layer. When analyzing custom architectures, a deterministic approach might yield great results on other architectural layers as well, but for the purpose of this study, we have focused only on MVC.

The non-deterministic approach which was inspired by [15] works well for finding similarities between components without using heuristics.

With those ideas in mind, we have concluded that the best way for those approaches to function well together and achieve good results is to apply the deterministic method for identifying the layers, and afterwards to apply the non-deterministic approach to those layers for which the deterministic approach did not work that well. The second stage of *HyDe* could be considered as a filter, enhancing the detection results.

To summarise, we have applied the deterministic approach first and obtained the components split into architectural layers based on the rules used by *MaCS*, afterward we have applied the non-deterministic method for the layers in which *MaCS* results were not confident – the Model and Controller layers.

RQ2 - How Effective and Performant is the *HyDe* Approach? We have applied the *HyDe* approach to 8 codebases of different sizes, to cover multiple types of applications from a size perspective, but also from functionality and the domain they operate in perspectives.

The proposed approach achieved good results on the analyzed codebases with three codebases that achieved over **90%** accuracy with the highest one at **97%**. The average accuracy for the analyzed set of applications was **85%** as seen in Table 3.

The layer which came from the deterministic approach and was left unaltered by the non-deterministic step, the View layer, has achieved a perfect precision score on all the analyzed codebase, indicating that *HyDe* does not produce false positives (it does not label as View components those that, conform the ground-truth, they belong to other layers). In respects to recall, the same layer achieved lower scores on some of the codebases, this was mainly caused by the fact that those codebases used external libraries for building their UI interfaces, and they did not rely solely on the SDK for implementing those features.

In the case of the other layers which were altered by the deterministic step, the precision and recall were heavily influenced by the way the codebase was structured, naming conventions, and coding standards.

The proposed method worked best for the Game codebase which was a medium-sized application. For larger codebase which had higher entropy due to their dimensions and used external libraries the method did not work as well.

For some of the smallest codebases, the method achieved the worst results, this is because the non-deterministic step did not have enough data to make accurate assumptions as the codebases were rather small.

From a View layer precision point of view, *HyDe* achieves perfect results, all the detected View layer elements are indeed views, there are no false positives. In respect to the recall of the View layer, the results are not perfect, there are some false negatives, this is because the analyzed codebases use external libraries for implementing certain UI elements and those libraries were not included in the analysis process.

Table 3. Results of the process in terms of detection quality [16].

Codebase	Model precision	Model recall	View precision	View recall	Ctrl precision	Ctr recall	Accuracy
Firefox	0,97	0,77	1,00	1,00	0,47	0,91	82,71
Wikipedia	0,79	0,74	1,00	0,66	0,74	0,95	80,00
Trust	0,86	0,89	1,00	0,70	0,66	0,72	82,86
E-commerce	1,00	0,80	1,00	1,00	0,81	1,00	90,97
Game	0,95	1,00	1,00	1,00	1,00	0,92	97,22
Stock	0,80	0,77	1,00	0,59	0,78	0,93	79,09
Education	0,87	0,95	1,00	1,00	0,92	0,90	93,60
Demo	0,91	0,77	1,00	1,00	0,25	0,67	78,79

Table 4. Results in terms of cohesion and coupling [16].

Codebase	Mean Silhouette Coef.	Davies-Bouldin index
Firefox	0,64	0,61
Wikipedia	0,67	0,51
Trust	0,68	0,52
E-commerce	0,63	0,58
Game	0,86	0,20
Stock	0,81	0,28
Education	0,80	0,29
Demo	0,52	1,55

Table 5. Homogeneity and Completeness on the analyzed codebases [16].

Codebase	Homogeneity score	Completeness score
Firefox	0,60	0,63
Wikipedia	0,50	0,56
Trust	0,20	0,18
E-commerce	0,66	0,73
Game	0,74	0,79
Stock	0,40	0,50
Education	0,17	0,31
Demo	0,80	0,90

In respect to performance, we have computed the Mean Silhouette Coefficient, the Davies-Bouldin Index as well as the Homogeneity and Completeness scores.

The Mean Silhouette Coefficient had the best values in the case of medium-sized codebases where the distinction between the 3 output layers was more pronounced as seen in Table 4. In the case of the large codebases, the accuracy was worse as we had many types of components in each architectural layer. The value for the smallest codebase was also poor, this is because it had small number of components.

As seen in Table 4, the results for the Davies-Bouldin Index were hand in hand with the ones for the Mean Silhouette Coefficient: the best performing codedbases were the medium-sized ones, the largest and smallest ones achieved worst results due to the same reasons that affected Silhouette metric.

In case of Homogeneity and Completeness, Table 5, *HyDe* did achieve good results for the medium-sized and small-sized codebase. The scores were better for the codebases which had a naming convention and coding standards in place.

RQ3 - What Are the Downsides of Using a Hybrid Approach for Architectural Layers and Components Detection? The most important downside of using a hybrid approach is that based on the analyzed codebase and the architecture it implements, the workflow might need to be adjusted in two places:

- the rules for the deterministic part of the process;
- the feature selection for the non-deterministic step.

In addition to those, an analysis would have to be conducted on the output of the deterministic step to identify the layers which should be feed to the non-deterministic step.

Another downside would be that this method only works if the deterministic step yields really good results for at least some of the layers, otherwise this part of the process becomes irrelevant.

From a computational performance point of view, the proposed approach is also heavier on the processing part as a simple singular process as it is composed of two separate steps; this also applies to the run time, as this is increased due to the same reasons.

In respect to the results, our proposal's main downside is the fact that for the output clusters from the non-deterministic step a manual analysis of those might be needed to match a cluster to an architectural layer if no heuristics can be found in the case of more specialized or custom architectural patterns.

Our proposed approach remains automatic in the case of more specialized software architectures, as it does not need the ground truth of the codebase. The feature extraction process needs to be enriched with information regarding the particularities of the analyzed architecture, in order for the process to yield good results.

5.3 Analysis - Stage

RQ4 - What is the Topological Structure of the Codebase after Applying *HyDe*? The same metrics were used as in the case of the other two approaches *MaCS* [13] and *CARL* [15]). From a topological structure point of view, *HyDe* split the codebase into architectural layers that had the fewest wrong dependencies between them as shown in Table 6.

Since *HyDe* is a combination of the first two approaches (*MaCS* and *CARL*), the results showed that it managed to combine the previous approaches successfully, by

Table 6. Analysis of codebases dependencies - *HyDe*.

#ExtDepends / #DiffExtDepend								
Dependency	Firefox	Wiki.	Trust	E-comm.	Game	Stock	Educ.	Demo
View-Model	24/9	9/5	21/14	63/25	1/1		11/4	1/1
View-Ctrl								
Model-View	94/7	1/1						
Model-Ctrl	65/14							3/1
Ctrl-Model	226/30	79/30	290/66	427/61	38/6	65/14	94/15	23/11
Ctrl-View	57/20	32/14	26/13	156/30	2/2	53/10	10/6	5/3
#CompleteExtDepends								
Model	2951	968	1200	814	111	177	229	138
View	677	258	280	293	42	107	79	8
Ctrl	2739	3114	1398	2691	196	681	416	283

Table 7. CCD and ACD metrics for the analysed codebases - *HyDe*.

Codebase	Metric	Model	View	Controller	Total
Firefox	CCD	2860	841	5506	9207
	ACD	7	7	22	12
Wiki	CCD	437	301	4776	5514
	ACD	3	5	19	9
Trust	CCD	2148	369	4027	6544
	ACD	6	6	22	11
E-comm	CCD	1011	612	6028	7651
	ACD	6	6	21	11
Game	CCD	94	28	90	212
	ACD	3	3	7	4
Stock	CCD	253	112	1323	1688
	ACD	5	5	16	9
Educ.	CCD	243	72	799	1114
	ACD	3	5	15	8
Demo	CCD	73	3	117	193
	ACD	2	1	8	4

achieving the best results from an architecture correctness point of view. In the case of the number of complete external dependencies, the results are comparable with the other two approaches.

RQ5 - What is the Extensibility and Maintainability of the Codebases by Using *HyDe* for Inferring Architectural Layers? For measuring the extensibility and maintainability of the hybrid approach, we have used the same metrics as for the other two approaches – CCD and ACD. The split into architectural layers made by *HyDe* achieved good results from a CCD and ACD point of view. In the case of one of the largest codebases, Firefox, *HyDe* matched the best result obtained by *MaCS*. The results obtained by *HyDe*, shown in Table 7, are comparable with the best results obtained by *MaCS* (in both approaches – SimpleCateg. and CoordCateg.). *HyDe* also achieved better results than *CARL*. As in the case of other approaches, the most complex analyzed system was Firefox, while the least one was Demo. In the case of the E-commerce codebase, *HyDe* managed to achieve the best score among all the other approaches, strengthening our previous findings that *HyDe* works best on medium and large-sized codebases.

5.4 Threats to Validity for Numerical Evaluation

Once the experiments were run and we've analyzed the entire process we have discovered the following threats to validity:

- **Internal** - the selection of features for the non-deterministic step was found using a trial and error approach, there might be another set of features that yield a better result. The selection of features can be improved by measuring the entropy of a feature for finding out its importance. Another reason for concern is the fact that in this approach we are only looking at the codebase, ignoring the external libraries used, and that can lead to wrongly detected components. This can be improved by also running the process on the libraries used by the analyzed codebase. We've also applied ML specific metrics to the results, including the View layer which was an output of the deterministic step. This might represent a threat to validity in respect to the results for the Silhouette Coefficient and Davies-Bouldin Index.
- **External** - Our study has focused only on Swift codebases on the iOS platform; other platforms and programming languages might come with their particularities which we have not encountered in the current environment. Furthermore, this study focuses on MVC alone. In the case of more specialized architectures, the rules from the deterministic step might need to be adjusted as well as the features selection involved in the non-deterministic phase.
- **Conclusions** - The experiments were run on a small number of applications that might have some bias, more experiments should be conducted to strengthen the results.

6 Empirical Evaluation

Our approaches were examined from an academic point of view *MaCS* in [13], *CARL* in [15], and *HyDe* in the current paper, however, since our work can have a significant impact on the way mobile applications are being built in an industrial context, it is also important to analyze the perspective of those end-users (developers).

There are often cases where academic research is not used in the industry not because it lacks performance or would not improve certain processes, but because is not presented in a user-friendly manner and researchers haven't got the time to polish their solutions to fit the real-world, production context. Even when our approaches are still in an initial stage, it is important to gather feedback and see if the current workflow of the approaches would fit an industrial context. In addition to this, we are also interested in the usefulness of the approaches from the developer's perspective. To find out more about the developers' points of view, we have conducted two interviews with senior iOS developers from a mobile applications development company. We have chosen iOS developers, as the approaches are configured for this platform and all our previous findings are on this platform. It's important to mention that with this empiric evaluation we were not interested in analyzing the performance of a certain approach (*HyDe*, *MaCS* nor *CARL*), our focus was on finding more about the practicality of the system resulted by using either one of the approaches in a real-world scenario.

When designing the interviews, we have directed our interviews on finding answers to the following questions:

- **IQ1** - Would a software architecture checker system be a valuable asset in a developer's toolkit?
- **IQ2** - When and how often would a developer use a software architecture checker system?
- **IQ3** - How can the current approach be improved?

We had 2 developers trying one of our approaches on real projects they are working on, and asked them to give us feedback about their experience. We have prepared a version of *MaCS* [13] as we have previously shown this approach worked well on all kinds of mobile codebases. Since we did not know the types of projects the developers are working on, we have decided to use a deterministic approach as those results are not influenced by the size of the codebase. In addition to this, it was also easier to port our solution to the developers' machines, as we did not have to install Machine Learning software for non-deterministic analyzing the codebases. Since the project is still in the research phase, we have made sure that it was properly configured on the computers used by the interviewed developers.

For assessing the performance and the usefulness of our proposal, we have asked them to run the system on their current projects, on the development branch. The reason for this is that in development, the code does not have yet the final form nor are all the architectural rules respected. Before the interview, the developers revealed that they approach each task with the following methodology *Make it work, make it right, make it fast!*, hence analyzing their current development branch could yield issues with their code and approaches. After the *MaCS* was applied, we have looked at the output and talked with the developers regarding the results. In our discussion, we have used the interview questions as starting points for conversation, but we were also interested in their general feedback.

6.1 Participants Background and Analyzed Data

We have conducted our study with the help of 2 senior iOS developers, who develop iOS mobile apps professionally for over 7 years. They work in the same software development company, and the focus of the company is on mobile apps and the backend services which serve those. They do both large-scale, enterprise projects, as well as smaller ones, minimum viable products for startups.

Developer 1. The first developer we have interviewed has started his IT career as an iOS developer. He has a Master's Degree in a Computer-Science related field and has worked his entire career as an iOS developer. When asked about what excites him the most about mobile development, his answer was *"the fact that you can see your work used by a lot of people, there are a few thousands of people every week which use a button implemented by me, and that's a great feeling"*. He works on a large project, the project started 4 years ago with an inherited codebase from another company, and together with his team, they refactored the codebase, changed the UI interface of the application, and have implemented a lot of new features. The project implements an MVC architecture using Coordinating Controllers for the navigation part. The project is a mobile application used in transportation, it handles multiple types of payments and real-time data. One of the important things for the project is to have as much as possible of the codebase covered by Unit Tests. When they inherited the codebase, it had no tests, and the codebase did not easily allow writing those, so they had to refactor a good part of the app.

Developer 2. The second developer we have interviewed does both iOS and Android development, with his current focus being iOS. He has started his career as a mobile developer over 8 years ago and has worked in multiple companies as a mobile developer on both iOS and Android platforms. He said he likes working on mobile applications *"because unlike back-end or Web development, on mobile I get to play with a full stack of technologies databases, networking, embedded devices, complex UI interfaces"*. He currently works on a minimum viable product for a startup, a small-sized project in the area of social networks, where they use MVC as an architectural pattern. The app makes it easier for its users to find interesting places to visit and ask for recommendations. The scope of the project is to launch a version as quickly as possible and to gather feedback from their audience. Mobile startups are built using a trial and error approach, where the scope of the application and the way the product functions is heavily influenced by the feedback received from early users, so it's really important that for these types of projects the architecture to allow great flexibility and extensibility.

6.2 Findings

After our initial discussion, we have ran the *MaCS* CoordCateg. approach on the codebases and analyzed the results and the feedback about the participants' experience.

IQ1 - Would a Software Architecture Checker System Be a Valuable Asset in a Developer's Toolkit?
Not necessarily related to the performance of the system, but more with the need for such a system, we have wanted to reinforce our assumptions. Both developers stated that a system that could help their teams better architecture their projects would be useful. In the case of **Developer 1** who works on a large project, he thinks that such a system would be of great value from both a development perspective as well as for the management-oriented metrics it can yield (the current state of architectural health of the codebase). **Developer 2** thinks that such a system would be a great tool for startup projects as well as they could easily see how flexible to change an app is and junior developers could write better code when working on those kinds of fast-paced product where code reviews are not that thoroughly made as in the case of large projects (due to time considerations).

IQ2 - When and How Often Would a Developer Use a Software Architecture Checker System?
The process of setting up the system was manual so it took a bit of time to get everything going on their machines. After the systems were run, they immediately saw its potential as a code quality gate. A quality gate is a process that runs periodically, usually when a new code is added to the central repositories, and before merging it into production, it will have to go through multiple quality gates, for validating that the new code does not break something else, that all the other integration and unit tests are working as expected, etc.. Both developers see an architecture check system more used as a quality gate in a CI/CD pipeline than to run it periodically on their machines. Both developers had a lot of experience in writing mobile apps, and they have a lot of architectural knowledge, which is why they might not find it useful for running it locally on their machines. However, **Developer 2** pointed out that the system might be useful for those who just start programming for mobile applications, as it will give them architectural guidelines.

IQ3 - How Can the Current Approach Be Improved?
When asked how the current approach can be improved, both developers had the same two mentions (**all approaches take the same input and yield the same output**). They have noticed that the output can be better formatted and instead of showing among which architectural layers there is a violation, it would be better to show the actual components involved. The other thing they mention is that the current way of running the system can be made more user friendly, instead of using the command line and running multiple commands, they would prefer to use something more graphic, like an IDE plugin, or at least the system packed as a command-line utility library. **Developer 2** also mentioned that for beginners, it would also be useful if the system would provide some suggestions on how could the identified issues be fixed.

6.3 Threats to Validity for Empirical Evaluation

After conducting the interviews and analyzing the results we have discovered the following threats to validity:

- **Internal** - When designing the interview we have focused more on the usability and practicability of the system. We were not necessarily interested in the exact performance of the system. By accurately analyzing the performance of the system, we could have obtained some more insights regarding its functionality.
- **External** - We have conducted the interviews on a small batch of developers. Validating the approach with more practitioners, with different experiences, and functions could yield much more comprehensive results.
- **Conclusions** - We have drawn our conclusions based on the feedback received from our set of participants. Having more diversity in the terms of participants to this study could bring to light some additional, new conclusions.

7 Conclusions and Further Work

With this extended study, we have strengthened the findings regarding our hybrid approach for detecting architectural layers from mobile codebases. As shown in this study, the combination between the deterministic and non-deterministic methods (*HyDe*) yields good results especially when is applied to medium-sized applications. Due to the blending of deterministic and non-deterministic algorithms, *HyDe* becomes the most our most promising approach for analyzing more complex architectural patterns and different platforms (that use SDKs for building their user interfaces). The good performance is an effect of the conjunction between the high accuracy of the deterministic method and the flexibility of the non-deterministic one. Moreover, our analysis stage showed that the layers' distribution of the codebase performed by *HyDe* are comparable with those of the two simple approaches (*MaCS* and *CARL*), which strengthens our findings even more.

HyDe leads the way towards creating a software architecture checker tool, that could highlight architectural issues early in the development phase, as it represents the core feature of such a system and could be applied to more architectural patterns and types of codebases. From our empirical evaluation, we reconfirm that a system that would validate the architectural health of a mobile codebase would be useful in an industrial context. The participants in the interview were pleased with the workflow of our approaches and have identified multiple areas in which it could be used.

Next, we plan to further improve the accuracy of *HyDe*, by also analyzing the external libraries used by the codebases, as this could provide more insights into the structure of the codebase and the purpose of components, especially in large-sized projects. Another idea we plan to pursue is analyzing not only the signature of the functions but also their body, for getting more insights into the scope of the components. Once we are satisfied with the accuracy of the system, we plan to integrate it into a CI/CD pipeline for testing it with real projects. In addition to this, based on the feedback obtained from our empirical validation, the output of *HyDe* and packing has to be further developed for a more user-friendly interaction. With the empirical evaluation, we were interested in discovering how the approach performs in a real-case scenario, we have not analyzed the codebases it was applied to, and we have no information as regards whether all the codebase issues were correctly identified as this was out of scope of the current research, but we plan to tackle this in one of our next studies.

HyDe can represent the basis of the future software architecture checker tool that could be used by developers, and managers for getting the status of architectural health in a mobile project. In addition to this, such a tool would be also suitable in an academic environment as it could provide insightful information to the students as to how the code should be structured and how to avoid architectural issues.

References

1. Anquetil, N., Lethbridge, T.C.: Recovering software architecture from the names of source files. J. Softw. Maint. Res. Pract. **11**(3), 201–221 (1999)
2. Apple: Model-view-controller (2012). https://apple.co/3a5Aox9
3. Apple: Placing objects and handling 3D interaction (2019). https://apple.co/3tJw8v2
4. Belle, A.B., El-Boussaidi, G., Desrosiers, C., Mili, H.: The layered architecture revisited: is it an optimization problem? In: SEKE, pp. 344–349 (2013)
5. Belle, A.B., El Boussaidi, G., Kpodjedo, S.: Combining lexical and structural information to reconstruct software layers. Inf. Softw. Technol. **74**, 1–16 (2016)

6. Belle, A.B., El Boussaidi, G., Mili, H.: Recovering software layers from object oriented systems. In: 2014 9th International Conference on Evaluation of Novel Approaches to Software Engineering (ENASE), pp. 1–12. IEEE (2014)
7. Campos, E., Kulesza, U., Coelho, R., Bonifácio, R., Mariano, L.: Unveiling the architecture and design of android applications. In: Proceedings of the 17th International Conference on Enterprise Information Systems, vol. 2, pp. 201–211 (2015)
8. Corazza, A., Di Martino, S., Maggio, V., Scanniello, G.: Weighing lexical information for software clustering in the context of architecture recovery. Empir. Softw. Eng. **21**(1), 72–103 (2015). https://doi.org/10.1007/s10664-014-9347-3
9. Daoudi, A., ElBoussaidi, G., Moha, N., Kpodjedo, S.: An exploratory study of MVC-based architectural patterns in android apps. In: Proceedings of the 34th ACM/SIGAPP Symposium on Applied Computing, pp. 1711–1720. ACM (2019)
10. Davies, D.L., Bouldin, D.W.: A cluster separation measure. IEEE Trans. Pattern Anal. Mach. Intell. **2**, 224–227 (1979)
11. DeLong, D.: A better MVC (2017). https://davedelong.com/blog/2017/11/06/a-better-mvc-part-1-the-problems/
12. Dobrean, D.: Automatic examining of software architectures on mobile applications codebases. In: 2019 IEEE International Conference on Software Maintenance and Evolution (ICSME), pp. 595–599. IEEE (2019)
13. Dobrean, D., Dioşan, L.: An analysis system for mobile applications MVC software architectures, pp. 178–185. INSTICC, SciTePress (2019). https://doi.org/10.5220/0007827801780185
14. Dobrean, D., Dioşan, L.: Model view controller in iOS mobile applications development, pp. 547–552. KSI Research Inc. and Knowledge Systems Institute Graduate School (2019). https://doi.org/10.18293/SEKE2019
15. Dobrean, D., Dioşan, L.: Detecting model view controller architectural layers using clustering in mobile codebases. In: Proceedings of the 15th International Conference on Software Technologies, pp. 196–203. INSTICC (2020). https://doi.org/10.5220/0009884601960203
16. Dobrean, D., Dioşan, L.: A hybrid approach to MVC architectural layers analysis. In: In Proceedings of the 16th International Conference on Evaluation of Novel Approaches to Software Engineering, pp. 36–46. INSTICC (2021). https://doi.org/10.5220/0010326700360046
17. El Boussaidi, G., Belle, A.B., Vaucher, S., Mili, H.: Reconstructing architectural views from legacy systems. In: 2012 19th Working Conference on Reverse Engineering, pp. 345–354. IEEE (2012)
18. Garcia, J., Popescu, D., Mattmann, C., Medvidovic, N., Cai, Y.: Enhancing architectural recovery using concerns. In: 2011 26th IEEE/ACM International Conference on Automated Software Engineering (ASE 2011), pp. 552–555. IEEE (2011)
19. Ghorbani, N., Garcia, J., Malek, S.: Detection and repair of architectural inconsistencies in Java. In: Proceedings of the 41st International Conference on Software Engineering, pp. 560–571. IEEE Press (2019)
20. Huang, A.: Similarity measures for text document clustering. In: Proceedings of the Sixth New Zealand Computer Science Research Student Conference (NZCSRSC2008), Christchurch, New Zealand, vol. 4, pp. 9–56 (2008)
21. GSMA Intelligence: 2019 raport (2019). https://www.gsmaintelligence.com/
22. Lakos, J.: Large-scale c++ software design. Reading MA **173**, 217–271 (1996)
23. Laval, J., Anquetil, N., Bhatti, U., Ducasse, S.: Ozone: layer identification in the presence of cyclic dependencies. Sci. Comput. Program. **78**(8), 1055–1072 (2013)
24. Le, D.M., Behnamghader, P., Garcia, J., Link, D., Shahbazian, A., Medvidovic, N.: An empirical study of architectural change in open-source software systems. In: 2015 IEEE/ACM 12th Working Conference on MSR, pp. 235–245. IEEE (2015)

25. Levenshtein, V.I.: Binary codes capable of correcting deletions, insertions, and reversals. Soviet Phys. Dokl. **10**, 707–710 (1966)
26. Lutellier, T., et al.: Comparing software architecture recovery techniques using accurate dependencies. In: 2015 IEEE/ACM 37th IEEE International Conference on Software Engineering (ICSE), vol. 2, pp. 69–78. IEEE (2015)
27. Mancoridis, S., Mitchell, B.S., Chen, Y., Gansner, E.R.: Bunch: a clustering tool for the recovery and maintenance of software system structures. In: Proceedings IEEE International Conference on Software Maintenance-1999 (ICSM 1999). Software Maintenance for Business Change (Cat. No. 99CB36360), pp. 50–59. IEEE (1999)
28. Mitchell, B.S., Mancoridis, S.: On the evaluation of the bunch search-based software modularization algorithm. Soft. Comput. **12**(1), 77–93 (2008)
29. Mozilla: Firefox iOS application (2018). https://github.com/mozilla-mobile/firefox-ios
30. Müller, H.A., Orgun, M.A., Tilley, S.R., Uhl, J.S.: A reverse-engineering approach to subsystem structure identification. J. Softw. Maint. Res. Pract. **5**(4), 181–204 (1993)
31. Murtagh, F.: A survey of recent advances in hierarchical clustering algorithms. Comput. J. **26**(4), 354–359 (1983)
32. Pruijt, L., Köppe, C., van der Werf, J.M., Brinkkemper, S.: The accuracy of dependency analysis in static architecture compliance checking. Softw.: Pract. Exp. **47**(2), 273–309 (2017)
33. Rathee, A., Chhabra, J.K.: Software remodularization by estimating structural and conceptual relations among classes and using hierarchical clustering. In: Singh, D., Raman, B., Luhach, A.K., Lingras, P. (eds.) Advanced Informatics for Computing Research. CCIS, vol. 712, pp. 94–106. Springer, Singapore (2017). https://doi.org/10.1007/978-981-10-5780-9_9
34. Rousseeuw, P.J.: Silhouettes: a graphical aid to the interpretation and validation of cluster analysis. J. Comput. Appl. Math. **20**, 53–65 (1987)
35. Sangal, N., Jordan, E., Sinha, V., Jackson, D.: Using dependency models to manage complex software architecture. In: ACM SIGPLAN Notices, vol. 40, no. 10, pp. 167–176. ACM (2005)
36. Sarkar, S., Maskeri, G., Ramachandran, S.: Discovery of architectural layers and measurement of layering violations in source code. J. Syst. Softw. **82**(11), 1891–1905 (2009)
37. Scanniello, G., D'Amico, A., D'Amico, C., D'Amico, T.: Using the Kleinberg algorithm and vector space model for software system clustering. In: 2010 IEEE 18th International Conference on Program Comprehension, pp. 180–189. IEEE (2010)
38. Schmidt, F., MacDonell, S.G., Connor, A.M.: An automatic architecture reconstruction and refactoring framework. In: Lee, R. (ed.) Software Engineering Research, Management and Applications 2011. Studies in Computational Intelligence, vol. 377, pp. 95–111. Springer, Heidelberg (2012). https://doi.org/10.1007/978-3-642-23202-2_7
39. Trust: Trust wallet iOS application (2018). https://github.com/TrustWallet/Trust-wallet-ios
40. Vewer, D.: 2019 raport (2019). https://iosdevsurvey.com/2019/
41. Wikimedia: Wikipedia iOS application (2018). https://github.com/wikimedia/wikimedia-ios/tree/master
42. Zapalowski, V., Nunes, I., Nunes, D.J.: Revealing the relationship between architectural elements and source code characteristics. In: Proceedings of the 22nd International Conference on Program Comprehension, pp. 14–25. ACM (2014)

Considerations for Indigenous Cultural Aspects in Software Development: A Case Study

Philemon Yalamu(✉), Abdullah Al Mahmud(✉), and Caslon Chua(✉)

Swinburne University of Technology, Hawthorn, VIC 3122, Australia
{pyalamu,aalmahmud,cchua}@swin.edu.au

Abstract. Requirements engineering (RE) is a human-centric domain and requires broader consultations. Oftentimes, focus of the process is on the software development perspectives and fails to consider how users view the requirements engineering process. This research examines whether cultural influences are important in the software development requirement engineering process from the users' perspective. A case study to elicit user requirements was conducted using design thinking and a human-centered approach, with data collected from university students from Papua New Guinea (PNG) and other Pacific Island nations. The findings reveal 11 cultural characteristics distinct to the indigenous cultures of participants have an impact on RE activities; six are related to Hofstede's cultural dimensions, while five are unclassified and unique to PNG. The study highlights the importance of culture in the RE process and why it is essential to consider users' cultural expectations in software development.

Keywords: Requirement Engineering · Design thinking · Human centered · Design · Culture

1 Introduction

1.1 Requirement Engineering

In order to develop effective software systems, designers and developers often spend time to understand how end-users perceive to use these systems. This procedure is usually referred to as the Requirement Engineering (RE) process, centered around the needs and requirements of people. According to Arthur and Gröner [1], Jiang, Eberlein [2], Davis, Hickey [3], RE is a human-centric domain that is considered a key aspect for the development of effective software systems. Davis, Hickey [3], Pandey, Suman [4] describe RE as an essential precondition for establishing a firm bond between products and services, customers and the organization, as well as for software developers to better understand user requirements. Studies have indicated RE to be the most critical and complex process within the development of socio-technical systems [4, 5]. Furthermore, RE is one of the most important processes that can influence whether software development is successful or not. [6]. Jiang, Eberlein [2], Agarwal and Goel [7] contend that the failure of a project is caused by poorly planned RE procedures. Poor requirement identification and inadequate requirements have been cited as the key reasons why systems

R. Ali et al. (Eds.): ENASE 2021, CCIS 1556, pp. 29–43, 2022.
https://doi.org/10.1007/978-3-030-96648-5_2

fail to satisfy user expectations [8, 9]. Therefore, to enable the success of systems, the RE techniques are often introduced in the different stages of the design and development process to accommodate users' expectations. Users become a significant component of the systems development lifecycle, just as they do in design, and concepts like design thinking and human-centered approaches are frequently used [10]. As a foundation for eliciting and modelling requirements, the context in which RE is achieved is dependent on cognitive and social familiarity [11, 12]. Whenever social aspects are included in a study, it is essential to consider cultural factors.

Kheirkhah and Deraman [13] highlight culture as one of the factors that influences the RE process because it affects how people act, think, and interact with systems and products. It can be argued that the RE conception was derived from the Western culture before taking into consideration other cultures [14]. Culture must be taken into account for the benefit of the intended users of systems and technology. RE can be regarded from two angles: from the developers' and the users' perspectives. To our knowledge, a lot of studies presented RE from the perspective of developers, and not much have been done from the users' standpoint. A prior study underlined the influences of culture on RE activities from software practitioners and academics [14]. Our research will fill a vacuum in the literature by presenting RE from the users' views who are deeply rooted in their indigenous cultures.

This paper examines whether indigenous cultural aspects are relevant in the software development requirements elicitation process from the users' perspective. According to [15], the notion of indigenous culture and practice relates to real-world knowledge associated with the practical engagement than the theoretical approach. Being indigenous (indigeneity) refers to the source of things or something that is natural/inborn to a certain context or culture. The specificity of indigenous cultures lies around "the ideas, customs, and social behavior of a particular people or society" [16]. In a more specific context, the term "culture" is used in this paper to refer to the indigenous knowledge and practices of students in Papua New Guinea (PNG) and other smaller Pacific Island countries, who are the target population for our study highlighted in this paper.

Our inspiration came from previous works associated to cultural influences on RE activities [14, 17–20]. These studies have brought new perspectives on culture and the RE process, particularly for web technologies used in higher education in underdeveloped countries.

The structure of this paper is organized as follows: Sect. 2 discusses the motivation and related study on RE pertinent to the web and cultural influences associated to it. Section 3 highlights the methodology adopted for the paper and also discusses the results for each of the studies. Section 4 provides the overall discussions of the study. Finally, Sect. 5 presents the conclusion of the paper and outlines plans for further studies.

2 Motivation and Related Study

This section highlights research on requirement engineering as the dominating approach for systems that support technologies for online learning in developing countries, and pays specific focus on culture. An overview of RE will be introduced in the context of web application development with reference to cultural influences on the RE process.

2.1 Phases of Requirement Engineering

In the software development life cycle, RE is the initial phase and forms the foundation of any software products [21]. Many studies capture the RE process highlighting several stages and among those, there are the five fundamental (sub) processes [22–25]: requirements elicitation, requirements analysis, requirements specifications, requirements validation, and requirements management. For this paper, more emphasis will be on requirements elicitation, analysis, and validation since requirements specifications and management were not part of our study. Figure 1 shows the RE process used for this paper, highlighting the users' and developers' activities [26].

This study is also guided by the international standard that manages the RE process. The standard ISO/IEC/IEEE 29148:2011 provides the standard guidelines for the process and activities for RE.

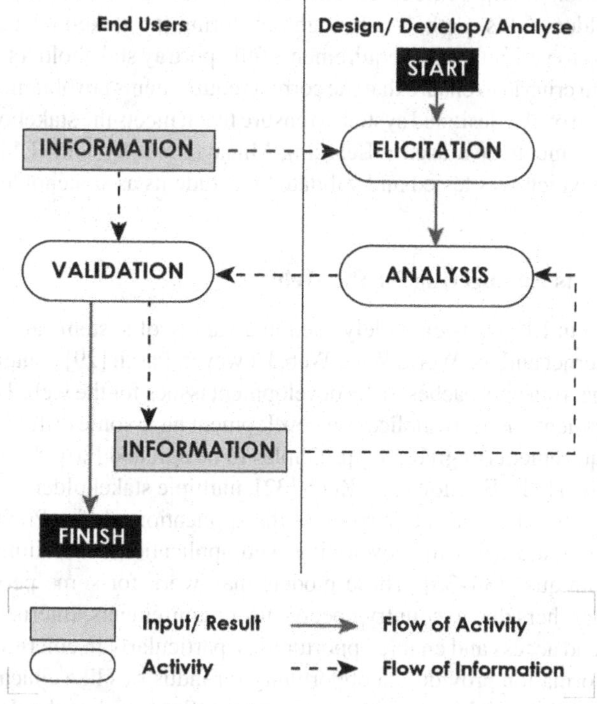

Fig. 1. The RE Process for the study (Adapted from [26])

Elicitation: One of the major processes in RE is requirements elicitation, which aims to determine the project scope and elicit user requirements [27]. According to Kasirun [28], this stage describes how to understand a problem and the circumstances in which it can be implemented. Kasirun [28] highlights that the goal of requirements elicitation is to collect as many requirements as possible so that different solutions to the challenges at hand might be considered. Often, the success of the requirements elicitation activity leads to better outcomes on the RE goals, culminating in the development of a suitable and effective application [28].

Analysis: The goal of the requirements analysis process was to gather stakeholder input on desired service requirements and translate that information into a technical view of a required product that could provide those services. This technique gives the impression of a system that will meet stakeholder needs in the future, but it does not advise any specific implementation as far as restrictions allow. It establishes quantitative framework requirements that indicate what traits the supplier must possess and to what extent stakeholder requirements must be met.

Validation: This activity verifies the authenticity, consistency, and validity requirements. It is at this point in the RE process when problems in the requirements document are frequently discovered. Whenever problems are identified, they must be rectified and corrected. Validation of requirements is contingent on the approval of project authorities and key stakeholders. This method is brought up during the stakeholder requirements definition process to verify that the requirements fully portray stakeholders' needs and to provide validation criteria to ensure that the correct requirements are obtained. Validation tests are performed on the designed system to ensure that it meets the stakeholder's expectations and requirements. We used a Learning Management System (LMS) prototype for our research, which was tested and validated by students as stakeholders.

2.2 Requirements Engineering for the Web

The process used in RE has been widely used in a variety of systems and applications, including the internet and the World Wide Web. However, Pasch [29] contends that there are several engineering approaches to the development issues for the web. The traditional software development and web application development have some differences that may cause classic requirements engineering principles to be agitated [30]. According to Srivastava and Chawla [31], Escalona and Koch [32], multiple stakeholders are involved in web applications, and the size and purpose of the applications differ. Previous research has offered several strategies for developing web applications, including procedures, models, and techniques [33–35]. These models may work for some people, but they may not work for others due to country-specific user requirements. Internet connectivity continues to extend access and enable opportunities, particularly in emerging economies [36]. This transformation provides an opportunity for industries like education to incorporate web apps and technology into their classrooms. Since web technology can break down educational barriers [37], learning institutions in emerging economies like PNG and other Pacific Island countries (PICs) are adamant about implementing technology like LMS to help with teaching and learning.

The PICs have several geographical challenges, such as their islands dispersed across the ocean and also other infrastructural challenges and therefore, using LMSs would allow learning resources to reach out to their citizens [38–40]. While access is still important, software developers and designers may face obstacles due to a variety of end-user requirements. One of these concerns is culture, which is regarded as an important aspect in efficient learning [41].

Culture is regarded as an important aspect of society in PICs [42]. As a result, cultural concerns should be considered in the RE process if web technologies are to be utilized.

2.3 Cultural Influences on Requirement Engineering Activities

Culture has a significant impact on how individuals and businesses work, including their preferences for RE approaches, methods, and practices. It affects the way people think, communicate, comprehend, and choose what is significant Hofstede, Hofstede [43]. Every culture has its own set of beliefs, practices, and communication methods. The behavioral practices within these cultures have an impact on their diversity. Hanisch, Thanasankit [20] contend that the social and cultural factors of RE cannot be ignored as it affects the success of software development. Previous research on the impact of culture on RE activities has revealed a link between the impact of cultural background on RE practice from the Saudi Arabian perspective [14].

Hofstede's Cultural Dimensions: One of the most wide-ranging research conducted by Hofstede, Hofstede [43] shows how culture influences values in the workplace. This study has been broadly used in numerous domains, including RE. Hofstede, Hofstede [43], Hofstede [44] defines culture as "the collective programming of the mind distinguishing the members of one group or category of people from others". Six dimensions of a nation's culture was proposed by Hofstede, Hofstede [43] that focus on:

- **Power Distance Index (PDI):** The degree to which members of a group or organization who are less powerful accept and anticipate power to be divided unequally, such as in a family or school context.
- **Individualism versus Collectivism (IDV):** The extent to which people in a community work with one another; for example, highly individualistic cultures would promote individual authority, achievement, and decision-making power. Individualism refers to the degree to which people feel self-sufficient rather than reliant as members of broader communities.
- **Masculinity versus Femininity (MAS):** The extent to which societal gender roles differ, particularly in masculinity, when the use of force is socially sanctioned.
- **Uncertainty Avoidance Index (UAI):** The degree to which members of society are either uncomfortable or at ease in chaotic or perplexing conditions. Uncertainty and ambiguity are dealt with by UAI.
- **Long- vs. Short-term Orientation (LTO):** The degree to which members of a society are tied to their own past while addressing current and future issues.
- **Indulgence versus Impulses (IND):** The extent to which members of a society have fun and enjoy life without being bound by rules and laws. It implies a long-term approach to dealing with change.

With this approach, each country is assigned a number score based on the above dimensions, which are used to define the country's society. The scale spans from 0 to 100, with 50 being the average. According to Hofstede's rule [43], if a score surpasses the average of a cultural dimension, the culture is high on that dimension. Although Hofstede's model only featured a few of the world's largest economies, it did reveal significant cultural parallels.

3 Methodology

This section presents the design of the methodology and procedures used in the study. To achieve the objectives of our study, we conducted two user studies during the requirement gathering phase in the design of the LMS prototype. These user studies were conducted to determine whether indigenous cultural factors are important in a software development requirement gathering from the perspective of the users. These user studies incorporated survey questionnaires, semi-structured interviews, focus groups, observations, and literature review. The user studies and their objectives include:

- **Exploratory Case Study (S1):** To elicit user requirements for technological solutions for teaching and learning.
- **User Experiment (S2):** To validate requirements gathered from the case study.

The user requirements from the participants in S1 and S2 were gathered based on the human-centric approach. The two studies were completed using the RE process presented in Fig. 1. The number of participants who completed the study using respective data collection methods is represented by 'n' in the below sections.

3.1 Exploratory Case Study

The first study was an exploratory case study (S1) conducted with students, lecturers, and university administrators at a higher learning institution PNG. Survey data for S1 was extracted from questionnaires (n = 58), focus groups (n = 15), and interviews (n = 2).

Specific to the objectives presented in this paper, the S1 explored different teaching and learning experiences from university students in PNG. Other growing economies face similar infrastructure and administrative issues, according to the results. In addition, various cultural influences on traditional knowledge and behaviors were discovered as a result of this research. The questionnaire and focus groups were used to acquire these needs.

S1 Result: In S1, participants shared different perspectives on how culture influences teaching and learning. Their perspectives contributed to an understanding of traditional cultures and learning approaches that could influence learning in PNG's HLIs. Most of the data came from the Likert scale ratings, survey comments and focus group sessions where participants openly shared their experiences. We found that cultural influences such as respect to the elders, gender differences, and hereditary statuses, pertinent to indigenous knowledge, practices and customs affect students' learning. In the focus groups, participants expressed that the influence of Bigman system, which gives certain men authority over others, affects the way they participate in university activities. They also highlighted the significance behind hereditary concerns where in few areas, women have power over the land and other hereditary privileges whilst in most, men obtain those privileges. Participants also stressed on the wantok system, a practice that appeared to have influenced the way teaching and learning is conducted; for example, favoritism in class. Moreover, they also highlighted that in traditional learning, knowledge transfer happens between the same gender where men and women are segregated into gender to learn certain skills. This influence is often brought into classroom learning. Comments were also made regarding cultural practices such as respect to elders, which students often reflect on their teachers. It has also been highlighted that often students fear making mistakes because to them, it denotes being stupid. Likert scale ratings (1 = not preferred to 5 = highly preferred) provided by students also reveal gender preference for group collaboration, whereby students prefer to work with the same gender.

The S1's user requirements were examined and transformed into a technical representation of a desired product, in this case, an LMS prototype. We divided the cultural influences into three areas in the LMS prototype: language, motifs and symbols [45, 46]. Participants were given a set of tasks to complete. Following the S1 study, we created a working prototype of an LMS in S2 that incorporated the cultural effects found in S1.

3.2 User Experiment (S2)

The second study (S2) was a user experiment that involved students from Papua New Guinea and other smaller Pacific Island nations who were studying at various universities in Victoria, Australia. This study was done to confirm and validate whether we have captured the relevant criteria in S1.

In S2, an LMS prototype was developed incorporating some of the cultural elements captured in S1 and tested on PNG and Pacific Island students from Fiji and Solomon Islands studying in Australia. The survey data for S2 was gathered from a questionnaire ($n = 22$) and observations ($n = 22$).

We incorporated aspects of traditional PNG culture into the design of the prototype in S2 by looking at how local language, traditional motifs, and cultural symbols affect HLI students' view of the interface on an LMS [45]. We presented a learning module incorporating these cultural elements (see Fig. 2. A: local language option, B: traditional motif, C: cultural symbols) into a learning user interface.

S2 Result: In S2, participants highlighted the essence of culture and its value in their society. These data came from the survey comments and Likert scale ratings provided by participants after attempting the learning activity. Forty-one percent of participants provided comments on their preference of a local language option on the interface. Of these, 36% were in favor of a local language, while the remaining 5% preferred English. The rest (59%) did not provide any comment. In reference to the use of traditional motifs, 77% provided a high rating for their experience interacting with an interface that has traditional motifs. The remaining 38% gave a neutral rating for their experience interacting with traditional motifs. Fifty-four percent provided a high effectiveness rating for using cultural symbols in learning. They gave comments like, "The use of cultural images brings a sense of pride from a cultural perspective". The other 46% provided lower ratings (32% = more effective and 14% = effective).

The two user studies that we conducted have been guided by Hofstede's cultural dimensions highlighted in Sect. 2.3, which sets the foundation for the framework for cultural requirements discovered in those studies.

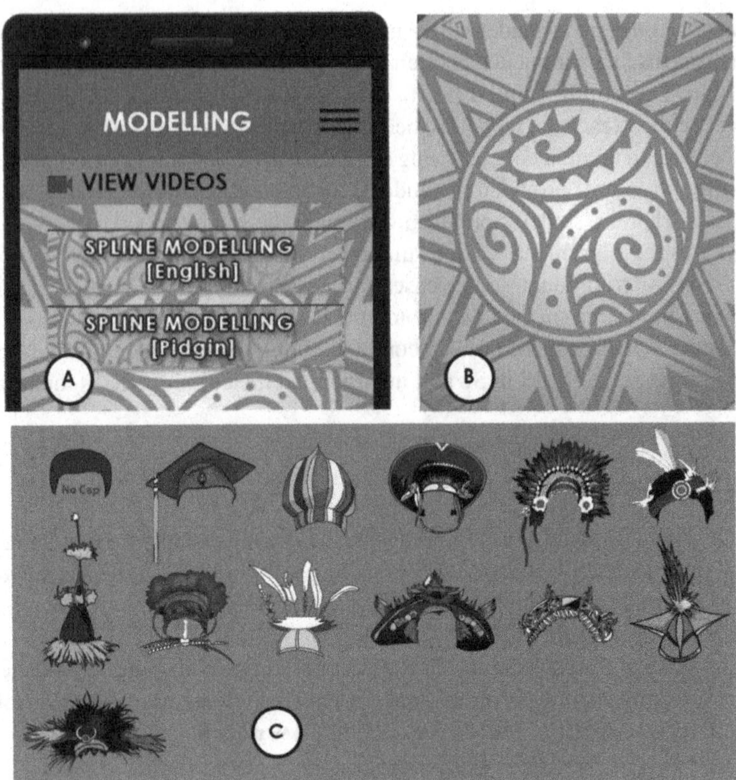

Fig. 2. Screenshots of the interface for the developed LMS prototype highlighting (A) local language option, (B) traditional motif, (C) cultural symbols

4 Discussion

The two user studies, which were conducted with PNG and other Pacific Island students from emerging economies, acquired information on teaching and learning experiences, as well as the role of culture in diverse RE activities that were influenced by indigenous cultural factors.

The data for S1 highlight how culture influences learning style; e.g.: from the focus groups, we provided the question, 'Can you think of any ways in which traditional culture affects the ways students communicate with each other and with their lecturers at your university?' Students' responses included things like, 'Teachers are considered elders, thus they are respected and cannot be questioned'. Apart from that, data from S2 [45] indicates how students value culture; e.g., the comments relating to participants' perception on interacting with the LMS prototype interface show 64% of PNG students indicated that cultural symbols gave them a sense of "identity, pride and belonging". These are two examples from our studies. According to the findings from these two research, 11 cultural characteristics specific to the indigenous culture of participants had an impact on RE activities [26], and those include:

1. Local language option for learning
2. Bigman system (e.g.: *man has higher status*)
3. Hereditary (e.g.: *patrilineal and matrilineal*)
4. Wantok system (e.g.: *Favouritism in class*)
5. Respecting teachers as elders
6. Gender preference for group collaboration
7. Learning styles
8. Knowledge transfer happens between the same gender
9. Students do not speak up
10. Making mistakes denotes stupidity
11. Cultural symbols – gives a sense of pride, identity, and belonging

These cultural influences were categorized into five groups, four of which were derived from Hofstede's dimensions (power distance, collectivism, masculinity, and short-term orientation), while a fifth dimension was proposed as a new dimension specific to PNG. Table 1 shows the influence of PNG culture on the main activities within the RE process. The "✔" signifies that the corresponding RE activity has an impact on the corresponding cultural dimension, whereas the "–" signifies that the corresponding cultural dimensions do not apply to the corresponding RE activity.

Table 1. Influences of cultural dimensions on the RE activities (from [26]).

RE activity	Hofstede's cultural dimensions				
	PDI	IDV	MAS	STO	Specific
Elicitation	✔	✔	✔	✔	✔
Analysis	✔	✔	✔	–	✔
Specification	–	–	–	–	–
Validation	✔	✔	–	–	✔
Management	–	–	–	–	–

We have excluded two of Hofstede's cultural dimensions: The Uncertainty Avoidance Index (UAI) and Indulgence versus Impulses (IND). The reason was that none of the data collected has any cultural factors from PNG that influences or has any correlations with these two dimensions. Instead, a specific cultural influence has been used. This added dimension was included to accommodate the cultural influences that are unique to PNG that were not captured by Hofstede's cultural dimensions. The next section details the cultural influences on RE.

Cultural Influences on Requirements Engineering

Hofstede's cultural dimensions [43, 47] unfortunately does not include all the emerging economies such as the smaller Pacific island nations, including PNG. Despite this, there are few identical characteristics similar to those presented by Hofstede. PNG, being in Melanesia, shares a lot of cultural similarities with many African and some Asian countries [48].

Power Distance Index (PDI). As mentioned above, Melanesian culture is similar to many African and some Asian countries in which PNG and other smaller Pacific Island nations come under. The 11 cultural influences from our S1 and S2 user studies that relate to the cultural dimensions are presented below.

In countries with high PDI, respecting teachers and elders is considered a basic and lifelong virtue [43]. We place PNG and the Pacific Island nations as ranging within the high PDI category.

Respecting Teachers as Elders. According to Hofstede, Hofstede [43], teachers are respected or even feared, and sometimes, students may have to stand when teachers walk into the classrooms. The data from our survey showed comments from student participants that relate to this where students find it difficult to criticize their teachers because of the way they grew up respecting their parents and elders in their villages. Hofstede, Hofstede [43] highlight, "students in class speak up only when invited to; teachers are never publicly contradicted or criticized and are treated with deference even outside school". Besides, student participants in the focus group also highlighted that a way to respect their elders was to keep a low profile and be humbled to avoid challenging their teachers.

Students do not Speak up in Class. Hofstede, Hofstede [43] highlighted that classroom situations often involve strict order, with the teacher initiating all communication. Students only speak up in class when they are invited. Teachers do not get public criticisms and are often treated with deference even outside school. In our study, similar statements were expressed and one of which, a lecturer participant in the focus group highlighted that "...students do not speak up when asked to. This is linked to traditional connotations whereby their thoughts are expressed by an elder or a village representative".

Collectivism (IDV). PNG, like other Melanesian islands, can be categorized as a Collective society due to the fact they live in traditions, consisting of a living society of men, sharing a common life as a member of the community [49]. Collectivism refers to "societies in which people from birth onward are integrated into strong, cohesive in-groups, which throughout people's lifetime continue to protect them in exchange for unquestioning loyalty" [43].

Wantok System. Data from the user studies show a range of wantok systems being practiced that would influence RE activities. Participants mentioned issues such as lecturers and students with common relationships support each other academically. Other times, it helps get people together for a common good. For example, a participant explained, "...the wantok system brings us together to live and care for each other's needs and even protects each other during times of need or when facing attacks". This system often comprises relationships between individuals characterized by certain aspects like a common language, kinship, geographical area, social association, and belief. Wantok system is one that is often regarded as vital in traditional PNG societies [Renzio 1999, as cited in 50].

Masculinity (MAS). Our user studies revealed the Bigman system where a male has a higher status than female counterparts in PNG context. The Bigman system resembles a type of leadership role where males, have certain personal qualities and status that are reflected in their character, appearance, and manner, enabling them to have power over others within their society [51]. The Bigman system is built around respect and regard to the Bigman for being the most respected person of worth and fame [50]. Supported by Hofstede, Hofstede [43], "Men are supposed to be more concerned with achievements outside the home – hunting and fighting in traditional societies. They are supposed to be assertive, competitive, and tough.

Short-Term Orientation (STO). Short-term orientation stands for the "fostering of virtues related to the past and present – in particular, respect for tradition, preservation of 'face,' and fulfilling social obligations" [43].

Hereditary Statuses. Data from our user studies show students and lecturer participants mentioned factors related to socio-cultural issues around the hereditary status of men and women. This is a form of a culture where people keep their traditions and preserve certain practices to fulfil the social obligation [43]. In specific contexts, PNG societies have the unilineal descent system which comprises of patrilineal and matrilineal societies, where men from patrilineal backgrounds inherit the land and other family obligations while from matrilineal, female owns the land and all other obligations.

Specific Cultural Influences (Specific). Apart from Hofstede's cultural dimensions model, this study identified four cultural influences that are specific to PNG's indigenous cultures and those are: local language, gender preference, and learning styles.

In countries with high PDI, showing respect for teachers and elders is considered a basic and lifelong virtue [43].

Local Language for Learning. The issue of language was considered to be an essential cultural factor that affects students learning. Although English is an official language taught in schools, participants expressed that it sometimes becomes difficult to understand, especially when it is the third, fourth, or fifth language for many. PNG has over 800 languages and it would be extremely difficult to include all the languages in the RE process and systems. However, there are four official languages and among those, *Tok-Pisin* is regarded as the widely spoken language throughout the country [52–55].

Besides, participants also used Tok-Pisin while attempting the surveys and focus groups and claimed that students and lecturers are speaking Tok-Pisin during course discussions when confronting situations where English could not be clearly understood.

Gender Preference. In the Likert-scale survey questions, female participants rated a higher preference for collaboration in any learning activity with their same gender instead of the opposite gender.

Learning Styles. There were also few comments and feedback regarding learning styles, such as the suggestion that traditional learning was accomplished through observation, storytelling, and practical means. For example, a participant in the focus group mentioned,"Learning is done through creative means through telling stories, arts & crafts, and performances". Furthermore, a comment on the gaming experience implies that the game resembles practice-based learning, which is similar to traditional learning and engages participants. Besides, one participant stated that people are hesitant to take on new challenges because they are afraid of being labelled as foolish and uneducated if they make mistakes.

Cultural Symbols. Participants discussed materialistic cultural objects, indicating that they have some value in their beliefs and feelings. For example, a student participant in the user study explains, "…having cultural icons/ motifs is another way of preserving culture by incorporating them in the interface…The icons are symbols and respectable ornaments that are used by culturally signifying cultural standing and elevation". This was supported by another, "Traditional learning is always done in a playful and engaging way. For instance, we learned to build houses by using clay and sticks, that basic knowledge provides the fundamental idea of building a proper house".

Transfer of Knowledge. Data from our user studies revealed that knowledge transfer usually occurs between the same gender where an elderly male teaches a young male or an elderly female training a young female. An example provided by a participant was, "…elders coached youths in the villages through various cultural activities". This can be supported by another, "traditional knowledge is imparted through oral, visual and hands-on activities which have interaction with the elders".

5 Conclusion and Future Plans

RE is a human-centered and socio-technical process that is essential to any software development projects. The process necessitates cultural sensitivity and a thorough understanding of user expectations. Consequently, it is critical to pay attention to the users' culture. In areas where culture is an important part of everyday life, the RE process should take cultural sensitivity into account.

This paper gathers perspectives from participants through two user studies on cultural influences of teaching and learning from university students from PNG and other smaller Pacific Island nations. University participants from PNG participated in a requirements elicitation study in S1. The requirements for this case study were examined, and used to design an LMS prototype. This prototype was then used in S2 on PNG and Pacific Island students studying in Victoria, Australia to test and verify the findings of S1. Four of the six cultural dimensions and three of the five core RE activities that were influenced were triangulated with the data gathered.

The findings highlight 11 cultural characteristics unique to PNG's indigenous culture, all of which have an impact on the RE activities. This supports our goal of emphasizing the importance of culture in the RE process and the importance of considering users' perspectives in choosing progressive RE activities. Six of these cultural influences were linked to Hofstede's cultural dimensions, while the other five were uncategorized and unique to PNG.

Following this research, future work will broaden the scope of this paper to include the impact of indigenous culture on RE activities from the perspectives of software practitioners and academics in PNG and other smaller Pacific Island countries. This would entail directly researching the impact of indigenous culture on RE efforts from the viewpoints of software practitioners and academics in the contexts of PNG and other smaller Pacific Island countries. For example, we hope to identify localization impediments associated to software design and development methods, and how indigenous knowledge, culture, and tradition contribute to guiding RE decisions that software practitioners and researchers make.

References

1. Arthur, J.D., Gröner, M.K.: An operational model for structuring the requirements generation process. Requirements Eng. **10**(1), 45–62 (2005)
2. Jiang, L., et al.: A methodology for the selection of requirements engineering techniques. Softw. Syst. Model. **7**(3), 303–328 (2008)
3. Davis, A., Hickey, A., Dieste, O., Juristo, N., Moreno, A.: A quantitative assessment of requirements engineering publications – 1963–2006. In: Sawyer, Pete, Paech, Barbara, Heymans, Patrick (eds.) REFSQ 2007. LNCS, vol. 4542, pp. 129–143. Springer, Heidelberg (2007). https://doi.org/10.1007/978-3-540-73031-6_10
4. Pandey, D., Suman, U., Ramani, A.: Social-organizational participation difficulties in requirement engineering process: a study. Softw. Eng. **1**(1), 1 (2010)
5. Juristo, N., Moreno, A., Silva, A.: Is the European industry moving toward solving requirements engineering problems? IEEE Softw. **19**(6), 70 (2002)
6. Li, Y., Guzman, E., Bruegge, B.: Effective requirements engineering for CSE projects: a lightweight tool. In: 2015 IEEE 18th International Conference on Computational Science and Engineering. IEEE (2015)
7. Agarwal, M., Goel, S.: Expert system and it's requirement engineering process. In: International Conference on Recent Advances and Innovations in Engineering (ICRAIE-2014). IEEE (2014)
8. Bubenko, J.A.: Challenges in requirements engineering. In: Proceedings of 1995 IEEE International Symposium on Requirements Engineering (RE 1995) 1995
9. Damian, D.E.H.: Challenges in requirements engineering (2000). https://doi.org/10.11575/PRISM/31288
10. Dobrigkeit, F., de Paula, D.: Design thinking in practice: understanding manifestations of design thinking in software engineering. In: Proceedings of the 2019 27th ACM Joint Meeting on European Software Engineering Conference and Symposium on the Foundations of Software Engineering, p. 1059–1069. Association for Computing Machinery: Tallinn, Estonia (2019)
11. Nuseibeh, B., Easterbrook, S.: Requirements engineering: a roadmap. In: Proceedings of the Conference on the Future of Software Engineering (2000)
12. Thanasankit, T.: Requirements engineering - exploring the influence of power and Thai values. Eur. J. Inf. Syst. **11**(2), 128–141 (2002)
13. Kheirkhah, E., Deraman, A.: Important factors in selecting requirements engineering techniques. In: 2008 International Symposium on Information Technology (2008)
14. Damiani, E., Spanoudakis, G., Maciaszek, L. (eds.): ENASE 2017. CCIS, vol. 866. Springer, Cham (2018). https://doi.org/10.1007/978-3-319-94135-6
15. Kimbell, R.: Indigenous knowledge, know-how, and design and technology. Des. Technol. Educ. Int. J. **10**(3) (2008)
16. Culture: In English Oxford Living Dictionaries, n.d [cited 2018 November 12]. https://en.oxforddictionaries.com/definition/culture

17. Alsanoosy, T., Spichkova, M., Harland, J.: A Detailed Analysis of the Influence of Saudi Arabia Culture on the Requirement Engineering Process. Springer International Publishing, Cham (2019). https://doi.org/10.1007/978-3-030-22559-9_11
18. Heimgärtner, R.: Culturally-Aware HCI Systems. In: Faucher, C. (ed.) Advances in Culturally-Aware Intelligent Systems and in Cross-Cultural Psychological Studies. ISRL, vol. 134, pp. 11–37. Springer, Cham (2018). https://doi.org/10.1007/978-3-319-67024-9_2
19. Rahman, N.A., Sahibuddin, S.: Challenges in requirements engineering for e-learning elicitation process. J. Math. Comput. Sci. **2**(2), 40–45 (2016)
20. Hanisch, J., Thanasankit, T., Corbitt, B.: Understanding the cultural and social impacts on requirements engineering processes-identifying some problems challenging virtual team interaction with clients. Eur. Conf. Inf. Syst. Proc. 43 (2001)
21. Malik, M.U., Chaudhry, N.M., Malik, K.S.: Evaluation of efficient requirement engineering techniques in agile software development. Int. J. Comput. Appl. **83**(3) (2013)
22. Sommerville, I.: Software engineering, Horton, M., et al. (eds.) Addison-Wesley: New York, Dubai, Delhi, Sydney, Tokyo. p. 773 (2011)
23. Abran, A., et al.: Software Engineering Body of Knowledge. IEEE Computer Society, Angela Burgess (2004)
24. Pandey, D., Suman, U., Ramani, A.K.: An effective requirement engineering process model for software development and requirements management. In: 2010 International Conference on Advances in Recent Technologies in Communication and Computing. IEEE (2010)
25. Sawyer, P., Kotonya, G.: Software requirements. SWEBOK, p. 9–34 (2001)
26. Yalamu, P., Doube, W., Chua, C.: Cultural Influences on requirement engineering in designing an LMS prototype for emerging economies: a papua new guinea and pacific islands' case study. In: Proceedings of the 16th International Conference on Evaluation of Novel Approaches to Software Engineering - ENASE, SciTePress: Portugal, p. 58–67 (2021)
27. Khan, S., Dulloo, A.B., Verma, M.: Systematic review of requirement elicitation techniques. Int. J. Inf. Comput. Technol. **4**(2), 133–138 (2014)
28. Kasirun, Z.M.: A survey on requirements elicitation practices among courseware developers. Malays. J. Comput. Sci. **18**(1), 70–77 (2005)
29. Pasch, G.: Hypermedia and the Web: an Engineering Approach. Internet Res. **10**(3) (2000)
30. Overmyer, S.P.: What's different about requirements engineering for web sites? Requirements Eng. **5**(1), 62–65 (2000)
31. Srivastava, S., Chawla, S.: Multifaceted classification of websites for goal oriented requirement engineering. In: Ranka, Sanjay, Banerjee, Arunava, Biswas, Kanad Kishore, Dua, Sumeet, Mishra, Prabhat, Moona, Rajat, Poon, Sheung-Hung., Wang, Cho-Li. (eds.) IC3 2010. CCIS, vol. 94, pp. 479–485. Springer, Heidelberg (2010). https://doi.org/10.1007/978-3-642-14834-7_45
32. Escalona, M.J., Koch, N.: Requirements engineering for web applications-a comparative study. J. Web Eng. **2**(3), 193–212 (2004)
33. Escalona, M.J., Mejías, M., Torres, J.: Methodologies to develop web information systems and comparative analysis. Eur. J. Inf. Prof. **III**, 25–34 (2002)
34. Koch, N.: A comparative study of methods for hypermedia development (1999). Citeseer
35. Retschitzegger, W., Schwinger, W.: Towards modeling of dataweb applications-a requirement's perspective. AMCIS Proceedings, p. 408 (2000)
36. Poushter, J.: Smartphone ownership and internet usage continues to climb in emerging economies. Pew Res. Center **22**(1), 1–44 (2016)
37. Vegas, E., Ziegler, L., Zerbino, N.: How Ed-Tech can help leapfrog progress in education. Center for Universal Education at The Brookings Institution (2019)
38. Kituyi, G., Tusubira, I.: A framework for the integration of e-learning in higher education institutions in developing countries. Int. J. Educ. Dev. Using Inf. Commun. Technol. **9**(2), 19–36 (2013)

39. Garnaut, R., Namaliu, R.: PNG universities review - report to the Prime Ministers Somare and Rudd. Australian Government - Department of Foreign Affairs and Trade, Australia (2010)
40. Gunga, S.O., Ricketts, I.W.: Facing the challenges of e-learning initiatives in African universities. Br. J. Educ. Technol. p. 896–906 (2007)
41. Chen, A.Y., et al.: Cultural issues in the design of technology-enhanced learning systems. Br. J. Edu. Technol. **30**(3), 217–230 (1999)
42. Rao, K.: Universal design for learning and multimedia technology: supporting culturally and linguistically diverse students. J. Educ. Multimedia Hypermedia **24**(2), 121–137 (2015)
43. Hofstede, G., Hofstede, G.J., Minkov, M.: Cultures and Organizations - Software of the Mind, 3rd edn (2010)
44. Hofstede, G.: Geert Hofstede cultural dimensions. Itim International: Itim online (2009)
45. Yalamu, P., Chua, C., Doube, W.: Does indigenous culture affect one's view of an LMS interface: a PNG and Pacific Islands Students' perspective. In: Proceedings of the 31st Australian Conference on Human-Computer-Interaction, pp. 302–306. Association for Computing Machinery: Fremantle, WA, Australia (2019)
46. Yalamu, P., Doube, W., Chua, C.: Designing a culturally inspired mobile application for cooperative learning. In: Luo, Y. (ed.) CDVE 2020. LNCS, vol. 12341, pp. 158–166. Springer, Cham (2020). https://doi.org/10.1007/978-3-030-60816-3_18
47. Hofstede, G.: The 6-D model of national culture. n.d. [cited 2020 July 14]. https://geerthofstede.com/culture-geert-hofstede-gert-jan-hofstede/6d-model-of-national-culture/
48. Rosenstiel, A.: Historical perspective and the study of Melanesian culture1. Oceania **24**(3), 172–189 (1954)
49. Denoon, D., Lacey, R.: Oral tradition in Melanesia. PNG: University of Papua New Guinea, Port Moresby (2017)
50. Nanau, G.L.: The wantok system as a socio-economic and political network in Melanesia. OMNES J. Multicultural Soc. **2**(1), 31–55 (2011)
51. Sahlins, M.D.: Poor man, rich man, big-man, chief: political types in Melanesia and Polynesia. Comp. Stud. Soc. Hist. **5**(3), 285–303 (1963)
52. The Economist. Papua New Guinea's incredible linguistic diversity (2017). [cited 2018 October 15] https://www.economist.com/the-economist-explains/2017/07/20/papua-new-guineas-incredible-linguistic-diversity
53. EMTV Online, Sign Language, Next official language for PNG. EMTV Online: Youtube (2015)
54. Paliwala, A.B.: Language in Papua New Guinea: the value of census data. J. Linguist. Soc. Papua New G. **30**(1) (2012)
55. Malone, S., Paraide, P.: Mother tongue-based bilingual education in Papua New Guinea. Int. Rev. Educ. Internationale Zeitschrift für Erziehungswissenschaft **57**(5/6), 705–720 (2011)

Modelling Age of End-Users Using Wire-Frames

Hourieh Khalajzadeh[1](✉), Tanjila Kanij[1], Aria YukFan Jim[2], Hyun Shim[2], Jue Wang[2], Lionel Richie Wijaya[2], Rongbin Xu[2], and John Grundy[1]

[1] HumaniSE Lab, Faculty of IT, Monash University, Melbourne, Australia
{hourieh.khalajzadeh,tanjila.kanij,john.grundy}@monash.edu
[2] Faculty of Information Technology, Monash University, Melbourne, Australia
https://www.monash.edu/it/humanise-lab

Abstract. The range of technology users is continuously increasing from adults to children as well as seniors. This introduces new age-related requirements and considerations. Modelling frameworks are used to assist the software development independently of the platform and the coding technology. However, very limited research has been done on age-related issues within the modelling and design frameworks. In this paper, we investigate how human-centric aspects regarding age can be better modelled by extending wire-frames. We collected both developers and end-users feedback through questionnaires and introduced an extension of wire-frames to cater for decisions regarding age within the modelling framework. We then conducted a usability testing by using the extended age-modelling wire-frame approach to design a news app. This shows that when using our extended wire-frames, developers can cater for different user types and their accessibility needs easily. We finally conducted cognitive walk-throughs with three personas, representing children, adults and seniors to evaluate the prototype app. The results proved the usability of the app for all age groups.

Keywords: Human aspects · Modelling · End-users age · Persona · Cognitive walk-through · Usability

1 Introduction

There is an increase in the average age of the Internet users, with 73% of United States adults over the age of 64 accessing the internet [37]. Elderly users can face issues such as screen readability due to visual impairments, which is not usually an issue for the mostly young developers who design and develop most software [36]. On the other hand, the number of teenagers growing up with technologies is also increasing. The study by Hussain et al. [18] compares web-browsing behaviour between different age groups and discusses the issues teenagers have with poor visual designs, such as font size, background colour and layout of certain websites. These provide evidence for a need to better cater for different age groups of software systems end-users and carefully consider the limitations and abilities of these groups when designing a software [22].

Modelling Languages are used to assist the development of complex software systems with implementation concerns such as usability, security, persistence, and business

R. Ali et al. (Eds.): ENASE 2021, CCIS 1556, pp. 44–66, 2022.
https://doi.org/10.1007/978-3-030-96648-5_3

rules independently of the platform and the coding technology [19]. Existing requirements modelling languages, including iStar 2.0 [12], and conventional modelling languages such as the Unified Modelling Language (UML), have been designed to model software functional and non-functional requirements. *Human-centric aspects* of end users of software, such as their age, satisfaction, preferences, working environment, and gender [22], are one of the most significant factors to the success of a software system. However, these have been largely ignored and not modelled properly during the system development process to date [15]. There have been works on modelling emotions and interactions of the users [26,32,33]. However, there is little or no provision to model diverse human-centric aspects of software end-users, including the age of the end-users.

In this paper, we present an extended wire-frame to improve the modelling process to better meet the human-centric issues regarding age. We critically analyse the existing models, present our own extended model, and eventually build a prototype, and evaluate it using personas and cognitive walk-through. Our research aim is to investigate how human-centric aspects regarding age can be expressed in current modelling frameworks. We initially investigate the type of modelling frameworks that are best fitted for adding human-centric aspects regarding age by collecting inputs from developers and relevant research papers. Next, we look into ways to best model user characteristics regarding age in software requirements and/or design models. Last, we discuss what application domains can benefit from human-centric aspects regarding age. Common applications include news apps, discussion forums, and social media. For the evaluation, we identify whether developers are easily able to create software systems with better usability for all age groups using our extended wire-frame. We also evaluate the prototype apps created using the extended wire-frame to understand whether the different user types are able to easily use the software systems. Finally, we apply cognitive walk-through with three personas, representing all three age groups, as a usability inspection method to evaluate the usability of our prototype app for users of different age groups.

This paper is an extended version of an earlier work that appeared at Evaluation of Novel Approaches to Software Engineering (ENASE) conference 2021 [20]. The key contributions of this paper include:

- Presenting an extended version of wire-frames to design the application specific to the age of the end-users
- Reviewing the literature on modelling the age of the users using personas
- Using personas to evaluate the usability of the method.

The rest of this paper is organised as follows. Section 2 provides a summary of the research papers that are related to our study. We present our approach in Sect. 3 and our evaluation approach in Sect. 4. Section 5 presents our extended modelling framework including examples of the artefacts resulting from the research. We also discuss evaluation responses from our developer survey questionnaires and the findings of our cognitive walk-throughs with personas. We will finally conclude the paper in Sect. 6.

2 Related Work

We reviewed a number of research papers related to extending modelling languages to support the modelling of different human-centric aspects, including modelling emotions, age, culture, language etc. [1,10,21,39]. We investigated how the languages were extended and which human-centric aspects were modified in these existing research papers. We also reviewed various works that extended existing modelling languages to capture additional non-functional characteristics [13,14,16]. We investigated what aspects could be changed in the existing modelling languages, in order to capture information about different age groups of end users. After our analysis, we developed a set of extensions to the widely used wire-frame based design notation [23] in order to model different end user ages, age-related implications on the design, and different design decisions based on user age characteristics.

2.1 Designing for Different Ages

We reviewed the key works done in three different categories related to designing for children, seniors and extending models to capturing emotions of end users. The age classification we used in this paper is called Life Cycle Groupings [40]. According to Statistics Canada, age groups can be defined as: Children aged from 0 to 14 years; youth aged from 15 to 24; adult aged from 25 to 64 years; and senior aged from 65 and above. The Australian Bureau of Statistics (ABS) uses a similar convention except they group both youth and adult as working-age population [2], which we named it as adult throughout the research.

Children. Mobile Educational Applications are used by Masood et al. [27] for usability testing. By recording with eye tracking glasses, they found some children had problems working with mobile applications. The system status is not apparent for them and they have a hard time finding out what to do next. They also had problems where they could not remember which page or button was accessed earlier. This children-oriented software needs to more clearly show the current state of the page, and sometimes the child users may need some guidance to do the next step. Help toolboxes and documentation were identified as necessary. Another important factor is to consider whether the buttons and menus are simple enough for children. Buttons and menu links should be easily identified as being clickable while items such as menu headings and titles should be easily identified as being not clickable.

A Fingerprint app [35] is used by Pan, to describe how to design the software user interface for the children. This work discusses four key points for the vision element regarding kids – integer vision effect, functional area design, icon and button design, and font design. For example, children may not understand the text inside a button but icons can be designed as buttons to show they are clickable.

The work of Michaels [31] and Boyatzis et al. [4] discusses colour preferences of children users as well as the effect of colour on children's emotions. They did colour tests with children around 6 years old, and found that their top three favorite colours are yellow, red, and green. Another type of testing they did was called the story test. If a child heard a happy story, most of them would select yellow. Using this research, they used yellow and red as the gradient colour for the theme colour, and made the whole app look funny and attractive.

Seniors. Boll et al. [3] provide a set of user interface design guidelines for people between 55 to 75 years old. They found 41 participants between 55 and 75 years to fill out questionnaires to research the actual requirement and the problems they have. They used the results to make the user interface design guidelines. According to the guidelines, for font design, the sans serif fonts provide good readability. For colour selection in the main content page, they recommended a light grey background with black fonts. Regarding the size of the icons and the buttons, most of the users reported that the icons are too small, and that double-clicking a small button is a problem for elderly people. The last important thing is the structure of the page. For example, in menu page, a good menu structure helps users to navigate through the user interface more easily. The menu needs to be put in conventional positions to make sure the position of the menus are consistent in the entire software.

Curumsing et al. [10] focus on designing emotion-oriented software, based on the smart home device for elderly. They used extended Goal models, Interaction models, Scenario models, Role models, and Behaviour models to keep track of the "cared for" to a list of emotions. Analysis of these emotions helps developers to understand the expectations of an older adult using the smart home. Using this approach, a goal model for the smart home device was created. The model includes different emotions for the elderly people to help get the elderly people to accept the device and feel like this is what they need. The software can catch the emotion of the user, and analyse their expectations. Thus, the software can make corresponding responses to meet the needs of users. The software can understand users' emotions, this could become one of the determinants of software success.

Curumsing et al. [11] demonstrate a case study of an emergency alarm system for elderly people, presenting the entire suite of models for this case study. They suggested a few important factors on designing the framework and also keeping the interest of the elderly people. Firstly, in order to encourage elderly people to adopt technological solutions, they have to be designed in such a way that they suit the needs of its users, are easy to use, and cost effective. The second important factor determining the successful adoption of technology consists of willingness and enthusiasm for acquiring new knowledge. However, this is rarely the feelings expressed by elderly people when it comes to using a system which is linked with a stigma. For example, some refused to use the pendant because of its visibility to others. It was viewed as a sign of stigma and old age. These are the way users perceived technology from an emotional aspect.

Wagner et al. [41] explain the impact of age on usability. It states that there is an increase in the average age of internet users which provides evidence that there is a need for catering elderly users for applications. Usability helps organisations by improving the job performance, gaining higher productivity and reduced costs by the users. There are five conceptualisations of age; Chronological or calendar age, Functional or performance-based age, Subjective or psycho social age, Organisational age, and Life span concept of age. Currently, mainly research chronological age is used to allow for consistency and comparison with the existing literature. We have also used chronological age as the other conceptualisations are mostly related to chronological age.

Finally, Holzinger et al. [17] aim to derive metric-based benchmarks for measuring usability. This study suggested two aspects of usability: passive and active interaction. Passive interaction means users are not directly interacting with it, but it helps out in the background. Active interaction means users directly interact with the technology. Several questions were developed to ensure it meets both passive and active interaction. They present an analogy between user anxiety and metrics.

2.2 Modelling Emotions of the Users

An emotion orientated software development method is developed by Chen et al. [8]. Existing emotion-aware applications lack accuracy in terms of emotion recognition due to the small scale of data collected. Through cloud-based computing and cloud assisted resources, mobiles phones can collect much more data. Combined with the architecture itself, applications can recognise user's emotional changes by big data analysis. Based on the user's current emotion, a common list of feedback is generated in the remote cloud. The information is transferred back to the local cloud, providing users with personalised services. Various in-home devices were used to accommodate the user's emotion.

Miller et al. [32] introduce the People Oriented Software Engineering (POSE) method to capture emotional desires by using emotional goals. The emotional goals are classified into two category of personal emotions and context-specific emotions. A survey is then used to evaluate and compare the proposed emotional model against iStar by implementing two domain models in both iStar and POSE. The survey results show that participants preferred to use POSE models since they are clearer, easier to understand, and not complicated to interpret. Participants mentioned that they were not confident to make modifications to iStar models, and would prefer to modify POSE model if required.

Lopez et al. [26] use personas within emotional scenarios to ensure that emotional desires are met. They describe their experience with three projects in the domains of aged well-being and mental health. Data are gathered form interviews and other ethnographic studies and personas are built based on composing textual description of personality traits. Emotional scenarios are script templates which explore how different personas react in identical situations.

Laurenzi et al. [33] propose a modelling language to support user interactions in heterogeneous physical scenarios. The model helps designers identify the services that will be required by the users to support their activities. It is assumed that systems modelled by this language are structured as Human-centric Wireless Sensor Network (HWSN). The nodes participating in an HWSN can be human-based sensors, regular sensors, mules, witness units and actuators.

Finally, a wire-frame extension method is presented in our previous work [20], to incorporate end-user diverse ages into the design of the software.

2.3 Personas for Usability Evaluation

Personas provide good information about the ends users the software engineers are designing the software for. Persona has also been used in evaluation of software interface using different usability inspection methods. Burnett et al. [5] reports multiple case studies to evaluate gender inclusiveness in problem solving software using GenderMag (Gender Inclusiveness Magnifier) approach [6]. According to the GenderMag approach they perform cognitive walk-through on three problem solving software from different domains with three personas provided with the GenderMag tool. They could identify gender inclusiveness issues in those software that had been in maintenance for years. They found most problems with the persona Abby that represented one group of users.

McIntosh et al. [29] also reported a study where they evaluated usability of popular e-commerce websites using cognitive walk-through with persona of different age groups. They could identify usability issues in the popular e-commerce websites for the persona representing users who are above 70 years of age. They also applied cognitive walk-through with persona representing users of different age groups. Mendez [30] has proposed a generalised framework called "InclusiveMag" that implements the main concepts of GenderMag approach, however is not focused on gender. InclusiveMag can be used to evaluate inclusiveness issues in any problem solving software with applying cognitive walk-through using persona. We used persona and individual user stories to guide the development of an improved smart parking app [25]. This resulted in a variety of individual user characteristics – age, language, physical and mental challenges, culture – being considered as first class requirements in the design and evaluation of a smart parking app prototype.

In summary there are some approaches and empirical research evidence of applying cognitive walk-through using persona on problem solving software to conduct usability evaluation.

3 Our Approach

3.1 End-Users and Developers Feedback

To evaluate our extended design modelling notation we used a set of different questionnaires, aimed at different classes, i.e., users and developers. We provided multiple solutions to modelling software design decisions regarding human-centric aspects related to age. We wanted to ask target end-users to identify the ones that are good for the age group, in their opinion. We used a range of target end users from different age groups to evaluate a prototype based on our augmented wire-frame design models. Using their feedback, we checked to see which solutions are the best fit for our prototype use cases.

Our extended wire-frame modelling frameworks are to be used by Software Engineers to create an end-product that is more age-aware and supports different interfaces and interface components for differently-aged end users. We prepared a different set of questions to ask a range of developers their opinion on the new modelling framework. We wanted to identify key current issues that can be found with the pre-existing model frameworks not supporting modelling of end user age. We also wanted their opinion on the new framework and whether it helped them in addressing these issues. Using the questionnaire results, we have refined our extended wire-frame-based design approach to better match the needs of the developers.

3.2 Extended Wire-Frames

There were multiple modelling frameworks that could be extended to support end user age difference modelling in our research. We decided that extending wire-frame-based design models would be the best option as most of the changes required for the different age groups were based on the application user interface. wire-frames provide a simple way for developers to create the basic design of an application and our extension point was to create a workflow that a developer can follow for each of the different age groups. In recent years, various other works have looked to extend the use of wire-frame-based UI design and to suggest wire-frame-based designs or partial designs [7,23]. None have focused on supporting different design decisions based on end user ages.

Based on the research review, our age groups are defined as: *1) Kids*; Under 15 *2) Adults*; Aged between 15 and 64; and *3) Seniors:* Aged above 64. To model different ages, age-related design considerations, and age-related design differences to wire-frame models, we added three features to the original wire-frame modelling framework:

1. Branching (Branch a screen into two or three pathways)
2. Merging (Merging two or three pathways into a single pathway)
3. Splitting (Splitting a screen into multiple screens).

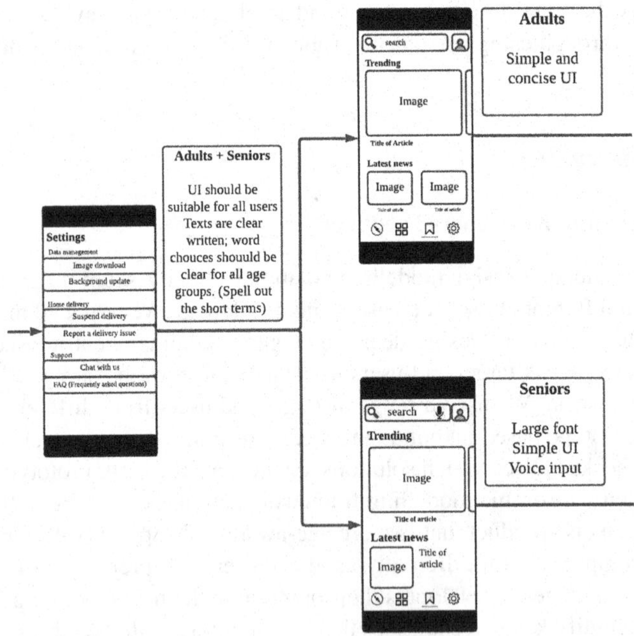

Fig. 1. Example of branching (from [20]).

Figure 1 shows an example of branching. A single pathway has been branched into two pathways. This is used when there is a need for different user interface or functionality for the same screen for different aged users. It thus gives developers a tool to express the need for a change in a single screen for different ages.

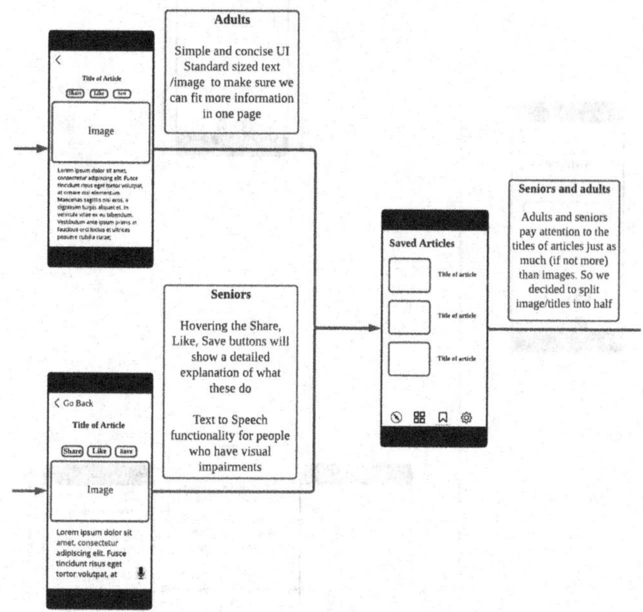

Fig. 2. Example of merging (from [20]).

Figure 2 shows an example of merging. Two pathways have been merged into a single pathway. This is useful when multiple pathways arrive at a specific screen that will be the same for multiple age groups that have been previously branched out. It saves the developers from creating the same screen design for different pathways. It also helps show that multiple screens will be the same across different age groups.

Figure 3 shows an example of splitting. A single screen is split into two screens. This is useful for age groups that require additional assistance in getting a task done. For example, adults may prefer a single register page as it allows them to quickly register. However, kids or seniors may need additional help when registering, e.g. by using a step by step multiple screen approach. Using multiple screens will give developers more room to explain key features within each screen, make items larger, or choose different interaction components. This will be a trade-off between speed and ease-of-use.

4 Evaluation Approach

4.1 Prototype News App

We created a prototype news app based on our extended wire-frame approach to evaluate how easy it was for a developer to use this extended wire-frame model. The prototype was also used to evaluate the final prototype system by different age group target

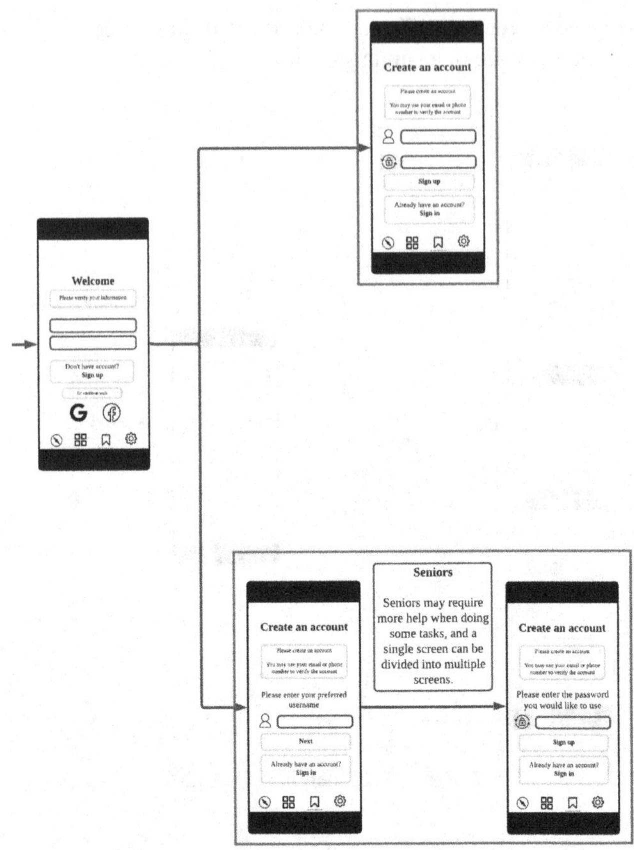

Fig. 3. Example of splitting (from [20]).

end-users. We chose a news app as the prototype as (i) most age groups use them or are interested to use them; (ii) despite their seaming simplicity, they often have quite complex interfaces and design decisions are not always fitting differently aged users; (iii) the interface design is reasonably detailed but not overwhelmingly so; and (iv) many lessons from news app development can be applied to social media, communications, education and other widely used apps [9]. Hence, the news reading app domain contains enough variation points between the three age groups to try out the use of our extended wire-frame modelling language features.

We used our extended wire-frames to design and develop a Figma-based prototype. The extended wire-frame designed to create the news app prototype is shown in Appendix. By using the extended modelling framework we captured key human-centric aspects regarding the age of the users and designed solutions to accommodate these. This news application has different functionality and user interface for different age groups of its users. In this prototype, we decided to keep the colours for each of the branches specific to the age groups even if a screen was for all three user types. For example, a screen that has not been branched out which is used for all three user types will still have different colour themes to allow for a more consistent experience for the end user.

In the extended wire-frame design model, we have many common pages for all three age groups. We needed to find a balance point for these age groups such as use of font size, user interface complexity, and any related points to ensure that the design for the common pages is clear enough for use from all three age groups. An age selector is presented to users at the start, as shown in Fig. 4.

Fig. 4. Age category selection page (from [20]).

Children. For the **kids application**, the key aim was to make the application enjoyable and attractive enough for the children. Some user interface design decisions that needed to be considered are:

- *Colour:* Research showed that children prefer colours like red and yellow and thus we used a rainbow gradient colour schema to catch the eyes of the children.
- *Font Style:* Use a fun looking font size to help children stay focused.
- *Icon selection:* We chose a more cartoonish icon for children to cater for their shorter attention span.

Figure 5a shows a user interface designed for kids, based on that specified in our extended wire-frame.

Adults. For the **adult application**, the key aim was to make the app clear and simple so that they will be able to quickly navigate between pages without too much overhead information. Thus key design decisions for the adult app user interface design included:

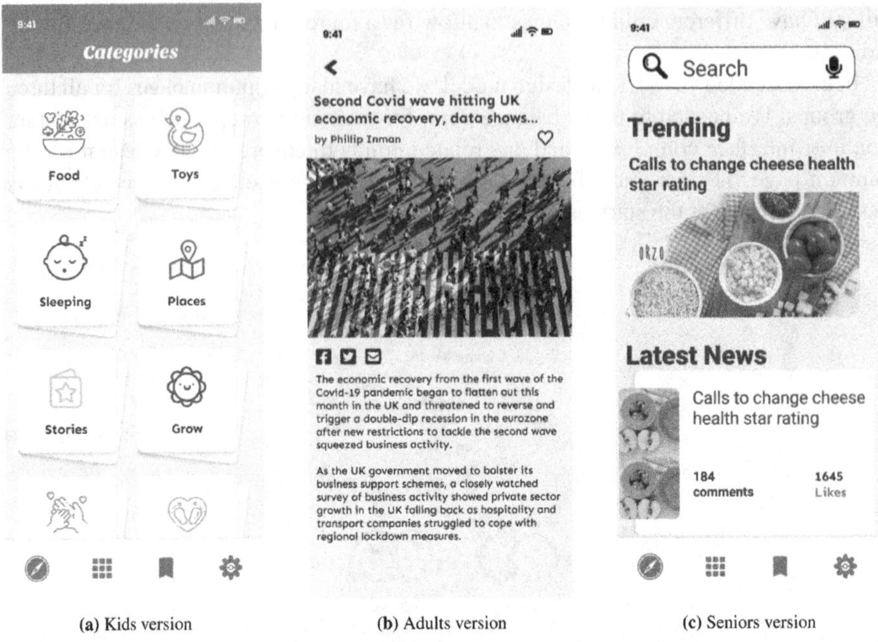

(**a**) Kids version (**b**) Adults version (**c**) Seniors version

Fig. 5. User interfaces adapted from the extended wire-frames (from [20]).

- *Font Size:* Normal size
- *Colour:* Simple and conventional colours. More professional compared to the kids version.

Figure 5b shows a user interface designed for adults, using our extended wire-frame.

Seniors. The **senior application** is similar to the adult application, but we needed to make sure that everything is large enough, easily accessible, and that the user interface is simple enough. We added some additional functionality to help aid seniors so that they can comfortably use aspects of the technology that they may not be familiar with. Some key design decisions for the senior age group include:

- *Colour:* Similar to adults, use simple and conventional colours.
- *Font Size:* use a larger font size to aid visual impairments.
- *Voice control:* Senior users may have trouble typing on a mobile device or reading smaller font sizes and speech-to-text and text-to-speech functionality would be good for them.
- *Larger components:* Make items such as buttons, and links large enough for them to easily click.

Figure 5c shows a user interface designed for seniors, using our extended wire-frame.

We also provided a toggle setting, shown in Fig. 10, so that users can customise the app styles such as the font size, font style, etc. This was necessary because there may be some users who do not require the customisations that were categorised within their user age groups. Other customisations that were determined necessary during our research are specified in the extended wire-frames. This allows developers to choose whether to include a customization within their applications (Fig. 6).

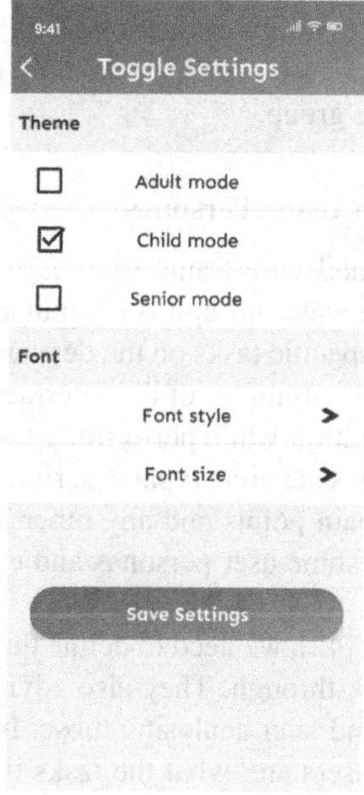

Fig. 6. Toggle setting (from [20]).

4.2 Usability Evaluation

To evaluate the news app prototype's usability, a usability test was conducted to gain insights into what went well and what needs to be improved in our extended wire-frame modelling approach. Users were asked to complete two tasks:

- Change the user mode along with some settings to match their preferences; and
- Find an article they are interested in, save the article, and open the article again using the saved articles page.

The details of the tasks given to the users were purposely given without too much detail on how to navigate within the application. This was so that we can see how a new user will act when using this application. These tasks helped us to gather user data on key age-based design decisions in the news app:

- Whether each user type is able to use the interaction flow designed for them within the application, as well as change the settings to match their accessibility needs; and
- whether the navigation supported within the application is easily understandable to new users.

The testers were asked to record whether the tasks were successfully completed as well as to describe any troubles that they encountered during performing the tasks. We conducted a preliminary test, and using the results, we enhanced our extended wire-frame models to increase the usability of the prototype. We plan to conduct a more comprehensive usability evaluation with developers to evaluate whether the extended wire-frame is applicable to different domains and can be easily used to create prototypes. We also plan to conduct usability evaluations with end-users from various age-groups to evaluate whether the created prototype actually increased the usability of the news app prototype for each age group.

4.3 Cognitive Walk-Through Using Personas

In order to evaluate our extended wire-frame designs we applied a cognitive walk-through process [38]. Cognitive walk-through is a popular usability inspection method that includes performing some specific tasks on the design or the user interface itself by an evaluator in order to assess the usability of the interface or the design. User characteristics are taken in to consideration while performing the walk-through. This is often done with user personas. Personas are archetypal descriptions of users that include their goals, general characteristics, pain points and any other information. In our cognitive walk-through approach we use some user personas and evaluate our wire-frame while accomplishing set tasks.

According to Wharton et al. [42], we need to define the cognitive walk-through process before conducting the walk-through. They also advise to record all critical information while walking though and later analysing those. In the first step Wharton et al. [42] advise to define who the users are, what the tasks they will perform, what is the design or interface they will perform the tasks on and the sequence of actions needed to accomplish the task. Since we want to evaluate our wire-frame design, the interface would be the wire-frame. The wire-frame is designed particularly for users of different age groups. We collect personas of different age group from a search in the existing literature.

Collection of Personas. Creating new personas for the evaluation of the wire-frame is out of scope for this study. We searched for existing personas representing end users of different age groups in the existing literature. We searched with “elderly persona”, “children persona” and “persona of news app?” on Google scholar and looked into the published research that describe personas. We then reviewed the quality of the persona and how the persona is created. Based on our reviews we selected three personas - one child, one senior and one adult persona. We will use these three personas in the cognitive walk-through process.

Children Persona: We collected children persona from [34]. This article was found while searching for children persona. The article focuses on persona creation for children and elderly end users. They describe different factors that can influence the decision of adopting a qualitative, quantitative or mixed method for data collection for creating personas. They provide several case studies as example. One of the case studies describe a project called “FamCannector”, where they have created some children persona. We take the persona called Sarah, as shown in Fig. 7, who is an eight years old school girl who uses computers for didactic games and information seeking. She often needs help using the system. We believe she represents the children end users for our news app wire-frame.

Name: Sarah
Age: 8
Location: Australia
Occupation: Third grade student in elementary school

Computer Experience: Sarah has initially learned how to handle computers through a computer for kids. Additionally, she uses the computer at school for didactic games and information seeking. She likes downloading music, which she learned from her older brother. She does not have her own Facebook account, but her mother does and sometimes they are on Facebook together. She would like to have her own account, but her mother does not want her to as she thinks Sarah is too young. Sarah has an email account for exchanging photos, but she does not use it to write or read text.

Goals: Love, security and independence. Therefore, Sarah needs to cope with leaving the security and safety of home and parents to enter the riskier but more exciting world of peers. To develop successfully, she must have the opportunity to safely explore beyond the world of her family, be exposed to a range of new experiences and be welcomed back when ready to return [1]. For Sarah, even her grandparents expand her world as they do not have a close relationship right now.

Frustrations and pain points: Needing frequent or a lot of help when using the system

Primary usage reasons: 1) establishing a steady relationship with her grandparents, getting to know them better and 2) communication supported by video (to see her grandparents, which is not possible on the phone)

Fig. 7. Children persona collected from [34].

Adult Persona: Mayas et al. [28] describes the opportunities and challenges of personas from several projects. They present an example persona Michael, as shown in Fig. 8, who is a 34 years old consultant. He is a commuter and a frequent traveller. We take his persona as an adult persona as commuters often read news during their travel.

Senior Persona: We collected one senior persona from [24]. The article reports a survey to understand elderly end users of mobile devices and to identify the factors that influence their interaction. They presented three personas with different level of literacy and interaction. We selected the persona Manoel, shown in Fig. 9 among those. Manoel enjoys using computing devices, however is reluctant to spend much time learning new

Commuter Michael Baumann

"The main thing is, that I arrive punctually at the destination!"

PERSONAL INFORMATION

34 years old, single
profession: corporate consultant
hometown: Stuttgart
hobbies: biking, gliding
characteristics: punctual, ecology-minded...

PUBLIC TRANSPORT PROFILE

Commuter
daily use of commuter traffic system
occasional use for business trips
knowledge of a place: good
knowledge of the system: good
ticket: monthly ticket
transport mode: street car, train
alternatives: bike, car
restriction: none
preferences: comfort, quietness, work en route

EXPECTATIONS

Michael expects...
- real time information about service disturbances
- quick alternative connections
- no unnecessary information

SUMMARY

Michael Baumann is a 34 year old, single corporate consultant from Stuttgart, who uses and prefers public transport over the car to get to work. He is punctual, endowed with technical affinities and tries to live ecology-minded. Due to his regular travel, Michael knows his daily routine and the public transport system well. His journey is about 35 minutes long and takes him to the center of Stuttgart. During his journey he has to transfer once and therefore he predominantly uses the street car, which gets him to work and back quickly.
Michael does not want any unnecessary information during his daily way to work, which already is familiar to him. He only uses passenger information in the event that something would not work out as planned. In that case, Michael expects that he would be informed about disturbances as soon as possible, ideally before setting off on a journey, so that he is able to avoid the disturbance by using an alternative connection.

DAILY ROUTINE

Every day Michael takes the street car to his place of work in downtown Stuttgart. He knows his daily travel routine by heart. He must transfer once every 20 minutes. Michael has attempted the same journey by car, but the constant traffic jams and the cumbersome search for a parking space became too stressful in the long run. In addition, he wants to travel ecology-minded and sees his best travel opportunities in public transport, in order to fulfill this desire. Public transport enables Michael a worry free daily routine. His monthly ticket enables him to travel stress free: the journey in general actually affords him relaxation in comparison to travel by car. He has gotten used to short delays and has scheduled 5 minutes of spare time, so as to get to his office at the latest by 8 o'clock. Major delays always get him in trouble with his boss and Michael's day schedule gets completely mixed up. This often continues to aggravate him on his way back home.

Fig. 8. Adult persona collected from [28].

things. He often struggles with the font size. Since the other two personas do not use computing devices frequently, we think Manoel will best represent the senior end users for our news app wire-frame.

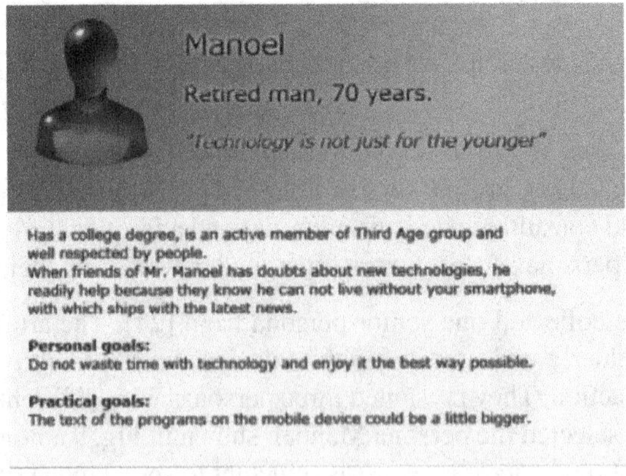

Manoel

Retired man, 70 years.

"Technology is not just for the younger"

Has a college degree, is an active member of Third Age group and well respected by people.
When friends of Mr. Manoel has doubts about new technologies, he readily help because they know he can not live without your smartphone, with which ships with the latest news.

Personal goals:
Do not waste time with technology and enjoy it the best way possible.

Practical goals:
The text of the programs on the mobile device could be a little bigger.

Fig. 9. Senior persona collected from [24].

Usability Tasks. In order to perform the cognitive walk-through we need to define some usability inspection tasks that we assume the selected personas perform using the prototype app. We define the following two tasks that we will perform on the prototype app:

- Task 1: User can change the font size from settings: For this task we assume that the user will be able to bring the setting interface and customise their font size.
- Task 2: User can search for desired news article: For this task we assume that the user can perform a keyword based news search on the prototype app interface.

5 Results

In this section, we present the results of our survey of developers and users, and the cognitive walk-throughs using personas. We collected a total of 27 responses – 6 from developers, 21 from app end users. We also conducted the cognitive walk-throughs by three personas: one child, one adult, and one senior.

5.1 Evaluation Results - Developer Questionnaires

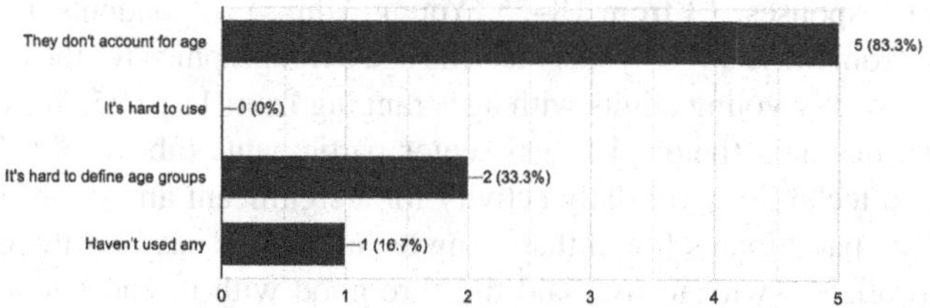

Fig. 10. Developer responses on designing in issues regarding different end user age during development (from [20]).

Six developers responded to our survey – 3 with 5 to 10 years development experience, 2 with 1 to 4 years, and 1 with more than 20 years of experience. Among all of these developers, 4 said they think there is a need for human-centric aspects regarding age in modelling frameworks e.g. UML diagrams, Wire-frames, User stories, etc. One had never thought of this issue, and one thought it is not important. We collected a list of approaches and frameworks they currently use to deal with age related issues of the users in the software that they develop. This included use of wire-frames (3 of the developers), UML (3), user stories (2), use cases (2), and BPMN diagrams (1).

We asked the 6 developers whether they have encountered any issues regarding age during software development. Based on their responses, as shown in Fig. 10, one of the key issues is that the majority of developers do not address differing age of their end users at all in their software development. To address this issue in this study, we captured a lot of end user requirements from our end user survey questionnaires. The second issue is that some developers believe it is hard to define an "age group". To address this, we decided to research more about the target audience of the particular software and then defined the age groups accordingly.

We asked developers what tool(s) they used to help them address differing age issues of their app and web site end users. They mostly stated they never used any tools. Some suggested that although they did not use any tools in particular, they tried to address age related problems such as security restrictions in the identity server (e.g. some websites are for adults only); and informally captured non functional requirements in text, annotate the odd use case/user story. For a news application, age selection is important to restrict inappropriate news from the children. Icons, text, and background colours might also need to be changed to accommodate different types of users sight limitations and preferences based on their age.

Regarding what other human-centric aspects they think could be a good addition to better support in software modelling frameworks, developers included gender, culture, end user language, physical and mental challenges of users, accessibility needs of end users, Convenience of usage, usability test (user test), cognitive load (mental effort) test (including performance measures in terms of user's response time taken to complete a task and its accuracy, or physiological measures, e.g. pupil dilation and blink rate).

5.2 Evaluation Results - End-User Survey

We received 21 responses, 13 from 18–25 (Young Adults) respondents, 6 from 26–49 (Adults), and 2 from those 50–64 years old. The age demographics for the questionnaire participants are mostly young adults with ages ranging from 18 to 25. We did not have any younger participants (below 18) and senior participants (above 65). Most of the participants used technology for daily activity for a significant amount of time (8 h+). A majority of the participants found that using technology is easy for them (14 people said they are proficient with it, five said they are good with it, and one said they are doing okay with it). We also found out that the most popular device is a smartphone used for social media, entertainment and news apps. We asked if any participant had any accessibility requirements. The majority of people saying they had visual impairments, such as needing glasses to read, having short sight, and one person answered that they needed to use voice output to "read" app text.

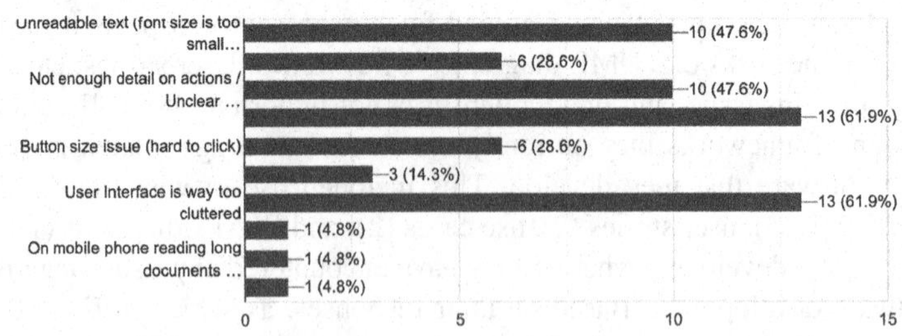

Fig. 11. Key pain points of using software systems (from [20]).

5.3 Evaluation Results - Cognitive Walk-Through

We performed cognitive walk-throughs on our news prototype app with the selected personas representing children, adult and senior users. We evaluated the usability of the news prototype app by performing the defined usability tasks as the persona. The cognitive walk-through is performed by one of the authors. Table 1 and 2 present the results of our cognitive walk-through process for the tasks defined in Sect. 4.3.

In our usability evaluation using cognitive walk-through with child persona "Sarah" we found evidence for all the related works summarised in Sect. 2. We used the colour theme advised by Michaels [31] and Boyatzis et al. [4] and found that the interface was intuitive for Sarah. We used icons for buttons as advised by [35] and made the title texts and clickable button distinguishable according to [27]. We found that Sarah could find the icons easily and could successfully conduct a search for news article using the search option. She could complete the usability tasks without help from others. We have implemented background colour and font suggestions provided by Boll et al. [3]. In our usability evaluation with senior persona "Manoel", we found that the font was suitable for him. In the description of "Manoel" persona we found that he prefers fonts bigger in size on mobile devices.

Table 1. Cognitive walk-through with selected personas - Usability task 1: Change the font size.

Persona	Cognitive walk-through	Notes
Children persona - Sarah	Opens news app wire-frame After signing in she lands on the "KidsNews" page. There is no option on this page to change the font size. She explores the four options available at the bottom. She finds the "profile" page where the second options says "Toggle Settings". She selects that and finds the option for "font size"	Sarah can complete the task without any help from others. The theme is intuitive and easy for Sarah to explore and find the functionalities
Adult persona	Opens news app wire-frame After signing in she lands on the "News" page. Although the font size is good for him, he often needs to make the fonts bigger while he reads news while travelling on public transport. He clicks on the settings icon, and finds the toggle settings option. He takes the short cut and selects senior mode presents the text in bigger font size. He likes the fact that he can change the settings with very fewer clicks and while on the move	Michael can change the font from toggle setting or can switch account settings to make the font bigger. He likes that he can do this with minimum effort on the app
Senior persona - Manoel	Opens news app wire-frame After signing in he lands on the "News" homepage. He likes the fonts since those are bigger than usual. He wants to play with the font size. He goes to profile page and checks "adult mode" and "child mode". He finds that fonts are smaller for adults. He goes to "Toggle Settings" and changes the font size for his profile to smaller as adult mode	Manoel can easily check all the font size options available on the app wire-frame and can change the font size for his profile

Based on the cognitive walk-through, we made the following findings about the user interface.

- The user interface is easy for children and intuitive enough that they are happy to explore and find functionalities they desire without help from others
- The user interface is easy for senior users who prefer larger fonts as well as for others who prefer normal fonts - they can toggle the setting very easily.

Table 2. Cognitive walk-through with selected personas - Usability task 2: Search for news article.

Persona	Cognitive walk-through	Notes
Children persona - Sarah	Opens news app wire-frame After signing in she lands on the "KidsNews" page. She wants to read the article about "calls to change cheese" that she heard from her friend. She likes the small categories icon at the bottom left of the screen. She finds it easy to select food since this is shown as a category on the main screen. She selects the category and finds all the articles related to food. She quickly finds the search icon at the top right and searches for the particular news she was looking for. She can find it easily	The interface layout and the options are intuitive and easy for children to figure out common functionalities
Adult persona	Opens news app wire-frame After signing in he lands on the "News" homepage. He writes his preferred keywords to search for news he enjoys to read. He does not have any difficulty in looking for the search options	The search option on top of the homepage is easy to locate
Senior persona - Manoel	Opens news app wire-frame After signing in he lands on the "News" homepage. He does not like the trending news that is highlighted on his homepage. He likes to read about sports so he clicks on the categories to find other categories of news. He finds "sports" category and selects that to find more on sports. He searches for the articles on yesterday's match by clicking top right search icon	The interface is designed in a way that the common functionalities can be found easily

5.4 Discussion

From the result in Fig. 11 we can see that most of the problems are User Interface related issues. This is one of the main reasons we decided to extend wire-frames since wire-frames provide early visuals that can help with these problems, they are also easy to adapt compared to conceptual designs. We used questionnaires for collecting data. We created both end user and developer questionnaires to capture data from multiple angles. We got a range of feedback from different age groups that indicated usability enhancement in the prototype news app for different age groups of target end users. However, we need to recruit more participants to gain a larger sample size, especially younger (under 18) and older (over 65) end users. According to our survey results in Fig. 12, we can see that our participants are commonly using a range of different application domains such as social, entertainment, study, etc. These results helped us in deciding on which domain our example extended wire-frame and prototype would focus on. Generalising our experiences to those other common domains would help to show if the approach can enhance different age group usability for them as well.

We chose to extend wire-frame design models with information about the age of target end users and alternative user interface design decisions based on these ages. However, other modelling frameworks such as interaction and sequence diagrams may help developers understand the human-centric aspects regarding age further and use similar approaches based on the wire-frame extensions we have created. For example, Fig. 13 contains an interaction diagram that is adapted from the extended wire-frames presented in this paper. Adapting other human-centric aspects, such as gender, emotion, and physical support, into the extended modelling framework presented in this paper may also be beneficial. Additional research can be done to increase the range of our

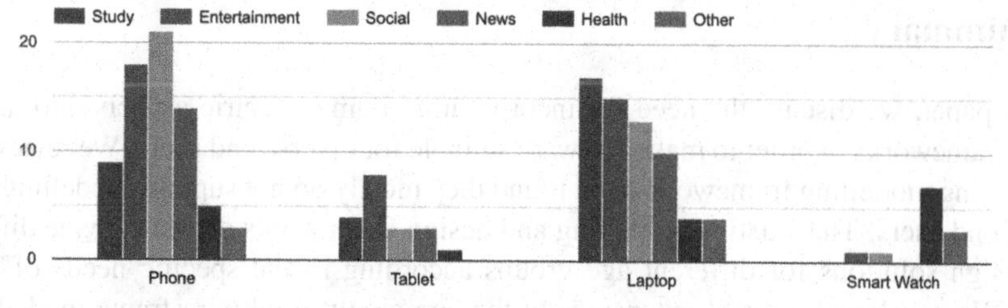

Fig. 12. Devices used by participants and for what purposes (from [20]).

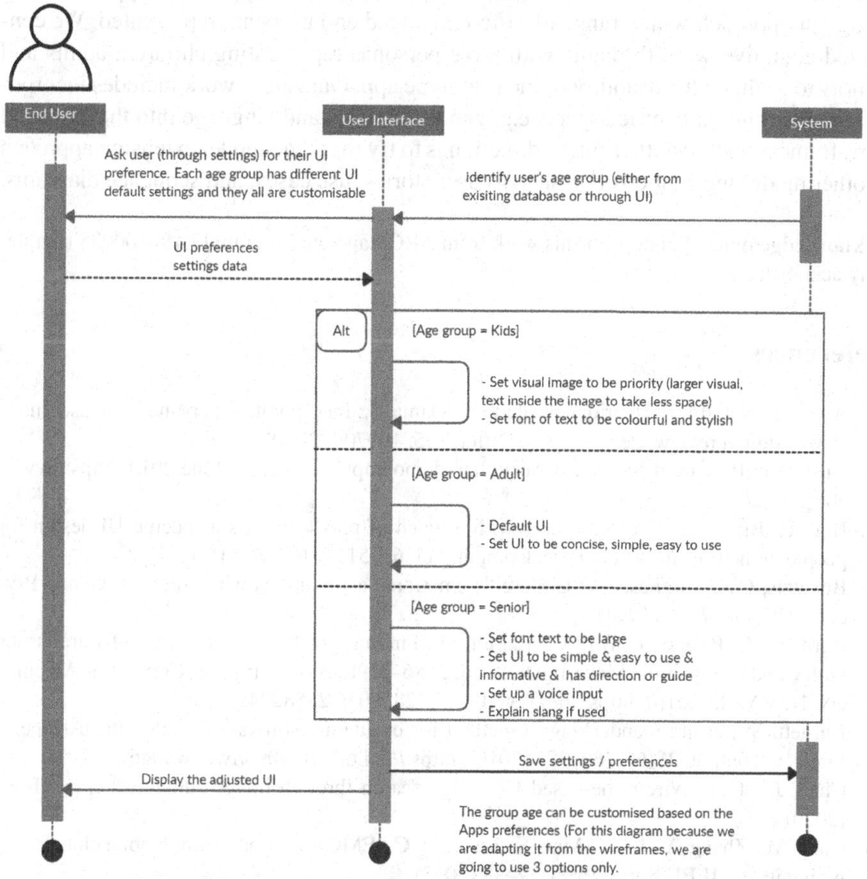

Fig. 13. Interaction diagram adapted from the extended wire-frames (from [20]).

user types and changes to the designs to accommodate their needs. Using approaches developed in the accessibility research field could also help us to better understand the needs of users with a range of disabilities. The specific requirements of these user types need to be identified so that the developers can create an appropriate pathway and design decisions for those users in our extended wire-frame models.

6 Summary

In this paper, we discuss the need for incorporating human-centric aspects into modelling frameworks in order to make software suitable for diverse end users. We reviewed the existing modelling frameworks, and found they mostly do not support modelling the age of end users. The existing modelling and design frameworks do not provide different design solutions for different age groups according to the specific needs of end users. We developed a set of extensions to the commonly used wire-frame modelling approach to incorporate different designs for child, adult and senior end users. Evaluation of our modelling approach with developers and a prototype news app developed using our approach with a range of differently aged end users are represented. We conducted cognitive walk-throughs with three personas representing children, adults and seniors to evaluate the usability of the prototype app. Our future work includes incorporating other human-centric aspects e.g. gender, culture, and language into the extended wire-frame model. Another future direction is to try the same model extension approach in other modelling frameworks, such as user stories, use cases, and sequence diagrams.

Acknowledgement. Support for this work from ARC Laureate Program FL190100035 is gratefully acknowledged.

References

1. Alves, T., Natálio, J., Henriques-Calado, J., Gama, S.: Incorporating personality in user interface design: a review. Pers. Individ. Differ. **155**, 109709 (2020)
2. Australian Bureau of Statistics: Australian demographic statistics, June 2019. https://www.abs.gov.au/
3. Boll, F., Brune, P.: User interfaces with a touch of grey?-towards a specific UI design for people in the transition age. Proc. Comput. Sci. **63**, 511–516 (2015)
4. Boyatzis, C.J., Varghese, R.: Children's emotional associations with colors. J. Genet. Psychol. **155**(1), 77–85 (1994)
5. Burnett, M., Peters, A., Hill, C., Elarief, N.: Finding gender-inclusiveness software issues with GenderMag: a field investigation, pp. 2586–2598. Association for Computing Machinery, New York (2016). https://doi.org/10.1145/2858036.2858274
6. Burnett, M., et al.: GenderMag: a method for evaluating software's gender inclusiveness. Interact. Comput. **28**(6), 760–787 (2016). https://doi.org/10.1093/iwc/iwv046
7. Chen, J., et al.: Wireframe-based UI design search through image autoencoder, pp. 1–31 (2020)
8. Chen, M., Zhang, Y., Li, Y., Mao, S., Leung, V.C.: EMC: emotion-aware mobile cloud computing in 5G. IEEE Netw. **29**(2), 32–38 (2015)
9. Constantinides, M., Dowell, J., Johnson, D., Malacria, S.: Exploring mobile news reading interactions for news app personalisation. In: Proceedings of the 17th International Conference on Human-Computer Interaction with Mobile Devices and Services, pp. 457–462 (2015)
10. Curumsing, M.K., Fernando, N., Abdelrazek, M., Vasa, R., Mouzakis, K., Grundy, J.: Emotion-oriented requirements engineering: a case study in developing a smart home system for the elderly. J. Syst. Softw. **147**, 215–229 (2019)
11. Curumsing, M.K., Lopez-Lorca, A., Miller, T., Sterling, L., Vasa, R.: Viewpoint modelling with emotions: a case study. Int. J. People-Orient. Program. (IJPOP) **4**(2), 25–53 (2015)

12. Dalpiaz, F., Franch, X., Horkoff, J.: iStar 2.0 language guide. arXiv preprint arXiv:1605.07767 (2016)
13. El-Attar, M., Luqman, H., Karpati, P., Sindre, G., Opdahl, A.L.: Extending the UML statecharts notation to model security aspects. IEEE Trans. Softw. Eng. **41**(7), 661–690 (2015)
14. Goncalves, E., Castro, J., Araujo, J., Heineck, T.: A systematic literature review of iStar extensions. J. Syst. Softw. **137**, 1–33 (2018)
15. Grundy, J., Khalajzadeh, H., Mcintosh, J.: Towards human-centric model-driven software engineering, pp. 229–238 (2020)
16. Grundy, J., Patel, R.: Developing software components with the UML, enterprise java beans and aspects. In: Proceedings 2001 Australian Software Engineering Conference, pp. 127–136 (2001)
17. Holzinger, A., Searle, G., Kleinberger, T., Seffah, A., Javahery, H.: Investigating usability metrics for the design and development of applications for the elderly. In: Miesenberger, K., Klaus, J., Zagler, W., Karshmer, A. (eds.) ICCHP 2008. LNCS, vol. 5105, pp. 98–105. Springer, Heidelberg (2008). https://doi.org/10.1007/978-3-540-70540-6_13
18. Hussain, A., Abd Razak, M.N.F., Mkpojiogu, E.O., Hamdi, M.M.F.: UX evaluation of video streaming application with teenage users. J. Telecommun. Electron. Comput. Eng. (JTEC) **9**(2–11), 129–131 (2017)
19. Iung, A., et al.: Systematic mapping study on domain-specific language development tools. Empir. Softw. Eng. **25**(5), 4205–4249 (2020). https://doi.org/10.1007/s10664-020-09872-1
20. Jim, A.Y., et al.: Improving the modelling of human-centric aspects of software systems- a case study of modelling end user age in wirefame designs. In: Evaluation of Novel Approaches to Software Engineering (ENASE) (2021)
21. Kamalrudin, M., Grundy, J., Hosking, J.: MaramaAI: tool support for capturing and managing consistency of multi-lingual requirements, pp. 326–329 (2012)
22. Kulyk, O., Kosara, R., Urquiza, J., Wassink, I.: Human-centered aspects. In: Kerren, A., Ebert, A., Meyer, J. (eds.) Human-Centered Visualization Environments. LNCS, vol. 4417, pp. 13–75. Springer, Heidelberg (2007). https://doi.org/10.1007/978-3-540-71949-6_2
23. de Lange, P., Nicolaescu, P., Rosenstengel, M., Klamma, R.: Collaborative wireframing for model-driven web engineering. In: Cheng, R., Mamoulis, N., Sun, Y., Huang, X. (eds.) WISE 2020. LNCS, vol. 11881, pp. 373–388. Springer, Cham (2019). https://doi.org/10.1007/978-3-030-34223-4_24
24. Leme, R.R., Amaral, A.R., Zaina, L.A.M.: Interaction with mobile devices on social networks by elderly people: a survey in Brazil with Facebook. In: 2014 XL Latin American Computing Conference (CLEI), pp. 1–7 (2014). https://doi.org/10.1109/CLEI.2014.6965103
25. Li, C., et al.: A human-centric approach to building a smarter and better parking application. In: 2021 IEEE International Conference on Computers, Software, and Applications Conference (COMPSAC2021), 12–16 July 2021. IEEE (2021)
26. Lopez-Lorca, A.A., Miller, T., Pedell, S., Mendoza, A., Keirnan, A., Sterling, L.: One size doesn't fit all: diversifying "the user" using personas and emotional scenarios. In: Proceedings of the 6th International Workshop on Social Software Engineering, pp. 25–32 (2014)
27. Masood, M., Thigambaram, M.: The usability of mobile applications for pre-schoolers. Proc. Soc. Behav. Sci. **197**, 1818–1826 (2015)
28. Mayas, C., Hörold, S., Krömker, H.: Personas for requirements engineering. In: Ebert, A., Humayoun, S.R., Seyff, N., Perini, A., Barbosa, S.D.J. (eds.) UsARE 2012/2014. LNCS, vol. 9312, pp. 34–46. Springer, Cham (2016). https://doi.org/10.1007/978-3-319-45916-5_3
29. McIntosh, J., et al.: Evaluating age bias in e-commerce. In: 2021 IEEE/ACM 13th International Workshop on Cooperative and Human Aspects of Software Engineering (CHASE), pp. 31–40 (2021). https://doi.org/10.1109/CHASE52884.2021.00012
30. Mendez, C.: The InclusiveMag method: a start towards more inclusive software for diverse populations (2020)

31. Michaels, G.M.: Colour preference according to age. Am. J. Psychol. **35**, 79–87 (1924)
32. Miller, T., Pedell, S., Lopez-Lorca, A.A., Mendoza, A., Sterling, L., Keirnan, A.: Emotion-led modelling for people-oriented requirements engineering: the case study of emergency systems. J. Syst. Softw. **105**, 54–71 (2015)
33. Monares, Á., Ochoa, S.F., Herskovic, V., Santos, R., Pino, J.A.: Modeling interactions in human-centric wireless sensor networks. In: Proceedings of the 2014 IEEE 18th International Conference on Computer Supported Cooperative Work in Design (CSCWD), pp. 661–666. IEEE (2014)
34. Moser, C., Fuchsberger, V., Neureiter, K., Sellner, W., Tscheligi, M.: Revisiting personas: the making-of for special user groups, p. 453–468. Association for Computing Machinery, New York (2012). https://doi.org/10.1145/2212776.2212822
35. Pan, X.: Research of iphone application UI design based on children cognition feature. In: 2010 IEEE 11th International Conference on Computer-Aided Industrial Design & Conceptual Design 1, vol. 1, pp. 293–296. IEEE (2010)
36. Parker Software: Key considerations for making age-friendly software (2019). https://www.parkersoftware.com/blog/key-considerations-for-making-age-friendly-software/
37. Pew Research Center: Internet, Science & Tec: Internet/broadband fact sheet (2019). https://www.pewresearch.org/internet/fact-sheet/internet-broadband/
38. Polson, P.G., Lewis, C., Rieman, J., Wharton, C.: Cognitive walkthroughs: a method for theory-based evaluation of user interfaces. Int. J. Man-Mach. Stud. **36**(5), 741–773 (1992)
39. Spichkova, M., Zamansky, A., Farchi, E.: Towards a human-centred approach in modelling and testing of cyber-physical systems, pp. 847–851 (2015)
40. Statistic Canada: Age categories, life cycle groupings (2017). https://bit.ly/3dopioH
41. Wagner, N., Hassanein, K., Head, M.: The impact of age on website usability. Comput. Hum. Behav. **37**, 270–282 (2014)
42. Wharton, C., Rieman, J., Lewis, C., Polson, P.: The cognitive walkthrough method: a practitioner's guide (1994)

A Framework for Privacy and Security Requirements Analysis and Conflict Resolution for Supporting GDPR Compliance Through Privacy-by-Design

Duaa Alkubaisy[1(✉)], Luca Piras[2(✉)], Mohammed Ghazi Al-Obeidallah[3(✉)], Karl Cox[4(✉)], and Haralambos Mouratidis[4,5(✉)]

[1] Department of MIS, College of Applied Studies and Community Service, Imam Abdulrahman Bin Faisal University, Dammam, Saudi Arabia
daalkubaisy@iau.edu.sa
[2] School of Computing, Robert Gordon University, Aberdeen, U.K.
l.piras@rgu.ac.uk
[3] Faculty of Engineering, Al Ain University, Abu Dhabi, United Arab Emirates
mohamed.alobeidallah@aau.ac.ae
[4] Centre for Secure, Intelligent and Usable Systems, University of Brighton, Brighton, U.K.
{K.Cox,H.Mouratidis}@brighton.ac.uk
[5] Department of Computer and Systems Science, Stockholm University, Stockholm, Sweden

Abstract. Requirements elicitation, analysis, and, above all, early detection of conflicts and resolution, are among the most important, strategic, complex and crucial activities for preventing software system failures, and reducing costs related to reengineering/fixing actions. This is especially important when critical Requirements Classes are involved, such as Privacy and Security Requirements. Recently, organisations have been heavily fined for lack of compliance with data protection regulations, such as the EU General Data Protection Regulation (GDPR). GDPR requires organisations to enforce privacy-by-design activities from the early stages and for the entire software engineering cycle. Accordingly, requirements engineers need methods and tools for systematically identifying privacy and security requirements, detecting and solving related conflicts. Existing techniques support requirements identification without detecting or mitigating conflicts. The framework and tool we propose in this paper, called ConfIs, fills this gap by supporting engineers and organisations in these complex activities, with its systematic and interactive process. We applied ConfIs to a realistic GDPR example from the DEFeND EU Project, and evaluated its supportiveness, with positive results, by involving privacy and security requirements experts (This research is an extension of the study conducted by Alkubaisy *et al.* [1] – which itself is a continuation of earlier studies [2, 3] and aims to aid the reader in comprehensively grasping the concepts laid out).

Keywords: Security requirements · Privacy requirements · Requirements conflicts · GDPR · Requirements modelling · Privacy by design

R. Ali et al. (Eds.): ENASE 2021, CCIS 1556, pp. 67–87, 2022.
https://doi.org/10.1007/978-3-030-96648-5_4

1 Introduction

Today's software systems are seen to be susceptible to attack and performance issues due to matters regarding their inherent dependability [4], meaning their availability and reliability can come across as questionable. Especially considering the large amounts of sensitive and personal information kept on the servers of information systems, the security of such systems becomes even more important. The requirement engineering process of Software Engineering (SE) includes a variety of activities, from client contact through definition of requirements for the design. Since software is vulnerable to various threats, security, privacy, and trustworthiness have become important consideration in recent years [5]. Many contemporary SE paradigms are concerned with requirements; however, security, privacy, and trust implementations have received less attention. In practice, much emphasis is placed on incorporating security considerations throughout the coding and testing stages. Some paradigms handle these problems, but they only examine one of the three requirements: security, privacy, or trust, not all three at the same time. Hence, we think that security, privacy, and trust needs should be thoroughly collected, evaluated, and defined at different phases of the RE process.

Though, as important as system security is, privacy of the users must also always remain intact. This differentiation of security and privacy – and their respective requirements – should thus be given focused attention, both at the levels of understanding and at various stages of system development [6, 7].

Every software system is characterized by its own security and privacy requirements, with the latter having become a bone of contention between many software developments companies, and their customers. Presumed misuse of personal data has garnered attention and action in the form of legislative controls to 'guarantee' privacy, especially as proposed by the EU's General Data Protection Regulation (GDPR) [8]. A common problem in the engineering process of software systems are conflicts arising between clashing requirements, such as privacy and security [9]. The nature of the software development process for realistic systems deems such conflicts inevitable and results in major inconsistencies [10]. Each requirement-based conflict is characterized by its own complex issues, understanding which is crucial to reaching their resolution [11]. Even in the presence of effective controls, such conflict may very well arise and adversely affect information systems [9–12]. Therefore, as mentioned above, conflict identification earlier in the development lifecycle becomes even more crucial. This becomes more important for highly data-sensitive businesses such as banks and governmental departments which make up for almost 80% of all data breach incidents recorded [13].

GDPR has regulations in place to both educate citizens on how they can control where their data is used and to force organizations to have robust data usage and protection mechanisms in place. An example of the former is user consent while that of the latter is keeping track of the user data involved. The regulations enforced by GDPR can be difficult to put into actions, however. Once again, the inherent complexities in such measures resurface and add to the conflicts needed to be addressed. The approaches devised by literature in this area [14, 15] seem to lack in-depth and applicable measures to identify and resolve the privacy-security conflicts, even though this identification and resolution, are crucial to minimize threats to the information system.

Considering this, the research questions (RQs) this paper will explore in the following sections are laid out as follows.

RQ1: How to design a framework supporting the analyst to identify and resolve conflicts between privacy and security requirements?
RQ2: How to support the analyst in the identification and resolution of conflicts between requirements in a systematic and tool-supported way in real cases?

Here, the requirement modelling tool SecTro [16, 17] is extended to address **RQ1**. The resultant framework then offers an avenue of conflict identification and resolution for the analyst and is validated using the relevant portions of the DEFeND project [18] to ensure compliance with GDPR. For addressing **RQ2**, however, contemporary methods for conflict identification and resolution are reviewed and the novel ConfIS framework is introduced phase by phase to aid the analysts in the conflict location process.

The following sections will discuss the basis of the research conducted highlighting privacy and security requirements, and conflicting requirement likely to arise. Next a conflict resolution framework is proposed and DEFeND is used to answer RQ1. Afterwards, we address RQ2 by the extension of DEFeND to identify, resolve, and apply conflicts via the Tool Supported Conflict Resolution approach, followed by a case study and the assessing proposed ConfIS framework via expert group. Finally, we discuss the related work and concluding remarks.

2 Privacy and Security Requirements: Analysis and Conflict Resolution (State of the Art)

A system's capabilities at maintaining security and privacy can be gauged by the robustness of its respective requirements [19]. The successful satisfaction of these requirements then results in the minimization of conflicts and adherence to regulatory controls. This satisfaction becomes the ever-important factor while adopting a new system. At this point, analysts are supported in identifying security-privacy requirement conflicts and in subsequently resolving them. The proposed framework is a CASE Tool for Modelling Security in Requirements Engineering. The software Secure Tropos (SecTro) is used as it caters both to the needs of the users and the security requirements of the organization [20] while also ensuring that the resultant system is effectively defensive against cyber-attacks.

The benefits of this framework will allow the analyst to define and segregate privacy and security requirements. This enables the analyst to dive into the required level of detail in both these avenues and to make and understand their relationship with each other. Additionally, the framework enhances the understanding of software engineers regarding both security and privacy requirements and how they can harmonically coexist in a fully functional system. While the former caters to the organization's security policy, the latter are necessary to comply with data privacy laws and the issues that arise in balancing out them both must be identified and addressed as early in the development process as possible.

2.1 Conflicting Requirements

Conflicts are a part of almost every software system environment. These are inevitable and to have a smooth environment, they need to be terminated. The entire process of software development faces many inconsistencies and irregularities and one of the prime reasons for these instabilities is conflicting requirements. This problem occurs when a requirement is inconsistent with any another requirement. In this case, security and privacy requirements are mandatory but they have resulted in conflicting requirements. This is because multiple goals can have conflicting elements [21]. This conflict needs to be resolved, the entire process is dependent upon this resolution and this needs to be implemented on a business level to fulfill all the business needs.

While both privacy and security requirements hold their own significance, their coexistence can inevitably lead to conflicts. For example, the security requirement of authentication warrant's identity disclosure while the privacy requirement of anonymity opposes it. Another example can be taken from the case of data integrity versus unobservability, where the former necessitates tracking user activity across networks while the latter strongly resists it.

The security and privacy requirements come head-to-head once again in the battle of authentication. While data security entails the user to reveal as much information about their identity as possible to ascertain authenticity, the user privacy requirements of anonymity and pseudonymity require that the personally identifiable information of a user be as unavailable and protected as possible to reduce exposure. This conflict seems to take inspiration from real life and is faced in many a scenario. For instance, governments may be keen on collecting as much information about their citizens as possible in the interest of national security. Contrarily, citizens may have to live with concerns of privacy encroachment and may thus resist such observatory policies.

Additionally, privacy requirements bring with them concerns related to unobservability and Unlinkability. These two concerns act to severely impact the security requirements converse to them, but if the security requirements are given precedence, the privacy requirements would undeniably suffer. Such concerns help us envisage the sources of conflict in the security-privacy domain that need pertinent attention to be resolved appropriately. If not given due importance, such conflicts can prove to be detrimental to system stability. And while the nature of the conflicts remains similar, the idiosyncrasies of specific situations demand situation-specific attention.

The security requirement of authorization is another issue for potential conflict, as it is directly in contradiction to the privacy requirement of unobservability. In this, authorization demands the user to reveal themselves to the adequate degree while the preservation of privacy of the user requires concealment. This negotiation complicates the authentication cover of approval while also putting the user's identity in threat.

Consequently, a lot of aspects of privacy and security requirements seem to conflict with each other. The long list of an organization's security requirements including authenticity, accountability, non-repudiation, and auditability for record-keeping purposes, activity logs are required. In direct contrast, however, the concurrent privacy requirements like unobservability and anonymity be visible. Moreover, the actions of separation of duties (SoD) and binding of duties (BoD) act to further these conflicts as they lie in contradiction to the privacy requirements of anonymity and Unlinkability as these comparative exercises demand the verification of identity of the involved parties.

Moreover, to identifying these conflicts at the requirements stage, there may be some aspects that become apparent at later stages in the (SDLC) Software Development Life Cycle. For instance, the intrinsic characteristics of the security requirements of integrity, confidentiality, and availability are dependent upon the act of authorisation itself, necessitating granting access or modifying resources. And while user identification is not necessary for these requirements, it may be the approach some developers employ. Consequently, this can lead to later-stage security-privacy requirement conflicts, especially when more concrete requirements must be considered. For instance, instead of requiring the user to access a service using their own identity, they can be given the leeway to sign in using an alias. However, since the alias is still a unique identity able to be attributed to the user, it again comes in conflict with the concept of anonymity. Nonetheless, if some aspects of privacy or security requirements supplement or overlap with aspects of the other, their conflicting characteristics may be able to be overlooked. For example, the requirements of integrity, anonymity, and confidentiality all aim towards the singular purpose of minimising data breaches, thereby acting in unison.

This section illustrates via visual maps, the most frequently conflicting requirements. Extending from literature, the five security requirements likely to conflict with multiple privacy requirements are depicted in Fig. 1. The most conflicting security requirement is seen to be availability as it directly conflicts with four privacy requirements, namely Unlinkability anonymity, undetectability, and unobservability. The next most conflicting security requirements are accountability, confidentiality, and auditability, each conflicting with three privacy requirements. These are followed by authentication which conflicts with two privacy requirements.

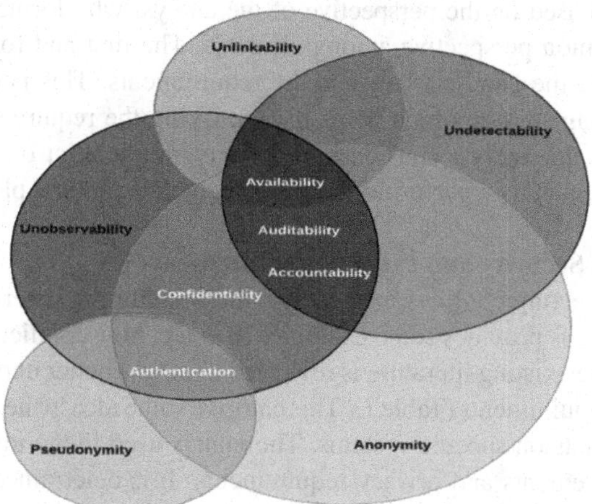

Fig. 1. Detecting conflicts between Security and privacy requirements (Venn diagram) (Alkubaisy et al. 2019).

It must be kept in mind that this list of security requirements is not exhaustive, but rather addresses the most common or frequently occurring and conflicting ones. Some security requirements are also not mentioned here since they do not seem to conflict with any privacy requirement.

2.2 Conflict Resolution - Framework and Process

The resolution process can give a clearer direction regarding other elements that were not previously discussed. This shows how prioritizing requirements is integral and which goal or element can be abandoned. This further highlight other important goals that can be achieved through this process. The overall change in business goals can alter the requirements, so the goals need to be achievable because if they are not achievable and realistic then the entire project can collapse.

The proposed framework has a sequence of phases to achieve conflict detection and resolution, presented in Fig. 2:

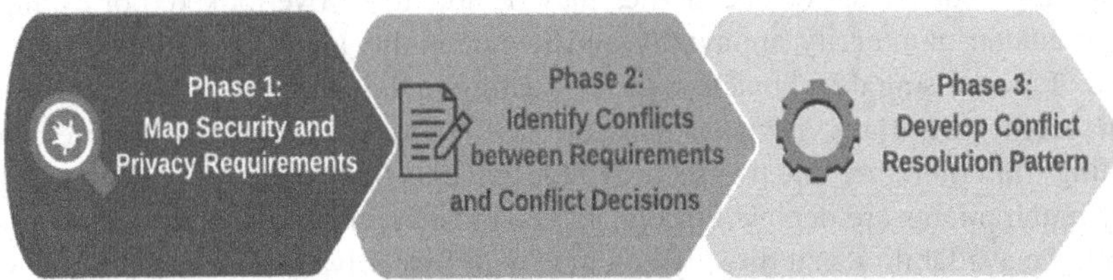

Fig. 2. The phases of the proposed theoretical framework- ConfIS framework (Alkubaisy et al. 2021).

The framework process has a combination of manual and semi-automated steps. These are majorly based on the perspective of the analyst who formed the theoretical framework. A common perspective among all these. The first and foremost step is to identify and analyze the conflicts between the requirements. This is established upon the matrix of existing studies which helps in identifying the requirements that can be conflict. Moreover, the analyst considers impacts of the conflict on the system. The software requirement analyst performs this phase, which is the first phase manually.

Phase 1: Mapping Security and Privacy Requirements

The first step of detecting conflicts is to review the literature to determine more about conflicting issues. This provides some examples to detect how conflict affects a system. In the first phase, the existing literature is reviewed to have a better understanding of the conflicts between requirements (Table 1). This can give some idea to the analyst regarding the impact of conflicts on specific systems. The matrix used in the identification helps map security requirements and privacy requirements. It is determined which conflicts exist between the two aspects.

Mapping Between Security and Privacy Requirements

The matrix maps conflicts between security requirements and privacy requirements. While there may indeed be conflicts among security requirements themselves, the matrix will focus on conflicts that cross the two aspects. The matrix helps us to visualize the

Table 1. Most frequent security and privacy requirements being in conflict.

Security requirements	Availability, Non-Repudiation, Confidentiality, Integrity, Authentication, AuthoriSation, Separation of duties (SoD), Binding of duties (BoD), Accountability, Auditability
Privacy requirements	Anonymity, Unlinkability, Pseudonymity, Unobservability, Undetectability

requirements with the most conflicts, which aids in identifying which deserve focus. From this matrix, anonymity and unobservability conflict the most with other security requirements (Table 2).

Table 2. Mapping conflicts between security and privacy requirements.

		Security Requirements:										*Privacy Requirements:*				
		Availability	Non repudiation	Confidentiality	Integrity	Authentication	Authorization	SOD	BOD	Accountability	Auditability	Anonymity	Unlinkability	Pseudonymity	Unobservability	Undetectability
Security Requirements:	Availability							o				o	o		o	o
	Non repudiation											o			o	
	Confidentiality											o			o	
	Integrity											o	o		o	
	Authentication						o					o		o	o	
	Authorization					o		o							o	
	SOD	o					o									
	BOD												o	o		
	Accountability											o			o	o
	Auditability											o			o	o
Privacy Requirements	Anonymity	o	o	o	o	o				o	o	o	o	o	o	
	Unlinkability	o			o				o			o		o		o
	Pseudonymity					o			o			o	o			
	Unobservability	o	o	o	o	o	o			o	o	o				o
	Undetectability	o								o	o		o		o	

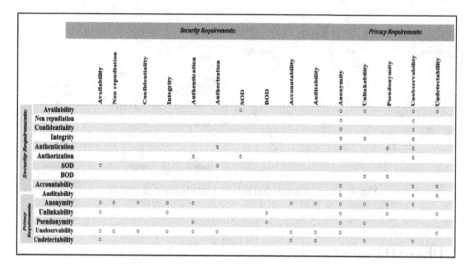

Phase 2: Identify Conflicts Between Requirements and Conflict Decisions
When we maintain security or privacy requirements, several challenges arise, according to an analyst's perspective. As discussed earlier, conflicts and problems are inevitable. Developers find it necessary to manage the conflicts that arise in this process and be compliant with GDPR. Identification of conflicts is essential and to do that, we analyze different scenario tasks to address conflicts. An example is used to explain this phase. We have to identify conflict in a situation where older people need to be taken care of by obtaining their personal information. This comes with security risks. Integrity and anonymity are the two requirements being conflict. Anonymity is a privacy requirement, and integrity is a security requirement.

Therefore, a conflict can arise if both the requirements have to be satisfied. It is vital to maintain the anonymity of the patient information according to privacy-by Design principles. Moreover, integrity is also important because sensitive information is being shared. Now, the requirements are mapped, and conflict is identified which is between integrity and anonymity. The analyst needs to evaluate all the scenarios related to this issue and evaluate them individually. The security and privacy requirements will be evaluated separately, and conflicts will be analyzed. This will assist the analyst in progressing to the resolution phase with all of the required information.

Phase 3: Tool Supported Conflict Resolution Patterns
Eventually, different solutions are proposed to deal with the conflict requirements. Thus, each type of conflict is set aside, and a model of patterns is found to connect the conflicting requirements with a supporting tool (Fig. 3). We need to find a tool that can satisfy both requirements without any sort of conflict. A relevant tool that can satisfy security and privacy requirements and resolve the conflict. The tool needs to be added to the Privacy Pattern Library for proper processing. The supporting tool needs to be added into the framework so that it is complete, and a conflict can be easily tackled through this tool.

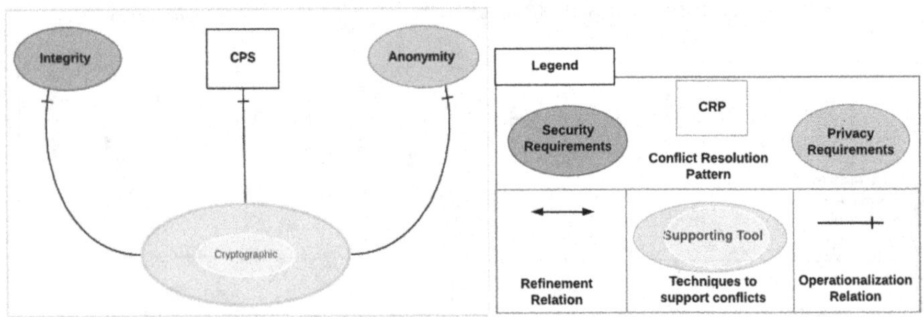

Fig. 3. Conflict resolution pattern (Alkubaisy et al. 2021).

3 DEFeND Project

Given the sensitivity of data and personal information organizations store of clients and customers, they are expected to comply with the European Union's General Data Protection Regulation (GDPR). DEFeND provides a platform to accredit organizations in different regions. This platform aims to have a plan to achieve GDPR compliance and raise awareness regarding its diverse features [22, 23]. All the scenarios are taken into consideration by the ConfIS framework which was not resolved by DEFeND project previously. By applying this framework, many conflicts are resolved now. The focus was on Data Scope Management (DSM), Data Protection Impact Assessment (DPIA), Privacy by Design and Security, and Privacy Threats. This research uses healthcare scenarios (mentioned in Sect. 5) of DEFeND project because it was more relevant, and it focused on sensitive user information and the personal data of the patient. There was also the potential to map requirements and identify conflicts related to this. Furthermore, the platform and the framework majorly support in discovering security and privacy requirements, identifying conflicts, and proposing legitimate solutions.

4 ConfIS Integration and SecTro

The SecTro tool has been used to aid in the modelling of conflicts resolution [1]. It implements the Secure Tropos Methodology which consists of an engineering approach for security and privacy requirements, starting from early-stage requirements of the (IS) Information System development process. Secure Tropos must be specified in the early phases of an IS development, as it is an organized approach for goal-oriented security and privacy requirement modelling. The Secure Tropos methodology supports a modelling language, security aware processes and automated processes. In fact, Secure Tropos methodology enhances our framework by translating conflicts between requirements in a goal model. SecTro presents models that contain security and privacy requirements [22]. It involves modelling views which are used to facilitate system design and elicitation of security and privacy requirements.

5 Motivation Scenario

There are a variety of scenarios where the conflicts arisen between security and privacy requirements can be seen to be exemplified. Neither one's respective significance can be ignored; however, each scenario accordingly demands individual attention. In our case study- Doctor and Patient, we have used the ConfIS framework on the DEFeND platform that aims to achieve conflict resolutions [23]. For maintaining confidentiality of Patient's record to avoid data breaches, a monitoring system must be installed in the hospitals. Another reason for installing a monitoring system is to remain in compliance with GDPR's regulations particularly when Third Parties are involved, for example external laboratories. For securing patient's data: The DEFeND platform introduces risk assessment, and Data Protection Impact Assessments (DPIA) along with validation process and proposed GDPR plan. A graphical representation of the model is achieved by the Hospital Analyst supporting doctors being able to change medical records by adding results from external parties (laboratories) and achieving approval from supervisors [24]. Furthermore, the DEFeND platform works with the organizational structure of the hospital, keeping hierarchy, and their interactions in check. The system comes with a configuration model for monitoring threats identified after Data Protection Impact Assessment (DPIA), Self-assessment, and related models for identifying potential threats.

The theoretical framework is built on the SecTro tool. Our case study in Phase 1 is supported by diagrams, and Privacy by Design tool to resolve conflicts. Phase 2 will identify security and privacy conflicts between these parties. The hospital analyst is supposed to make a sound decision based on the content of the identified conflict. In Phase 3, all concepts are added together, and solutions are presented to mitigate the identified conflict. After all of this, a case study is presented which implements all these three phases for an in-depth study. In Phase 1 to 3, ConfIS framework is introduced.

Based on the motivation example, we will illustrate the security and privacy requirements, following the phases of the ConfIS framework to resolve conflicts, using the extended supported tool. The first phase aims to map the security and privacy requirements [2]. This assumes the existence of a matrix to find out the potential conflicts between security and privacy requirements, based on our recent study [18]. The next sections show the application of our proposed framework phases in identifying and resolving conflicts, discusses the application of the motivation example in SecTro, and presents the theoretical framework to identify and resolve conflicts.

Phase 1: Mapping Security and Privacy Requirements
The privacy and security conditions are implicated in the determination of conflicts using a Mapping Matrix. To find out the reason for conflicting requirements, we have formed an outline by using Fig. 4 where the organization view of SecTro is exhibited. In the given flowchart each bubble depicts an actor which in our examples are doctor, supervisor, and an employee. To identify conflicts we have split the scenario to specify certain tasks to actors (doctor, employee, and supervisor). The tasks specified to them have distinct and precise requirements. The doctor requires medical history, data, and results from an Employee the main concern here is the privacy and integrity to send such confidential data, so the patient's privacy is not breached at any cost. Additionally, the data that is recorded after the doctor's careful examination or the update of a patient's medical record in the system should always be confidential. At the same time, the data recorded by the doctor needs to be authenticated by the supervisor. The long chain of action demands responsibility.

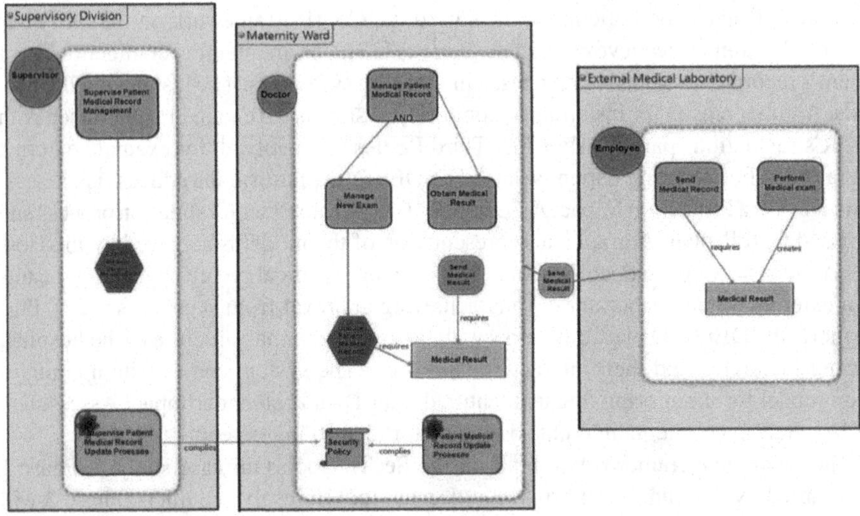

Fig. 4. Organization view of managing patient records (Alkubaisy et al. 2021).

Even the doctor's update of a patient's medical record in the system necessitates obligations. All these activities need to be compliance by GDPR principles. From seeing the above management process, we can conclude that each task has a different set of privacy requirements. From there, we can recognize and distinguish conflicting requirements. For instance, the confidentiality of the patient's record conflicts with the accountability principles as the accountability requires validation of the data. Considering the following scenario: Patient's medical record is met with a conflict for anonymity. Validation of

Medical examination is met with the conflict for accountability. Sending Medical results is met with the conflict for confidentiality and integrity.

Phase 2: Identify Conflicts Between Requirements and Conflict Decisions
We have divided a few key terms to help you figure out which ones are in conflict between security and privacy as presented in Table 2. For instance, Authentication and Undetectability are in conflict. Another example is of a conflict between Anonymity and Availability. According to the motivation scenario in terms of security and privacy requirements, assume a patient's doctor has ordered some medical test. A lab test was required for the patient. As a result, the lab will send the doctor's report with the patient's results; by maintaining the report's integrity and confidentiality. Next, the doctor will update patient's record according to GDPR's accountability principles. Privacy by design principles recommend anonymity to be top priority for updating a patient's medical record while results should be approved by a senior supervisor, and therefore accountability is a must in this case. Therefore, there is conflicts between accountability as security requirement and anonymity as privacy requirement. While the patient's record must be updated anonymously but there should also be an accountability record to cross-check drug recommendation when an audit is conducted or there is a need for an investigation for Doctor's misconduct. Many cases, like the one involving the doctor, patient, and lab examiner, have more than one requirement. Thus, it must follow both security and privacy principles, which is a difficult decision, and thus a major conflict arises. The case of anonymity and accountability is significant because the former allows users to use resources or make decisions without revealing their identity while the latter contradicts and relates each action to a participant. To conclude, Phase 2 discussed identification of the conflict between a Doctor and his Supervisor in terms of accountability and anonymity.

Phase 3: Conflict Resolution Patterns
In Phase 3 we discuss Conflict Mitigation by addressing the requirements to be followed, and then presenting possible solutions for mitigating the conflict. In order to mitigate the conflict with the help of a supporting tool, each conflict case must first define the problem and identify the restrictions that must be followed. This supporting tool will be added to a Privacy Pattern Library and will be applied in a scenario in SecTro. It will provide to requirements of both sides and will relate to each individual conflict to produce feasible solutions as depicted in Fig. 5. First, requirements analyst must identify measures related to security and privacy concerns to support and improve constraints. Then, related to support and execution of the established route of plan by following mechanisms identified in security and privacy domains. According to [7] alongside identifying measures with the help of experts, a security and privacy catalogue is recommended to be used if need arises in such complex situations. A Design Pattern Library (DPL) is formulated and added in SecTro2. Various experts develop models according to the identified conflict and can save it for later use. These models as available on DPL are then accessed by the Developer to resolve security and privacy conflicts.

In this case we were able to identify two supporting tools, titled: IDEMIX and Cryptography Supporting Tool. Cryptography couldn't address the anonymity concern even though it was suitable for maintaining confidentiality and integrity. IDEMIX was established as the more suitable one because it adheres to GDPR's Data minimization principle by making the medium of file sharing anonymous [27] between users and service provider, this resolving the conflict between the Doctor and his supervisor while also maintaining the accountability perspective. In addition, we added supporting tools in Privacy by Design View in Fig. 5 in which we can add new concepts/tools to import a suitable mechanism according to the conflict identified. Additionally, DBL also supports Data Record Action along with IDEMIX were identified as supporting tools in DBL.

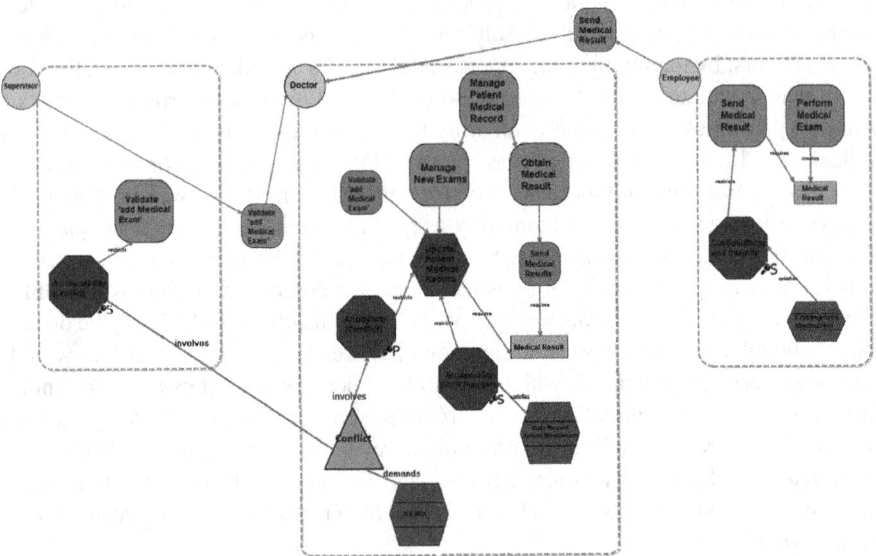

Fig. 5. Integrating conflict resolution in privacy-by-design view of managing patient records (Alkubaisy et al. 2021)

Discussion

For the entire process of updating the Patient Medical Record, there is a strong need to deal with the anonymity concern. The anonymity of the doctor is important so that no one knows who made the change on the records. This concern is fulfilled through a mechanism. IDEMIX is there to cater to this concern. For the accountability requirement, the supervisor needs to authorize the change. This is where the conflict lies because anonymity is compromised in this case. There is a conflict between anonymity and accountability. This problem can be resolved by the IDEMIX mechanism [24]. This will ensure minimized release of personal information hence keeping the anonymity intact. IDEMIX is an optimizing cryptographic compiler that provides a great level of assurance. This keeps the transport medium between the users and service providers anonymous. This technique ensures anonymity, authenticity, and accountability of transactions between the users and service providers. Furthermore, the requirements of integrity and anonymity are also fulfilled by cryptographic mechanisms while sending medical records. Lastly, the concern of accountability is catered through the Record Data

Action mechanism. Using these combinations of mechanisms and techniques we can meet all the requirements and resolve all the conflicts that may arise in this process. These mechanisms help us achieve anonymity, integrity, and accountability in the whole process.

6 Evaluation

6.1 Evaluation Strategy

We employ qualitative and quantitative analyses to achieve a comprehensive evaluation. For the qualitative aspect, we designed a focus group session, with participants who are experts in software engineering and researchers. Before we undertook the evaluation, we constructed a pilot focus group evaluation with three participant groups – PhD student, PhD doctor and Research Fellow. This revealed to us the possibilities of improving the focus group evaluation according to the participants' feedback. Moving forward, we could perform the full-scale focus group evaluation of fifteen participants. The fifteen participants were active researchers in the fields of software engineering and were practicing at different universities across various countries to add multi-dimensional and multi-perspective value to our heterogeneous approach.

Qualitative and quantitative analysis are critical parts of the evaluation strategy. Based on qualitative and quantitative analysis, each complete evaluation is scaled. Both aspects are approached in different methods by the researchers. The objective is to establish a critique of the frameworks and highlight the flaws which can be fixed for improvements. A pilot focus group has to be created before the evaluation begins.

According to the policy for ethical research in the United Kingdom, parts of the research methods and data of a research study are subject to ethical review because of the involvement of human participants. Ethical review self-assessment forms and a data management plan were submitted to the Ethics and Integrity Officer of the University. The ethical review forms included details of the project and self-assessment questions.

6.2 Full Evaluation

To design the evaluation of the framework, we have mentioned that some of the steps of ConfIS framework are semi-automated, while others are manual steps, based on the analyst's point of view. First, the conflicts between requirements are identified, based on a matrix presented by a previous study [3]. Hence, we sort the requirements that could lead to a potential conflict. After identifying the requirements which are in conflict, the analyst must decide whether this kind of conflict would affect the system, based on the presented scenarios. Therefore, the first phase of the framework is performed manually by the software requirements analyst. Phase 2 identifies the potential conflicts between requirements that were detected in the previous phase. The final phase proposes conflict resolution patterns by matching the problem to a resolution pattern for each conflict that the analyst might face. These patterns act as a reference for the analyst to resolve conflicts between requirements. The final phase of our framework is automated by using SecTro tool (by importing a privacy pattern library).

6.3 Results

A summary analysis of the evaluation survey reveals that the majority of respondents were research fellows (47%), followed by PhD students (33%) and doctor (20%). All participants found the research design questions were appropriate, useful, well presented (87%) and the research field quite interesting (93%) in gaining their feedback. On the other hand, just 54% agreed that the results were clearly presented; this leaves room for improvement (Fig. 6).

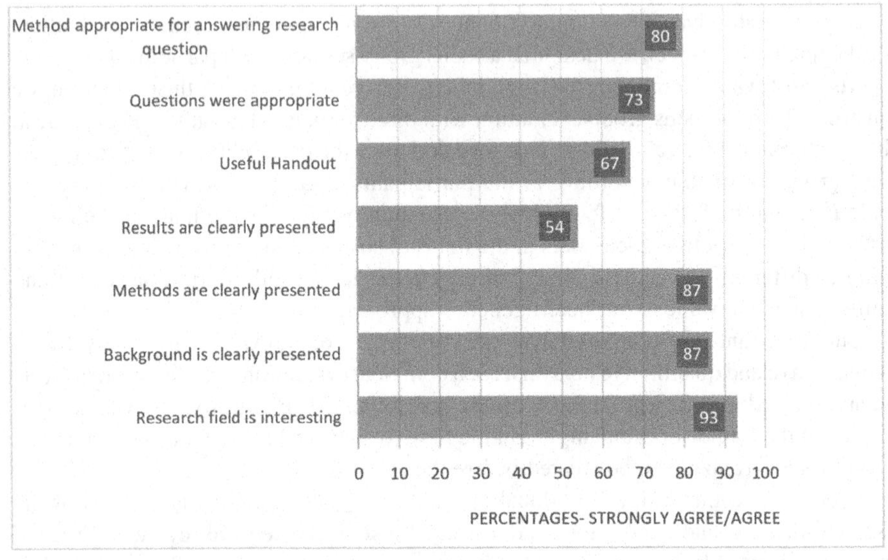

Fig. 6. Research design questions.

More than 80% of the research fellows who participated highly agreed with the research design saying that the research field is interesting, background and methods are clearly presented and appropriate for answering the research questions, the handout is useful, and questions are appropriate. Furthermore, 100% of the PhD doctors who participated highly agreed that the research field is interesting, and that the background is clearly presented. Moreover, over 60% (the majority) did agree to the method being clearly presented and appropriate for answering the research questions. A neutral response was provided, however, to whether the results were clearly presented, the usefulness of the handout and appropriateness of questions. Additionally, most PhD students, over 60%, agreed with the research design, Figure above. In instances of participants disagreeing with it to some degree. Additionally, the general framework was well received by the majority, proving to be sequentially in order (87%), clear and well defined (80%), easy to analyze (80%) and for making feasible decisions such as reducing cost, conflict, and faster development processing (73%) (Fig. 7).

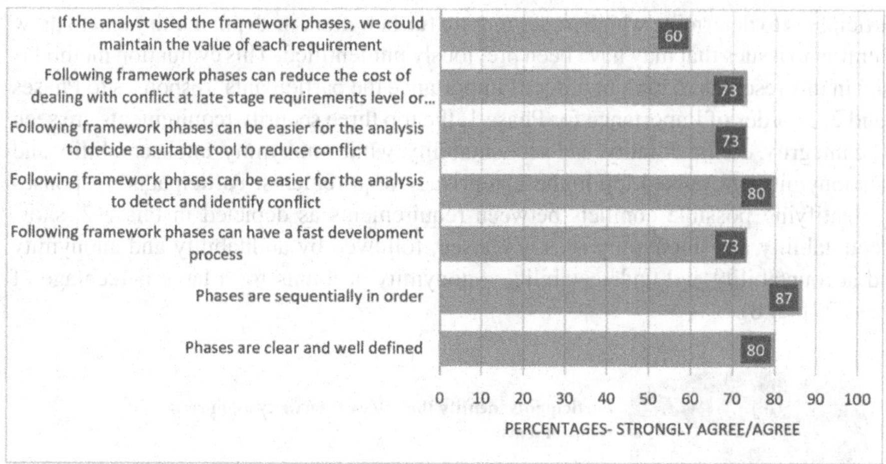

Fig. 7. General framework (Alkubaisy et al. 2021).

The majority share, well over 70% of research fellows, agreed with the general framework. They approve of the statements that the relevant phases are clear, well defined, sequentially in order, can have a fast development process, are easy for identifying conflict, reducing it and its relevant costs, and maintaining the value of each requirement. Additionally, more than 80% of PhD students agreed with the design of the general framework and its phases. Phase 1, mapping security and privacy requirements, showed 70–87% of participants agreeing to the presentation of Phase 1 while Phase 2 was well received with the majority (80–86%) agreeing that the researcher adequately addressed conflicts between requirements and decisions. Additionally, feedback on Phase 3 showed varying responses (67–87%), yet the participants still agreed that there was an ease to understanding conflict resolutions patterns and its supporting tools (Table 3).

Table 3. ConfIS framework phases and survey responses.

Phase 1: Mapping Security and Privacy Requirements	70–87% (strongly/agree)
Phase 2: Identify Conflicts between Requirements and Conflict Decisions	80–86% (strongly/agree)
Phase 3: Conflict Resolution Patterns	67–87% (strongly/agree)

Analysis of ConfIS Framework Phases' Focus Group Results and Survey Responses
Ven and Delbecq [25] found that a two-stage combination of focus group and the nominal group technique (NGT), coined as 'nominal focus group', was particularly effective as an evaluation method. The nominal group process is a structured meeting which seeks to provide an orderly procedure for obtaining qualitative information from target groups who are most closely associated with a particular issue. It allows the meetings'

participants to determine which issues require further, more in-depth inquiry and to draw attention to issues that may have been previously unidentified. This evaluation method is used in this research to rank in order of importance the participants' responses to Phases 1 and 2. In order of importance for Phase 1, the top three security requirements are seen to be integrity, confidentiality, and accountability, while anonymity, unobservability and pseudonymity are ranked top highest in privacy requirements. Participants' responses to identifying possible conflicts between requirements as depicted in Phase 2, show accountability and anonymity mostly chosen, followed by auditability and anonymity and accountability and undetectability. Anonymity accounts for a large percentage of Phase 2 (Fig. 8).

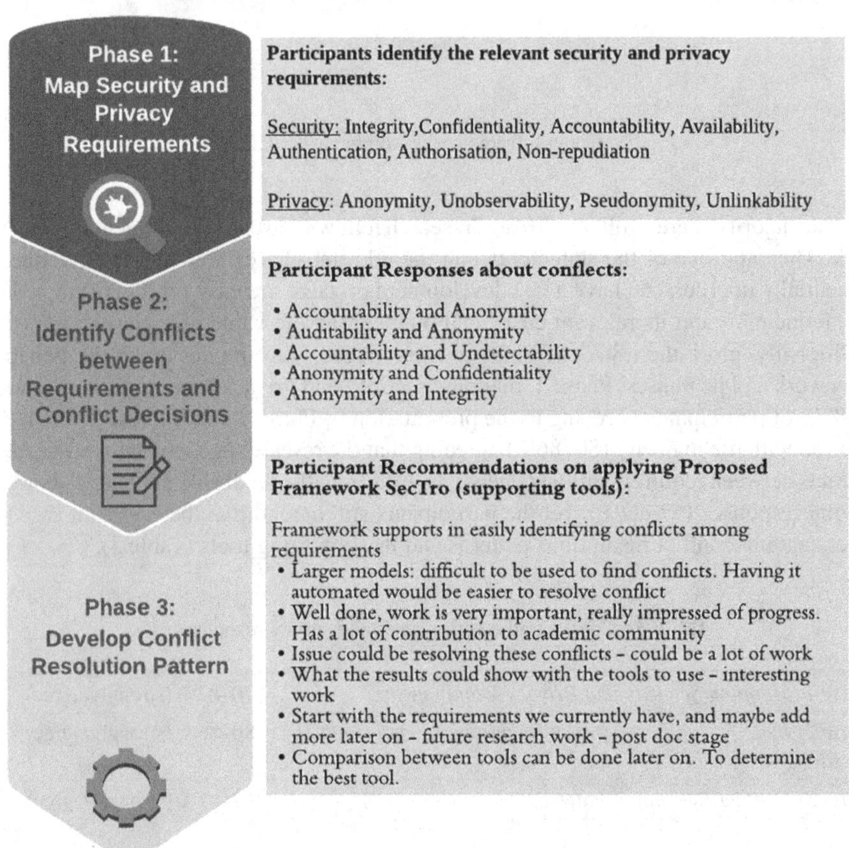

Fig. 8. ConfIS framework and focus group response using nominal ranking evaluation method.

7 Application to ConfIS Framework

In pursuit of answering **RQ1:** How to design a framework supporting the analyst to identify and resolve conflicts between privacy and security requirements? A list of Security and Privacy Requirements, supported by the literature review we conducted, has been developed as a part of **Phase 1: Mapping Security and Privacy Requirements**. This list is presented in Table 1. Additionally, **RQ1** is also supported by the mapping matrix we stipulated in **Phase 1: Mapping Conflicts between security and privacy requirements**. **RQ1** addressed by employing SecTro as mentioned earlier. SecTro creates models of the requirements for information systems [17]. By extending SecTro to our proposes framework, we offer the analyst a way forward to identify and resolve conflicts using a mapping matrix presented in Table 2. The framework is then validated according to the DEFeND project's stipulations [18], ensuring compliance with GDPR in the process. Moreover, we aim to answer **RQ2**: How to support the analyst in the identification and resolution of conflicts between requirements in a systematic and tool-supported way in real cases? In **Phase 2: Identify Conflicts between Requirements and Conflict Decisions**, we provide the analyst with the necessary and pertinent tools. It is seen that our proposed framework also seeks to mitigate conflicts, under the condition that both the Phases 1 and 2 are adequately fulfilled. Lastly, with **Phase 3: Conflict Resolution Patterns**, including its table and design view, we provide an approach to mitigating conflicts.

8 Related Work

Many types of research have been conducted in this field of study. Many researchers have come up with their theories and worked hard on constructing mechanisms to deal with conflicts and find their solutions. Professionals with knowledge in requirements elicitation methodologies, based on systematic procedures and methods, are required, according to a recent study [26], to enhance software requirements with crucial security and privacy aspects.

Ramadan *et al.* conducted several studies in this field of study [27, 28]. Their data showed how conflicts can be detected between data-minimization and security requirements. This was investigated in business process models and conflicts between security and privacy requirements in a system were examined. Salnitri and fellow researchers had conducted a study related to this same subject in 2020 [29]. They had come up with an innovative method which was called SePTA (Security, Privacy and Trust Approach). As the name suggests, this procedure supported all three aspects which are security, privacy, and trust. These requirements were supported under only one framework. This framework was majorly designed for sociotechnical systems because this helped software designers and security experts to satisfy these requirements. In terms of dealing with such conflicts involving goals and/or requirements, we introduced risk based on the user concern, trustworthiness goals, and requirements as determinants to TrustSoFt in our previous work.

In the work of Horkoff, 246 top-cited papers were examined in the span of 20 years [30]. They have focused their study on the Goal-oriented requirements engineering (GORE) area. In this field, goals are used as the main subject. Goals are utilized and used as a baseline to elicit, model, and analyze requirements. A survey paper compared recent studies in this field [31]. This talked about the conflict between requirements in the early stage of development. The survey consisted of various case studies regarding software engineering under the requirement gathering techniques. It further talked about how conflicts could be resolved at the early phase. Regarding resolving the conflicts, usage of the agile software development method was also elaborated. Maxwell *et al.* also includes the identification of conflicting software requirements [32]. They highlighted the rules and laws which made them easier to handle. They further mentioned that the reputation of a company highly depends on the rules and ethics that they follow, which increases the importance of these rules. We can't ignore the extra costs that these laws and regulations might bring. According to their perspective of Schon *et al.* [33], agile software development made the changing of requirements easy and fast which further made it simple to handle. But with the rapidness it provided, more complexities were also created because a hybrid development model was used in this.

It is important to mention that privacy became an important aspect at this time, as we mentioned in introduction section. As we find out that there are more that regulation and laws concern privacy disclosure. For instance, Brazilian citizens' complaints regarding data privacy are rising by the day, particularly with the access into force of the General Data Protection Law (LGPD) [34]. The purpose of the Act is to regulate the handling of personal data. If personal data processing is not done in compliance with this regulation, it might have a lot of consequences in technical fields. LGPD is a piece of legislation that gives Brazilian citizens privacy, allowing them to identify and amend data processing at any anytime. Organizations that apply the LGPD will demonstrate their integrity and dedication to their users. Therefore, LGPD provides numerous principles that will help both citizens and organizations, in addition to showing how risk management has improved and organizational techniques have improved. Some aspects may have affected organizations' LGPD requirement specification in the Brazilian environment. Moreover, The California Consumer Privacy Act (CCPA) [35], a digital privacy regulation that offers consumers more control over their online personal information, was approved by California lawmakers in 2018. In the United States, the CCPA is a major rule that regulates how technology firms acquire and use data. (CCPA) recognizes various categories of personal information. The CCPA, on either hand, exempts public access information, which is described as "information lawfully made available from federal, state, or provincial government records, but not if the aim of data processing is incompatible with its declared purpose". Regulations may be required for such organisations to comply. Additionally, it is in companies' best interests to establish compliance strategies beforehand and rather than be caught unawares by last-minute implementation or significant complaints.

9 Conclusion

The nature of software development for realistic systems presents a complex phenomenon of conflict resolution. Usually in engineering software systems, the conflict arises between security and privacy. This article presented a three -phases framework, called ConfIS, to identify conflicts between security and privacy requirements and to find solutions that could mitigate these conflicts. This framework allows the analyst to look at the potential conflicts beforehand that may arise in the future. ConfIS has been applied to a case study from the DEFeND project. A step-by-step demonstration of the phases of ConfIS has been presented. We plan to add CCPA and LGPD support to the ConfIS framework in the future. Using different case studies that are in accordance with the regulations.

Acknowledgement. This work has received funding from the European Union's Horizon 2020 research and innovation program under grant agreement No. 787068.

References

1. Alkubaisy, D., Piras, L., Al-Obeidallah, M.G., Cox, K., Mouratidis, H.: ConfIs: a tool for privacy and security analysis and conflict resolution for supporting GDPR compliance through privacy-by-design. In: 16th International Conference on Evaluation of Novel Approaches to Software Engineering (ENASE) (2021)
2. Alkubaisy, D.: A framework managing conflicts between security and privacy requirements. In: 2017 11th International Conference on Research Challenges in Information Science (RCIS), pp. 427–432. Institute of Electrical and Electronics Engineers (2017). https://doi.org/10.1109/RCIS.2017.7956571
3. Alkubaisy, D., Cox, K., Mouratidis, H.: Towards detecting and mitigating conflicts for privacy and security requirements. In: Kolp, M., et al. (eds.) Proceedings: RCIS 2019 - IEEE 13th International Conference on Research Challenges in Information Science: Towards a design science for information systems. Brussels, 29–31 May 2019. Institute of Electrical and Electronics Engineers Computer Society, Belgium (2019). https://doi.org/10.1109/RCIS.2019.8876999. Accessed 05 Dec 2020
4. Noll, T.: Safety, dependability and performance analysis of aerospace systems. In: Artho, C., Ölveczky, P.C. (eds.) FTSCS 2014. CCIS, vol. 476, pp. 17–31. Springer, Cham (2015). https://doi.org/10.1007/978-3-319-17581-2_2
5. Tejas, R.S., Patel, S.V.: Security, privacy and trust oriented requirements modeling for examination system. In: 2012 Nirma University International Conference on Engineering (NUiCONE). IEEE (2012)
6. Dubois, E., Mouratidis, H.: Guest editorial: security requirements engineering: past, present and future, pp. 1–5 (2010)
7. Mouratidis, H., et al.: A framework to support selection of cloud providers based on security and privacy requirements. J. Syst. Softw. **86**(9), 2276–2293 (2013)
8. Albrecht, J.P.: How the GDPR will change the world. Eur. Data Prot. L. Rev. **2**, 287 (2016)
9. Kim, M., Park, S., Sugumaran, V., Yang, H.: Managing requirements conflicts in software product lines: a goal and scenario-based approach. Data Knowl. Eng. **61**(3), 417–432 (2007)
10. Egyed, A., Boehm, B.: A comparison study in software requirements negotiation. In: Proceedings of the 8th Annual International Symposium on Systems Engineering, INCOSE 1998 (1998)
11. Lamsweerde, A., Darimont, R., Letier, E.: Managing conflicts in goal-driven requirements engineering. IEEE Trans. Softw. Eng. **24**(11), 908–926 (1998)
12. Schär, B.: Requirements engineering process: HERMES 5 and SCRUM. Master's thesis. University of Applied Sciences and Arts (2015)
13. Botha, J., Grobler, M., Eloff, M.: Global data breaches responsible for the disclosure of personal information: 2015 & 2016. In: European Conference on Cyber Warfare and Security. Academic Conferences International Limited (2017)
14. Aldekhail, M., Azzedine, C., Djamal, Z.: Software requirements conflict identification: review and recommendations. Int. J. Adv. Comput. Sci. Appl. **7**(10), 326–335 (2016)

15. Mairiza, D., Zowghi, D., Gervasi, V.: 'Conflict characterization and analysis of non functional requirements: an experimental approach. In: IEEE 12th International Conference on Intelligent Software Methodologies, Tools and Techniques (SoMeT), pp. 83–91. Institute of Electrical and Electronics Engineers, Budapest (2013)
16. Pavlidis, M., Islam, S.: SecTro: a CASE tool for modelling security in requirements engineering using secure Tropos. In: CEUR Workshop Proceedings, vol. 734, pp. 89–96 (2011)
17. Mouratidis, H.: Secure software systems engineering: the secure tropos approach. J. Softw. **6**(3), 331–339 (2011)
18. Piras, L., et al.: DEFeND architecture: a privacy by design platform for GDPR compliance. In: Gritzalis, S., Weippl, E.R., Katsikas, S.K., Anderst-Kotsis, G., Tjoa, A.M., Khalil, I. (eds.) TrustBus 2019. LNCS, vol. 11711, pp. 78–93. Springer, Cham (2019). https://doi.org/10.1007/978-3-030-27813-7_6
19. Yahuza, M., et al.: Systematic review on security and privacy requirements in edge computing: state of the art and future research opportunities. Inst. Electr. Electron. Eng. Access **8**, 76541–76567 (2020)
20. Mouratidis, H., Giorgini, P.: Secure Tropos: a security-oriented extension of the Tropos methodology. Int. J. Softw. Eng. Knowl. Eng. **17**(02), pp. 285–309 (2007). http://www.worldscientific.com/doi/abs/10.1142/S0218194007003240. Accessed 10 Feb 2016
21. Salado, A., Nilchiani, R.: The concept of order of conflict in requirements engineering. Inst. Electr. Electron. Eng. Syst. J. **10**(1), 25–35 (2014)
22. Piras, L., et al.: DEFeND DSM: a data scope management service for model-based privacy by design GDPR compliance. In: Gritzalis, S., Weippl, E.R., Kotsis, G., Tjoa, A Min, Khalil, Ismail (eds.) TrustBus 2020. LNCS, vol. 12395, pp. 186–201. Springer, Cham (2020). https://doi.org/10.1007/978-3-030-58986-8_13
23. Piras, L., et al.: A data scope management service to support privacy by design and GDPR compliance. J. Data Intell. **2**(2), 136–165 (2021)
24. Camenisch, J., van Herreweghen, E.: Design and implementation of the idemix anonymous credential system. In: Proceedings of the 9th ACM Conference on Computer and Communications Security, pp. 21–30. Association for Computing Machinery, New York (2002). https://doi.org/10.1145/586110.586114
25. van de Ven, A.H., Delbecq, A.: The nominal group as a research instrument for exploratory health studies. Am. J. Public Health **62**(3), 337–42 (1972)
26. Mendes, L.M., de Franco Rosa, F., Bonacin, R.: Enriching financial software requirements concerning privacy and security aspects: a semiotics based approach. In: Latifi, S. (ed.) ITNG 2021 18th International Conference on Information Technology-New Generations. Advances in Intelligent Systems and Computing, vol. 1346, pp. 85–90. Springer, Cham (2021). https://doi.org/10.1007/978-3-030-70416-2_11
27. Ramadan, Q., Strüber, D., Salnitri, M., Riediger, V., Jürjens, J.: Detecting conflicts between data-minimization and security requirements in business process models. In: Pierantonio, A., Trujillo, S. (eds.) ECMFA 2018. LNCS, vol. 10890, pp. 179–198. Springer, Cham (2018). https://doi.org/10.1007/978-3-319-92997-2_12
28. Ramadan, Q., Strüber, D., Salnitri, M., Jürjens, J., Riediger, V., Staab, S.: A semi-automated BPMN-based framework for detecting conflicts between security, data-minimization, and fairness requirements. Softw. Syst. Model. **19**(5), 1191–1227 (2020). https://doi.org/10.1007/s10270-020-00781-x
29. Salnitri, M., et al.: Modelling the interplay of security, privacy and trust in sociotechnical systems: a computer-aided design approach. Softw. Syst. Model. **19**(2), 467–491 (2020)
30. Horkoff, J., et al.: Goal-oriented requirements engineering: an extended systematic mapping study. Requirements Eng. **24**(2), 133–160 (2017). https://doi.org/10.1007/s00766-017-0280-z

31. Bhavsar, R., et al.: Resolving conflicts in requirement engineering through agile software development: a comparative case study. In: Bhattacharyya, S., et al. (eds.) International Conference on Innovative Computing and Communications, vol. 55, pp. 349–357. Springer, Singapore (2019). https://doi.org/10.1007/978-981-13-2324-9_35
32. Maxwell, J.C., Antón, A.I., Swire, P.: A legal cross-references taxonomy for identifying conflicting 160 software requirements. In: 2011 IEEE 19th international requirements engineering conference, vol. 161, pp. 197–206 (2011)
33. Schon, E.-M., Thomaschewski, J., Escalona, M.J.: Agile requirements engineering: a systematic literature review. Comput. Stand. Interfaces **49**, 79–91 (2017)
34. Ferrão, S.É.R., Carvalho, A.P., Canedo, E.D., Mota, A.P.B., Costa, P.H.T., Cerqueira, A.J.: Diagnostic of data processing by Brazilian organizations—a low compliance issue. Information **12**(4), 168 (2021)
35. Mulgund, P., et al.: The implications of the California Consumer Privacy Act (CCPA) on healthcare organizations: lessons learned from early compliance experiences. Health Policy Technol. **10**(3), 100543 (2021)

The Relevance of Privacy Concerns, Trust, and Risk for Hybrid Social Media

Angela Borchert[1(✉)], Aidmar Wainakh[3], Nicole Krämer[2], Max Mühlhäuser[3], and Maritta Heisel[1]

[1] Software Engineering, University of Duisburg-Essen, Duisburg, Germany
angela.borchert@uni-due.de

[2] Social Psychology, University of Duisburg-Essen, Duisburg, Germany
nicole.kramer@uni-duisburg-essen.de

[3] Telecooperation Lab, Technical University of Darmstadt, Darmstadt, Germany
{aidmar.wainakh,max.muhlhauser}@tu-darmstadt.de

Abstract. Users generate a massive amount of personal, partly sensitive data in online social media. In the past, data breaches made evident that service providers of social media lack in adequately protecting this data leading to user concerns in regards to their privacy. Privacy-preserving social media emerged to address this issue by providing more secure environments for private social exchanges. However, these platforms often fall short of attracting users away from conventional social media and establishing users' trust in them. In this work, we aim to enhance the trustworthiness of privacy-preserving social media, in particular a hybrid social media application. For this purpose, we first analyze the relationships between *privacy concerns*, *trusting beliefs*, *risk beliefs*, and *willingness to use*. Second, we examine the effect of user characteristics on these relationships. Third, we mitigate privacy concerns via trust-related software features developed with the TrustSoFt method. We conduct a thorough user study to assess the impact of these features on the privacy concerns and trustworthiness. Our findings indicate the special importance of addressing particular privacy concerns, such as "Awareness of Privacy Practices". Furthermore, results suggest that older individuals as well as individuals that have experience with privacy incidents, are more susceptible to trust-related software features.

Keywords: Hybrid social media · Information privacy concerns · Trustworthiness · Requirements engineering

1 Introduction

In an increasingly interconnected world, social media plays an essential role in our societies by enabling social interaction, exchanging information, and online self-presentation. With these unique services, the ever-growing user base of social media was tripled in the last decade to cover more than half of the world population [11]. This increase led also to an exponential rise in the data generated by users. However,

A. Borchert and A. Wainakh—Funded by the Deutsche Forschungsgemeinschaft (DFG, German Research Foundation) - 251805230/GRK 2050 and 2167.

R. Ali et al. (Eds.): ENASE 2021, CCIS 1556, pp. 88–111, 2022.
https://doi.org/10.1007/978-3-030-96648-5_5

several pioneer social media providers (e.g., Facebook) have consistently shown insufficient commitment to adequate protection of user data and privacy [36]. That is evident by numerous data breaches especially in the last few years, such as Cambridge Analytica [18], leaking Facebook user personal data [22], and Facebook tokens hack [19]. User data was frequently prone to unauthorized accessed, has been used without informed consent, and was passed to third parties like data brokers. This has led to a remarkable increase in the users' privacy concerns [29]. Moreover, the nontransparent way these incidents are handled by providers increased the damage of their reputation, thus, their trustworthiness. For example, in the infamous Cambridge Analytica incident [18], Facebook deliberately did not inform users about the breach until it was exposed two years later by whistleblowers and journalists.

As an alternative, a number of privacy-preserving social media were proposed in the research community [10,33,44] and the market [2,41]. The main objectives of these solutions are to eliminate the control of central providers and empower users with more means of control. That is mainly achieved by establishing decentralized social media on top of Peer-to-Peer networks. The user data is protected from unauthorized access by encryption and outside the control of single authorities on distributed entities [44]. Despite the extensive efforts and the advanced technologies used to build this kind of social media, they fall short of clearly conveying their privacy practices, and thus, gaining the users' trust. This is due to various reasons, such as introducing novel, and sometimes complex concepts and technologies [44]; users usually hesitate to use a novel technology, as they are not sure it is safe and works as expected (aka penguin effect) [8]. Furthermore, since some of these social media applications are still evolving, their user interfaces need to be improved in some cases. In the process, the user experience must be supplemented with user-friendly functionalities and insightful explanations of the technologies used. Therefore, it is important to enhance these social media in their design to better show people that their privacy concerns are properly addressed and thereby gaining their trust.

Malhotra et al. [35] have found that decreasing privacy concerns positively impact people's trusting beliefs in online companies. Their findings indicate how the issue of privacy-preserving social media, which is mostly not perceived as trustworthy although it protects users' privacy, can be dealt with. An approach is to develop software features that mitigate specific privacy concerns, and, thus, improve trustworthiness in technology and service provider [5]. However, the study of Malhotra et al. was conducted in 2004 [35], even before the existence of modern online social media, e.g., Facebook and Twitter. The huge number of new technologies introduced in the last decade has shaped society and different user groups more than ever before [12]. Hence, it is likely that various user groups also differ in their cognitions regarding privacy-preserving social media. Therefore, it is essential to revisit the conclusions of [35] for the new context. Here, it is especially important to focus on how the relations of privacy concerns, trust, risk an the willingness to use privacy-preserving social media varies for different user types.

1.1 Contributions

This work is an extension of our recent publication [6]. In the previous work [6], we first analyzed the relationships between the privacy concerns, trust beliefs, risk beliefs, and the willingness to use a privacy-preserving social media application. Second, we developed trust-related software features, which focus on the graphical user interface. By applying the software engineering method Eliciting Trust-Related Software Features (TrustSoFt) [5], features are specified that address users' privacy concerns [35]. We showcased the validity of our approach by conducting a user study with over 2300 participants, who use an exemplary privacy-preserving social media application, which is Hybrid Social Media (HSM) [44]. Then, we measured the impact of the elicited features on the privacy concerns and the trustworthiness of the application.

This work substantially extends the previous work with an advanced analysis of the relationships between the constructs: privacy concerns, trust beliefs, risk beliefs, and the willingness to use. More precisely, we investigate how the relations differ for various user groups. This investigation is essential for building user-centred HSM, i.e., tailored to the needs of different user groups. This work has the following additional contributions.

- We examine differences regarding sex, age, and education in terms of how the aforementioned constructs impact each other.
- We analyze the impact of two privacy-related covariates: (1) Identification misrepresentation: how often individuals provide falsified personal identifiable information to a marketer, and (2) privacy invasion: how often the privacy of subjects has been invaded in the past.

We proceed with the paper as follows. We start with providing theoretical background on the HSM concept and information privacy concerns in Sect. 2 and 3. In Sect. 4, we introduce TrustSoFt under our problem setting to elicit trust-related software features. Then, we present the user study for examining our hypotheses and evaluating the features in Sect. 5. The results are reported in Sect. 6, followed by an analysis and discussion in Sect. 7. Finally, we conclude the paper in Sect. 8.

2 Hybrid Social Media

Commercial Social Media (CSM) employ the users' data to make profits, mainly by realizing targeted advertisements. Pioneer CSM have attracted a massive number of users and dominated the market. Consequently, they are imposed as almost inevitable tools in our modern societies. While being inevitable, the providers show consistently insufficient commitment to the users' privacy [31,32].

The Privacy-Preserving Social Media (PPSM) alternatives [17,41] focus on empowering users and protecting their data. One of the key techniques of PPSMs to achieve privacy is the elimination of central entities. As such, there is no central provider that controls user data. Instead, PPSMs are mainly based on distributed technologies to realize the essential functionalities for social media: (1) storage, (2) access control, and (3) connectivity. However, PPSM are not well-adopted by the users because of several reasons [44], such as poor functionality (e.g., [34]), high complexity (e.g., [41]), and low scalability (e.g., [10]).

Hybrid Social Media (HSM) addresses these issues by combining CSM and PPSM [44]. That combination enables users to profit from both the market penetration of the commercial ones and the privacy features of the privacy-preserving ones.

CSM provides the user base, while PPSM is established logically above and provides users with means of private communication beyond the knowledge of the provider of CSM. In other words, the objective of HSM is providing the users of commercial media with additional functionality to preserve their privacy while enjoying the same social experience. Wainakh et al. [44] have demonstrated the viability of the HSM concept by a prototype. They have built an Android app on top of Twitter, and it was later called *hushtweet*. The app allows users to seamlessly switch between Twitter and PPSM. More precisely, the main additional functionalities of hushtweet are:

1. Anonymous like: a user can like a tweet without disclosing their identity. Thus, this like cannot be used to track their behavior or preferences.
2. Private tweet: a user can tweet to a private network, where only their followers can access the tweet. In the private network, the tweet is encrypted and stored on a distributed database.
3. Statistical information: hushtweet collects information about the user population that is unlinkable to individuals. Example: 30% of hushtweet users mentioned the U.S. election in a tweet. This information is passed to Twitter as compensation for using their services by hushtweet users.

3 Privacy Concerns, Trust, and Risk

Smith et al. [42] and Malhotra et al. [35] have identified the most prominent privacy concerns as follows.

Awareness of Privacy Practices. This refers to the degree to which an individual is aware of the privacy practices taken by the organization.

Collection. Users are concerned about the amount of their personal data possessed by the organization. They weigh the cost of disclosing personal data against the benefit of the received services.

Control. Control concerns encompass whether individuals are able to decide on certain procedures concerning their personal data, e.g., approving, modifying, or opting-out.

Errors. This concern stems from the apprehension that the organization makes an insufficient effort to minimize the errors in personal data.

Improper Access. This concern focuses on the availability of personal data to people who are not authorized to view or process it.

Unauthorized Secondary Use. Here, users are concerned that personal data is collected for one purpose but is used for another.

Malhotra et al. [35] examined the relation of *privacy concerns* with *trusting beliefs*, *risk beliefs* and behavioral *intention* to disclose personal information. The context of the study was e-commerce. They showed that the greater the privacy concerns, the less trust people have in online companies (see Fig. 1, H1) and the greater the perceived risk of data disclosure is (H2). Furthermore, trusting beliefs have a positive impact on the behavioral intention to disclose information (H4), while risk beliefs affect it negatively (H5). Trusting beliefs and risk beliefs are also negatively related (H5).

In addition to the tested model (see Fig. 1), Malhotra et al. [35] analyzed the effects of demographic and issue-related variables on the examined constructs. The

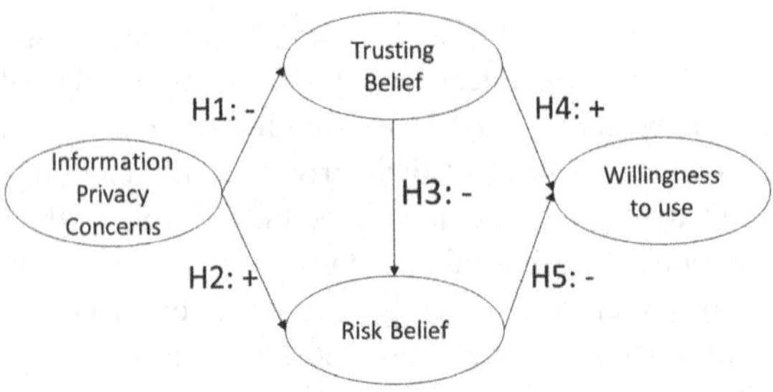

Fig. 1. Overview of hypotheses H1–H5 based on the work of Malhotra et al. [6,35].

demographic variables included *sex*, *age* and *education*. The other variables were *Internet use* in hours per day, the amount of *media exposure* concerning reports of privacy violations, frequency of experienced *privacy violations* and occurence of *misrepresentation of identification* in percentage - meaning how often people provide false identification information when asked by a marketer. They found negative relations between age and intention, education and trusting beliefs, Internet use and trusting beliefs, misrepresentation of identification and intention, and media exposure and trusting beliefs.

3.1 Hypotheses on the Constructs' Relationships in HSM

Understanding the underlying mechanisms of the constructs privacy concerns with trusting beliefs, risk beliefs and the behavioral intention to make use of technology is crucial for developing privacy-preserving applications. Hence, we reanalyze the work of Malhotra et al. [35] by transferring their hypotheses to the context of HSM. This results in the following hypotheses:

H1: Privacy concerns are negatively related to trusting beliefs in an HSM application.
H2: Privacy concerns are positively related to risk beliefs in an HSM application.
H3: Trusting beliefs are negatively related to risk beliefs in an HSM application.
H4: Trusting beliefs are positively related to the willingness to use the HSM application.
H5: Risk beliefs are negatively related to the willingness to use the HSM application.

4 Eliciting Trust-Related Software Features with TrustSoFt

Another research objective is to mitigate the aforementioned privacy concerns by developing adequate software features. For the development, we use the method *Eliciting Trust-Related Software Features (TrustSoFt)*.

TrustSoFt is a step-wise, iterative method for developing user-centred social media applications [5]. It aims to support users in assessing the trustworthiness of other users, the application and the service provider to mitigate user concerns. Figure 2 shows the major steps of TrustSoFt: (1) First, user concerns are identified. (2) For each concern, software goals must be determined. (3) The next step is to specify which attributes parties involved in the specific concern should possess so that the concern would be

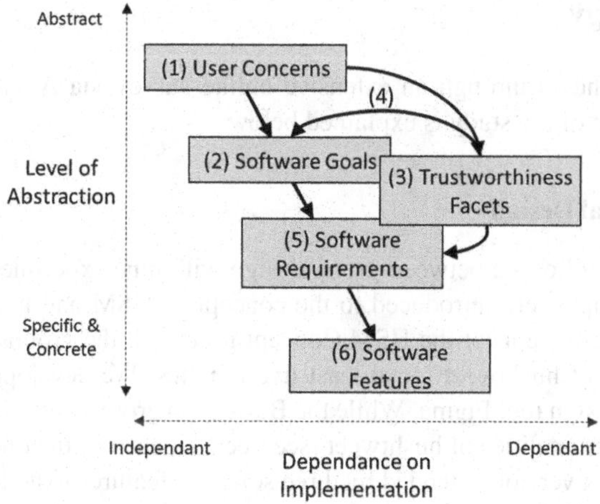

Fig. 2. Overview of the workflow of the TrustSoFt [5] method, which consists of six steps [6].

mitigated. These attributes are called *trustworthiness facets* [4]. They are evaluated during the trustworthiness assessment. (4) Trustworthiness facets and software goals are then related with each other. (5) Afterwards, software requirements must be determined. They specify what the system should do in order to achieve a software goal while addressing related facets. (6) Lastly, TrustSoFt results in software features. They describe front- or backend elements by which requirements can be realized.

The application of TrustSoFt for hushtweet is described in our previous work [6]. It resulted in a multitude of software features. For each privacy concern, we chose three comparable software features, which we then implemented in the HSM application hushtweet for the user study.

4.1 Hypotheses on the Privacy Concerns Addressed by Software Features

Aiming to develop software features that reduce users' privacy concerns in the HSM application hushtweet, we formulate the following hypotheses:

H6: An HSM application that has software features implemented, which aim to reduce a particular privacy concern, has a positive impact on the user perception that this concern is countered.

H7a & H7b: An HSM application that includes software features aiming to counter all privacy concerns is a) trusted the most b) perceived the least risky compared to HSM applications addressing fewer concerns by software features.

Compared to the hypotheses of Sect. 3, we do not analyze users' privacy concerns here, but those being addressed. Therefore, hypotheses H1 and H2 must be adapted to this context:

H1.1: Counteracted privacy concerns are positively related to the trusting beliefs in an HSM application.

H2.1: Counteracted privacy concerns are negatively related to risk beliefs in an HSM application.

5 Methodology

We test our hypotheses through an extensive online survey via Amazon Mechanical Turk. The structure of the study is explained below.

5.1 Experimental Design

The online survey follows a between-group design with nine experimental groups (see Table 1). The groups were introduced to the concept of HSM and hushtweet through a short description. Except for the HSM Concept group, all the groups interacted with a mockup version of hushtweet for at least five minutes. We developed the mockups using the online design tool Figma. While the Basic App group received a mockup with only the basic functionalities of hushtweet (see Sect. 2), each of the other groups interacted with a distinct version extended by three software features to address one privacy concern. We carefully selected the implemented features to cover all trustworthiness facets identified during TrustSoFt. Due to comparability reasons, a software feature for each concern is a *FAQ* section answering questions that treat the nature of the respective concern. The names of the experimental groups correspond to the concern the mockup addresses. The Full-featured group received a mockup including all the elicited features. An overview of this mockup is shown in Fig. 3.

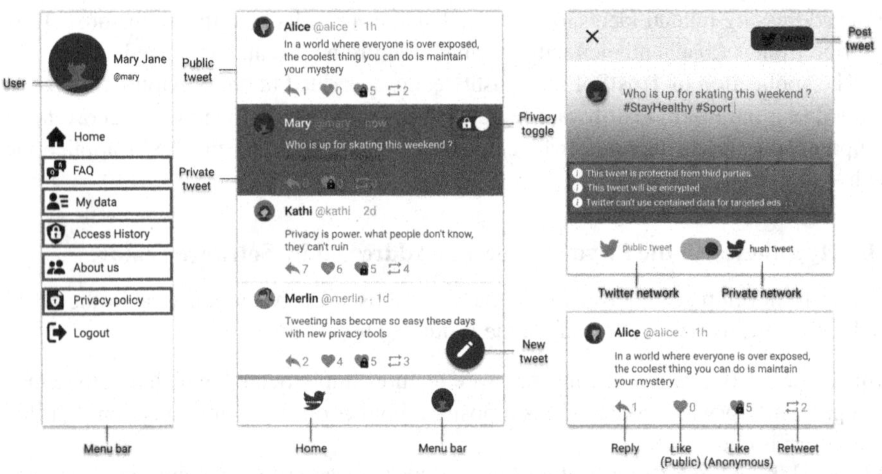

Fig. 3. Overview of the hushtweet mockup for the Full-featured group. The red frames highlight included software features [6]. (Color figure online)

5.2 Scales

For questionnaire selection, we mainly adopted the scales used by Malhotra et al. [35], namely: General Information Privacy Concern (GIPC) [42], Internet Users' Information Privacy Concerns (IUIPC), Concern for Information Privacy (CFIP) [42], trusting and risk beliefs [24]. Additionally, we added a trustworthiness scale introduced by Buttner et al. [7] to measure how the trustworthiness of hushtweet is perceived. The scale includes subscales measuring *ability, benevolence, integrity*, and *predictability*. These have been partially considered as trustworthiness facets in the application of TrustSoFt. Moreover, we developed an eight-questions scale to measure the willingness to use hushtweet. For each questionnaire, we used a 7-point Likert scale (1 = "strongly disagree" to 7 = "strongly agree"). The questionnaires were adapted in the wording to the hushtweet context. As an example, we replaced words like "online companies" and "computer databases" with "hushtweet" and "distributed databases".

The IUIPC and CFIP scales were used for two purposes: first, to measure the privacy concerns of the HSM Concept group. Second, for the rest of the groups, the scales were used to measure to what extent the hushtweet mockup the participants were confronted with has addressed the privacy concerns. For that, the scales were modified by omitting the expectational modal verb "should".

Last but not least, we included the questions and corresponding scales for the additional demographic and issue-related variables from Malhotra et al. [35]. For sex, we added the answering option "divers". For age, we adjusted the response options from predefined age groups to free entry for statistical reasons after the study with the HSM Concept Group.

5.3 Procedure

After briefing the participants about the context of the study, they received the GIPC scale. Then, they were introduced to the concept and basic functionalities of hushtweet. Afterwards, we checked their comprehension of hushtweet with six questions. The purpose of this check is to include only the participants, who understood the concept of hushtweet for the follow-up analysis. As a next step, every experimental group–except the HSM Concept group–received a distinct task to use hushtweet depending on the respective hushtweet mockup version. The task includes hints regarding the privacy concern features. Each participant had a minimum of five minutes to interact with the mockup. Afterwards, all groups received the remaining scales in the following order: trustworthiness scale, IUIPC and CFIP, trusting beliefs scale, the scales for risk beliefs and the willingness to use. Finally, the participants were also asked about their gender, age, and education level.

6 Study Results

In this section, we report details on the population of the participants, as well as our findings concerning the descriptive analysis and our hypotheses H1–H7b.

6.1 Population

The study was conducted via Amazon Mechanical Turk. 300 participants make up the HSM Concept group. For the other experimental groups, we asked 250 participants each. Only experienced Amazon Mechanical Turk users were allowed to participate to ensure high-quality data. Participants were only allowed to take part in one of the experimental groups. For further analysis, we considered participants, who absolved the hushtweet comprehension test with three or fewer mistakes. Furthermore, only complete data sets were analyzed. This reduced the various populations by 7% to 19%. The final population of each experimental group is shown in Table 1 along with information on their gender, age, and education level. The average gender distribution of 62,3% men and 32,8% women resembles the actual population of Twitter users in 2021 with 68,5% men and 31,5% women [38]. Nonetheless, we cannot guarantee that all the attributable characteristics of the actual Twitter population apply to our study population.

Table 1. Overview of the experimental groups and characteristics of the surveyed populations [6].

Group	Population (n)	men (%)	women (%)	Age (M)	Bachelor's degree or higher (%)
HSM Concept	245	61.2	38.4	35-44	52.7
Basic (control)	205	68.3	31.2	33.6	84.5
Awareness	222	63.1	36.0	33.5	67.1
Collection	223	63.2	36.3	35.6	66.9
Concern Control	223	58.3	39.5	37.6	70.8
Error	211	58.7	39.8	32.6	87.7
Improper Access	202	58.4	41.6	35.9	72.8
Unauthorized S. Use	216	64.8	35.2	33.8	83.8
Overall	233	63.9	35.2	35.6	68.3

6.2 Descriptive Analysis of the Studied Constructs

Here, we investigate the users' privacy concerns regarding HSM. For that, we conducted a descriptive analysis for the results of the "HSM Concept" group. We found that GIPC has a mean of M = 4.89, SD = .93., while the mean of IUIPC is higher M = 5.73, SD = .74. The two types of concerns are found to be strongly related (r = .561, p<.001).

The participants rated the importance of the individual concerns about hushtweet in the following order (from highest to lowest): (1) Unauthorized secondary use (M = 6.26, SD = .93), (2) awareness for privacy practices (M = 6.16, SD = .84), (3) improper access (M = 5.89, SD = 1.03), (4) control (M = 5.87, SD = .86), (5) errors (M = 5.14, SD = 1.30), and (6) collection (M = 5.04, SD = 1.17).

With regard to the other constructs, trusting beliefs have a mean of M = 5.14, SD = 1.08. The trustworthiness of hushtweet is rated with M = 5.24, SD = .97, where the trustworthiness facets are ordered as follows: integrity (M = 5.42, SD = 1.12), benevolence (M = 5.40, SD = 1.11), ability (M = 5.33, SD = 1.02), and predictability (M = 5.07, SD = 1.07). Lastly, risk beliefs are rated with M = 3.58, SD = .94.

Overall, the participants showed moderated general privacy concerns with high variance. Whereas, they conveyed that hushtweet should address individual privacy concerns. The participants trusted hushtweet and slightly disagree that it is risky.

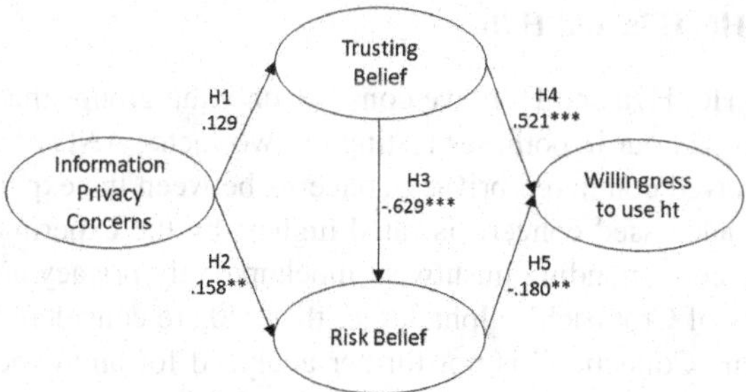

Fig. 4. SEM for hypotheses testing for the HSM Concept group ** $p < .01$, *** $p < .001$ [6].

6.3 Hypotheses H1–H5

We test the hypotheses H1-H5 (including H1.1 and H2.1) using a Structural Equation Model (SEM) for each experimental group. We omitted the items (questions) that did not contribute to an acceptable internal scale consistency of at least $\alpha = .70$. Also, we excluded constructs with factor loadings less than .70. As a result, the privacy concern "Collection" was excluded from all SEMs. The privacy concern "Errors" was only relevant for the experimental groups "Control", "Errors" and "Improper Access". Furthermore, we checked the model fit of SEMs by calculating a confirmatory factor analysis [23]. All SEMs are at least acceptable with a comparative fit index (CFI) and Tucker-Lewis index (TLI) higher than .90, a root-mean-square error of approximation (RMSE) lower than .80 and a normed chi-square (X^2/df) lower than 5.

We depict, as an example, the SEM of the HSM Concept group in Fig. 4. The model fit is good (X^2/df = 1.943, TLI = .949, CFI = .956, RMSEA = .062). Based on this SEM, we cannot confirm the hypothesis H1, as the relationship between privacy concerns and trusting beliefs is not significant. However, privacy concerns have a small positive effect on risk beliefs (H2). Hypothesis H3 is also supported as trusting beliefs highly negatively influence risk beliefs. Lastly, the willingness to use hushtweet is positively impacted by trusting beliefs with a medium effect (H4), while it is slightly negatively influenced by risk beliefs (H5).

For the experimental groups that interacted with the hushtweet mockups, the mitigation of privacy concerns positively affects trusting beliefs (H1.1), and trusting beliefs positively influence the willingness to use (H4)–both in a strong way. Therefore, hypotheses H1.1 and H4 are confirmed. The relationship between addressed privacy concerns and risk beliefs was not statistically significant for any experimental group. Thus, we cannot confirm hypotheses H2.1. Hypothesis H3 is significant only in the Full-featured group. Therefore, a negative impact from trusting beliefs on risk beliefs can only be partially supported. With regard to H5, in some of the experimental groups, risk beliefs do not significantly influence the willingness to use hushtweet. However, in the groups where the influence is statistically significant, it is always positive with a weak effect. This is the case for the groups Basic App (r = .208, p = .001), "Control" (r = .178, p = .007) and "Unauthorized Secondary Use" (r = .110, p = .044). Therefore, hypothesis H5 can partly be falsified.

6.4 Hypotheses H6, H7a and H7b

To test hypotheses H6, H7a and H7b, we consider only the groups that interacted with the mockups. We based our hypotheses testing on two-factor ANOVAs [3] to examine differences in perceived countered privacy concerns between the experimental groups. We expect that an addressed concern is rated highest by the experimental group that was exposed to the corresponding hushtweet mockup. Only privacy concerns with the internal consistency of Cronbach's alpha larger than .70 are considered. Consequently, the privacy concern "Collection" is not further analyzed for any experimental group. Moreover, the privacy concern "Control" has an unsatisfying internal consistency in the experimental groups "Collection", "Control", and "Improper Access".

Hypothesis H6 can only be supported for the privacy concern "Errors". This group rated the errors concern to be addressed the most (F(7,1727) = 4.249, p = .000, partial $\eta^2 = .017$). However, only 1.3% of the variation of the addressed errors concern around the total mean value can be explained by the implemented errors software features (adjusted R-square). The effect size of the model is f = .13 and can be interpreted as weak. Post-hoc tests with the Bonferroni correction show significant differences ($p < .05$) between the "Errors" group (M = 5.34, SD = .98) with the groups "Awareness" (M = 4.95, SD = 1.11), "Collection" (M = 4.97, SD = 1.05), "Control" (M = 4.82, SD = 1.06), and "Unauthorized Secondary Use" (M = 4.95, SD = 1.21).

Furthermore, ANOVA has shown that the privacy concern "Control" is also evaluated significantly different by the experimental groups (F(7, 1727) = 2.063, p = .044, partial $\eta^2 = .008$). However, contrary to what is assumed in H6, it is not the "Control" group that evaluates hushtweet the highest in providing users with means of control (second place with M = 5.83, SD = 1.01), but the "Awareness" group (M = 5.86, SD = .91).

For hypotheses H7a and H7b, we calculated two-factor ANOVAs for the Full-featured group. The ANOVAs for trusting beliefs and the trustworthiness are not statistically significant for any of the experimental groups. Thus, hypothesis H7a cannot be confirmed. The only significant ANOVA model in the context of trust is for the trustworthiness facet *integrity* (F(7, 1727) = 2.017, p = .05, partial $\eta^2 = .008$). Interestingly, the "Awareness" group has rated integrity the highest (M = 5.89, SD = .93), while the "Errors" group rated it the lowest (M = 5.60, SD = .97). The same can be observed for hypothesis H7b concerning risk beliefs (F(7, 1727) = 10.364, p = .000, partial $\eta^2 = .040$). The "Awareness" group believes hushtweet to be the least risky compared to the other groups (M = 3.32, SD = .11), while the "Errors" group evaluates it the most risky (M = 4.35, SD = .11). It should be mentioned that the Basic App group has the second-highest value in their risk beliefs (M = 4.11, SD = .11). Nonetheless, hypothesis H7b is rejected.

6.5 Moderation Analysis for Demographic and Privacy-Related User Variables

Following the research of Malhotra et al. [35], we were also interested in the impact of the demographic and issue-related variables of the population concerning the constructs of privacy concerns, addressed privacy concerns, trusting beliefs, risk beliefs and the willingness to use. Analyzing user differences may result in insights for future

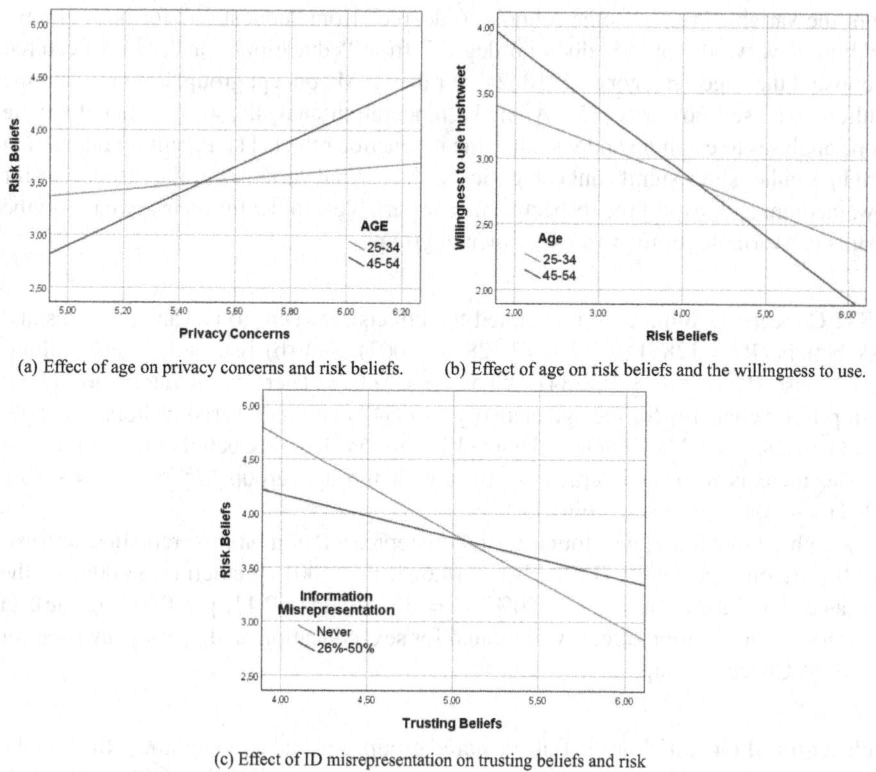

(a) Effect of age on privacy concerns and risk beliefs. (b) Effect of age on risk beliefs and the willingness to use.

(c) Effect of ID misrepresentation on trusting beliefs and risk beliefs.

Fig. 5. HSM concept group - simple slopes for the moderations of age and ID misrepresentation.

HSM application development. For that reason, we conducted an exploratory moderation analysis for the two boundary groups, namely HSM Concept and Full-Featured groups. In the HSM Concept group, the participants are only introduced to the fundamentals of HSM. Whereas the Full-Featured group served as a counterpole, because the participants used a hushtweet mockup with all the developed features to address their privacy concerns.

The analysis was employed for the demographic variables *sex*, *age* and *education*. Focusing on the privacy issue, we also included *privacy invasion* and *identification misrepresentation* variables. Whereas *Internet use* and *media exposure* were excluded from the analysis due to the lack of timeliness of the questions and scales given by Malhotra et al. [35] at the time.

For moderation analysis, we used the PROCESS procedure in SPSS with standardized variables [20]. Dummy coding was used for the categorical variables in our analysis [26]. We chose the folling reference variables for the dummy coding method: "Never" for "ID misrepresentation", "highschool" for "education", and "25–34" for "age" in the HSM Concept group (age is a metric variable for the Full-Featured Group). Some categories of ordinal variables could not be considered representative because of the very small number of associated participants. Therefore, we excluded "divers" from the variable "sex", "some school, no degree" from "education" for both groups. Additionally, we discarded "doctoral degree" from "education" for the Full-Featured group and the "age" category of "18–24" for the HSM concept group. To omit extreme outliers, we used boxplots [15]. After the moderation analysis, we conducted simple slope analyses to examine and visualize the interaction effects [1]. Resulting interaction graphics either show significant categories of the ordinal variables or the percentiles for low, medium and high of the respective metric variables. In the following, we report the results per variable for the two experimental groups.

HSM Concept Group. Age moderated the effects between (a) privacy concerns and risk beliefs ($R^2 = .128$, $F(9, 234) = 3.828$, $p = .002$), and (b) risk beliefs and willingness to use ($R^2 = .254$, $F(9, 234) = 8.858$, $p < .001$). There is an interaction effect with privacy concerns for the age category "45–54" that predicts risk beliefs ($\beta = .523$, $t(244) = 2.28$, $p = .023$), which is depicted in Fig. 5a. For risk beliefs and willingness to use, there is also an interaction effect with the age group "45–54" ($\beta = -.353$, $t(244) = -2.04$, $p = .043$, see Fig. 5b).

Another moderation was found for ID misrepresentation on the prediction of trusting beliefs on risk beliefs ($F(9, 234) = 14.625$, $p < .001$, predicting 36,00% of the variance) for the category "26%–50%" ($\beta = .367$, $t(244) = 2.11$, $p = .036$; Fig. 5c). In contrary, no moderation effects were found for sex, education, and privacy invasion for the HSM Concept group.

Full-featured Group. For the Full-Featured group, age had a moderating effect on the predictions of (a) addressed privacy concerns on trusting beliefs ($F(3, 228) = 133.541$, $p < .001$, predicting 63.73% of the variance), (b) addressed privacy concerns on risk beliefs $F(3, 226) = 6.176$, $p < .001$, predicting 7.58% of the variance), and (c) trusting beliefs on the willingness to use ($F(3, 228) = 53.415$, $p < .001$, predicting 41.27% of the variance). The interaction effects with each dependent variable (first variable) for predicting the independent one (latter variable) are as follows (a) $\beta = .09$, $t(232) = 2.40$, $p = .017$ (Fig. 6a), (b) $\beta = -.13$, $t(230) = -2.26$, $p = .025$; (Fig. 6b), and (c) $\beta = -.13$, $t(232) = -2.63$, $p = .009$ (Fig. 6c).

For education, a moderating effect could be observed regarding addressed privacy concerns on risk beliefs ($F(9, 218) = 3.640$, $p < .001$, predicting 13.06% of the variance). The interaction effect was found for people having a Master's degree compared to those with a highschool graduation ($\beta = .144$, $t(228) = 2.02$, $p = .044$, Fig. 6d).

ID misrepresentation moderated the relationships of addressed privacy concerns and trusting beliefs ($F(9, 219) = 50.684$, $p < .001$, predicting 67.56% of the variance). Misrepresentation of over 75% of all cases interacted with addressed privacy concerns when predicting trusting beliefs ($\beta = 1.37$, $t(229) = 3.09$, $p = .002$; Fig. 6e). For addressed privacy concerns and risk beliefs ($F(9, 223) = 4.338$, $p < .001$, predicting 15.05% of the variance), interaction effects with addressed privacy concerns were found for the categories "26%–50%" ($\beta = .396$, $t(233) = 2.62$, $p = .010$) and "51%–75%" ($\beta = .778$, $t(233) = 3.08$, $p = .002$; Fig. 6f). For the moderation with trusting beliefs and risk beliefs ($F(9, 219) =$ $p < .001$, predicting 19.80% of the variance), the interaction effect with trusting beliefs was significant for the categories "26%–50%" ($\beta = .386$,

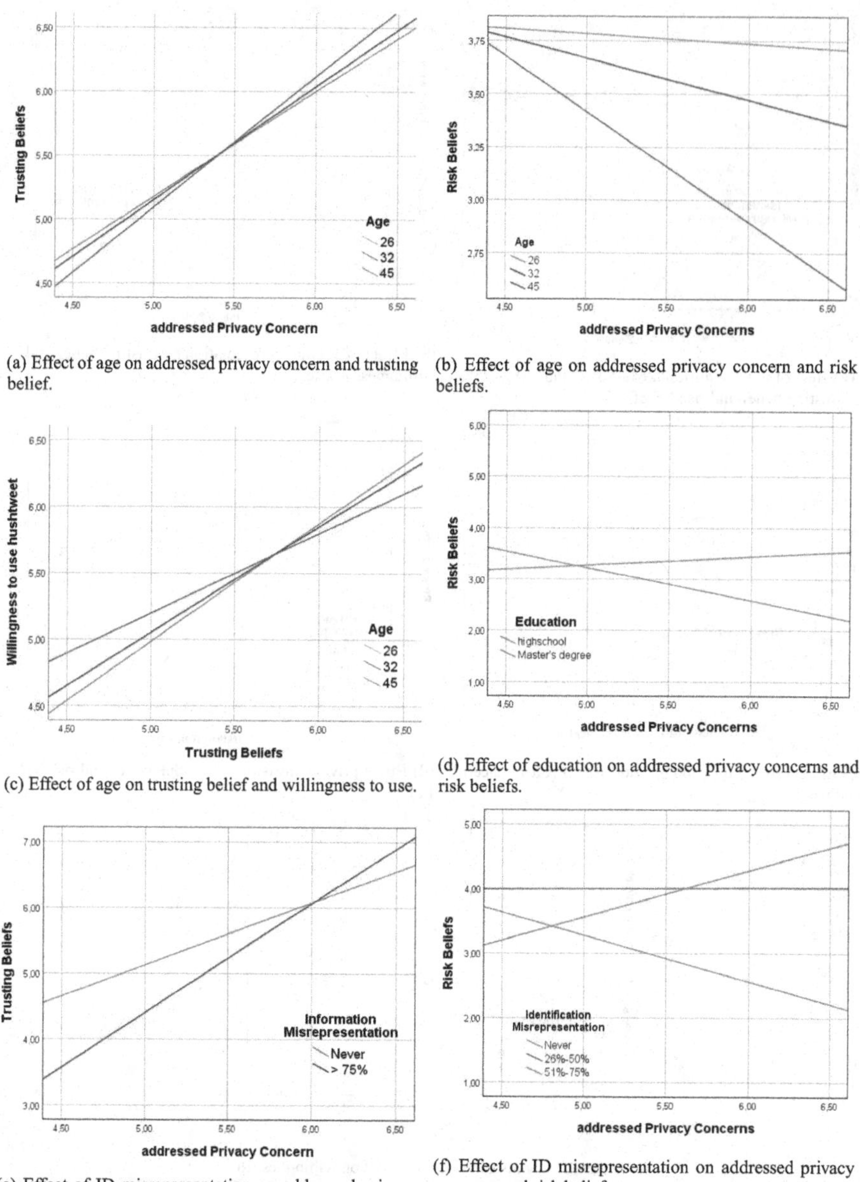

(a) Effect of age on addressed privacy concern and trusting belief.

(b) Effect of age on addressed privacy concern and risk beliefs.

(c) Effect of age on trusting belief and willingness to use.

(d) Effect of education on addressed privacy concerns and risk beliefs.

(e) Effect of ID misrepresentation on addressed privacy concern and trusting beliefs.

(f) Effect of ID misrepresentation on addressed privacy concerns and risk beliefs.

Fig. 6. Full-featured group - simple slopes for the moderations of age, education, and ID misrepresentation.

t(229) = 2.42, p = .016) and "51%–75%" (β = .534, t(229) = 2.09, p = .038; Fig. 7a) The last moderation of "ID misrepresentation" was found for trusting beliefs and the willingness to use (F(9, 219) = 20.968, p < .001, predicting 46.29% of the variance). The

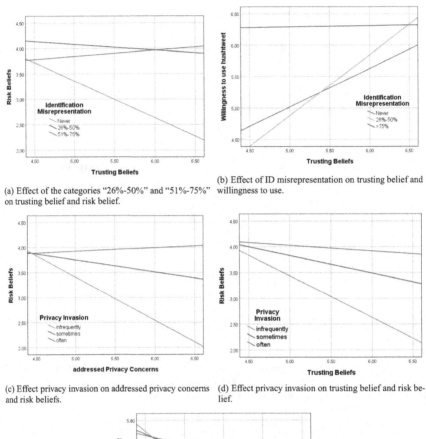

(a) Effect of the categories "26%-50%" and "51%-75%" on trusting belief and risk belief.

(b) Effect of ID misrepresentation on trusting belief and willingness to use.

(c) Effect privacy invasion on addressed privacy concerns and risk beliefs.

(d) Effect privacy invasion on trusting belief and risk belief.

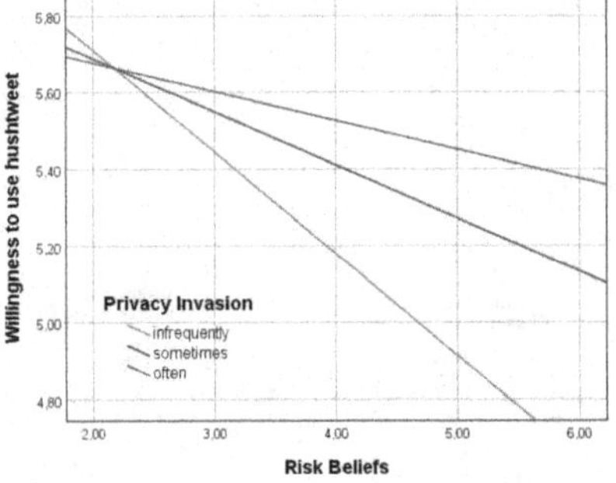

(e) Effect privacy invasion on risk belief on willingness to use.

Fig. 7. Full-featured group - simple slopes for the moderations of ID misrepresentation and privacy invasion.

categories "26%–50%" ($\beta = .302$, $t(229) = 2.32$, $p = .021$) and "over 75%" ($\beta = -.501$, $t(229) = -2.04$, $p = .042$) significantly interacted with trusting beliefs for the prediction of willingness to use (Fig. 7b).

For privacy invasion, we found moderations for: (a) addressed privacy concerns and risk beliefs ($F(3, 228) = 23.812$, $p < .001$, predicting 23.86% of the variance), (b) trusting beliefs and risk beliefs ($F(3, 228) = 29.362$, $p < .001$, predicting 27.87% of the variance), and (c) risk beliefs and the willingness to use ($F(3, 228) = 4.575$, $p = .004$, predicting 5.68% of the variance). The interaction effects are as follows: (a) ($\beta = .315$, $t(232) = 4.83$, $p < .001$; Fig. 7c), (b) $\beta = .27$, $t(232) = 4.42.$, $p < .001$; Fig. 7d, and (c) $\beta = .159$, $t(232) = 2.27$, $p = .024$; Fig. 7e.

7 Discussion

This work tackles two major research objectives. First, we examined the relationships between privacy concerns, trusting beliefs, risk beliefs, and the willingness to use in the HSM context. Second, we applied TrustSoFt to elicit trust-related software features to address users' privacy concerns in an HSM application. In this section, we discuss the results of our user study on (1) the relevance of the privacy concerns, (2) the relations between the constructs, (3) the impact of the developed features on privacy concerns, and (4) the impact of user variables. Lastly, we conclude the section by describing the limitations of this work and articulating suggestions for future work.

7.1 Relevance of Privacy Concerns

Our results show that "Unauthorized Secondary Use" is the most important concern, followed by "Awareness of Privacy Practices" and "Improper Access", while "Errors" and "Collection" were the least relevant. These findings are aligned with the results of Smith et al. [42], where they found that "Unauthorized Secondary Use" and "Improper Access" affect privacy concerns more than "Errors" and "Collection". The prominence of "Awareness of Privacy Practices" in HSM supports the suggestion that the context slightly impacts the relevance of privacy concerns [14].

In addition, our SEM analysis supports the low expression of the two concerns "Collection" and "Errors", as their factor loadings weakly contribute to the representation of privacy concerns. For the "Collection" concern, we assume, based on unacceptable internal consistency, that the scale used is not sufficient to validly measure the construct. The low rating of the "Errors" concern can be due to the fact that HSM leverages encrypted and distributed data storage, which contributes to a lower risk of malicious attacks on personal data. Therefore, people are less concerned about errors in their data.

7.2 Relationships of the Constructs

For people only knowing HSM without ever using it, the relationships of privacy concerns with trusting beliefs, risk beliefs, and the willingness to use were partly unexpected. It cannot be confirmed that privacy concerns regarding hushtweet affect trusting beliefs negatively. It seems as if privacy concerns are detached from trust in hushtweet. This finding conforms with a study on a sample of Facebook users [30], where it is discussed that the trust in Facebook and in its privacy policy exceeds the privacy concerns. For our context, we argue that although the participants expressed inherited concerns about hushtweet, as yet another social media application, its purpose leads to trust given in principle and thus is detached from the concerns. This argumentation is additionally supported by our results, which show that addressing privacy concerns by software features does have an impact on the trust in hushtweet.

For risk beliefs, on the one hand, our findings suggest that privacy concerns slightly increase risk beliefs in hushtweet. This conforms with the conclusions of Malhotra et al. [35]. On the other hand, we found that addressing privacy concerns does not necessarily reduce the risk beliefs. A possible explanation for this might be that users are still aware of the existing risks accompanying information processing during social media use as the implemented software features refer to their existence. Risk awareness is identified as a relevant factor in research about privacy concerns [39].

Interestingly, we observe that sometimes participants are a bit more willing to use hushtweet the higher their risk beliefs are. Curiosity can be one reason for this phenomenon, because it induces people to tolerate more risk, which in turn promotes the willingness to use [13]. However, a positive relation of risk beliefs to the willingness to use is not always confirmed.

Another salient finding is that trusting beliefs reduce risk beliefs in two cases; first, when the participants are only introduced theoretically to the concept of HSM. Second, when they interact with the application where all privacy concerns are addressed. We conclude that the principle of HSM is essential to establish the relationship between trusting and risk beliefs. For this, an application should convey the HSM concept in an encompassing way so that the benefits are emphasized and a multitude of concerns are addressed.

7.3 Impact of Software Features on Privacy Concerns

Looking at the impact of the software features on the users' opinions regarding the extent to which privacy concerns are addressed, the results differ from our expectations. Only features that address concerns about errors in data processing were rated as most strongly addressing those concerns. Remarkably, we found that features meant to address a specific concern greatly affect also other concerns. This can be related to how direct a particular feature addresses a concern. Some features confront users explicitly with the targeted concern, e.g., we deliberately included an error in the application to present how the application addresses the "Errors" concern. In contrast, other features indirectly present concerns by displaying the way they are handled with. Therefore, we assume that concerns need to be emphasized stronger in order to make it more apparent to users that they are being taken into account. In general, we rate features addressing errors as special, because they are associated with undesired software behavior. Therefore, it is not surprising that such features were perceived the lowest concerning the trustworthiness facet "Integrity" compared to other features.

In contrast, the "Awareness for Privacy Practices" features are rated the highest concerning integrity and the lowest regarding risk beliefs. Surprisingly, these features are also found to be remarkably mitigating the "Control" concern. Thus, we conclude that raising the users' awareness positively contributes to an enhanced feeling of control, stronger trusting beliefs, and weaker risk beliefs. This conforms with the research of

Kani et al. [28], who pointed out that software features creating privacy awareness also support users in managing their privacy concerns.

7.4 Impact of User Variables

We found that the user variables, i.e., demographics and privacy-related variables, have an impact on the relationships between the constructs we study in this work. This impact also differs between (1) people who only know HSM, and (2) those who additionally have used an HSM application. According to the findings of Junco [27], differences between these two groups are likely due to the contextual gap between hypothetically using an application and actually using it [27].

In total, we identified user differences for the demographic variables, age and education. We could not find any gender differences. In addition, there are user differences regarding the privacy-related variables, ID misrepresentation and privacy invasion. Next, we discuss the differences per variable for both aforementioned groups of participants.

Age. There are age differences for people introduced solely to the HSM concept and who used hushtweet. People who only knew the concept had increasing risk beliefs the stronger their privacy concerns were. At the same time, the riskier they believed hushtweet to be, the less willing they were to use it. These effects were stronger for people aged 45 to 54 than among those aged 25 to 34.

People who actually used hushtweet and perceived their privacy concerns as addressed had higher trusting beliefs which decreased their risk beliefs. This applies more strongly with the increase of people age. However, it is the younger people who were more willing to use hushtweet with higher trusting beliefs than the older ones. Still, older people were also interested in using it.

Our findings imply that older people are more cautious concerning the HSM concept and app usage. Simultaneously, they are easier to convince by privacy-preserving software features in terms of trusting and risk beliefs. Similar age tendencies were found by Goldfarb and Tucker [16]. Older people had higher privacy concerns and were less willing to disclose private information. Their explanation was that older people have other privacy preferences than younger ones, more experiences with information technology, and are thus more aware of potential privacy concerns.

Education. User differences were found for the people with high-school graduation and Master's degree, who have used hushtweet. People with high-school graduation believed hushtweet to be less risky the more their privacy concerns were addressed. This is slightly the opposite for people with a Master's degree, whose risk beliefs slightly increased the more their privacy concerns were addressed. The negative effect of addressed privacy concerns on risk beliefs for people with high-school graduation complies with the findings of Malhotra et al. [35]. Whereas the positive effect for people with a Master's degree can be explained by the fact that people with a higher level of education are more aware of their information security and associated risks [40]. As the implemented software features sensitized users to privacy risks that hushtweet emphasizes reducing, people with higher education might become even more aware of them and thus more cautious. In contrast, people with a lower educational level might be comforted by the features, since they promise to mitigate the risks.

Identification Misrepresentation. Individuals who differed in the frequency of ID misrepresentation showed different expressions concerning the constructs studied. This applied both to the people who were only introduced to the HSM concept and to those who actually used hushtweet.

For the ones who were only introduced to the HSM concept, risk beliefs decreased the more the people believed hushtweet to be trustworthy. This effect could be observed for people who never have misrepresented their identity and who sometimes did this. However, the effect was smaller for the latter. The results comply with the ones of Malhotra et al. [35].

In the case of the participants who have used hushtweet, trusting beliefs similarly affected risk beliefs in a negative way. The trusting beliefs of people who sometimes falsified their identity had a smaller impact on their risk beliefs than that of individuals who never misrepresented their identity. However, people who often misrepresented their identity slightly believed hushtweet to be riskier when they actually trusted it. Although the positive effect is weak, it is surprising that it is not negative and differs from the findings of Malhotra et al. [35]. We assume that people who more often misrepresent their personal information have generally a higher risk awareness. As the selected hushtweet software features emphasized the associated risks that are aimed to be reduced, people with general high-risk awareness might be strengthened in their cautiousness. Nonetheless, their trusting beliefs simultaneously increase.

This explanation could also apply to the prediction of addressed privacy concerns on risk beliefs, as the previously described effect can be observed again. People, who never misrepresented their identity believed hushtweet to be less risky the more their privacy concerns were addressed. For those, who sometimes falsified their identity, addressed privacy concerns did not have any effect on their risk beliefs at all. This is in contrast to those who often intentionally disclosed false IDs. With higher addressed privacy concerns, their risk beliefs slightly increased as well.

With respect to the addressed privacy concerns and trusting beliefs, the former positively predicts the latter for both individuals who never misreported their identity and those who misreported it very often. Yet, the level of trusting beliefs was in general higher for people who never misrepresented their identity. We assume that this is related to a high *trust propensity*, i.e., a general personal predisposition to trust others [9]. Trust propensity might further be the reason why some people entrust personal data to others while others do not. This is supported by Heirman et al. [21]. They found that both privacy concerns and trust propensity predict self-disclosure of personal information in exchange for commercial incentives. The trusting beliefs of people who never falsified identifiable information is only exceeded by the trusting beliefs of those who very often misrepresented their identity–but only when their privacy concerns were highly mitigated.

Lastly, differences can be found in the prediction of trusting beliefs on the willingness to use. In general, it can be said that for people who never, sometimes and very often misrepresented their ID, the more they beliefs hushtweet to be trustworthy, the more they were willing to use it. However, trusting beliefs were less relevant for people who very often falsified their ID regarding their willingness to use the application. Their willingness to use hushtweet is generally exceptionally high. We again relate this to our assumption that this set of people are highly aware of their privacy and social media risks, and they use ID misrepresentation as a privacy protection strategy [25]. Therefore, HSM application might be especially appealing to them due to its privacy-preserving characteristics.

Privacy Invasion. Moderating effects of privacy invasion were only found when people interacted with hushtweet. With increasing experiences of privacy invasions, the following impacts became weaker: (a) addressed privacy concerns on risk beliefs, (b) trusting beliefs on risk beliefs, and (c) risk beliefs on the willingness to use. Nonetheless, the predictions all remained negative. The only exception is for people, who experienced privacy invasions often. They slightly believed hushtweet to be riskier the more their privacy concerns were addressed.

To explain the results, it is important to consider that people who have had experiences of privacy invasion have become more sensitive to the issue of privacy in social media. They are more aware of social media risks and tend to use it less often [45]. These findings reflect why risk beliefs are higher among users who have experienced more privacy invasions than among users who have experienced them infrequently–even though privacy concerns are addressed and trusting beliefs in hushtweet exist. In the end, hushtweet is still a social media application, but with the purpose of privacy protection. Its functionalities to enable more privacy control and to hamper privacy invasion might lead people with more experiences to be more willing to use hushtweet, because they might perceive these functionalities as more relevant especially due to their high-risk beliefs. Lastly, people who often experienced privacy violations believed hushtweet to be riskier the more their privacy concerns were addressed. Again, similar to age and ID misrepresentation variables, the high-risk awareness of these people may serve as an explanation for this finding.

7.5 Limitations and Future Research

HSM is a technology that is not widely known, relatively complex and thus not easy to understand for regular users [44]. For this reason, we introduced participants to the exemplary HSM application hushtweet to facilitate the understanding of the HSM concept. In addition, we were able to evaluate the impact of the software features that we elicited with TrustSoFt on the examined constructs within the user studies. However, participants were thus only indirectly able to respond to the HSM technology itself. Their answers could be biased based on the design and usability of hushtweet. On these grounds, our work is limited to the scope of hushtweet. Nonetheless, we are optimistic that the participants considered the HSM technology within their answers, since the analysis only included the participants who understood the concept.

Regarding the design and usability of hushtweet, participants gave us positive feedback. Their feedback implied fun during usage and that they like the application. This indicates that we developed hushtweet in regards to *situational normality*–meaning that the application is perceived as proper, normal or originating from a serious, success-oriented service provider [37]. Providing an appealing interface is significant for positively impacting users' perception and their performance in terms of software use [43]. As one of our objectives was to demonstrate to users the privacy-preserving advantages of HSM and thereby mitigating privacy concerns, situational normality was necessary. However, this might introduce some bias in our work, as intervening variables like branding or marketing can have impacted the participants' privacy concerns and trusting beliefs, as well.

Another potential limitation is due to our selection of examined privacy concerns and software features. These limited our research to the context of information processing, which is a key characteristic of HSM. However, our participants stated additional concerns regarding HSM, for example, the economical aspects of the service provider that might impact information processing. Therefore, future work needs to elicit further user concerns, which in turn can additionally be considered for the development of HSM applications. In regards to the choice of implemented software features, we carefully selected those that clearly addressed the concerns in a similar design and message to ensure comparability. Nonetheless, we cannot ensure that the features impacted participants similarly or contribute to the various concerns in the same way. Here, it is interesting to examine each feature and its impact individually. Additionally, features could be modified and tested for their various impact on the users. An approach for modification could be in regards to different user differences. Based on our findings, tailored features for age groups and for people with experiences of privacy invasion might be useful to better address their trusting and risk beliefs.

As we analyzed user differences in the context of HSM, we found that additional variables might be relevant to consider. Variables like risk and privacy awareness, privacy practices and trust propensity seem to be decisive for various user types in the interplay of privacy concerns, trust, risk and the willingness to use HSM. Therefore, future research should address this research gap, which we especially found for ID misrepresentation as a privacy protection strategy. Knowledge about these variables regarding the different user types can be regarded as meaningful for developing tailored software features and enhancing HSM applications.

Our results of the demographic and privacy-related variables provide future work indications concerning user differences, which need to be proven and further analyzed. In our analysis, we closely followed the work of Malhotra et al. [35], but in the HSM context. We adopted their questions and scales so that some of our statistical calculations were restricted to categorical variables, like education or ID misrepresentation. Some of the categories of these variables were less represented than others, which might have led to artifacts in the results. We tried to balance this by only considering those categories that were well represented. Future work should consider user studies with a larger population or design the scales for metric variables. On these grounds, some of our findings should be regarded as trends that need further analysis.

8 Conclusion

In this work, we modeled the relationships between *privacy concerns*, *trusting beliefs*, *risk beliefs*, and *willingness to use* in the context of privacy-preserving social media, particularly, a hybrid social media application. Furthermore, we investigated the impact of various user characteristics on these relationships and developed trust-related software features using the novel TrustSoFt method to mitigate users' privacy concerns. By that, we contributed to a better understanding for the users' concerns and behavior in this emerging kind of social media. This is relevant to develop hybrid social media that convince with its privacy-preserving attributes and increase its trustworthiness compared to profit-oriented social media like Facebook or Twitter.

Our results showed that addressing users' privacy concerns with the developed software features increases the trustworthiness of the respective platform and the users' willingness to use it. Moreover, findings indicate that addressing a specific concern, namely the awareness of privacy practices, played an essential role in improving the perceived integrity of the service provider and also provided users with the feeling of control. Overall, the software features particularly affected older people and those with more experience regarding privacy-related incidents in the past. Future work needs to consider additional variables, such as users' risk awareness, to be equally responsive to all people through tailored software features.

References

1. Aiken, L.S., West, S.G., Reno, R.R.: Multiple Regression: Testing and Interpreting Interactions. Sage (1991)
2. Alisie, M.: Unveiling AKASHA, May 2016. https://akasha.org/blog/2016/05/03/unveiling-akasha. Accessed 21 Mar 2019
3. Anderson, J.C., Gerbing, D.W.: Structural equation modeling in practice: a review and recommended two-step approach. Psychol. Bull. **103**(3), 411 (1988)
4. Borchert, A., Díaz Ferreyra, N.E., Heisel, M.: Building trustworthiness in computer-mediated introduction: a facet-oriented framework. In: International Conference on Social Media and Society, pp. 39–46 (2020)
5. Borchert, A., Ferreyra, N.E.D., Heisel, M.: A conceptual method for eliciting trust-related software features for computer-mediated introduction. In: ENASE, pp. 269–280 (2020)
6. Borchert, A., Wainakh, A., Krämer, N., Mühlhäuser, M., Heisel, M.: Mitigating privacy concerns by developing trust-related software features for a hybrid social media application. In: ENASE, pp. 269–280 (2021)
7. Büttner, O.B., Göritz, A.S.: Perceived trustworthiness of online shops. J. Consum. Behav.: Int. Res. Rev. **7**(1), 35–50 (2008)
8. Choi, J.P.: Herd behavior, the "penguin effect", and the suppression of informational diffusion: an analysis of informational externalities and payoff interdependency. Rand J. Econ. 407–425 (1997)
9. Colquitt, J.A., Scott, B.A., LePine, J.A.: Trust, trustworthiness, and trust propensity: a meta-analytic test of their unique relationships with risk taking and job performance. J. Appl. Psychol. **92**(4), 909 (2007)
10. Daubert, J., Bock, L., Kikirasy, P., Mühlhäuser, M., Fischer, M.: Twitterize: anonymous micro-blogging. In: 2014 IEEE/ACS 11th International Conference on Computer Systems and Applications (AICCSA), pp. 817–823. IEEE (2014)
11. Dean, B.: Social network usage & growth statistics: how many people use social media in 2021? (2021). https://backlinko.com/social-media-users. Accessed 24 June 2021
12. Donath, J.: How social media design shapes society. In: CHI 2014 Extended Abstracts on Human Factors in Computing Systems, pp. 1057–1058 (2014)

13. Dowling, G.R.: Perceived risk: the concept and its measurement. Psychol. Mark. **3**(3), 193–210 (1986)
14. Ebert, N., Ackermann, K.A., Heinrich, P.: Does context in privacy communication really matter?-A survey on consumer concerns and preferences. In: Proceedings of the 2020 CHI Conference on Human Factors in Computing Systems, pp. 1–11 (2020)
15. Elliott, A.C., Woodward, W.A.: Statistical Analysis Quick Reference Guidebook: With SPSS Examples. Sage (2007)
16. Goldfarb, A., Tucker, C.: Shifts in privacy concerns. Am. Econ. Rev. **102**(3), 349–53 (2012)
17. Graffi, K., Podrajanski, S., Mukherjee, P., Kovacevic, A., Steinmetz, R.: A distributed platform for multimedia communities (2008)
18. Guardian, T.: Facebook to contact 87 million users affected by data breach, April 2018. https://www.theguardian.com/technology/2018/apr/08/facebook-to-contact-the-87-million-users-affected-by-data-breach. Accessed 07 Dec 2020
19. Guardian, T.: Huge Facebook breach leaves thousands of other apps vulnerable, October 2018. https://www.theguardian.com/technology/2018/oct/02/facebook-hack-compromised-accounts-tokens. Accessed 18 Nov 2020
20. Hayes, A.F.: Introduction to Mediation, Moderation, and Conditional Process Analysis: A Regression-Based Approach. Guilford Publications (2017)
21. Heirman, W., Walrave, M., Ponnet, K.: Predicting adolescents' disclosure of personal information in exchange for commercial incentives: an application of an extended theory of planned behavior. Cyberpsychol. Behav. Soc. Netw. **16**(2), 81–87 (2013)
22. Holmes, A.: 533 million Facebook users' phone numbers and personal data have been leaked online (2021). https://www.businessinsider.com/stolen-data-of-533-million-facebook-users-leaked-online-2021-4?r=US&IR=T. Accessed 24 June 2021
23. Hu, L.T., Bentler, P.M.: Cutoff criteria for fit indexes in covariance structure analysis: Conventional criteria versus new alternatives. Struct. Eqn. Model.: A Multidisc. J. **6**(1), 1–55 (1999)
24. Jarvenpaa, S.L., Tractinsky, N., Saarinen, L.: Consumer trust in an internet store: a cross-cultural validation. J. Comput.-Mediat. Commun. **5**(2), JCMC526 (1999)
25. Jiang, Z., Heng, C.S., Choi, B.C.: Research note-privacy concerns and privacy-protective behavior in synchronous online social interactions. Inf. Syst. Res. **24**(3), 579–595 (2013)
26. Jose, P.E.: Doing Statistical Mediation and Moderation. Guilford Press (2013)
27. Junco, R.: Comparing actual and self-reported measures of Facebook use. Comput. Hum. Behav. **29**(3), 626–631 (2013)
28. Kani-Zabihi, E., Helmhout, M.: Increasing service users' privacy awareness by introducing on-line interactive privacy features. In: Laud, P. (ed.) NordSec 2011. LNCS, vol. 7161, pp. 131–148. Springer, Heidelberg (2012). https://doi.org/10.1007/978-3-642-29615-4_10
29. Kozlowska, I.: Facebook and data privacy in the age of Cambridge analytica. The University of Washington, Seattle (2018). Accessed 1 Aug 2019
30. Kusyanti, A., Puspitasari, D.R., Catherina, H.P.A., Sari, Y.A.L.: Information privacy concerns on teens as Facebook users in Indonesia. Proc. Comput. Sci. **124**, 632–638 (2017)
31. Larson, S.: Every single Yahoo account was hacked - 3 billion in all, October 2017. http://money.cnn.com/2017/10/03/technology/business/yahoo-breach-3-billion-accounts/index.html. Accessed 07 Dec 2020
32. Larson, S.: Fitness app that revealed military bases highlights bigger privacy issues, January 2018. http://money.cnn.com/2018/01/29/technology/strava-privacy-data-exposed/index.html. Accessed 09 May 2019
33. Luo, W., Xie, Q., Hengartner, U.: FaceCloak: an architecture for user privacy on social networking sites. In: International Conference on Computational Science and Engineering, CSE 2009, vol. 3, pp. 26–33. IEEE (2009)

34. Luo, W., Xie, Q., Hengartner, U.: FaceCloak download, August 2011. https://crysp.uwaterloo.ca/software/facecloak/download.html. Accessed 07 Dec 2020
35. Malhotra, N.K., Kim, S.S., Agarwal, J.: Internet users' information privacy concerns (IUIPC): the construct, the scale, and a causal model. Inf. Syst. Res. **15**(4), 336–355 (2004)
36. McCandless, D.: World's biggest data breaches & hacks, April 2019. https://informationisbeautiful.net/visualizations/worlds-biggest-data-breaches-hacks. Accessed 07 Dec 2020
37. McKnight, D.H., Chervany, N.L.: What trust means in e-commerce customer relationships: an interdisciplinary conceptual typology. Int. J. Electron. Commer. **6**(2), 35–59 (2001)
38. Noyes, D.: Distribution of Twitter users worldwide as of January 2021, by gender (2021). https://www.statista.com/statistics/828092/distribution-of-users-on-twitter-worldwide-gender/. Accessed 10 Feb 2021
39. Olivero, N., Lunt, P.: Privacy versus willingness to disclose in e-commerce exchanges: the effect of risk awareness on the relative role of trust and control. J. Econ. Psychol. **25**(2), 243–262 (2004)
40. Rezgui, Y., Marks, A.: Information security awareness in higher education: an exploratory study. Comput. Secur. **27**(7–8), 241–253 (2008)
41. Salzberg, M.: Diaspora - kickstarter pitch, April 2010. https://web.archive.org/web/20110814222702/, http://blog.joindiaspora.com/2010/04/27/kickstarter-pitch.html. Accessed 07 Dec 2020
42. Smith, H.J., Milberg, S.J., Burke, S.J.: Information privacy: measuring individuals' concerns about organizational practices. MIS Q. 167–196 (1996)
43. Sonderegger, A., Sauer, J.: The influence of design aesthetics in usability testing: effects on user performance and perceived usability. Appl. Ergon. **41**(3), 403–410 (2010)
44. Wainakh, A., Grube, T., Daubert, J., Porth, C., Mühlhäuser, M.: Tweet beyond the cage: a hybrid solution for the privacy dilemma in online social networks. In: 2019 IEEE Global Communications Conference (GLOBECOM), pp. 1–6. IEEE (2019)
45. Yang, H.: Young American consumers' prior negative experience of online disclosure, online privacy concerns, and privacy protection behavioral intent. J. Consum. Satisf. Dissatisf. Complain. Behav. **25**, 179–202 (2012)

From Business Process Textual Description to BPEL Models

Wiem Khlif[1] (✉), Nadia Aloui[1], and Nourchène Elleuch Ben Ayed[2]

[1] Mir@Cl Laboratory, University of Sfax, Sfax, Tunisia
[2] Higher Colleges of Technology, ADW, Abu Dhabi, UAE
nbenayed@hct.ac.ae

Abstract. Creating BPEL model based on a Textual Description (TD) is crucial to its consistent analysis particularly by making information accessible to different stakeholders. However, producing or preserving TD-BPEL alignment is a problem especially when an organization develops or modifies a BEPL model. In fact, it is possible to identify misalignment between BPEL model and its documentation when modifications are not applied to both representations. In this paper, we propose a new methodology that helps business analyst to generate BPEL models that are aligned with their textual description. It applies an enriched structured template of a business concept to define a set of transformation rules. In addition, our methodology offers a complete alignment, which covers all BPEL elements. It is evaluated experimentally using the recall and precision rates as well as COSMIC Functional Size Measurement (FSM) method.

Keywords: BPEL model · Textual description · Alignment · COSMIC FSM · Method

1 Introduction

Business process modelling represents a crucial asset to describe software requirements. Nevertheless, the issue of the Business Process Models (BPM) is their representation based on different notations such as Business Process Modelling Notation (BPMN) and Business Process Execution Language (BPEL).

Recall that the business analyst uses BPMN notation for designing and improving the business process, whereas BPEL is used by the technical analyst and programmer when implementing it. These BPMN models are as blueprints to define the BPEL model.

In this context, several approaches were proposed in the literature [1–8] to reduce the complexity of defining a model and increase the agility. These approaches are organized in two categories: the first one represents the derivation of a business process model from its textual description [9] and vice versa [1, 3, 5, 6, 8], while the second category expresses the generation of BPEL model based on the BPMN model and vice versa [2, 4, 7].

Apropos the first category, the derivation of the textual description corresponding to BPMN model can be either automatic [5] or semi-automatic [1, 6] combining manual

R. Ali et al. (Eds.): ENASE 2021, CCIS 1556, pp. 112–131, 2022.
https://doi.org/10.1007/978-3-030-96648-5_6

and automatic tasks to produce a textual process description based on Natural Language Generation System (NLGS). For the generation of the BPMN model associated to its documentation, [3, 8] present an automatic approach that combines existing tools from natural language processing in an innovative way and augments them with a suitable anaphora resolution mechanism.

For the second category, several researchers [2, 4] propose BPMN patterns and their corresponding BPEL structured constructs. What becomes challenging with business process modelling is differences between these two languages: BPMN process models are graph-oriented (with only minor topological restrictions), while BPEL process definitions are block-structured. Few works [7] have used COSMIC Functional Size Measurement (FSM) method [10] to check the conformity of BPMN and BPEL models.

To overcome these limitations, this paper, which is a revised and extended version of our paper presented at the 16th International Conference on Evaluation of Novel Approaches to Software Engineering (ENASE 2021) [11], addresses the challenge of producing a BPEL model from a textual description.

To end this purpose, we aim to improve MONET (a syste**M**atic derivati**O**n of a bpm**N** mod**E**l from business process Textual description) methodology [12] that helps business designer to derive BPMN models from their corresponding textual descriptions. The latter is based on decomposing business process textual description into goals. Each goal is associated to a business concept that is described by an enriched structured template. This template respects linguistic patterns that are used to define a set of transformation rules.

The improvement of MONET methodology goes through differents steps. First, proposing new transformation rules that are used to generate BPEL model from a textual decription. Second, assessing the quality of the produced model using the recall and precision rates. Third, applying COSMIC FSM [10] method to measure the consistency between BPEL and its textual description based on formula and heuristic.

The remainder of the paper is organized as follows: Sect. 2 starts by an overview of MONET methodology (a syste**M**atic derivati**O**n of a bpm**N** mod**E**ls from business process Textual description) and the related works. Section 3 defines a set of business transformation rules that aim to generate BPEL model based on the enriched structured template corresponding to each business concept. Section 4 assesses the quality of the derived BPEL model by calculating the recall and precision rates, and the application of COSMIC FSM method to verify the consistency of the transformation. Section 5 presents our tool MONEET that implements the transformation rules and the ontology to produce BPEL model. Section 6 enumerates the threats to validity of our methodology. Finally, Sect. 7 summarizes the research results and draws the future works.

2 Background

2.1 Overview of MONET

MONET (a systeMatic derivatiOn of a bpmN modEls from business process Textual description) is a methodology that generates BPMN model from its corresponding documentation [12]. It is composed of two phases: BPMN model derivation phase and evaluation phase.

The derivation phase is organized around a set of three steps that are a pre-processing, a definition of the transformation rules, and their implementations. A pre-processing step during which the business analyst cleans first the business process description, written with a natural language. The cleaning is based on a simple Natural Language Processing (NLP) technique (Stanford CoreNLP tool [13]). Then, the business analyst identifies business goals to divide the business process description into different business concepts. For each business concept, the business analyst prepares its textual description according to a specific template [12] (See Fig. 1).

Overview
ID of the business concept: *<Unique ID assigned to a business concept>*
Name of the business concept: *<Unique name assigned to a business concept>*
Purpose of the business concept: *<Summary of the business concept purpose>*
Trigger/Precondition for execution: *<List of conditions that must be true to initialize the business concept>*
Participants: *<Actors and/or units involved in the business concept execution>*
Relationships between BC and its successors: *<Sequence flow or control structure>*

Main Scenario
Begin at
<Steps of the scenario of the trigger to goal>
[<Pre-condition>] <Task$_i$> < Task Description > <Task Type>
....
[<Pre-condition>] <Task$_{i+k}$> < Task Description > <Task Type>
Relationships between each task and its direct successors:<Sequence flow or control structure>
End
Alternative Scenario
Begin at < Task$_i$ >
[<Pre-condition>] < Task$_j$> < Task Description > <Task Type >
....
[<Pre-condition>] <Task$_{j+1}$> < Task Description > <Task Type>
Relationships between each task and its direct successors:<Sequence flow or control structure>
End
Error Scenario
Begin at < Task$_i$>
The main scenario fails
End

Post-condition :<A list of business objects as result of BC execution>

Fig. 1. Detailed description of a business concept [12].

This template expresses the semantic information related to the business logic. It is composed of three blocks. The first block summarizes the business concept that aims including information such as its id, name, purpose, pre-conditions, participants involved in its execution, and its relationships with business concept's successors. The second block describes the main scenario expressed by sub tasks and their sequence, the alternative, and the error scenarios. The third block illustrates the list of business objects as result of the execution of the business concept. For more details, reader can refer to [12].

A transformation-definition step during which the business designer defines an ontology, which represents the entities related to BPMN metamodel, to analyze the semantic of the business concepts' template. The ontology and the linguistic syntactic patterns are used to define business transformation rules.

A Transformation-implementation step during which the business engineer formalizes/implements the transformation rules, which provide for the automated generation of the BPMN model.

To evaluate our methodology, we examined the performance of the transformations experimentally through the calculation of recall and precision rates.

2.2 Related Works

Several authors define a set of methods for deriving BPMN model from its textual description and vice versa [1, 3, 5, 6, 8], and from model to another at different abstraction levels (i.e. from BPMN to BPEL and vice versa) [2, 4, 7].

On the one hand, model-to-text transformation [1, 5, 6] allows an effective way of directing the requirements and enhancing their completeness and correctness. The authors of [1, 2] proposed a technique that automatically transforms process models into intuitive natural language texts. It conducts a two-step evaluation. First, they utilize a test collection of model-text pairs from [3] and a set of text metrics to investigate in how far the generated texts are comparable to manually created texts. [6] generated textual descriptions of 552 process models using two approaches (1) manual textual description approach and (2) automatic textual description approach where Natural Language Generation System (NLGS) is used to produce a textual process description of the given process model. Results show that the content of manual and auto generated textual descriptions are the same, but the ordering of texts and topical similarity between them is low. [1] defined a semi-automated approach that consists of two main phases. In the manual preparation phase, users identify the automatable activities in the input process model(s) and specify the associated responsibilities, data needs, system interactions, and execution constraints. The requirements model, resulting from this analysis, serves as input for a generation algorithm, which automatically provides the user with a well-organized natural language requirements document.

On the other hand, text-to-model transformation techniques also cover a diversity of models. [3, 8] offered an approach that derives automatically BPMN models from natural language text. They developed a tailored Natural Language Processing (NLP) technique that identifies activities and their inter-relations from textual constraint descriptions.

The authors of [2, 4] address the issues related to model-to-model transformation from BPMN to BPEL and vice versa. [2] claim that the proposed model transformations between the two languages BPMN and BPEL fulfil the evaluation criteria: completeness, correctness, readability and reversibility. [4] proposed pattern-based transformation from BPMN to BPEL using ATL.

What become problematic with these works [2, 4] is the patterns identification and the different types of process models: BPEL (block-based) and BPMN (graph based). To overcome these limits, [14] present a unified framework, namely UniFlexView, for supporting automatic and consistent process view construction. Based on this framework, process modellers can use the proposed View Definition Language to specify their view construction requirements disregarding the types of process models.

In [7], the authors propose the application of COSMIC FSM method [10] to verify the conformity of the modelling levels: BPMN design, BPEL runtime. The presented approach is based on the measurement procedures and heuristics for measuring the functional size of BPMN and BPEL models.

In summary, many researchers studied the transformation between BPMN model and its textual description or between BPMN and BPEL models. However, there is no works that focus on the generation of BPEL from the documentation of the business process. Our objective is to facilitate the task of the business designer and developer to obtain BPEL model at a high level of granularity.

3 From Textual Description to BPEL Model

We propose to extend MONET methodology to generate BPEL model from its textual description. We called the new methodology MONEET (a systeMatic derivatiOn of a bpmN and bpEl modEls from business process Textual description). MONEET is composed of two phases: BPEL model derivation phase and evaluation phase. As MONET, the derivation phase is organized around a set of three steps that are a pre-processing, a definition of the transformation rules, and their implementations. The pre-processing step is quite similar to MONET. However, we defined new transformation rules to generate the BPEL model and we enhanced the evaluation phase by the use of COSMIC FSM method to measure the alignment of the generated BPEL model with its textual description. We describe in the following sections the transformation rules and the evaluation phase.

We defined eighteen transformation rules. Each transformation rule operates on the different components of the template (See Sect. 2).

R1. Each trigger is transformed into an event that will be linked to the first element of the current business concept. Based on the trigger type, we add the corresponding event.

R1.1. If the trigger type describes the time, so add the following code:

• Case of start event, which is only applied on an Event Sub-Process [9]:

```
<eventHandlers>
<onAlarm>[timer-spec]
<scope> [current business concept]
</scope>
</onAlarm>
</eventHandlers>
```

• Case of intermediate event:

```
<wait name = "[trigger-name]" for="[trigger-TimeCycle]"/>
```

R1.2. If the trigger type describes any action that refers to a specific addressee and represents or contains information for the addressee, so add the following code:

• Case of start event:

```
<receive name= [trigger-name] partnerLink = [Participant] createInstance="yes|no"/>
```

• Case of intermediate event

```
<receive name= [trigger-name] partnerLink = [Participant] createInstance="no"/>
```

We note that several event types such as conditional and signal event cannot be mapped to BPEL [9].

R2. Each participant is transformed into partner link depending on its type.

R2.1. If a participant invokes the BPEL process, so add the following code:

```
<process name=[process.name]/>
<partenerLink name="[participant name]" myRole = "[processNameProvider]"/>
```

R2.2. if a participant is invoked by the BPEL process, so add the following code:

```
<partnerLink name="[participant name]" myRole = "[processNameProvider]"
partnerRole= "[ParticipantNameRequester]"/>
```

R3. Each relationship between a business concept and its successors respects the linguistic pattern: **[<Pre-condition>] <Current Business Concept ID> is related <sequentially | exclusively | parallel | inclusively> to <Business Concept ID>**.

R3.1. If the relationship is <sequentially>, then add the following code:

```
<sequence>
  <scope> [current BC] </scope>
  <scope> [successor of the current BC] </scope>
</sequence>
```

R3.2. If the relationship is <parallel>, then add the following code:

```
<flow> [current BC] [successor of the current BC] </flow>
```

R3.3. If the relationship is <exclusively> and there is a precondition, then add following code:

```
<if >[precondition] [current BC]
 <else> [BC successor] </else>
</if>
```

R3.4. If the relationship is <inclusively> and there is a precondition, add the following code:

```
<flow>
 <links>
   <link name= "link1" >
   <link name= "link2" >
   <link name= "link3" >
   <link name= "link4" >
  </links>
  <source linkName="link1"> <transitioncondition>precondition1 <transitioncondition>
</source>
  <source linkName= " link2" >
   <transitioncondition>precondition2 <transitioncondition> </source>
<flow>
  <target linkName= "link 1" > </target>
  <source linkName= "link 3" > </source>
  [current BC]
</flow>
<flow>
  <target linkName= " link 2" > </target>
  <source linkName= " link 4" > </source>
  [business concept successor]
</flow>
<target linkName= " link3" ></target>
<target linkName= " link4" ></target>
</flow>
```

R4. For each step of a BC's scenario respecting the linguistic pattern: **[<Pre-condition>] <Task#> <Task Description> <Task Type>**, then add the following:

R4.1. If the task description is «Action verb + BusinessObject», then add an invoke activity presented by the following BPEL code and call R4.4, R4.5, and/or R4.6.

```
< invoke name="[Action verb + BusinessObject]"
  portType="[Task-operation-interface]" operation="[Task-operation]" >
</invoke>
```

R4.2. If the task description is «Action verb + NominalGroup», then add an invoke activity that has the same name of the pattern and call R4.4, R4.5 and/or R4.6. If the pre/post-modifier is a noun that merely represents a pure value, so there is no variable (data object) to add. Otherwise, if the pre/post-modifier is a complex noun (an entity) then add a variable corresponding to the data object.

```
<invoke name="[Action verb + NominalGroup]"
   partnerLink="[participant]"
   portType="[Task-operation-interface]" operation="[Task-operation]">
 </invoke>
```

R4.3. If the task description is «CommunicationVerb + BusinessObject | Nominal-Group + [[to ReceiverName(s)] | [from SenderName]]», then add the following code corresponding to an invoke or receive activity that has the same name of the pattern and a variable for each BusinessObject or NominalGroup.

```
<invoke  name="[CommunicationVerb+BusinessObject|NominalGroup]"  partenerLink=
"[ReceiverName]">
    <toPart part ="[variable.name]" fromVariable="[variable.name]"/>
</invoke>
```

Or

```
<receive name="[CommunicationVerb+BusinessObject|NominalGroup]"
partnerLink=[SenderName] portType="[Task-operation-interface]" operation="[Task-oper-
ation]" >
    <fromPart part ="[variable.name]" fromVariable = "[variable.name]"/>
</receive>
```

R4.4. If the task type is ActivePER, then add a variable presented by the following code:

```
<fromPart part = "[variable.name]" fromVariable = "[variable.name]"/>
```

R4.5. If the task type is ActiveRET, then add a variable expressed as follows:

```
<toPart part = "[variable.name]" fromVariable = "[variable.name]"/>
```

R4.6. If the task type is ActiveREP, then add a reply activity represented as follows:

```
<reply> </reply>
```

R5. Each relationship between the task and its successors respects the linguistic pattern: **[<Pre-condition>] <Current Task ID> is related <sequentially | exclusively | parallel | inclusively> to <Task ID>**

R5.1. If the relationship is <sequentially> and if the current activity and its direct successor are in the same main process, then add the following code:

```
</sequence> [current task] [successor task] </sequence>
```

Otherwise add

- Receive activity

```
<receive name="[direct successor task]" partenerLink="[participant]"></receive>
```

• Invoke activity

```
<invoke name= "[direct successor task]" partenerLink="[participant]" ></invoke>
```

R5.2. If the relationship is <parallel>, then add

```
<flow> [current task] [successor task] </flow>
```

R5.3. If the relationship is <exclusively> and there is a precondition, add the following code:

```
<if >[precondition][current task]
 <else> [ task successor] </else>
</if>
```

R5.4. If the relationship is <inclusively> and there is a precondition, then add the following code:

```
<flow>
<links>
<flow>
<links>
<link name= " link1" >
<link name= " link2" >
 <link name= " link3" >
<link name= " link4" ></links>
<source linkName="link1">
<transitioncondition>precondition1 <transitioncondition> </source>
<Source linkName= " link2" >
<transitioncondition>precondition2 <transitioncondition> </source>
<flow>
<target linkName= " link 1" > </target>
<source linkName= " link 3" > </source>
[current task]
</flow>
<flow>
<target linkName= " link 2" > </target>
<source linkName= " link 4" > </source>
[task successor]
</flow>
<target linkName= " link3" ></target>
<target linkName= " link4" ></target>
</flow>
```

R5.5. If the relationship is <sequentially>, and there is a <complete> construct related to a task, then add an end event based on the following code:

• None end event

```
<empty name="[e-name]"> </empty>
```

• Message End Events

```
<invoke name="[e-name]"
partnerLink="[Q, e-operation-interface]"
portType="[e-operation-interface]" operation="[e-operation]">
</invoke>
```

• Error end event:

```
<throw faultName="[e -name]"> </throw>
```

• Compensation end event

```
<compensate/> or <compensateScope target="[referencedActivity]"/>
```

• Terminate End Events

```
<exit> </exit>
```

4 Evaluation

The evaluation of our methodology is mainly composed of two activities: an experimental comparison by using the recall and precision rates and the COSMIC Functional Size Measurement (FSM) method [10] that calculates their functional size. The following subsections provide a brief description of these methods and their results.

4.1 Experimental Performance

We examined the performance of the transformations experimentally through the calculation of recall and precision rates. These measures aim to compare the performance of our method to the human performance by analyzing the results given by our methodology to those supplied by the expert.

For each BPEL element, the recall and precision rates are calculated according the following equations:

$$\text{Precision} = \text{TP}/(\text{TP} + \text{FP}) \tag{1}$$

$$\text{Recall} = \text{TP}/(\text{TP} + \text{FN}) \quad (2)$$

Where:

- True positive (TP) is the number of existing real elements generated by our transformation;
- False Positive (FP) is the number of not existing real elements generated by our transformation;
- False Negative (FN) is the number of existing real elements not generated by our transformation.

4.2 COSMIC Functional Size Measurement

Recall that COSMIC FSM method proposes a standardized measurement process to determine the functional size of any software. The software functional size is derived by quantifying the Functional User Requirement (FURs). FURs represent the "user practices and procedures that the software must perform". A FUR involves a number of functional processes. Each Functional Process (FP) consists of a set of functional sub-processes that move data or manipulate data. A data movement moves a single data group from/to a user (respectively Entry and eXit data movement) or from/to a persistent storage (respectively Read and Write data movement). The unit of measurement is one data movement for one data group, referred to as one CFP. The size of a FP is equal to the number of its data movements. Consequently, the software size is equal to the sum of the sizes of all its functional processes.

To facilitate the functional size measurement of a BPEL model, [7] use the COSMIC concepts mapping to those of the BPEL notation shown in Table 1.

Then, we decompose the BPEL model into a set of blocks. Each fragment in the BPMN corresponds to a block in the BPEL. A block hierarchy for a process model is a set of blocks of the process model in which each pair of blocks is either nested or disjoint and which contains the maximal block (i.e., the whole process model). Each block has an interface representing the public tasks. A public task is defined as a task sending or receiving a message flow. The functional size of a BPEL model composed of n blocks is given by:

$$FS(BPEL) = \sum\nolimits_{i=1}^{n} FS(B_i) \quad (3)$$

where:

- *FS(BPEL)*: functional size of the BPEL model.
- $FS(B_i)$: functional size of block B_i.
- *n*: the total number of blocs in a BPEL model.

The functional size of a functional process block B_i in *BPEL* is:

$$FS(Bi) = FS(event) + \sum_{j=1}^{m} FS(PTj) + \sum_{y=1}^{z} FS(Oy) \quad (4)$$

Table 1. Mapping of COSMIC on BPEL [7].

COSMIC	BPEL
Functional User	<partnerLinks>: Participant that interacts with the process
Boundary	Frontier between the <process> and the participants <partnerLinks>
Triggering Event	The first <invoke> message without <partnerLinks>
Functional Process	<process>: a process node presented in the first level
Data group	<variable>: name of a resource or data object
	operation = "[e-operation]" in <invoke>: name of a message sequence flow: Information provided as part of a flow
Entry	<invoke>: receive message from <partnerLinks>
eXit	<receive>: send message to <partnerLinks>
Read	<toPart part = "[dataInput-name]" fromVariable = "[DataObject name]"/>: read from a data object
Write	<formPart part = "[dataOutput-name]" fromVariable = "[DataObjectname]"/>: write to a data object

where:

- FS (B_i): functional size of block.
- m: number of public tasks in a block B_i. (j = 1,… m)
- FS(event) is the FS of the event triggering the functional process in block B_i. It is represented by <invoke>, <receive> or <wait>. Its FS is equal to 1 CFP.
- FS(PT_j) is the functional size of the public task PT_j. A public task can be <invoke>, <receive>. The functional size of <invoke> and <receive> task is equal to 1 CFP.
- FS (Oy): is the functional size of associations from/to a data object. The functional size of <toPart…from> or <fromPart… to> is equal to 1 CFP.
- z: number of associations in a block B_i. (y = 1,… z).

5 MONEET Tool

For a better use of our methodology, we enhance MONET tool [12] by a module that generates BPEL model from its corresponding textual description (See Fig. 2). We called MONEET Tool, which is implemented as an EclipseTM plug-in [15] and is composed of three main modules: Parser, generator, and evaluator.

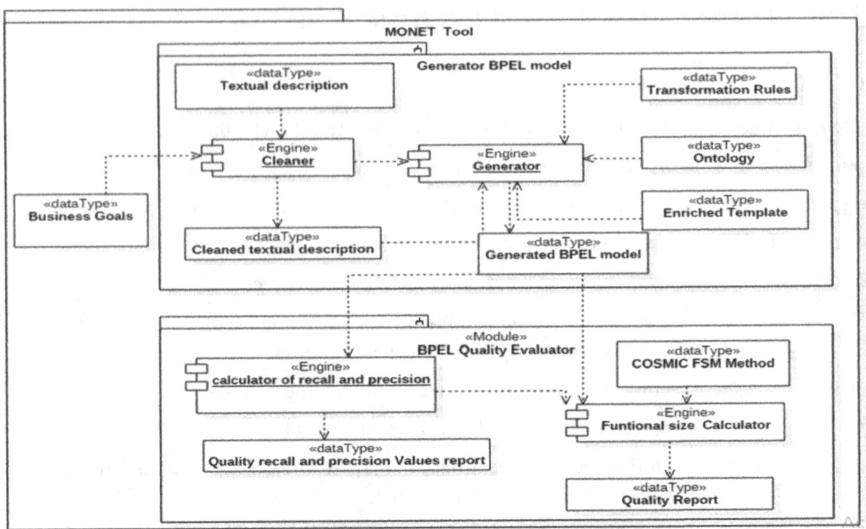

Fig. 2. Architecture of MONEET tool.

The pre-processing engine uses as input the textual description of a BPEL model written in a natural language. It cleans the file using the Stanford CoreNLP tool [13]. The cleaned file is used by the business analyst to manually determine the business goals. Figure 3 illustrates the Business Goal (BG4) definition and its description.

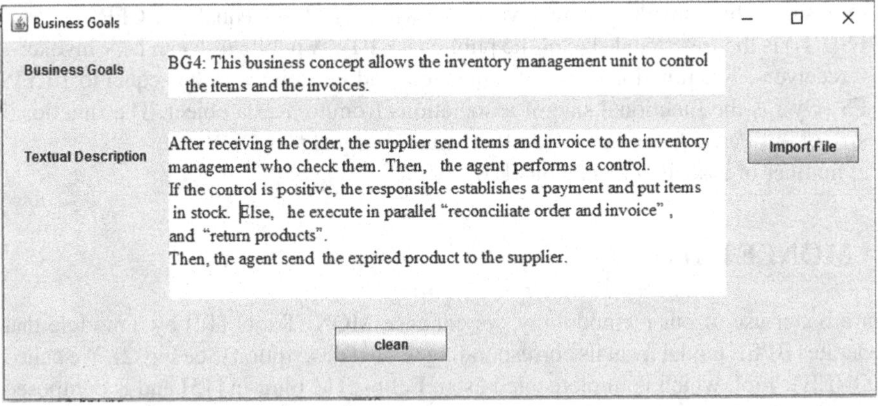

Fig. 3. Business goal definition [12].

Each business goal has its corresponding Business Concept (BC). The business analyst creates the enriched template corresponding to each BC. Figure 4 shows the template corresponding to BC4.

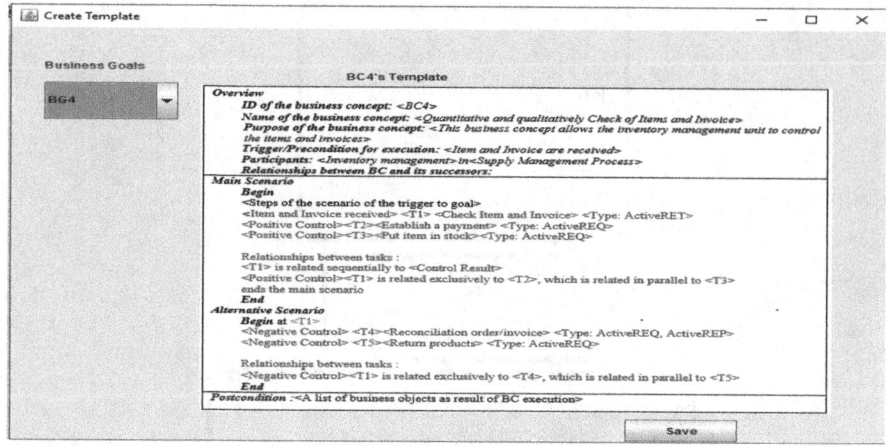

Fig. 4. BC4's enhanced template [12].

Next, the analyst selects one or more BCs. If he selects one BC, the corresponding fragment is generated. Else, the business analyst can select all business concepts to transform.

The generator engine uses the ontology and applies the transformation rules to derive the BPEL model. Figure 5 illustrates the generated BPEL model: "Supply Management Process".

First, by applying **R2.1** we add a process name "*Supply Management Process*" and a partnerLink "*Inventory Management*". Second by applying **R1,** the process is activated by the trigger "*Item and Invoice are received*". The transformation of the main scenario calls **R4.2** and **R4.5** that generate an invoke activity labelled "*Check item and invoice*". Then, we add two variables labelled "*item*" and "*invoice*" to this activity. **R4.2** produces an invoke activity labelled "*Establish a payment*" (respectively, "*Put items in stock*"). By applying **R5.1,** we generate an orchestration logic between "*Control result*" and "*Check item and invoice*". Then, by applying **R5.2**, we add a flow activity between "*establish payment*" and "*put item in stock*". The transformation of the alternative scenario calls **R4.2, R4.5** and **R4.6** that produces an invoke activity labelled "Reconciliation order/invoice". Then, we add two variables labelled "order" and "*invoice*" to this activity and we add a reply activity "send expired product". **R4.1** produces an invoke activity labelled "return products". Then, by applying **R5.2**, we add a flow activity between "reconciliation order/invoice" and "return products". Table 2 illustrates the BPEL code corresponding to BC4.

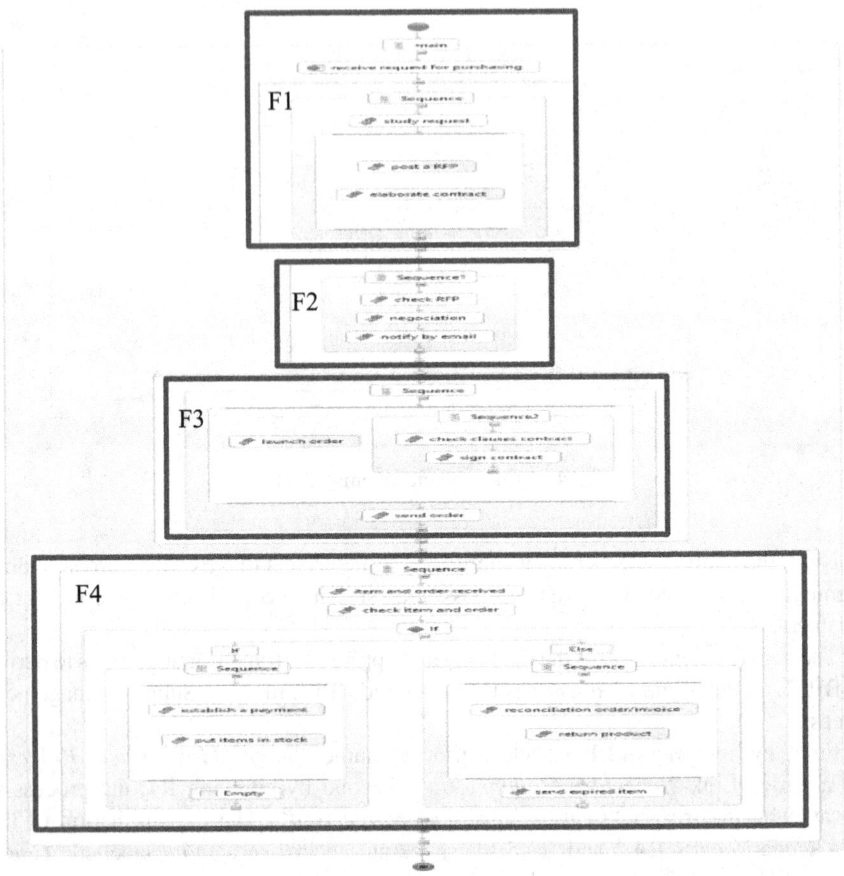

Fig. 5. The generated BPEL model: "Supply Management Process" [11].

Table 2. BPEL code corresponding to BC4 [11].

BC4	Textual description	Rules	Code BPEL
Overview	Participants: <Inventory management> In<SupplyManagement Process>	R2.1	<process name= "SupplyManagementProces" </process> <partnerLink name= "InventoryManagemen" myRole="SupplyManagementProcesPro-vider" />
	<Item and Invoice are re-ceived>	R1	<receive name= item and invoice received partnerLink= "supplier" createIn-stance=*"yes"*/>
Main scenario	<T1> <Check Item and In-voice> <Type: ActiveRET>	R4.2 R4.5	<invoke name="check item and invoice " <toPart part = "item" fromVariable = "item"/> <toPart part = "invoice" fromVariable = "in-voice"/>
	<Positive Control> <T2><Establish a pay-ment> <Type: Ac-tiveREQ>	R4.2	< invoke name="establish a payment" port-Type="[T2-operation-interface]" opera-tion="[T2-operation]"> </invoke>
	<T3><Put item in stock><Type: Ac-tiveREQ>	R4.2	< invoke name="put item in stock" port-Type="[T3-operation-interface]" opera-tion="[T3-operation]"> </invoke>
	<T1> is related sequen-tially to <Control Result>	R5.1	<sequence><T1><control result></sequence>
	which is related in parallel to <T3>	R5.2	<flow> [T2] [T3] </flow>
Alternative scenario	<T4><Reconciliation or-der/invoice> <Type:ActiveRET, Ac-tiveREP>	R4.2 R4.5 R4.6	<invoke name="reconciliation order/invoice " portType="[T4-operation-interface]" operation="[T4-operation]"> </invoke> <toPart part = "order" fromVariable = "or-der"/> <toPart part = "invoice" fromVariable = "in-voice"/> <reply name="send expired product"> </reply>
	<T5><Return products> <Type: ActiveREQ>	R4.1	< invoke name="return products" portType="[T5-operation-interface]" operation="[T5-operation]"> </invoke>
	<T4> is related in parallel to<T5>	R5.2	<flow> [T4] [T5] </flow>

The evaluator evaluates experimentally the BPMN model through the calculation of recall and precision rates (See Fig. 6). The high scores for both ratios mean that the generated BPMN model covers the whole domain precisely in accordance with the experts' perspective (See Fig. 7). We can deduce that the performance of our methodology approaches the human performance.

Recall-Precision measurement.

BPEL Model C:User/bob/Monet/bpel/bp.bpel Import

Expert BPEL Model C:User/bob/Monet/bpel/bp1.bpel Import

Recall	Precision
TP/(TP+FN)=40/46=0.86	TP/(TP+FP)=40/42=0.95

Interpret : the generated BPEL model covers the whole domain precisely in accordance with the experts' perspective

Fig. 6. Recall-precision measurement.

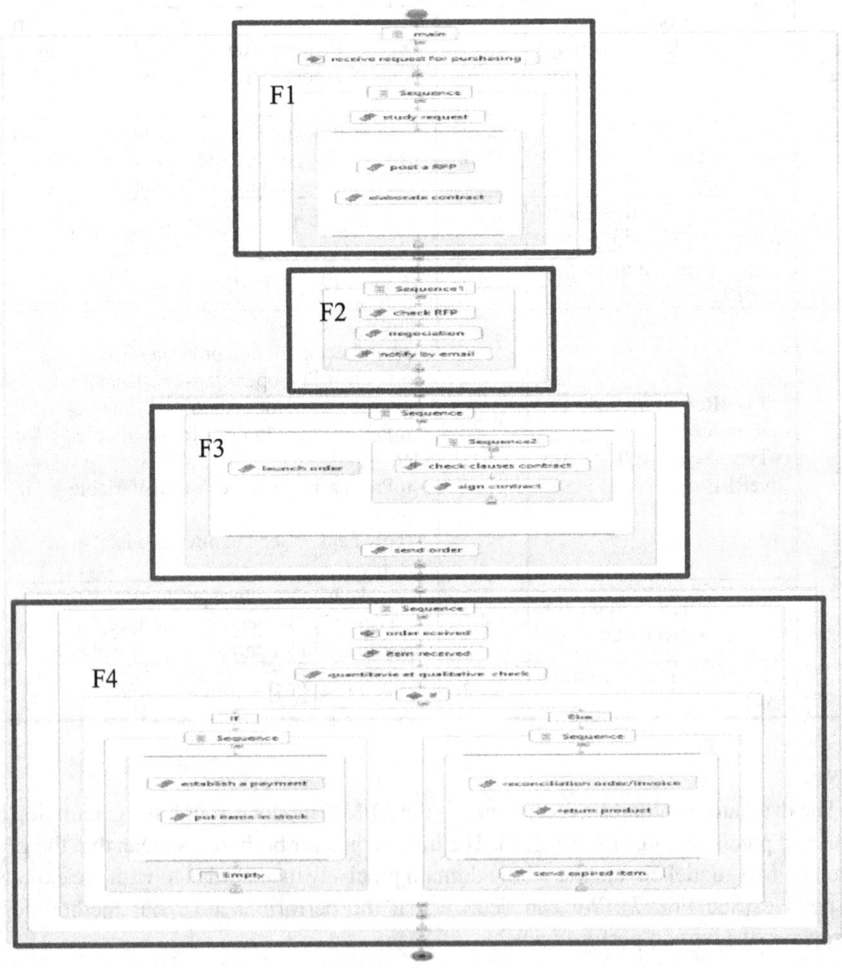

Fig. 7. The elaborated BPEL model by the expert [11].

In addition, we verify the alignment between the generated BPEL model and its corresponding textual description based on COSMIC FSM method. To do this, we calculate the functional size of each fragment FS(F_i) and its corresponding business concept FS(BC_i). Table 3 expresses measurement results for the BPEL model "Supply Management Process".

The obtained values show that BPEL model and its corresponding textual description are equal, which prove the alignment between them.

The obtained values show that BPEL model and its corresponding textual description are equal, which prove the alignment between them.

Table 3. Measurement results for the "Supply Management Process".

BC in textual description	Functional sub-process	FS(F_i) in BPEL model	FS (BCi)	Type
BC1	Receive request for purchasing	1 CFP	1 CFP	E
	Study request	1 CFP	1 CFP	E
	Post a RFP	1 CFP	1 CFP	W
	Elaborate contract	1 CFP	1 CFP	W
BC2	Check RFP	1CFP	1CFP	R
	negotiation	0 CFP	0 CFP	–
	Notify by email	1 CFP	1 CFP	X
BC3	Launch order	1 CFP	1 CFP	W
	Check clauses contract	1CFP	1CFP	R
	Sign contract	1CFP	1CFP	W
	Send order	1CFP	1CFP	X
BC4	Item and invoice received	1 CFP	1 CFP	E
	Check item and invoice	2 CFP	2 CFP	R
	Control result	1 CFP	1 CFP	E
	Establish a payment	0 CFP	0 CFP	–
	Put items in stock	0 CFP	0 CFP	–
	Reconciliation order/invoice	2 CFP	2 CFP	R
	Return products	0 CFP	0 CFP	–
	Send expired products	1 CFP	1 CFP	X
Total		17 CFP	17 CFP	

6 Threats to Validity

We identified several validity threats of our study including the internal and external validity [16].

The internal validity threats are related to four issues: the first issue expresses that despite the advantages generated by defining a specific template, the usage of multiple descriptions of the same process can also lead to considerable problems. In fact, stakeholders may develop different expectations about the purpose of the process and the manner of the process execution [3]. The second issue is due to the use of imprecise process descriptions. Therefore, considerable effort is required to maintain process descriptions and clear up any conflicts. The third issue concerns the costs of creating the template. A manual creation of a template is, depending on the size of the model, associated with considerable effort. In addition, it is also important to note that process is typically subject to changes. Hence, the describing texts must be adapted accordingly and therefore the manual adaptation does not appear to be a reasonable solution and might be a cumbersome task. The fourth issue is related to the impact of an error-prone generation of a BPEL model. This case may lead to misalignment and inconsistency between the textual description and business process model.

The external validity threats deal with the possibility to generalize this study results to other case studies. The limited number of case studies used to illustrate the proposed methodology could not generalize the results. Automation of our methodology needs to be considered even it is easy to use manually given its simplicity.

7 Conclusion

In this paper, we propose a methodology to derive BPEL models from their corresponding textual descriptions. Compared to existing work, our methodology starts by defining an enriched template based on structured linguistic patterns. Next, it proposes transformation rules that operate on the different components of the template to derive the corresponding BPEL elements. These transformation rules are implemented in MONEET tool which generated BPEL model and assesses its quality experimentally through the calculation of recall and precision rates, as well as COSMIC FSM method.

References

1. Aysolmaz, B., Leopold, H., Reijers, H.A., Demirörs, O.: A semi-automated approach for generating natural language requirements documents based on business process models. J. Inf. Softw. Technol. **93**, 14–29 (2018)
2. Dumas, M.: Case study: BPMN to BPEL model transformation (2009)
3. Friedrich, F., Mendling, J., Puhlmann, F.: Process model generation from natural language text. In: Mouratidis, H., Rolland, C. (eds.) CAiSE 2011. LNCS, vol. 6741, pp. 482–496. Springer, Heidelberg (2011). https://doi.org/10.1007/978-3-642-21640-4_36
4. Doux, G., Jouault, F., Bézivin, J.: Transforming BPMN process models to BPEL process definitions with ATL. In: Proceedings of the 5th International Workshop on Graph-Based Tools (2013)

5. Leopold, H., Mendling, J., Polyvyanyy, A.: Supporting process model validation through natural language generation. J. IEEE Trans. Softw. Eng. **40**, 818–840 (2014)
6. Zaheer, S., Shahzad, K., Nawab, R.M.A.: Comparing manual- and auto-generated textual documentations of business process models. In 6th International Proceeding of the 6th International Conference on Innovative Computing Technology, Dublin, Ireland, August 2016
7. Khlif, W., Ben-Abdallah, H., Sellami, A., Haoues, M.: A COSMIC-based approach for verifying the conformity of BPMN, BPEL and component models. In: Abramowicz, W., Corchuelo, R. (eds.) BIS 2019. LNBIP, vol. 353, pp. 381–396. Springer, Cham (2019). https://doi.org/10.1007/978-3-030-20485-3_30
8. van der Aa, H., Di Ciccio, C., Leopold, H., Reijers, H.A.: Extracting declarative process models from natural language. In: Giorgini, P., Weber, B. (eds.) CAiSE 2019. LNCS, vol. 11483, pp. 365–382. Springer, Cham (2019). https://doi.org/10.1007/978-3-030-21290-2_23
9. OMG. Business Process Modeling Notation Specification 2.0 (2011). http://www.omg.org/spec/BPMN/2.0/PDF/
10. COSMIC v 4.0.2 ISO/IEC 19761: Common Software Measurement International Consortium. COSMIC Functional Size Measurement Method, Version 4.0.2 (2020)
11. Khlif, W., Aloui, N., Ayed, N.E.B.: A methodology for generating BPEL models from a business process textual description. In: 16th International Conference on Evaluation of Novel Approaches to Software Engineering, pp. 323–330 (2021)
12. Khlif, W., Elleuch Ben Ayed, N., Chihi, F.: Towards a systematic derivation of BPMN model from business process textual description. In: International Conference on Software Engineering and Knowledge Engineering, Virtual Venue 2020, 9–19 July 2020 (2020)
13. Manning, C.D., Surdeanu, M., Bauer, J., Jenny Rose Finkel, J.R., Bethard, S., McClosky, D.: The stanford CoreNLP natural language processing toolkit. In: The 52nd Annual Proceedings of t Meeting of the Association for Computational Linguistics, 22–27 June 2014, pp. 55–60 (2014)
14. Yongchareon, S., Liu, C., Zhao, X.: UniFlexView: a unified framework for consistent construction of BPMN and BPEL process views. J. Concurr. Comput. Pract. Exp. **32**(1), e5646 (2020)
15. Eclipse Specification (2011). http://www.eclipse.org/
16. Wohlin, C., Runeson, P., Höst, M., Ohlsson, M.C., Regnell, B., Wesslén, A.: Experimentation in Software Engineering: An Introduction (2000)

XtraLibD: Detecting Irrelevant Third-Party Libraries in Java and Python Applications

Ritu Kapur[1(✉)], Poojith U. Rao[1], Agrim Dewam[2], and Balwinder Sodhi[1]

[1] Indian Institute of Technology, Ropar, Punjab, India
{ritu.kapur,poojith.19csz0006,sodhi}@iitrpr.ac.in
[2] Punjab Engineering College, Chandigarh, India

Abstract. Software development comprises the use of multiple Third-Party Libraries (TPLs). However, the irrelevant libraries present in software application's distributable often lead to excessive consumption of resources such as CPU cycles, memory, and modile-devices' battery usage. Therefore, the identification and removal of unused TPLs present in an application are desirable. We present a rapid, storage-efficient, obfuscation-resilient method to detect the irrelevant-TPLs in Java and Python applications. Our approach's novel aspects are *i)* Computing a vector representation of a .class file using a model that we call Lib2Vec. The Lib2Vec model is trained using the Paragraph Vector Algorithm. *ii)* Before using it for training the Lib2Vec models, a .class file is converted to a *normalized* form via semantics-preserving transformations. *iii)* A e*Xtra Lib*rary *D*etector (XtraLibD) developed and tested with 27 different language-specific Lib2Vec models. These models were trained using different parameters and >30,000 .class and >478,000 .py files taken from >100 different Java libraries and 43,711 Python available at MavenCentral.com and Pypi.com, respectively. XtraLibD achieves an accuracy of 99.48% with an F1 score of 0.968 and outperforms the existing tools, viz., LibScout, LiteRadar, and LibD with an accuracy improvement of 74.5%, 30.33%, and 14.1%, respectively. Compared with LibD, XtraLibD achieves a response time improvement of 61.37% and a storage reduction of 87.93% (99.85% over JIngredient). Our program artifacts are available at https://www.doi.org/10.5281/zenodo.5179747.

Keywords: Third-party library detection · Code similarity · Paragraph vectors · Software bloat · Obfuscation

1 Introduction

Third Party Libraries (TPLs) play a significant role in software development as they provide ready-made implementations of various functionalities, such as image manipulation, data access and transformation, and advertisement. As reported by [16], 57% of apps contain third-party ad libraries, and 60% of an application's code is contributed by TPLs [25]. However, as the software development process progresses through multiple iterations, there is generally a change in the requirements or technology. In the process of performing modifications to embed the changes into the application, an unused (or irrelevant) set of libraries (which were used earlier) often remains referenced in

R. Ali et al. (Eds.): ENASE 2021, CCIS 1556, pp. 132–155, 2022.
https://doi.org/10.1007/978-3-030-96648-5_7

the application's distributable. Such unused TPLs have become a prominent source of software bloat. We refer to such unused TPLs as irrelevant-TPLs. Resource wastage is a critical problem for mobile devices that possess limited computing resources and significantly impact the performance by affecting the execution time, throughput, and scalability of various applications [18,26]. Therefore, the **identification and removal of the irrelevant TPLs** present in an application are desirable.

1.1 Motivation

Our primary objective is to develop a technique for detecting *irrelevant TPLs* present in a software application's distributable binary. An essential task for achieving this objective is to *develop a robust technique for TPL-detection.* The existing TPL-detection methods [5,17] generally depend, directly or indirectly, on the package names or the library's structural details and code. Thus, they are potentially affected by various obfuscations, such as package-name obfuscation and API obfuscation. Also, most of the works are restricted to Android applications [5,15,17,27].

Definition 1 (Irrelevant-TPL). *We define an* ***irrelevant TPL*** *as the one bundled in the distributable binary of a software application A but not relevant to it. The examples of such TPLs would be the Mockito*[a] *or JUnit*[b] *Java ARchives (JARs) that get packaged in the deployable release archive of a Java or Python application.*
The relevance of a TPL is based on its application in different contexts. For instance, relevant vs. irrelevant, reliable vs. unreliable, anomalous vs. non-anomalous, bloat vs. non-bloat, used vs. unused etc. The idea is to compare with a reference list of relevant libraries or white-listed libraries[c] *in an automated manner.*

[a] https://site.mockito.org/.
[b] https://junit.org/.
[c] Black libraries matter.

Definition 2 (Paragraph Vector Algorithm). ***Paragraph Vector Algorithm (PVA)*** *is an unsupervised algorithm that learns fixed-length feature representations from variable-length pieces of texts, such as sentences, paragraphs, and documents. The algorithm represents each document by a dense vector trained to predict words in the document [14].*

In our recent work, we proposed an obfuscation-resilient tool, Bloat Library Detector (BloatLibD) [10][1], that detects the TPLs present in a given Java application by identifying the similarities between the source code of the "available TPLs" and the TPLs used in the given application. To obtain this set of "available TPLs," we leverage the TPLs present at MavenCentral repository[2] that hosts TPLs for various functionalities,

[1] Tool and dataset available at https://www.doi.org/10.5281/zenodo.5179634.
[2] https://mvnrepository.com/repos/central.

which we assume to be a trustworthy source. In our previous work [10], we also validated the efficacy of PVA in computing a reliable and accurate representation of binary and textual code. The current work aims to extend the existing method for Python applications. We name our new tool as eXtra Library Detector (XtraLibD) which is capable of detecting irrelevant libraries in both Java and Python applications. In our current work, we also compare XtraLibD for some new TPL detection tools for Python and Java applications. One of the reasons for choosing these very languages is their popularity with the professional programmers [23] and the availability of a large volume of OSS source code written using these languages[3].

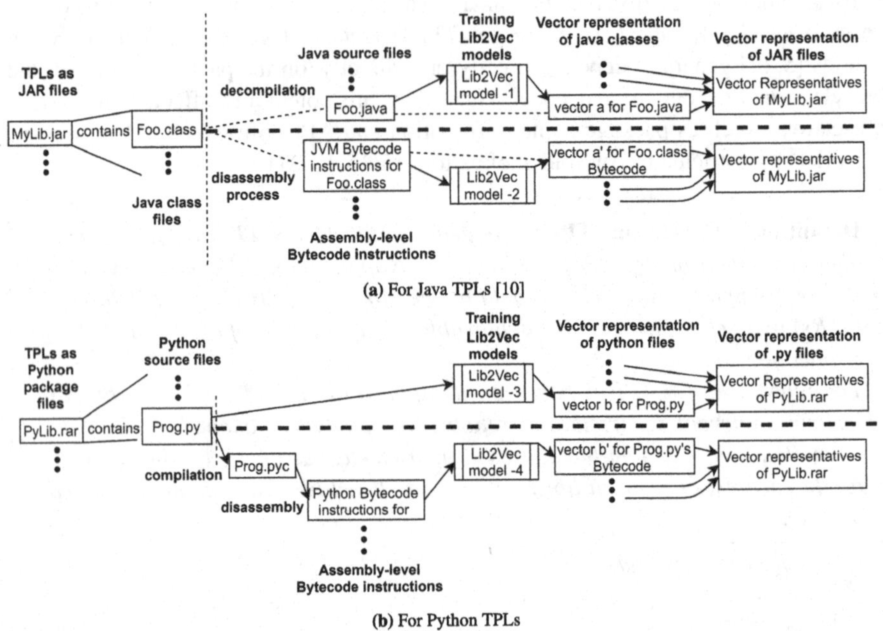

Fig. 1. Basic idea of our method.

1.2 Basic Tenets Behind Our System

In this paper, we present a novel TPL-detection technique by creating a *library embedding* using PVA – we named it Lib2Vec. The central idea underlying our approach is illustrated in Fig. 1 and stated as follows:

1. Each of the TPLs consists of a collection of binary .class files or source code files, which we refer to as TPL-constituent files.
2. Semantics-preserving transformations (such as compilation, decompilation, and disassembly) are applied to the TPL-constituent files to obtain their *normalized* textual form(s), viz., the textual forms of source code and bytecode instructions.

[3] Sources of stats: https://octoverse.github.com/projects.html and https://githut.info/.

3. With a large corpus of such text, we train Lib2Vec models, using which a vector representation of any TPL-constituent file can be computed.
4. Further, the vector representations of a TPL can be computed as a suitable function of the vector representations of all the TPL-constituent files contained in that TPL.
5. If the vector representations of a TPL T in an application, have a considerable cosine similarity[4] with the vector representations of the set of "available TPLs," we label T as *likely-to-be-non-irrelevant-TPL* or else *likely-to-be-irrelevant-TPL*.

1.3 Handling Obfuscated Libraries

One of the significant issues faced in TPL-detection is the obfuscation of the library code. The TPL-detection techniques that rely on the obfuscation-sensitive features of a library would fail to detect a library under obfuscation. The key idea underlying our approach towards handling obfuscated libraries is to produce a "normalized" textual representation of the library's binary .class files before using it to train the Lib2Vec models and when checking an input .class using a Lib2Vec model. We perform the decompilation and disassembly of .class files to obtain their "normalized" textual forms, viz., source code and bytecode instructions as text. These operations on a .class file are obfuscation-invariant. Similarly, for Python cose, we perform compilation operation on .py files present in .zip package of a Python TPL to obtain .pyc files, from which th bytecode instructions are obtained by performing the dissassembly operation. For example, we transform a .class file using a decompiler [24] (with suitable configuration), which produces almost identical output for both obfuscated and unobfuscated versions. The decompiler can emit either bytecode or the Java source code for the .class files.

2 Related Work

Most of the existing works that target TPL-detection assume that "*the libraries can be identified, either through developer input or inspection of the application's code.*" The existing approaches for TPLs detection can be categorized as follows:

1. *Based on a "reference list" of TPLs:* The techniques presented in [6,7,12,16] are significant works in this category. A "reference list" comprises libraries known to be obtained from a trustworthy source and useful for software development. The basic idea behind the approach is first to construct a "reference list" of libraries and then test the application under consideration using the list. In this process, it is evaluated that the application's constituent libraries are present in the "reference list" or not. All the constituent libraries, which are not present in the list, are deemed to be irrelevant-TPLs. In practice, this approach requires keeping the "reference list" up-to-date. Since these methods require manually comparing the libraries with the "reference list" and a periodic update of this list, they tend to be slower, costly, and storage-inefficient.

[4] http://bit.ly/2ODWoEy.

2. *Features-Based approaches:* [5,15,17] are some of the approaches that work by extracting individual libraries' features and then use them to identify libraries that are similar to another. The feature-based methods generally depend, directly or indirectly, on the package names or the structural details of the application and source code. A brief description of these works is provided below:
   (a) **LibScout** [5] presents a TPL-detection technique based on Class Hierarchical Analysis (CHA) and hashing mechanism performed on the application's package names. Though the method has been proven to be resilient to most code-obfuscation techniques, it fails in certain corner cases. For example, modification in the class hierarchy or package names, or when the boundaries between app and library code become blurred. Another recent work is [11], which relies on the obfuscation-resilient features extracted from the Abstract Syntax Tree of code to compute a code fingerprint. The fingerprint is then used to calculate the similarity of two libraries.
   (b) **LibRadar** [17] is resilient to the package name obfuscation problem of LibScout and presents a solution for large-scale TPL-detection. LibRadar leverages the benefits of hashing-based representation and multi-level clustering and works by computing the similarity in the hashing-based representation of static semantic features of application packages. LibRadar has successfully found the original package names for an obfuscated library, generating the list of API permissions used by an application by leveraging the API-permission maps generated by PScout [4]. Though LibRadar is resilient to package obfuscation, it depends on the package hierarchy's directory structure and requires a library candidate to be a sub-tree in the package hierarchy. Thus, the approach may fail when considering libraries being packaged in their different versions [15]. An alternate version of LibRadar, which uses an online TPL-database, is named as LiteRadar.
   (c) **LibD** [15] leverages feature hashing to obtain code features, which reduces the dependency on package information and supplementary information for TPL-detection. LibD works by developing library instances based on the package-structure details extracted using Apktool, such as the direct relations among various constituent packages, classes, methods, and homogeny graphs. Authors employ Androguard [3] to extract information about central relationships, viz., inclusion, inheritance, and call relations. LibD depends upon the directory structure of applications, which leads to the possibility of LibD's failure due to obfuscation in the directory structure.
   (d) **DepClean** [22] detects the presence of bloated dependencies in Maven artifacts. Given an input maven project, DepClean analyzes the bloat library dependencies through API member calls to identify the actual used libraries by the project. The final output from the tool is new maven POM file containing only the used bloat libraries along with a dependency usage report. Authors conduct a qualitative assessment of DepClean on 9,639 Java projects hosted on Maven Central comprising a total of 723,444 dependency relationships. Some key observations of the study were that it is possible to reduce the number of dependencies of the Maven projects by 25%. Further, it was observed that when pointed out, developers were willing to remove bloated dependencies.

(e) **JIngredient** [13] detects the TPLs present in a project's JAR file and proposes their origin TPLs. Basically, given an input TPL (in .jar format) z, JIngredient identifies the source TPLs containing source files similar to those present in z. To determine the similarity in source code, JIngredient uses class names (as class signatures) for classes present in z. As the tool depends on class names, which can easily be obfuscated, it is not resilient to source code obfuscations (also reported by the authors). JIngredient when compared with an existing software Bertillonage technique [9], it achieves an improvement of 64.2% in terms of precision metrics.

(f) **Autoflake** [19] removes unused TPL imports and unused variables from the code written in python. However, the removal of unused varables is disabled by default. Authoflake uses Pyflakes [20] in its implementation. Pyflakes analyzes python programs to detect errors present in them by parsing them.

(g) **PyCln** [2] is another tool used to detect and remove unused TPL import statements in python source code.

Limitations of the Current Works. While the TPL-detection based on "reference list" methods tend to be inefficient and costly, the feature-based methods are potentially affected by various types of obfuscations and are mostly developed for Android applications. Therefore, it is desirable to develop TPL-detection techniques that are resilient against such issues. Also, while surveying the literature, we observed that there are very few TPL detection tools for Python, and most of the solutions exist for Java or Android based applications. Therefore, there exist a need to develop efficient, obfuscation-resilient TPL detection tools for applications developed in other programming languages, such as Python, C#, etc. To the best of our knowledge, we were not able to find any tools that detect TPLs for Python-based applications, i.e., applications having source code written in Python. AutoFlake and PyCln were the closest tools related to our work as they too work with TPLs, though they detect the bloatness or Irrelevance in terms of the usage of TPLs. In contrary, XtraLibD aims to detect the irrelvant TPLs by comparing with a certain collection of white-listed TPLs. Nevertheless, XtraLibD provides a novel solution for detection of irrelevant TPLs present in python applications.

3 Proposed Approach

Our system's primary goal can be stated as follows: Given a TPL T, determine if T is likely-to-be-irrelevant-TPL or a non-irrelevant-TPL in the given application. Our approach's central idea is to look for source code similarity and bytecode similarity between T and the set of "available TPLs." However, analyzing the detailed usages of the TPLs in the application is currently out of scope of this work. Our method can be considered as similar to the "reference list" methods, but the similarity here is determined on the basis of source code present in the TPL, and not merely the TPL names or package-hierarchial structure. Table 1 shows the notation used for various terms in this paper.

Table 1. Table of Notations.

T	$\triangleq$ A TPL in its JAR, RAR, or ZIP file format
L	$\triangleq$ Set of considered programming languages, {Java, Python}
C	$\triangleq$ The collection of TPLs files fetched from MavenCentral or PyPi
Z	$\triangleq$ The set of PVA tuning-parameter variation scenarios, listed in Table 4
$F^j_{bc}, F^j_{sc}, F^p_{bc}, F^p_{sc}$	$\triangleq$ The collections of bytecode (bc) and source code (sc) data obtained by disassembling and decompilation of .class and .pyc files f, respectively, such that $f \in T$, and $T \in C$. Note: j refers to Java (j) and p refers to Python (p)
$M^j_{bc}, M^j_{sc}, M^p_{bc}, M^p_{sc}$	$\triangleq$ The collections of Lib2Vec models trained on $F^j_{bc}, F^j_{sc}, F^p_{bc}, F^p_{sc}, \forall Z$
$\hat{M}^j_{bc}, \hat{M}^j_{sc}, \hat{M}^p_{bc}, \hat{M}^p_{sc}$	$\triangleq$ The best performing Lib2Vec models among all $M^j_{bc}, M^j_{sc}, M^p_{bc}, M^p_{sc}$
$\phi^j_{bc}, \phi^j_{sc}, \phi^p_{bc}, \phi^p_{sc}$	$\triangleq$ The PVA vectors corresponding to source files' bytecode and source code
$\phi^{\hat{j}}_{sc}, \phi^{\hat{j}}_{bc}, \phi^{\hat{p}}_{sc}, \phi^{\hat{p}}_{bc}$	$\triangleq$ The reference PVA vectors for source code and bytecode representations
D	$\triangleq$ The database containing the source files' vectors ($\phi^j_{bc}, \phi^j_{sc}, \phi^p_{bc}, \phi^p_{sc}$) for C
β	$\triangleq$ The number of training iterations or epochs used for training a PVA model
γ	$\triangleq$ The PVA vector size used for training a PVA model
ψ	$\triangleq$ The number of training samples used for training a PVA model
α	$\triangleq$ The cosine similarity score between two PVA vectors
$\hat{\alpha}$	$\triangleq$ The threshold cosine similarity score

3.1 Steps of Our Approach

The central ideas behind our approach were presented in Sect. 1.2. Here we expand those steps in more detail and highlight the relevant design decisions to be addressed while implementing each step.

1. **Preparing the Dataset of "available TPLs"**
   (a) Download a set of Java TPLs C from MavenCentral, and Python TPLs from Pypi[5].
   Design decision: Why use MavenCentral or Pypi to collect TPLs? How many TPLs should be collected from different software categories?
   (b) For each TPL $J \in C$, obtain the Java or Python source code and bytecode collections (F_{sc}, F_{bc}) by performing the decompilation and disassembly transformation operations.
   Design decision: Why are the decompilation and disassembly transformations appropriate?
   (c) Train the PVA models M_{sc} and M_{bc} on F_{sc} and F_{bc}, respectively, obtained in the previous step.
   Design decision: Why use PVA, and what should be the PVA tuning-parameters for obtaining optimal results in our task?
   (d) For each source file $f \in F_{sc}$ and the bytecode record $b \in F_{bc}$, obtain the corresponding vector representations (ϕ_{sc}, ϕ_{bc}) using suitable PVA models trained in the previous step. ϕ_{sc} and ϕ_{bc} obtained for each source code and bytecode instance are stored in the database D.

[5] https://pypi.org/.

2. **Determining if an Input TPL (T) is a Irrelevant-TPL or Not for a given Application**
   (a) Compute the vector representation $\langle \phi'_{bc}, \phi'_{sc} \rangle$ for the bytecode and source code representations of T.
   (b) Obtain all the vectors $\langle \phi_{bc}, \phi_{sc} \rangle \in D$, such that the respective similarity scores between $\langle \phi'_{bc}, \phi_{bc} \rangle$ and $\langle \phi'_{sc}, \phi_{sc} \rangle$ are above specific threshold values ($\hat{\alpha_{bc}}$ and $\hat{\alpha_{sc}}$).
   Design decision: What are the optimal values of similarity thresholds ($\hat{\alpha_{bc}}$ and $\hat{\alpha_{sc}}$)?
   (c) Determine whether T is a irrelevant-TPL or not for the given application.
   Design decision: How is the nature of T determined?

3.2 Design Considerations in Our Approach

In this section, we address the design decisions taken while implementing our approach.

Collecting TPLs from MavenCentral and Pypi. The libraries used for training our models (named Lib2Vec) were taken from MavenCentral and Pypi software repository hosts. We use MavenCentral to fetch Java-TPLs and Pypi for Python-TPLs. We choose these portals as these are the public hosts for a wide variety of popular Java and Python libraries. Further, MavenCentral categorizes the Java libraries based on the functionality provided by the libraries. However, our method is not dependent on MavenCentral or Pypi; the TPLs could be sourced from reliable providers. To collect the TPLs, we perform the following steps:

1. Crawl the page https://mvnrepository.com/open-source and https://pypi.org/, and download the latest versions of TPLs in JAR and .rar (or .zip) formats, respectively. We download top k (=3) libraries listed under each category at MavenCentral. Similarly, we downloaded a random collection of python TPLs from PyPi. Pypi categorizes the TPLs based on different programming languages and frameworks used while developing them. While collecting the TPLs, we made sure to download Python libraries belonging to different frameworks to obtain a heterogeneous TPL dataset. Further, we applied the following constraints to obtain a useful (non-trivial) collection of TPLs:
   (a) *Size constraint:* The size of library should be greater than a threshold ($\geq$9 KB). Please note that repository size here stands for the total size of only the source files present in the repository. All the binary files such as multimedia and libraries are excluded.
   (b) *Source file count constraint:* The repository should contain at least one source file written in Java or Python.
   (c) *Reputation constraint:* The repository should have earned $\geq$1 star. This constraint was applied to ensure that the selected repositories are popular and are being used by a minimum number of programmers.
2. Extract and save in a database table the metadata associated with the downloaded TPLs. The metadata includes details of the TPL, such as the category, tags, and usage stats.

Rationale for Choosing PVA for Training Models. We train Lib2Vec models using PVA on the source code and bytecode textual forms of the .class files obtained by the decompilation and disassembly of various JAR TPLs. In case of Python-TPLs (available in .zip or .rar formats), we directly obtain the source files by uncompressing them. We then obtain the bytecode by first performing the compilation and then the disassembly process as shown in Fig. 1, and discussed in Sect. 1.2. For our experiments, we train language-specific and type-specific PVA models, i.e., a Lib2Vec model trained on python source code M^p_{sc}, a Lib2Vec model trained on python bytecode M^p_{bc}, and similarly for Java (M^j_{sc}, M^j_{bc}). The key reasons for choosing PVA are i) It allows us to compute the fixed-length vectors that accurately represent the source code samples. Keeping the length of vectors same for every source code sample is critical for implementing an efficient and fast system. ii) Recent works [1] propose a close variant of PVA, and have proven that it is possible to compute accurate vector representations of source code and that such vectors can be very useful in computing semantic similarity between two source code samples.

Tuning Parameters for PVA. Performance, in terms of accuracy, efficiency, and speed of PVA, is determined by its input parameters such as β, γ, and ψ (see Table 1). Therefore, one of the major tasks is to select the optimal values of β, γ, and ψ that can result in the best performing Lib2Vec models ($\hat{M}^j_{bc}, \hat{M}^j_{sc}, \hat{M}^p_{bc}, \hat{M}^p_{sc}$). The experiments' details to determine β, γ, and ψ are provided in the Appendix.

Rationale for Using the Decompilation and Disassembly Transformations. It is necessary to derive a "normalized" and obfuscation-resilient textual form of the source files to compute a reliable vector representation. The normalization applies a consistent naming of symbols while preserving the semantics and structure of the code. We use the decompilation (*giving a source code text*) and disassembly (*giving a bytecode text*) as transformations to extract such normalized textual forms of .class (or source) files.

Employing the Use of Vector Representations for Performing Similarity Detection Between TPLs. To determine the similarity between libraries efficiently, we create a database (D) of vectors. These vectors correspond to the source files present in a target repository of libraries (such as MavenCentral, or an in-house repository maintained by an organization). We obtain the vector representations for both the source code and bytecode of source files present in TPLs using suitably trained PVA models and store them in D. The PVA vectors enable fast and efficient detection of TPL similarity.

Computing the Threshold Similarity Measure $\hat{\alpha}$. Our method detects two libraries' similarity by inferring the similarity scores for source files contained in those libraries. To check if two source file vectors are similar or not, we compute their cosine similarity[6]. An important design decision in this context is:

For reliably detecting a library, what is the acceptable value of Lib2Vec similarity scores for decompiled source code and bytecode inputs?

[6] https://bit.ly/2RZ3W5L.

We deem two source files (.java or .py files) as highly similar or identical when the similarity score for the files is higher than a threshold value $\hat{\alpha}$. Note: In these comparisons, we compare the files written in the same language only. The value of $\hat{\alpha}$ is determined by running several experiments to measure similarity scores for independent testing samples. The details of the experiments are discussed in the Appendix.

Determining the Nature of an Unseen TPL T for a given Application A. To determine if a given TPL (T) is "irrelevant-TPL" for an application (A), we leverage the best performing Lib2Vec models ($\hat{M}_{bc}$ and $\hat{M}_{sc}$) and the vectors database D.

If L contains .class or .py files depicting considerable similarity ($\geq\hat{\alpha}$) with the "available TPLs," it is deemed to be as "likely-to-be-relevant" for A. If for at least N source files in T, the similarity scores are $\geq\hat{\alpha}$, we label T as a *likely-to-be-relevant* TPL for A, else a *irrelevant-TPL*. In our experiments, we take N as half of the count of source files present in T. For a more strict matching, a higher value of N can be set. The complete steps for the detection procedure are listed in Algorithm 1.

Selection of the Top-Similar "available TPLs": We explain it with an example. Suppose we have four "available Java TPLs", with $C := \{$M1.jar, M2.jar, M3.jar, M4.jar$\}$, such that these contain 15, 6, 10, and 10 .class files, respectively. Now, D will contain the PVA vectors corresponding to the source code and bytecode representations of all the .class files present in all the JARs in C. Next, suppose we want to test a JAR file Foo.jar that contains ten .class files, and that we have the following similarity scenarios:

1. All ten .class files of *Foo.jar* are present in M1.jar.
2. All six .class files of *M2.jar* are present in Foo.jar.
3. Seven out of ten .class files of *M3.jar* are present in Foo.jar.
4. For *M4.jar*, none of these files is identical to those present in Foo.jar, but they have similarity scores higher than the threshold.

Which of the JAR files (M1–M4) listed above will be determined as the most similar to Foo.jar?

Our approach determines the most-similar JAR file by measuring the total number of distinct .class file matches. So with this logic, the similarity ordering for Foo.jar is M1, M4, M3, M2.

In this setting, determining the similarity of two JARs is akin to comparing two sets for similarity. Here the items of the *sets* would be the PVA vectors representing .class files. We apply the following approach to determine the TPL-similarity:

1. For each .class c in Foo.jar, find each record $r \in D$ such that the similarity score between c and r is higher than a threshold. Let $R \subset D$ denote the set of all such matched records.
2. Find the set Y of distinct JARs to which each $r \in R$ belongs.
3. Sort Y by the number of classes present in R.
4. Select the top-k items from Y as similar JARs to Foo.jar.

Algorithm 1 presents the above logic in more detail. The same algorithm works for both the JAR-based and Python-based TPLs.

Algorithm 1. Steps for determining the nature of a TPL T.

Input: $T :=$ A TPL file provided as input by an end-user.
$L :=$ Set of considered programming languages, {Java, Python}
$\hat{M^j_{bc}}, \hat{M^j_{sc}}, \hat{M^p_{bc}}, \hat{M^p_{sc}} :=$ The best performing Lib2Vec models.
$\alpha^{\hat{j}}_{sc}, \alpha^{\hat{j}}_{bc}, \alpha^{\hat{p}}_{sc}, \alpha^{\hat{p}}_{bc} :=$ Threshold similarity scores for source code and bytecode for Python and Java.
$\phi^{\hat{j}}_{sc}, \phi^{\hat{j}}_{bc}, \phi^{\hat{p}}_{sc}, \phi^{\hat{p}}_{bc} :=$ Reference PVA vectors for source code and bytecode for Python and Java.
$D :=$ Database containing the vector representations of source files in C.
Output: $d :=$ Decision on the nature of J.
/*Please see Table 1 for notation*/
$S_{sc} := S_{bc} := NULL$
for all .class files or .py files $f \in T$ **do**
  l := Detect Programming Language of f.
  Obtain the PVA vectors $\langle \phi^l_{bc}, \phi^l_{sc} \rangle$ for $\langle f_{bc}, f_{sc} \rangle$ using $\langle \hat{M^l_{bc}}, \hat{M^l_{sc}} \rangle$, where $l \in L$.
  Query the database D for top-k most similar vectors to ϕ^l_{sc} and ϕ^l_{bc}.
  $\alpha^l_{sc}, \alpha^l_{bc} :=$ Compute the cosine similarity between $\langle \phi^l_{sc}, \phi^{\hat{l}}_{sc} \rangle$ and $\langle \phi^l_{bc}, \phi^{\hat{l}}_{bc} \rangle$.
  $S_{sc} := S_{sc} \cup \langle \alpha_{sc} \rangle$
  $S_{bc} := S_{bc} \cup \langle \alpha_{bc} \rangle$
end for

$$d := \begin{cases} \text{relevant} & \text{if for at least } N \text{ source file records in both } S_{sc} \text{ and } S_{bc} \text{ individually, } \alpha^l_{sc} > \alpha^{\hat{l}}_{sc} \text{ and } \alpha^l_{bc} > \alpha^{\hat{l}}_{bc} \text{ respectively.} \\ \text{irrelevant} & \text{otherwise} \end{cases}$$

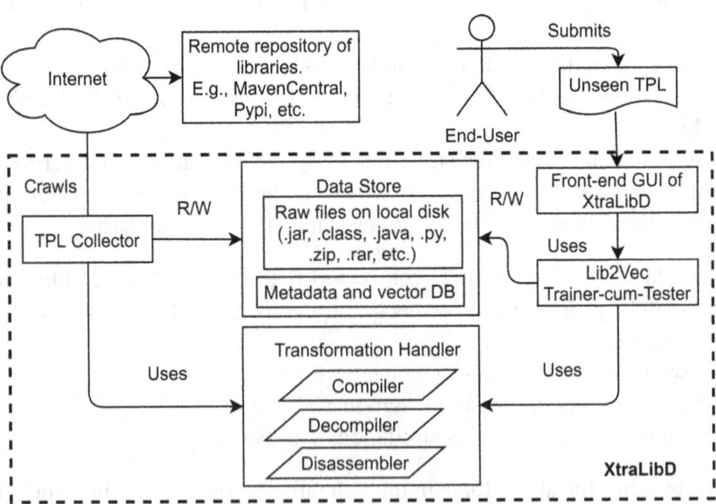

Fig. 2. Logical structure of the proposed system [10].

3.3 Implementation Details

The logical structure of the proposed system is shown in Fig. 2. All components of the system have been developed using the Python programming language. Details of each of the components are as follows:

1. **TPL File Collector.** We developed a crawler program to collect the TPLs and the metadata associated with each file. The files were downloaded from www.mavencentral.com and https://pypi.org/, reputed public repositories of Open Source Software (OSS) Java and Python libraries. MavenCentral has about 15 million indexed artifacts, which are classified into about 150 categories. Some examples of the categories include JSON Libraries, Logging Frameworks, and Cache Implementations. The metadata about each JAR includes the following main items: License, Categories, HomePage, Date of Availability, Files, Used By (count, and links to projects using a library).
   Similarly, Pypi has $300 + K$ python projects classified by programming languages, topics, frameworks, etc., used while developing them. Django, Dash, CherryPy, Flask, and IDLE are some of the example Pypi frameworks. The metadata about each Python project on Pypi comprises release-history, project readme, the count of stars, forks, pull requests, Date of Release, Latest Version, HomePage, License, Author information, Maintainers information, Programming Environment, Programming Framework, Intended Audience, Operating System, and Programming Language used.
2. **Transformation Handler.** This module provides the transformations and preprocessing of the source files present in the input TPL files (in JAR or .zip/.rar formats). Three types of transformations implemented are a) Decompilation of the .class file present in JAR files to produce a corresponding Java source, b) Compilation of the .py files present in .rar/.zip Python TPLs to produce the corresponding compiled .pyc files, and c) Disassembling the .class and .pyc files into human-readable text files containing bytecode instructions for the .class files and .pyc files, respectively. We used the Procyon [24] tool for performing the decompilation and disassembling of the .class files. The respective transformation output is further preprocessed to remove comments and adjust token whitespaces before storing it as a text file in a local repository. The preprocessing was done for the decompiled Java source to ensure that the keywords and special tokens such as parentheses and operators were delimited by whitespace. Similar, we removed the comments from the python source code (in .py) files during the preprocessing phase. The preprocessing provides proper tokenization of the source into meaningful "vocabulary words" expected by the PVA.
3. **Lib2Vec Trainer-cum-tester.** We use an open-source implementation of the PVA – called Gensim [8], to train our Lib2Vec models. The Lib2Vec trainer-cum-tester module's primary task is to:
   (a) Train the Lib2Vec models using bytecode and source code produced by various disassembling, compilation, and decompilation operations.
   (b) Infer the vectors for unseen .class files' bytecode and source code by using the respective models.

4. **Metadata and the Vectors' Database.** The information about libraries fetched from MavenCentral is stored in a relational database. The following are the essential data items stored in the database:
   (a) Name, category, version, size, and usage count of the library.
   (b) Location of the library on the local disk as well as a remote host.
   (c) For each .class file f in a JAR or .py file f in a Python project:
      i. The fully qualified name of the f.
      ii. Sizes of f, and the textual form of its decompiled Java source code (f^j_{sc}), python source code (f^p_{sc}), and the disassembled bytecode for both Java and Python TPLs (f^j_{bc}, f^p_{bc}).
      iii. Inferred PVA vectors $\langle \phi^l_{sc}, \phi^l_{bc} \rangle$, $l \in L$ for the above files.
      iv. Cosine similarity scores $\alpha^{\hat{l}}_{sc}$ and $\alpha^{\hat{l}}_{bc}$ between $\langle \phi^l_{sc}, \alpha^{\hat{l}}_{sc} \rangle$ and $\langle \phi^l_{bc}, \alpha^{\hat{l}}_{bc} \rangle$, respectively. The values $\alpha^{\hat{l}}_{sc}$ and $\alpha^{\hat{l}}_{bc}$ are scalar.

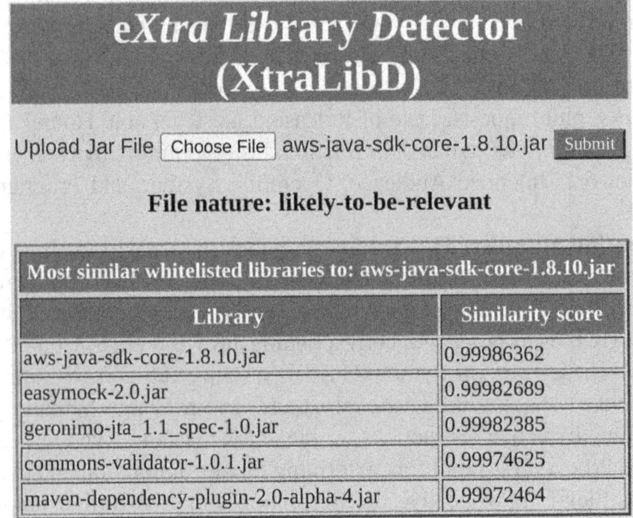

Fig. 3. Top similar TPLs detected by XtraLibD.

5. **XtraLibD's GUI:** The user interface of XtraLibD is a web-based application. End-user uploads a TPL using this GUI, which is then processed by our tool at the server-side. The tool requires the TPLs in JAR, .zip, or .rar formats as input. Figure 3 displays the results for a test file[7] submitted to our tool. As shown by the figure, XtraLibD displays the input file's nature and the top-k (k = 5) similar essential libraries along with the corresponding similarity scores. As we achieve higher accuracy with the source code Lib2Vec models than the bytecode models (discussed in the Appendix), we use the best performing source code Lib2Vec model for developing our tool.

[7] https://bit.ly/2yb2eHY.

4 Experimental Evaluation

The primary goal of our experiments is to validate the correctness and accuracy of our tool – XtraLibD. For a given input file, XtraLibD labels it as ⟨ likely-to-be-irrelevant-TPL, likely-to-be-non-irrelevant-TPL⟩, and lists the top-k similar libraries and the respective similarity scores shown in Fig. 3. The efficacy of our tool depends on its accuracy in performing the task of detecting similar TPLs. XtraLibD achieves this by detecting the similarity between the PVA vectors of the .class files present in the TPLs. The Lib2Vec models used by XtraLibD are responsible for generating different PVA vectors. Therefore, we perform various parameter-tuning experiments to obtain the best performing Lib2Vec models (discussed in the Appendix). To evaluate the performance of XtraLibD, we develop a test-bed using the TPLs collected from MavenCentral and PyPi (discussed in Sect. 4.1) and perform the following experiments:

1. Test the performance of Lib2Vec models (and thus XtraLibD) in performing the TPL-detection task (discussed in the Appendix).
2. Compare the performance of XtraLibD with the existing TPL-detection tools (discussed in Sect. 4.2).

4.1 Test-Bed Setup

To compare the performance of XtraLibD on Java-based and Python-based tools, we setup Java and Python testbeds separately for our experiments. In this section, we provide the details of setting these testbeds.

Developing Test-Bed for Comparison with Java-Based Tools. We crawled https://mvnrepository.com/open-source?p=**PgNo**, where **PgNo** varied from 1 to 15. Each page listed ten different categories from the list of most popular ones, and under each category, the top-three libraries were listed.

We started by downloading one JAR file for each of the above libraries. That is, a total of $15 \times 10 \times 3 = 450$ JAR files were fetched. In addition to the above JAR files, we also included the JDK1.8 runtime classes (`rt.jar`). After removing the invalid files, we were left with 97 JAR files containing 38839 .class files.

We chose random 76 JAR files out of 97 plus the `rt.jar` for training the Lib2Vec models, and the remaining 20 JAR files were used for testing. We used only those .class files for training whose size was at least 1kB since such tiny .class files do not give sufficient Java and byte code, which is necessary to compute a sufficiently unique vector representation of the .class contents. The training JARs had 33,292 .class files, out of which only 30,427 were of size 1kB or bigger. The testing JARs had 4,033 .class files.

Developing Test-Bed for Comparison with Python-Based Tools. We crawled https://pypi.org/search/?c=Programming+Language+%3A%3A+Python&o=&q=&page=PgNo, where **PgNo** varied from 1 to 500. Since Pypi also categorizes the projects based on the *Developing Framework*, we made sure to select top 10 libraries belonging to

Table 2. TPL Data summary.

Item	Java count [10]	Python count
Downloaded TPLs	450	43,711
TPLs selected for experiments	97	43,711
TPLs used for training	76 + 1 (`rt.jar`)	30,597+ 1 (`rt.zip`)
TPLs used for testing	20	13,113
.class (or .py) files used for training	30427	478,031
.class (or .py) files used for generating test pairs of bytecode and source code	4033	204,870
Unique pairs of bytecode files used for testing	20,100	200,000
Unique pairs of source code files used for testing	20,100	200,000

each framework on different pages, resulting in a total of 43,711 python TPLs. By applying the constraints during the selection of these libraries (discussed in Sect. 3.2), we made sure that each library contains atleast one source file written in python. These libraries were available in .zip or .rar formats, and by uncompressing them we obtained 42,497,414 .py files. Out of the total 42,497,414 .py files, only 682,901 .py had size ≥1 kB, which we considered for training and testing our python Lib2Vec models. From these 682,901 .py files, we choose random 30,598 .py for training and rest 13,113 for test our python Lib2Vec models.

Note: We chose the minimum source file size as 1 kB because we observed that the files smaller than 1 kB did not significantly train an accurate Lib2Vec model. A summary of the TPL data is shown in Table 2. Note: the training and testing of Lib2Vec models were performed on the source code and bytecode extracted from the respective number of source files.

4.2 Performance Comparison of XtraLibD with the Existing TPL-detection Tools

To the best of our knowledge, no work leverages the direction of using code similarity (in TPLs) and the vector representations of code to detect the irrelevant-TPLs for Java and Python applications. We present our tool's performance comparison (XtraLibD) with some of the prominently used tools, viz., LiteRadar, LibD, and LibScout, DepClean, JIngredient, Autoflake, and PyCln. The details about these tools have been discussed in Sect. 2. We already conducted the experiments with LiteRadar, LibD, and LibScout in our previous research work [10], and extend our previous work by providing the TPL-detection support for python-based TPLs. In this section, we provide the details of new experiments performed with some of the recent Java-based and Python-based TPL detection tools, viz., DepClean, JIngredient, Autoflake, PyCln, and also a summarized comparison of performance results obtained in our previous comparisons [10] with LiteRadar, LibD, and LibScout.

Though PyCln and Autoflake work in detection of used/ unused import TPLs, and not the detection of TPLs, we included them as in our research, we found them to be the closest available python tools working with TPLs. For experiment with PyCln and Autoflake we experimented by developing different import scenarios, for instance, direct imports, secondary imports, and both with used and unused cases.

Objective. To compare the performance of XtraLibD with the existing TPL-detection tools. Through this experiment, we address the following:

How does XtraLibD perform in comparison to the existing TPL-detection tools? What is the effect on storage and response time? Is XtraLibD resilient to the source code obfuscations?

Procedure. To perform this experiment, we invited professional programmers and asked them to evaluate our tool. One hundred and one of them participated in the experiment. We had a mixture of programmers from final year computer science undergraduates, postgraduates, and the IT industry with experience between 0–6 years. The participants had considerable knowledge of Java programming language, software engineering fundamentals, and several Java and Python applications. The experiment was performed in a controlled industrial environment. We provided access to our tool for performing this experiment by sharing it at https://www.doi.org/10.5281/zenodo.5179747. The tools' performance was evaluated based on their *accuracy*, *response time*, and the *storage requirement* in performing the TPL-detection task. We compute the tool's storage requirement of the tools by measuring the memory space occupied in storing the relevant "reference TPLs." The TPL-detection tools – LibD, LibScout, and LibRadar, require the inputs in an Android application PacKage (APK) format. Therefore, APK files corresponding to the JAR versions of the TPLs were generated using the Android Studio toolkit[8] (listed in Step 13 of Algorithm 2). Similarly, DepClean requires the input TPLs in maven project format and JIngredient in JAR file format. Both PyCln and Autoflake require the input files in .py format.

The programmers were requested to perform the following steps:

1. Randomly select a sample of 3–5 TPLs from the test-bed developed for the experiments (discussed in Sect. 4.1).
2. Test the TPLs using Algorithm 2.
3. Report the tools' accuracy and response time, as observed from the experiment(s).

Evaluation Criteria. In the context of the TPL-detection, we define the accuracy as [10]:

$$Accuracy = \frac{Number\ of\ TPLs\ correctly\ detected}{Total\ number\ of\ TPLs\ tested} \tag{1}$$

[8] https://developer.android.com/studio.

Algorithm 2. Steps for performing the comparison.

Input: C = Set of TPLs (T) downloaded randomly from MavenCentral and Pypi.
X = Set of XML files required as input by LibScout.
$\hat{M}^j_{bc}, \hat{M}^j_{sc}, \hat{M}^p_{bc}, \hat{M}^p_{sc}$:= The best performing Lib2Vec models for Java and Python.
$\hat{\phi}^j_{sc}, \hat{\phi}^j_{bc}, \hat{\phi}^p_{sc}, \hat{\phi}^p_{bc}$:= Reference PVA vectors for source code and bytecode.
/*Please see Table 1 for notation*/
Output: Terminal outputs generated by the tools.
$F^p_{sc} := F^p_{bc} := F^j_{sc} := F^j_{bc} := NULL$
for all TPLs $T \in C$ **do**
  for all .class and .py files $f \in T$ **do**
    l := Detect the programming language of f_u.
    f^l_{bc}, f^l_{sc} := Obtain the textual forms of the bytecode and source code of f_l.
    f'_{bc}, f'_{sc} := Modify f^l_{bc} and f^l_{sc} using transformations listed in Section 4.1.
    $F^l_{sc} := F^l_{sc} \cup \langle f'_{sc} \rangle$
    $F^l_{bc} := F^l_{bc} \cup \langle f'_{bc} \rangle$
  end for
end for
Y := Convert F^l_{sc} into the respective input formats required by the tools.
Test with the considered tools using X and Y.
Test F^l_{sc} and F^l_{bc} with XtraLibD using Algorithm 1.

Similarly, for the detection of used/unused TPL imports, we define accuracy as follows:

$$Accuracy = \frac{Number\ of\ correctly\ identified(used/unused)\ TPL\ imports}{Total\ number\ of\ TPL\ imports} \tag{2}$$

By a correctly identified TPL import we imply to a scenario when a used import is labelled (or identified or marked) as a used import, and an unused import is labelled as an uned import by a considered tool.

Results and Observations. Table 3 lists the *accuracy*, *response time*, and *storage space requirement* values observed for the tools. We now present a brief discussion of our results.

Accuracy of the TPL-Detection Tools. Some of the key observations from the experiments are:

1. LiteRadar cannot detect the transformed versions of the TPLs and fails in some cases when tested with the TPLs containing *no transformations*. For instance, it cannot detect exact matches in the case of zookeeper-3.3.0.jar library[9] and kotlin-reflect-1.3.61.jar library[10].

[9] http://bit.ly/2VymUmA.
[10] http://bit.ly/32MvkZe.

Table 3. Performance comparison of various TPL-detection tools.

TPL detection tools	Performance Metrics values		
	Accuracy (in %)	Response Time (in seconds)	Storage requirement (in MBs)
LiteRadar	68.97	12.29	1.64
LibScout	25.23	6.46	3.93
LibD	85.06	100.92	12.59
DepClean	99	4.458	Not applicable
JIngredient	99.75	0.001	1000
Autoflake	99.29	0.002	Not applicable
PyCln	99.29	0.002	Not applicable
XtraLibD (Java)	99.48	12.043	1.52
XtraLibD (Python)	99.5	12.043	401.94

2. LibScout detects the *TPLs without any transformations* but suffers from package-name obfuscations as it cannot detect the modified versions of TPLs containing package-name transformations.
3. LibD substantially outperforms LibRadar and LibScout in capturing the similarity between the TPLs but does not comment on their nature, i.e., ⟨likely-to-be-irrelevant-TPL, likely-to-be-non-irrelevant-TPL⟩. It also comes with an additional cost of manually comparing the TPLs with the "reference set."
4. DepClean is able to detect 99% of the direct dependency cases, but is unable to detect transitive dependency cases as observed by us and an existing research [21].
5. JIngredient detects the TPLs and their class reuse with an accuracy of 99.75%. However, its dependence on class names to form the class signatures used to detect TPL similarity, makes it prone to obfuscations. Also, its use is constrained by huge storage and processing requirements (discussed shortly in detail).
6. Since PyCln and Autoflake do not perform TPL detection and both perform the detection of used/ unused TPL imports, we analyze them independently and compare them with each other. In our experiments, PyCln was unable to detect the import statements present in a try-except structure, whereas Autoflake was successful in detecting them. Further, both the tools miss the import statements where one library imports another but does not use all the models of it. For instance, when a file A.py imports from B.py (as from B import *), and does not use all the modules imported in B.
7. XtraLibD detects the TPLs for 99.5% of the test cases. As observed from the table values, XtraLibD outperforms LiteRadar, LibScout, and LibD with the improvement scores of 30.33%, 74.5%, and 14.1%, respectively. Though XtraLibD has a comparable accuracy rate as DepClean, JIngredient, Autoflake, and PyCln, its benefits in terms of low storage requirements and small response time make it more feasible for use. Also, XtraLibD performs equally well on the obfuscated test-inputs, the results validate that it is resilient to the considered obfuscation types.

Storage Requirement of the TPL-Detection Tools. XtraLibD leverages the PVA vectors to detect the similarity among the TPLs, while the tools used for comparison, viz., LibD, LibScout, and LiteRadar, use the "reference lists" of TPLs. These tools contain the "reference lists" of TPLs as files within their tool packages. As observed from the storage requirement values, XtraLibD has the lowest storage requirement due to the vector representation format. XtraLibD reduces the storage requirement by 87.93% compared to LibD, 61.28% compared to LibScout, and 7.3% compared to LiteRadar. As DepClean is based on the TPL dependency usage rather than the comparison with a reference list of libraries, storage requirement comparison is not applicable to it. Similarly, PyCln and AutoFlake are based on code analysis for TPL import detection, hence the storage requirement comparison is not applicable in their case.

JIngredients performs TPL detection by using the source code class names as signatures to match with a reference database for determining TPL reuse. However, JIngredients has a storage requirement of 1 GB for its database, and needs a high performance hardware and memory support to implement its approach. It was originally implemented on a high end workstation with 2 Six core processors with a 64 GB RAM on a large corpus size of 1 GB (which itself was constructed from an original repository data of size 77.8 GB with a total of 172,232 JAR files). To perform our experiments, we used a database of 214 JAR files from which 192 JAR files were used in JIngredient's database. We performed the experiments on a machine having an AMD Ryzen 5 4600H 3.0 Ghz 6 Cores 12 Threads processor with an 8 GB RAM. JIngredients was unable to detect any instances of reuse on this machine, though it is able to identify the classes within the JAR files. Thus, JIngredient's working is constrained by its high storage and processing requirement. However, XtraLibD has only 1.52 MBs storage requirement for its Java version at a comparable accuracy rate as JIngredient. Thus, when compared in terms of storage requirement, XtraLibD outperforms JIngredient by 99.85%.

Response Time of the TPL-Detection Tools. For DepClean, the average response time mentioned in Table 3 includes only the time involved in running the actual dependency analysis on the maven projects. XtraLibD has an average response time of 12.043 s with a 61.37% improvement in the response time over LibD while delivering higher response times than the rest of the tools.

4.3 Threats to Validity

For developing our Lib2Vec models and D, we utilize a subset of Java TPLs (i.e., JAR files) present in the MavenCentral repository, and a subset of Python TPLs from Pypi.org. We assume that these TPLs cover a reasonably wide variety of Java and Python code such that the Lib2Vec models that we train on them will be accurate. However, there could still be many other Java and Python code types that could have improved the Lib2Vec models' accuracy. For training the Lib2Vec models, we obtain the normalized textual forms of the source code and bytecode representations of the .class files present in the JAR files and .py files present in Python TPLs (in .zip/ .rar/ /tar.gz forms). We obtain the source code and bytecode by using the compilation, decompilation and disassembly operations. Therefore, our Lib2Vec models' accuracy is subject to the accuracy of the decompilation and disassembly operations.

Next, we treat an unseen TPL that shows considerable similarity with the set of "available TPLs" as *likely-to-be-non-irrelevant-TPLs*. Thus, the labeling of a TPL as *likely-to-be-non-irrelevant-TPL* or *irrelevant-TPL* is strongly dependent on its use in the considered application. We do not consider the TPL-usage as per now, but have included it as part of our future work.

While training the Lib2Vec models, we consider only the .class and .py files of size 1 kB or larger. However, there may exist Java and Python libraries where the average class size is lower than this limit. Excluding such a group of TPLs from the training might give inaccurate results when the input TPL being checked happens in such a group. The main reason for excluding such tiny source files is that they do not give sufficient Java and byte code, which is necessary to compute a sufficiently unique vector representation of the source code contents.

By reviewing the literature [5, 15, 17], we realized that there are a significant amount of TPL-detection tools designed for Android Applications, requiring the input file in an APK format. To the best of our knowledge, very few tools perform the TPL-detection for software applications existing in JAR format or for Python applications. Therefore, we converted our TPLs present from JAR to APK format using the Android Studio toolkit and choose LibD, LibRadar, and LibScout – some of the popular TPL-detection tools for our comparison. However, due to the fast advances of research in this area, we might have missed some interesting TPL-detection tool that works with the JAR file formats.

5 Conclusions

Software Development is immensely supported by the functionalities provided by various TPLs. However, as the software progresses through various releases, there tend to remain some irrelevant TPLs in the software distributable. These irrelevant TPLs lead to the unnecessary consumption of various resources such as CPU cycles, memory, etc., and thus its desirable to remove them. We propose a novel extra-library detector (XtraLibD) tool that detects the irrelevant libraries present in an application distributable. XtraLibD detects these libraries by performing code similarity detection with a reference dataset of 450 Java and 43,711 Python TPLs collected from MavenCentral. We use PVA to train language-specific code similarity detection model on the source code and byte code of these MavenCentral libraries. To the best of our knowledge, we are the first to apply PVA for detecting code similarity in TPLs.

We used source code and byte code representations of TPLs to train our models as these preserve the semantics and are free from source code obfuscations. We successfully leveraged the semantics-preserving Java decompilers (and Python compilers) to transform the binary .class files and .pyc files into an obfuscation-invariant textual form, viz., source code and byte code. We verified our approach's efficacy by testing it with more than 30,000 .class files and 478,031 .py files, where we have achieved detection accuracy above 99.48% and an F1 score of 0.968 for Java, and 99.5%

accuracy for Python. XtraLibD outperforms the existing TPL-detection tools, such as LibScout, LiteRadar, and LibD, with an accuracy improvement of 74.5%, 30.33%, and 14.1%, respectively. XtraLibD achieves a storage reduction of 87.93% over LibD and of 99.85% over JIngredient.

As part of the future work, we plan to explore the direction of actual TPL-usage within the application to detect the unused parts of TPL-code. The idea can be leveraged to develop various software artifacts for automating the SDLC activities, such as software code review, source code recommendation, and code clone detection.

Appendix

Objective. The objective here is to seek an answer to our questions:

1. *For reliably detecting a library, what is the acceptable value of Lib2Vec similarity scores for source code and bytecode inputs?*
2. *Does the threshold similarity score ($\hat{\alpha}$) vary with the input parameters (β, γ, and ψ) of PVA?*
3. *What are the optimal values for the PVA tuning-parameters β, γ, and ψ?*

Please refer to Table 1 for notation definitions.

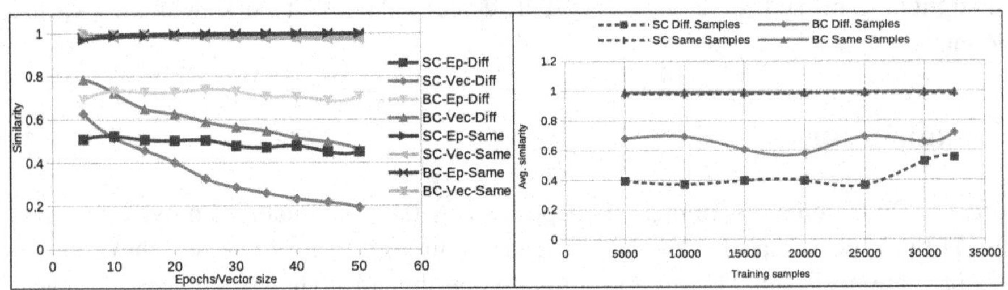

Fig. 4. Variation of *average similarity* with PVA tuning-parameters [10].

Table 4. Scenarios for training Lib2Vec models using PVA [10].

Parameters varied			
Epochs β	Vector size γ	Training samples ψ	Models
Fixed at 10	Fixed at 10	Vary 5000 to- `CorpusSize` in- steps of 5000	`CorpusSize` ÷ 5000
Vary 5- to 50 in- steps of 5	Fixed at 10	Fixed at- `CorpusSize`	10
Fixed at 10	Vary 5- to 50 in- steps of 5	Fixed at- `CorpusSize`	10

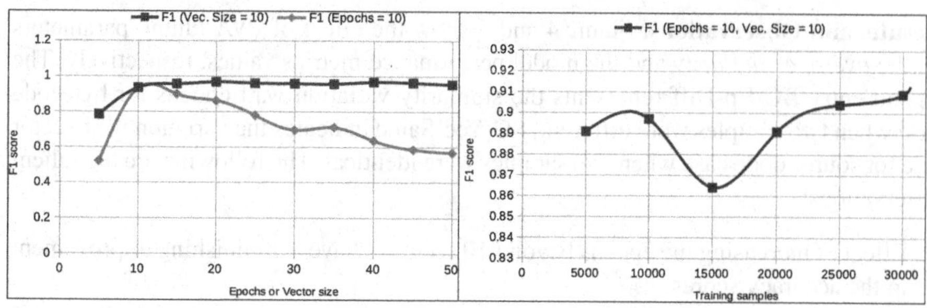

Fig. 5. Performance metrics with PVA models trained on *source code* [10].

Test-Bed Setup: Using the test partition of the test-bed developed in Sect. 4.1, we generate a test dataset (Y) containing $same, different$ file pairs in 50:50 ratio. Further, to check if our tool is resilient to source code transformations, we test it for the following three scenarios:

1. *Package-name transformations:* Package names of the classes present in TPLs are modified.
2. *Function (or method) transformations:* Function names are changed in the constituent classes' source code, and function bodies are relocated within a class.
3. *Source code transformations:* Names of various variables are changed, source code statements are inserted, deleted, or modified, such that it does not alter the semantics of the source code. For instance, adding print statements at various places in the source file.

We test Lib2Vec models' efficacy in detecting similar source code pairs (or bytecode pairs) using Y.

Procedure. The salient steps are [10]:

1. F_{bc}, F_{sc} := Obtain the textual forms of bytecode and source code present in source files of training JARs of the test-bed (developed in Sect. 4.1).
2. For each parameter combination $\pi \in Z$ (listed in Table 4):
   (a) $S^{\pi}_{sc} := S^{\pi}_{bc} := NULL$
   (b) $M^{\pi}_{bc}, M^{\pi}_{sc}$:= Train the Lib2Vec models using F_{bc}, F_{sc}.
   (c) Save M^{π}_{bc} and M^{π}_{sc} to disk.
   (d) For each file pairs $\langle p_i, p_j \rangle \in Y$:
      i. ϕ_i, ϕ_j := Obtain PVA vectors for p_i, p_j using $M(\pi)$
      ii. $\alpha_{i,j}$:= Compute cosine similarity between $\langle \phi_i, \phi_j \rangle$
      iii. if $p_i == p_j$: $S_{same} = S_{same} \cup \langle \alpha_{i,j} \rangle$
      iv. else: $S_{different} = S_{different} \cup \langle \alpha_{i,j} \rangle$
   (e) $\hat{\alpha^{\pi}_{bc}}, \hat{\alpha^{\pi}_{sc}}$:= Obtain the average similarity scores using S^{π}_{bc} and S^{π}_{sc} and save them.
   (f) Using the $\hat{\alpha^{\pi}_{bc}}, \hat{\alpha^{\pi}_{sc}}$ as thresholds, compute the accuracy of M^{π}_{bc} and M^{π}_{sc}.
   (g) Plot the variation of $\hat{\alpha_{bc}}, \hat{\alpha_{sc}}$, the accuracy of PVA models for different values of β, γ, and ψ used in the experiment, and analyze.

Results and Observations. Figure 4 and 5 show the effect of PVA tuning-parameters on the *average similarity* and the model performance metrics values, respectively. The legend entry BC-Ep-Diff represents the similarity variation w.r.t epochs for bytecode case when two samples were different. SC-Vec-Same indicates the variation w.r.t vector size for source code case when two samples were identical. The following are the salient observations:

1. Effect of increasing the epochs beyond 10 seems to have a diminishing improvement in the accuracy scores.
2. A noticeable decrease in similarity scores was observed by increasing the vector count beyond 5, and the epochs count beyond 10.
3. As anticipated, the accuracy (indicated by F1 scores[11]) improves with the size of training samples.

Therefore, we take $\hat{\alpha_{sc}} = 0.98359$ and $\hat{\alpha_{bc}} = 0.99110$ as the similarity threshold values for source code data and bytecode data, respectively. Further, the best accuracy (99.48% for source code and 99.41% for bytecode) is achieved with the Lib2Vec model trained using 30427 samples, 10 epochs, and the vector size of 10. The precision and recall values, in this case, were 99.00% and 99.00%, respectively, resulting in an F1 score of 99% for the source code case. As we achieve the highest accuracy scores at $\beta = \gamma = 10$, we take these as the optimal input parameter values for PVA.

References

1. Alon, U., Zilberstein, M., Levy, O., Yahav, E.: Code2vec: learning distributed representations of code. Proc. ACM Program. Lang. **3**(POPL), 40:1–40:29 (2019)
2. Alqattan, H.: Pycln (2020). https://hadialqattan.github.io/pycln/. Accessed 09 Aug 2021
3. Desnos, A., Geoffroy Gueguen, S.B.: Welcome to Androguard's Documentation! (2018). https://androguard.readthedocs.io/en/latest/
4. Au, K.W.Y., Zhou, Y.F., Huang, Z., Lie, D.: PScout: analyzing the Android permission specification. In: Proceedings of the 2012 ACM Conference on Computer and Communications Security, pp. 217–228. ACM (2012)
5. Backes, M., Bugiel, S., Derr, E.: Reliable third-party library detection in Android and its security applications. In: Proceedings of the 2016 ACM SIGSAC Conference on Computer and Communications Security, pp. 356–367. ACM (2016)
6. Book, T., Pridgen, A., Wallach, D.S.: Longitudinal analysis of Android ad library permissions. arXiv preprint arXiv:1303.0857 (2013)
7. Chen, K., Liu, P., Zhang, Y.: Achieving accuracy and scalability simultaneously in detecting application clones on Android markets. In: Proceedings of the 36th International Conference on Software Engineering, pp. 175–186. ACM (2014)
8. Dai, A.M., Olah, C., Le, Q.V.: Document embedding with paragraph vectors. In: NIPS Deep Learning Workshop (2015)
9. Davies, J., German, D.M., Godfrey, M.W., Hindle, A.: Software bertillonage. Empir. Softw. Eng. **18**(6), 1195–1237 (2013)
10. Dewan, A., Rao, P.U., Sodhi, B., Kapur, R.: BloatLibD: detecting bloat libraries in Java applications. In: ENASE, pp. 126–137 (2021)

[11] https://bit.ly/3kHqkNg.

11. Feichtner, J., Rabensteiner, C.: Obfuscation-resilient code recognition in Android apps. In: Proceedings of the 14th International Conference on Availability, Reliability and Security, p. 8. ACM (2019)
12. Grace, M.C., Zhou, W., Jiang, X., Sadeghi, A.R.: Unsafe exposure analysis of mobile in-app advertisements. In: Proceedings of the Fifth ACM Conference on Security and Privacy in Wireless and Mobile Networks, pp. 101–112. ACM (2012)
13. Ishio, T., Kula, R.G., Kanda, T., German, D.M., Inoue, K.: Software ingredients: detection of third-party component reuse in Java software release. In: 2016 IEEE/ACM 13th Working Conference on Mining Software Repositories (MSR), pp. 339–350. IEEE (2016)
14. Le, Q., Mikolov, T.: Distributed representations of sentences and documents. In: International Conference on Machine Learning, pp. 1188–1196 (2014)
15. Li, M., et al.: LibD: scalable and precise third-party library detection in Android markets. In: 2017 IEEE/ACM 39th International Conference on Software Engineering (ICSE), pp. 335–346. IEEE (2017)
16. Liu, B., Liu, B., Jin, H., Govindan, R.: Efficient privilege de-escalation for ad libraries in mobile apps. In: Proceedings of the 13th Annual International Conference on Mobile Systems, Applications, and Services, pp. 89–103 (2015)
17. Ma, Z., Wang, H., Guo, Y., Chen, X.: LibRadar: fast and accurate detection of third-party libraries in Android apps. In: Proceedings of the 38th International Conference on Software Engineering Companion, pp. 653–656. ACM (2016)
18. Mitchell, N., Sevitsky, G.: The causes of bloat, the limits of health. In: Proceedings of the 22nd Annual ACM SIGPLAN Conference on Object-Oriented Programming Systems and Applications, pp. 245–260 (2007)
19. Myint, S.: Autoflake (2016). https://pypi.org/project/autoflake/. Accessed 09 Aug 2021
20. Phil Frost, M.A., et al.: Pyflakes (2014). https://pypi.org/project/pyflakes/. Accessed 09 Aug 2021
21. Serena Elisa Ponta, W.F., et al.: The used, the bloated, and the vulnerable: reducing the attack surface of an industrial application (2021)
22. Soto-Valero, C., Harrand, N., Monperrus, M., Baudry, B.: A comprehensive study of bloated dependencies in the maven ecosystem. Empir. Softw. Eng. **26**(3), 1–44 (2021)
23. StackOverflow: Stackoverflow developer survey results 2020: most popular technologies (2020). https://insights.stackoverflow.com/survey/2020#technology
24. Strobel, M.: Procyon: a suite of java metaprogramming tools focused on code generation, analysis, and decompilation, June 2019. https://bitbucket.org/mstrobel/procyon/src/default/
25. Wang, H., Guo, Y., Ma, Z., Chen, X.: Wukong: a scalable and accurate two-phase approach to Android app clone detection. In: Proceedings of the 2015 International Symposium on Software Testing and Analysis, pp. 71–82. ACM (2015)
26. Xu, G., Mitchell, N., Arnold, M., Rountev, A., Sevitsky, G.: Software bloat analysis: finding, removing, and preventing performance problems in modern large-scale object-oriented applications. In: Proceedings of the FSE/SDP Workshop on Future of Software Engineering Research, pp. 421–426 (2010)
27. Zhang, Y., et al.: Detecting third-party libraries in Android applications with high precision and recall. In: 2018 IEEE 25th International Conference on Software Analysis, Evolution and Reengineering (SANER), pp. 141–152. IEEE (2018)

Automation of the Software Development Process from ReLEL Using the Praxeme Approach

Rapatsalahy Miary Andrianjaka[1], Mahatody Thomas[1], Livaniaina Razanakolona[1,4], Ilie Mihaela[2], Razafimahatratra Hajarisena[1], Ilie Sorin[2(✉)], and Razafindrakoto Nicolas Raft[3]

[1] Laboratory for Mathematical and Computer Applied to the Development Systems, University of Fianarantsoa, Fianarantsoa, Madagascar

[2] Department of Computers and Information Technology, University of Craiova, Craiova, Romania
sorin.ilie@software.ucv.ro

[3] Laboratory of Multidisciplinary Applied Research, University of Antananarivo, Antananarivo, Madagascar

[4] Laboratory for Mediations, Informations, Communication and Arts, University of Bordeaux Montaigne, Pessac, France

Abstract. Praxeme is an enterprise methodology designed to overcome the difficulties associated with the construction of enterprise information systems. The aspect that specifies the company's intentions represents the initial phase of the software development process in Praxeme. The use of the eLEL lexicon to express the intentional aspect of Praxeme enables the knowledge in the following aspects to be clarified. However, the logical modeling (logical aspect) from the intentional aspect represented by eLEL is largely lacking in conceptual information to be exploited in the purely IT aspect of Praxeme. In this paper, we propose the use of the ReLEL lexicon to specify the intentional aspect of Praxeme in order to automate the process covering the business and IT aspects of the enterprise. ReLEL is an enterprise terminology database and has precise information concerning the conceptual representation of an information system. For this purpose, we have proposed rules to automate the articulation that covers the intentional, semantic, logical and software aspects of Praxeme. We made use of the ATL and Acceleo language for the implementation of the transformation rules. The result obtained in this article is a SOAP web service of the software aspect of Praxeme.

Keywords: Acceleo · ATL · MDA · Praxeme · Relel · Requirements · Engineering · SOA · SOAP · UML

1 Introduction

Developing a company's information system is a complex task [1]. Among the difficulties is the permanent evolution of needs, which forces the company's information

R. Ali et al. (Eds.): ENASE 2021, CCIS 1556, pp. 156–182, 2022.
https://doi.org/10.1007/978-3-030-96648-5_8

system to remain flexible in the face of this progression. Hence the need for a methodological framework within the enterprise in order to control its structure and manage its transformation [2]. This article makes use of Praxeme as a methodology for the software development process. Indeed, Praxeme provides enterprises with a tool to absorb changes by pushing the design of information systems towards a service-oriented approach [4]. Consequently, in order to correctly coordinate the role of the software architecture, Praxeme focuses on the process of logical modeling based on a set of high-level models from the business itself [5]. In a certain way, the logical model ensures the decoupling of the conceptual solution from the technology used for the implementation, which makes the design of the information system perennial. It specifies the logical aspect of the Praxeme methodology. The logical aspect models the service architecture known as SOA (Service Oriented Architecture) and consequently structures the information system with the elementary unit called the logical service. However, the automatic localization of logical services at the time of logical modeling remains a difficult task [7]. The dispersion of information at the level of the representation of the enterprise's intentions in Praxeme is the cause. It is essential to group together in the intentional aspect all the terms and their precise definitions specifically used in the enterprise and its field of activity [9]. Hence the importance of a lexicon based on natural language to represent the intentional aspect of Praxeme [8]. The lexicon is a source of reference for the stakeholders and can take several forms, namely the glossary in a linear form or the LEL (Language Extended Lexicon) [10], eLEL (elaborate Lexicon Extended Language) [11], SBVR (Semantic Business Vocabulary and Rules) [12] in a more complex form [13]. Nevertheless, the consideration of the highest level of abstraction of Praxeme (intentional aspect) is rarely discussed in the research topics that exploit the Praxeme methodology. Consequently, there is no approach that instantiates the SBVR or LEL requirement models in the Praxeme methodology. Moreover, Razafindramintsa [14] already dismisses the hypothesis of using LEL in Praxeme due to the lack of conceptual views which makes difficult the automatic derivation to static and dynamic UML models. Since eLEL is a more elaborate natural language requirements model than the classical LEL and has a dedicated UML metamodel, Razafindramintsa [14] proposes an approach that instantiates eLEL in Praxeme in order to represent the intentional aspect of the methodology. This approach obviously facilitates the automatic localization of the logical service (logical aspect) from eLEL (intentional aspect) at the time of the logical modeling. The result obtained using this approach is a logical model composed of a logical factory, logical workshop, logical machine, logical service and data structure [7]. However, the logical business services automatically located from eLEL are not exploitable in code (software aspect) of an object-oriented application [8]. However, all the information which constitutes the Praxeme logical services is already described in eLEL [7]. Consequently, the problem lies at the level of the intentional aspect specified by eLEL, whose conceptual level does not conform to object-oriented conventions [6, 8].

The ReLEL (Restructuring extended Lexical Elaborate Language) requirements model is an extension of eLEL. It records the terms used by the company and models the conceptual information of the future system to be developed according to the object-oriented principle [6]. Therefore, in this article, we have discarded eLEL from Praxeme and replaced it with the ReLEL natural language oriented requirements model in order to represent its intentional aspect. Our objective in this article is to automate the software development process from ReLEL using the Praxeme business methodology. Since Praxeme absorbs the MDA (Model Driven Architecture) approach for the articulation of its aspects, this article presents two very distinct approaches. In the first approach, we have used Rapatsalahy's [8] approach for logical modeling (logical aspect) from ReLEL (intentional aspect) which articulates the intentional, semantic and logical aspects of Praxeme. For this purpose, we have used transformation rules described in human language and ATL, known as model-to-model (M2M), defined by Rapatsalahy [8]. Subsequently, we proposed the implementation of the Praxeme logical model by a SOAP (Simple Object Access Protocol) web service which articulates the logical, technical and software aspects of Praxeme. Thus, in order to automate the process, we have proposed M2M transformation and translation rules described from the Acceleo template engine, known as model-to-text (M2T). This approach uses both top-down and bottom-up approaches to build the SOAP web service from the logical model of the methodology. Indeed, the choice of implementation of the logical model into a SOAP web service (top-down or bottom-up) depends on the decision taken in the technical aspect of Praxeme. Finally, this article only deals with the purely IT (Information Technology) aspects of Praxeme, compared to Rapatsalahy's article in [8] which explores the business part of the methodology. But as a common point, both articles make use of the logic aspect to realize the role of the bridge between the business and IT aspects of Praxeme.

2 Background

This section introduces the two concepts developed in this work. Firstly, it describes the ReLEL lexicon, the artifact used to model the domain knowledge. At the end, it describes the Praxeme methodology that orients the design of enterprise information systems towards a service-oriented approach.

2.1 Restructuring Extended Lexical Elaborate Language

The ReLEL natural language oriented requirements model is a set of symbols that records the significant terms of the universe of discourse (UofD). The ReLEL symbol classifies the input terms in the model into four categories such as subject, object, verb and state. Requirements are extracted from the ReLEL subject (and/or) verb (and/or) object symbols [15]. Each term in the ReLEL lexicon can be described according to its type by the heuristics presented in Tables 1, 2, 3, and 4. Table 1 describes the subject ReLEL.

Table 1. Subject type ReLEL.

ReLEL typology	Subject
Description	It is an active entity with an associated role in the application. The subject is either an actor or a software component or any other system with which it must interact
Notion	It describes the subject (who is the subject?), the properties of the subject (what are their characteristics?) as well as the objects it manipulates (what are the objects it manipulates?)
Behavioral response	It relates the definition of functions supported by the subject
Attribute	It indicates the properties of the subject. The attribute type can be either an existing ReLEL object type or a simple type. A parameter is a particular attribute
Method	It develops the details of the actions defined by a behavioral response described by a symbol of type subject. Indeed, it represents the operation that allows to manipulate an attribute

Table 2 represents the heuristics associated with the ReLEL object type.

Table 2. Object type ReLEL.

ReLEL typology	Object
Description	It is an entity manipulated by a ReLEL subject type. Therefore, a ReLEL object type does not act with respect to an action
Notion	It describes the object (who is the object?), the properties of the object (what are its characteristics?) and the other objects with which it is related (what objects are related to it?)
Behavioral response	It describes the actions applied to this object
Attribute	It indicates the properties of an object. The attribute type can be either an existing ReLEL object type or a simple type. A parameter is a particular attribute
Method	It specifies the operation to access or modify a ReLEL object

Table 3 represents the heuristic associated with the verb type ReLEL object.

Table 4 represents the heuristic associated with the state type ReLEL object.

The ReLEL objective is to unify the domain language (dictionary), to specify the requirements and to represent the conceptual information corresponding to each domain term. Indeed, it is based on eLEL but models the information of the UofD in order to have a conceptual view in accordance with the object-oriented principle for attribute typing and the construction of a method [6]. The process of the ReLEL construction is composed of fourteen steps that conform to the metamodel presented in Fig. 1.

The basic metaclasses that compose the ReLEL metamodel is explained above:

Table 3. Verb type ReLEL.

ReLEL typology	Verb
Description	The verb type ReLEL object describes a functionality that is executed by the subject ReLELs with its impacts in the operational environment
Notion	It describes what acts when an event happens or occurs, the object manipulated by the subject (what is the object manipulated by the subject?), as well as the goal to be reached (what is the goal to be reached?)
Behavioral response	It describes the environmental impact, the resulting condition, and the satisfactory conditions for achieving the objective or goal
Attribute	It represents the subjects or objects concerned by the verb
Method	It represents the actions to be carried out by the subject on the objects participating in the realization of the objective or the goal to be reached

Table 4. State type ReLEL.

ReLEL typology	State
Description	The ReLEL object of type state is characterized by rather large attributes that contain values at different times during the execution of the system
Notion	It describes what it represents and then the actions that led to it
Behavioral response	It allows the identification of other states that can be reached by the current state
Attribute	It represents subjects or objects that change their state
Method	It represents the actions taken to produce this state

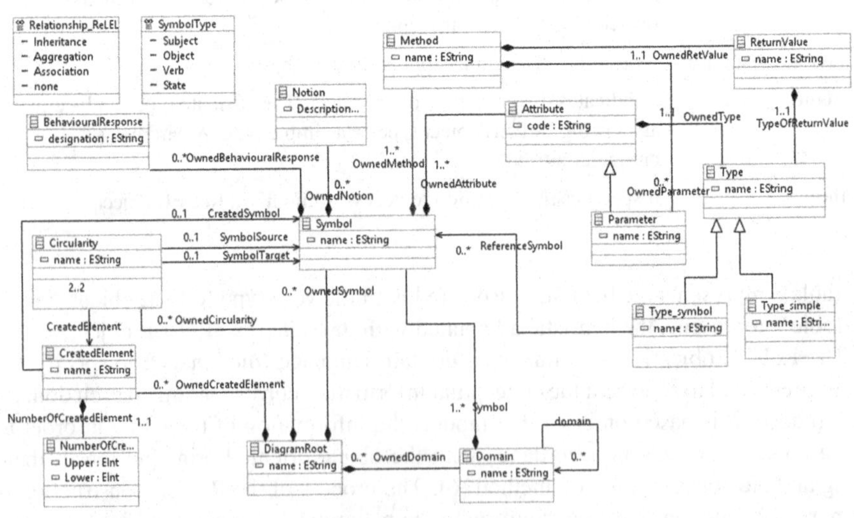

Fig. 1. ReLEL metamodel [6].

- Metaclass symbol: it constitutes the basic notion of the ReLEL lexicon. Indeed, each significant term of the UofD is recorded in the form of a ReLEL symbol classified as subject and/or object and/or verb and/or state and then described through the metaclass notion, behavioral response, attribute and method. Therefore, the symbol metaclass is composed of the notion, behavioral response, attribute and method metaclass;
- Notion metaclass: its purpose is to describe the denotation of a term captured by a ReLEL symbol;
- Behavioral response metaclass: it aims to describe the connotation of a term recorded by a ReLEL symbol;
- Attribute metaclass: represents the conceptual view of the ReLEL and metamodels the characteristics of the ReLEL symbol;
- Method metaclass: it represents the conceptual view of the ReLEL. Consequently, it constitutes the operation allowing to manipulate an attribute metaclass;
- Metaclass circularity: this concept is necessary when there is a relation between two ReLEL symbols. Therefore, its role is to link the symbol metaclass (target and source) two by two. It also stores a reference to the created element metaclass;
- CreatedElement metaclass: this concept is used to register each created ReLEL symbol. Therefore, it stores a reference of the ReLEL symbol metaclass. It is composed of the NumberCreatedElement metaclass;
- Metaclass NumberCreatedElement: it is used to indicate the minimum and maximum number of the target element created object occurrences in the circularity;
- The SymbolType enumeration: it allows to list all possible values of the classification for a ReLEL symbol. It can be either subject, object, verb or state. Thus the enumeration value assigned to a ReLEL symbol is unique;
- The Relation enumeration: it allows to list all possible values of the relation between two ReLEL symbols in the concept of circularity. The value can be inheritance, aggregation, association or none. The enumeration value assigned to the circularity concept is unique.

2.2 Praxeme Methodology

Praxeme is an enterprise methodology that enables the perfect alignment of its business architecture with its technical architecture. For this purpose, it proposes a TSE (Topology System Enterprise) framework that respects certain rules, such as focusing on the enterprise, taking into account all of its reality, the uniqueness of any element in a repository within the framework, assistance with the transformation of one model into another, the linking of elements to each other and finally the existence of a reference metamodel. The TSE constitutes the theoretical basis of the Praxeme methodology and identifies seven aspects of the enterprise [7].

By definition, an aspect is a component of the system that is linked to a viewpoint, a type of concern, a specialization [3]. The TSE indicates the possibility to move from one aspect to another via a link. These links express the dependencies between aspects. The articulation of aspects shows how information, representations and decisions flow from one end of the software production chain to the other [3]. Thanks to the adoption of the MDA approach by the Praxeme methodology, derivation rules can be defined on these relationships, which allow us to move from one aspect to another. The derivation rules are first expressed in human language. Then they can be implemented by model transformation languages to be semi-automated or even automated. This article is particularly interested in some articulation fixed by the topology of the enterprise system, namely the intentional aspect represented by the CIM model (Computation Independent Model), semantic and logical by the PIM model (Plateform Independent Model), software by the PSM model (Plateform Specific Model). Indeed, the key principle of MDA consists in the use of different types of models in the development cycle of a software, namely the CIM requirements model, the PIM analysis and design model and the PSM code model [8]. Therefore, the derivation of the intentional aspect into the semantic aspect is a so-called vertical transformation in MDA that induces a change of abstraction level. Then the derivation of the semantic aspect into the logical aspect is a horizontal transformation in MDA because the source model (semantic model) and target model (logical model) involved in the transformation are at the same level of abstraction. Finally, the derivation of the logical aspect into the software aspect is a vertical transformation. Figure 2 represents the Enterprise System Topology Framework of the Praxeme methodology.

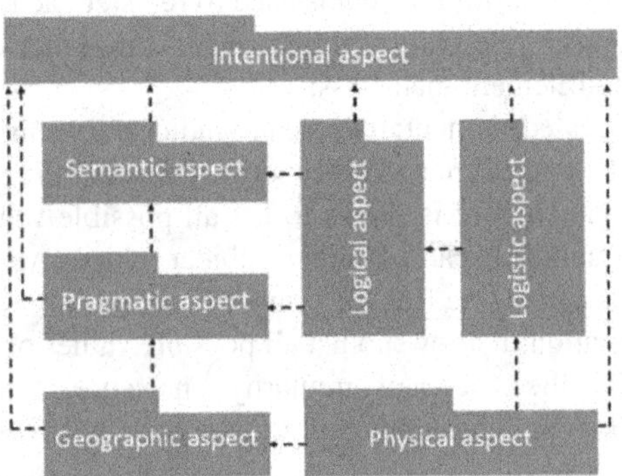

Fig. 2. Enterprise System Topology [7].

The intentional aspect is the source of all business knowledge in the semantic (object at the heart of the business) and pragmatic (business processes) aspects of Praxeme. Thus, it requires a model described in natural language which has a dedicated UML metamodel to guarantee the durability of the SOA model of the logical aspect of Praxeme.

Indeed, Praxeme provides for three derivation paths from the semantic model, namely towards the pragmatic aspect and the innovative design of processes, and then two others towards the logical aspect for data modeling and service design. In this article, we have oriented the semantic modeling towards the design of services, since our initial problematic is based on the inability of the logical business service automatically localized from eLEL to be exploited in the software aspect of Praxeme [8]. Certainly Praxeme aims to design the system using an SOA approach [16]. It uses basic units called logical services to build systems. The logic model is composed of several logic services that are arranged in logic aggregations on three levels of aggregation, namely logic machines, logic shops and logic factories. By definition, the logical machine is a coherent set of logical services. Then the logical workshop groups each logical machine. Finally, the logical factory is a set of logical workshops. The logistics aspect encompasses the technical and software aspects of the Praxeme methodology. The technical aspect indicates how to convert artifacts from the logical model into software. Then, the software aspect covers all the software components that automate part of the system's action [3]. The relationship between the technical, logical and software aspects, whatever their level, are obtained by deriving logical components, for a given architecture.

3 Related Work

The integration of the natural language oriented requirements model in a software development process is a very promising approach in the field of software engineering. It allows to reduce the gap between the developed software and the requirements specified by the stakeholders. However, this hypothesis requires a methodology capable of mastering the usual complexity of the development of an enterprise information system. Therefore, this section summarizes the research literature based on the integration of lexicons such as SBVR and eLEL into the methodology intended for the enterprise software development process noted Praxeme.

Biard [2] proposes in his approach a method that consists in using the Praxeme methodology and recommends some new modeling tools that facilitate its use. The permanent evolution of needs obliges companies to make their information systems agile in the face of these continual changes. Nevertheless, the problem with adapting the company's information system to changing needs lies in the fact that the company's knowledge is not formally expressed and poorly structured. Biard [2] solves this problem in this article by using the Praxeme enterprise methodology, which proposes the appropriate framework to carry out this explicitation and structuring of knowledge. Thanks to the TSE, Praxeme structures the enterprise in seven aspects and divides them into aspects representing the business architecture and the technical architecture. The article by Biard [2] focuses rather on the business architecture, which deals with the knowledge of the enterprise.

To make the knowledge explicit in this architecture, Biard's strategy [2] starts with the pragmatic aspect of the Praxeme methodology. Therefore, the sequence of elaboration of the semantic aspect and the pragmatics is opposite to their dependence. The authors claim that participants generally have a more precise idea of how they intervene in the business process than to spontaneously express the business objects and data they are dealing with. Consequently, in this approach, Biard [2] proposes an extraction of the business objects and their data according to the messages exchanged between the different actors in the business process to constitute the semantic aspect of Praxeme. After the formalization of the semantic aspect, it is then the turn of the business and organizational rules, which the actors often find difficult to formalize. Thus, in this article, Biard [2] proposes a language close to natural language such as SBVR to establish the business and organizational rules in the semantic and pragmatic aspect of Praxeme. Indeed, the researcher indicates that the Praxeme method, the approach they have proposed as well as the adapted tools allow for the construction of a solid base on which to build the enterprise architecture. This allows all the assets to align the information system with the company's strategy and increase its agility.

Razafindramintsa [14] focused on the integration of the natural language oriented requirements model in the Praxeme methodology. Indeed it is a very interesting approach to improve the software development process, as Biard [2] even asserts the usefulness of natural language at the level of the intentional aspect of Praxeme in order to make explicit the intentions of the enterprise by all stakeholders. Consequently, their strategy in this article consists of specifying the intentional aspect of Praxeme through the eLEL requirements model in order to make the automatic derivation of the business knowledge source into the semantic aspect of this methodology easy. The eLEL requirements model allows this derivation to be satisfied perfectly, because Razafindramintsa [14] maintains that it is a terminological database that provides all the specific terms used by the company and has a UML metamodel. This strategy also solves the problem mentioned by Biard [2] related to the graphical representation of the intention in the company, which is not yet very common. The researchers state that in this approach, they have moved away from the hypothesis of using the LEL requirements model to specify the intentional aspect of Praxeme, since they have observed that not only does the LEL model not present the conceptual level of a domain, but also it cannot directly derive the static and behavioral model of the UML language. Thus, in order to realize their proposal, they established rules expressed in natural language to derive the eLEL model into a UML class diagram and transition state machine. The UML class diagram and transition state machine specify the semantic aspect of the Praxeme methodology. In order to automate the derivation of the eLEL model into the semantic aspect, they have used the ATL model transformation language. Indeed, this transformation is an M2M approach within the framework of MDA, as the eLEL requirements model of the intentional aspect of Praxeme represents the CIM, and then the UML class diagram and the transition state machine are models of the PIM.

For the ATL transformation, Razafindramintsa [14] used the eLEL metamodel in ecore format as the source model and two ecore metamodels for the semantic aspect as the target. The class diagram and the UML transition state machine in XMI format are the first results of the transformation. Then, they proposed to transform the recently obtained UML diagrams with the PlantUML script in order to obtain a concrete UML diagram.

Razafindramintsa [7] proposed an approach to automatically locate the logical service from the eLEL natural language oriented requirements model. Indeed, this is a very interesting approach in a service architecture (SOA), because Razafindramintsa [7] assert that the automatic localization of services at the time of logical modeling is a difficult task because of the complexity of the model and the dispersed nature of enterprise architecture information in organizations, systems as well as actors and applications. Especially since the location of logical services during the modeling process is still done in a manual or semi-automatic way. However, they argue that all the information that makes up the logical services is described in eLEL as well as in the business architecture aspects of the Praxeme methodology. Therefore, in this article Razafindramintsa [7] made use of the semantic aspect and obtained from eLEL in order to automatically derive the logical aspect of the Praxeme methodology. They proposed four rules described in natural language for the transformation of the UML class diagram into a logical factory. Subsequently, they transposed the rules described in natural language into ATL rules in order to automate the derivation process defined previously. The results obtained are UML logical factory diagrams at the Praxeme logical aspect level [7]. As a work perspective, the researchers suggest the realization of the SOA from the logical aspect derived automatically from eLEL.

4 Proposed Approach

This section presents the approach proposed in this article which consists in integrating the ReLEL natural language requirements model into the Praxeme methodology. The objective of this approach is to automatically obtain the Praxeme software aspect component from the intentional aspect specified by ReLEL. Therefore, this section outlines our approach for M2M and M2T model transformation. Obviously, the approach proposed in this article is entirely based on the MDA approach that is used by Praxeme to articulate each aspect of the TSE. The model transformation rule proposals in this section are first expressed in human language (natural language) and then translated into model transformation language.

4.1 Proposed Methodology for the M2M Approach

The basic principle of the M2M approach proposed in this paper is to generate target PIM models (semantic and logical) from the source CIM and PIM models (intentional and semantic). Theoretically, the derivation process is done in two steps.

The first consists of the derivation of the intentional aspect into Praxeme semantics. Then, the second derives the semantic aspect into the logical aspect. Figure 3 illustrates the first part of the synoptic of the proposed M2M approach for model transformation.

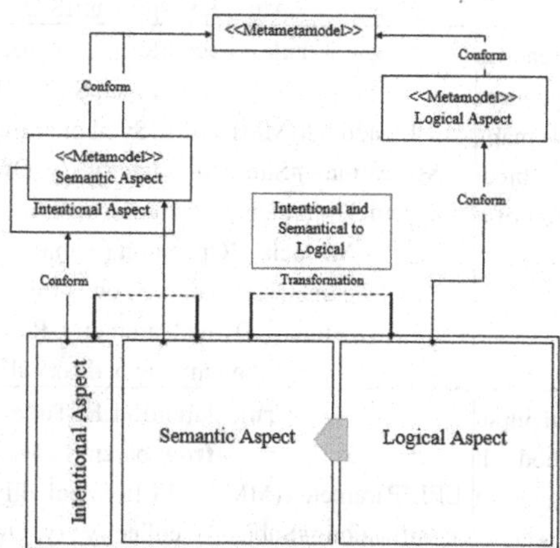

Fig. 3. Overview of the first part of the M2M approach [8].

The process of derivation of the intentional aspect in semantics. The semantic aspect hosts the business knowledge of the enterprise which excludes the organization

Table 5. Rule for transforming the ReLEL into a UML class diagram.

Natural language transformation rule	ATL transformation rule
R1: "The domain is a concept that allows the grouping of subject and object type ReLEL symbol. Therefore, the domain concept becomes a UML package for transformation".	**rule** DomainReLELToPackageUML { **from** domain : MMReLEL!Domain **to** package : MMdclass!Package (name<- domain.name, ownedClass<- domain.Symbol, import<- domain.domain)}
R2: "An actor described in the UofD is defined as a subject ReLEL. Then a passive entity is registered as an object ReLEL. Therefore, a subject and/or object ReLEL type is mapped to a UML class in the transformation".	**rule** SymbolReLELToClassUML { **from** symbolSubj : MMReLEL!Symbol(symbolSubj.classification=#Subject) **to** classSubj : MMdclass!Class (name<- symbolSubj.name, attribute<- symbolSubj.OwnedAttribute, operation<- symbolSubj.OwnedMethod)}
R3: "The attribute concept determines the properties of ReLEL symbols. Rule 3 allows to map the attributes of the ReLEL subject and/or object into an attribute of a UML class. However, the type of the attribute according to the object-oriented principle is only obtained in rule 7."	**rule** AttributeReLELToAttributeUML { **from** attrS : MMReLEL!Attribute((MMReLEL!Symbol.allInstances()->select(x | x. classification =#Subject)->collect(y | y. name)->flatten()->includes(attrS. ownerSymbol)=true) **and** (attrS.oclIsTypeOf (MMReLEL!Attribute))) **to** attrC : MMdclass!Attribute(code <- attrS.code, name<- attrS. ownerSymbol, size<- attrS.size, AttributeType<- attrS.OwnedType)}
R4: "The action that reaches ReLEL objects is the concept method. Therefore, rule 4 maps the method of a ReLEL subject and/or object to the operation of a UML class."	**rule** MethodReLELToOperationUML { **from** methS : MMReLEL!Method((MMReLEL!Symbol.allInstances()->select(x | x. classification =#Subjet)->collect(y | (y. OwnedMethod)->collect(z | z. name))->flatten()->includes(methS.name)=true)) **to** methC : MMdclass!Operation (name <- methS.name, nameClass<- methS. ownerSymbol, Parameter<- methS.OwnedParameter, ReturnValue <- methS.OwnedRetValue)}
R5: "A parameter is an input value of a ReLEL method. It corresponds to the parameter of an operation of a UML class."	**rule** ParamReLELToParamUML{ **from** paramS : MMReLEL!Parameter((MMReLEL!Symbol.allInstances()->select(x | x. classification=#Subject)->collect(y | (y. OwnedMethod)->collect(z | z. name))->flatten()->includes(paramS. name)=true) **and** (MMReLEL!Symbol.allInstances()->select(x | x. classification=#Subject)->collect(w | (w. OwnedAttribute)->collect(q | q. name))->flatten()->includes(paramS. name)=true)) **to** paramC : MMdclass!Parameter (--inheritance

(*continued*)

Table 5. (*continued*)

	code <- paramS.code, name<- paramS. ownerSymbol, size<- paramS.size, AttributeType<- paramS. OwnedType --Binding name<- paramS.name)}
R6: "The return value is an output value of a ReLEL method. It logically corresponds to the return value of an operation of a UML class."	**rule** ValRetReLELToValRetUML { **from** RetValS : MMReLEL!ReturnValue(MMReLEL!Symbol.allInstances()->select(x |x. classification =#Subject)->collect(y | (y. OwnedMethod)->collect(z | z. name))->flatten()->includes(RetValS. name)=true) **to** RetValC : MMdclass!ReturnValue(name<- RetValS.name, nameClass<- RetValS. ownerSymbol, ReturnType<- RetValS.TypeOfReturnValue)}
R7: "The type of an attribute or the return value of a ReLEL method is a ReLEL symbol (subject or object) or a simple type. Therefore, the type of a ReLEL attribute corresponds to the type of an attribute of a UML class. The type of a ReLEL return value corresponds to the type of a return value of a UML class."	**rule** SimpleTypeReLELToPrimTypeUML { **from** typeS : MMReLEL!Type_simple((MMReLEL!Symbol.allInstances()->select(x | x. classification=#Subject **or** x. classification=#Object)->collect(y | (y. OwnedAttribute)->collect(z | z. name))->flatten()->includes(typeS. name)=true) **or** (MMReLEL!Symbol.allInstances()->select(x | x. classification =#Subject **or** x. classification=#Object)->collect(w | (w. OwnedMethod)->collect(q | q. name))->flatten()->includes(typeS. name)=true)) **to** typeC : MMdclass!Type_primitif (-- inheritance name<- typeS.name, nameClass<- typeS. ownerSymbol, -- Binding nameTypePrim<- typeS.name, type_prim<- typeS.type_simple)}
R8: "The circularity links two ReLEL symbols target and source. Therefore, it is mapped into a UML class association in the transformation."	**rule** CircularityReLELToAssociationUML { **from** y : MMReLEL!Circularity ((y.SymbolSource. classification <>#State) **or** (y. SymbolTarget. classification<>#State)) **to** association : MMdclass!Association (name<-y.CreatedElement.first ().name+'_To_'+y. CreatedElement.last ().name, Type<- y. CircularityType, ReferenceEndAssociation<-y. CreatedElement ->collect(t | Tuple{r=t, n=t.NumberOfCreatedElement}))}
R9: "The concept of the number of elements created is the	**rule** NbrElemCreatedReLELToAssociationEndUML{ **from** r : MMReLEL!CreatedElement,

(*continued*)

Table 5. *(continued)*

cardinality of a UML class."	n: MMReLEL! NumberOfCreatedElement (r. NumberOfCreatedElement =n) **to** assEnd : MMdclass! AssociationEnd(name<- r.name, lower<- n.Lower, upper<- n.Upper, AssociationEndReference<- r. CreatedSymbol)}

related reference [8]. The extraction of information from the ReLEL into a UML class diagram is composed of a total of nine transformation rules [6, 8].

The second process of the derivation consists in transforming the ReLEL requirements model of the intentional aspect into a UML transition state machine of the semantic aspect of Praxeme. The extraction of information from the ReLEL into a UML transition

Table 6. Rule for transforming the ReLEL into a UML transition state machine diagram.

Natural language transformation rule	ATL transformation rule
R1: "The state type ReLEL symbol determines values at several moments of the system execution. Therefore, a ReLEL symbol classified as state is mapped to state in the UML state machine diagram."	**Rule** SateReLELToStateUML{ **from** symb : MMReLEL!Symbol (symb. classification =#State) **to** state : MMState!State (name<- symb.name, trigger<- symb. OwnedMethod)}
R2: "Each state object ReLEL (source and target) registered in the circularity concept becomes an event transition in the UML state machine diagram."	**rule** CircularityToTransition { **from** circularity : MMReLEL!Circularity(circularity.SymbolSource.classification =#State **and** circularity.SymboleTarget. classification =#State) **to** transition : MMState!Transition (name<-circularity. CreatedElement.first ().name +'_To_'+ circularity. CreatedElement.last ().name, source<- circularity.SymboleSource, target<- circularity.SymboleTarget, ownEvent<- circularity.SymboleTarget. OwnedMethod)}
R3: "A state is an event trigger. The method of a state ReLEL is mapped to an event of a UML transition state machine diagram."	**rule** MethodToEvent { **from** method : MMReLEL!Method((MMReLEL!Symbol.allInstances()->select(x | x. classification=#State)->collect(y | (y. OwnedMethod)->collect(z | z. ownerSymbol))->flatten()->includes(method. ownerSymbol)=true)) **to** event : MMState!Event (name<- method.name)}

Table 7. Rule for transforming the UML class diagram into a Praxeme logic factory.

Natural language transformation rule	ATL transformation rule
R1: "The UML class diagram package becomes a logical factory for the logical aspect of Praxeme." BLM: Business Logic Machine, LF: Logical Factory.	**rule** PackageToLogicalFactory { **from** s : MMdclass!Package **to** c : LogicalFactory!LF (name<-s.name, ownedBLM<-s.ownedClass)}
R2: "The class of the UML class diagram contained in the UML package is mapped into a business logic machine in the Praxeme logic aspect." BLS: Business Logic Service.	**rule** ClassToBusinessLogicalMachine { **from** s : MMdclass!Class(s. root=#Package) **to** c : LogicalFactory!BLM (name<-s.name, ownedBLS<-s. operation)}
R3: "The operation of the UML class diagram contained in the UML package is mapped into the business logic service of the Praxeme logic aspect."	**rule** OperationToBusinessLogicService { **from** s : MMdclass!Operation (s. root=#Package) **to** c : LogicalFactory!BLS (name<- s.name, ownedParameter <- s. Parameter, ownedReturnValue<- s. ReturnType)}
R4: "The parameter of the UML class diagram contained in the UML package is mapped as a parameter of a logical business service of the logical aspect of Praxeme."	**rule** ParamUMLToParamBLS { **from** s : MMdclass!Parameter((s. root=# Package) **and** (MMdclass!Class.allInstances()->select(x |x. root=# Package) ->collect(y | (y.operation)->collect(z | z.name)) ->flatten()->includes(s.name)=true)) **to** c : LogicalFactory!Parameter(name<-s.code, ownedTypeParameter<- s. AttributeType)}
R5: "The return value of the UML class diagram contained in the UML package is mapped to the return value of a logical business service of the logical aspect of Praxeme."	**rule** ReturnValToRetValBLS { **from** s : MMdclass! ReturnValue ((s. root=#Package) **and** (MMdclass!Class.allInstances()->select(x | x. root=#Package) ->collect(y | (y. operation)->collect(z | z. name)) ->flatten()->includes(s. name)=true)) **to** c : LogicalFactory! ReturnValue (name<- s.name, ownedReturnValue<-s. ReturnType)}
R6: "The primitive type of the UML class diagram contained in the UML package is mapped to the primitive type of a parameter or a return value of a BLS of the logical aspect of Praxeme."	**rule** TP_ClassToTP_BLS { **from** s : MMdclass!Type_primitif((s. root=#Package) **and** (s.ownedType =#Method) **and** (MMdclass!Class.allInstances()->select(x|x. root=#Package) ->collect(y | (y.operation)->collect(z | z.name)) ->flatten()->includes(s.name)=true)) **to** c : LogicalFactory!Type_primitive (--inheritance from primitive Type to Type name<- s.name, nameBLM<- s.name, --BLS primitive standard link name<- s. nameTypePrim, type<- s. type_prim)}

(*continued*)

Table 7. (*continued*)

<table>
<tr><td>R7: "The class type of the UML class diagram contained in the UML package is mapped to the BLM type of a parameter or a return value of a BLS of the Praxeme logic aspect."</td><td>rule TypeClassToTypeBLM {
from s : MMdclass!Type_Class((s. root=#Package) and (s.ownedType =#Method) and (MMdclass!Class.allInstances()->select(x|x. root=#Domain)->collect(y | (y.operation)->collect(z | z.name))->flatten()->includes(s.name)=true)) to
c : LogicalFactory!Type_BLM (
-- inheritance from BLM Type to Type
name<- s.name, nameBLM<- s.name,
--BLS TypeBLM link
name<- s. nameTypePrim, referenceBLM<-s.ReferenceType)}</td></tr>
</table>

state machine diagram is composed of a total of three transformation rules [8]. Table 6 summarizes the rules described in human and ATL language of the transformation.

The process of deriving the semantic **aspect into a logical aspect.** The logical aspect of the Praxeme methodology is an advantage in terms of opening up the system. Indeed, it leads to the production of software components distributed in the form of services, in the logical continuity of web services technology. The process of deriving the semantic aspect into the logical aspect of Praxeme is composed of a total of seven rules. It consists of the extraction of the information that makes up the UML class diagram to constitute the Praxeme logical factory model.

Table 8 gives the definition of the basic elements that make up the Praxeme logic model used in the transformation described in Table 7.

Table 8. Elements used by WSDL for web service description.

Element	Description
Business logic factory	It is a logical aggregate corresponding to a domain in the upstream models. It derives from the object domain which is the decomposition unit of the semantic model
Business logic machine	It is a coherent set of logical business services, built around a strong notion of an upstream model. Its origin comes from the Praxeme semantic class
Business logic service	It is the elementary grain in the service architecture. Everything that can be requested from the information system, action or transformation, is obtained through a service. As its origin, the logical business service comes from the operation having been found on a semantic class of Praxeme

The process of deriving the logical aspect in software aspect. The approach proposed in this article implements the logical model obtained from ReLEL from the SOAP web service technology. In this section, we will present the top-down approach which consists in establishing first of all a contract that says everything about the service operation before implementing it. Consequently, our approach is still based on the philosophy of the M2M transformation, which consists of deriving the logical model (PIM) of the logical aspect into a WSDL model (PSM) of the software aspect of Praxeme. The basic principle of this transformation consists of extracting the elements of the logical model, such as the logical factory, logical business machine, logical business service, parameter as well as the return values, in order to constitute the WSDL structure. Generally speaking, the derivation process is composed of five rules in all. Figure 4 illustrates the second part of the synoptic of the M2M approach proposed in this article for model transformation (Table 9).

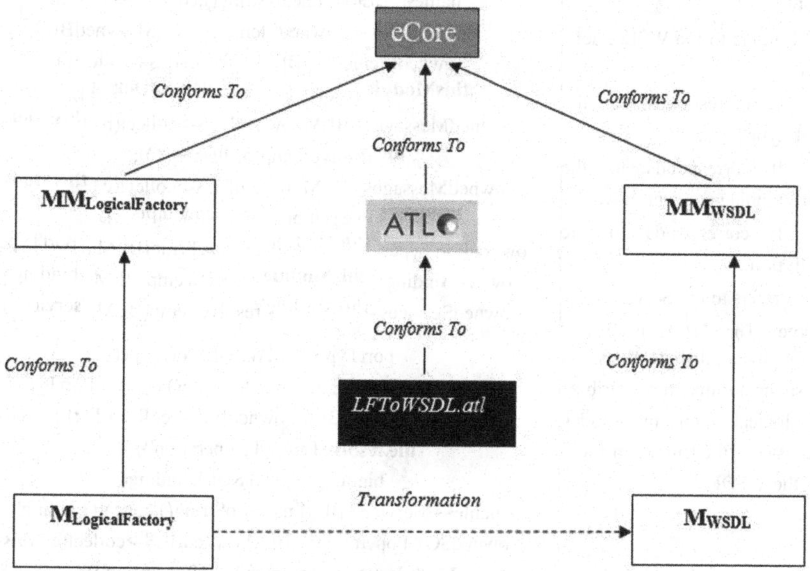

Fig. 4. Overview of the transformation from logical to WSDL model.

In WSDL, the abstract information is separated at two levels such as the abstract and concrete part. The root of the document is represented by the definitions tag whose child information is detailed in Table 10 below.

Table 9. Rule for transforming the logical factory into the Praxeme WSDL model.

Natural language transformation rule	ATL transformation rule
R1: "The logical factory corresponds to the WSDL package."	**rule** LFToWSDLPackage { **from** LF : LogicalFactory!LF **to** ContainerWSDL : MMWSDL!WSDLPackage (name<- LF.name, ownedDefinition<- LF. ownedBLM)}
R2: "The business logic machine corresponds to several elements of the WSDL model, namely 1. It refers to the WSDL definition. 2. It corresponds to the WSDL type port. 3. It corresponds to the WSDL binding concept. 4. It corresponds to the WSDL port. 5. It refers to the Service. Note: The NameSpace and location meta-attribute does not correspond to any meta-attribute of the logical factory metamodel, but must be filled in when modeling the WSDL."	**rule** BLMToDefinition { **from** BLM : MMLogicalFactory!BLM **to** definition : MMWSDL!Definition (name<- BLM.name.toString().concat('Service'), NameSpace<- '', ownedElement<- BLM.ownedBLS, ownedElement<- BLM. ownedBLS->collect(a |**thisModule**.resolveTemp(a, 'elementOutput')), ownedMessage<- BLM. ownedBLS->collect(b | **thisModule**.resolveTemp(b, 'message')), ownedMessage<- BLM. ownedBLS->collect(c | **thisModule**.resolveTemp(c, ' elementOutput ')), ownedPortType<-**thisModule**.resolveTemp(BLM , 'portType'), ownedBinding<-**thisModule**.resolveTemp(BLM, 'binding'), ownedService<-**thisModule**.resolveTemp(BLM, 'service')), portType: MMWSDL!PortType(name<- 'Service'+BLM.name.toString().concat('PortType'), ownedOperation<- BLM. ownedBLS->collect(d | **thisModule**.resolveTemp(d , 'operation'))), binding : MMWSDL!Binding(name<- 'Service'+BLM.name.toString().concat('binding'), ownedSOAPoperation<- BLM.ownedBLS->collect(e | **thisModule**.resolveTemp(e, 'SOAPoperation'))), service : MMWSDL!Service(name <- 'Service'+BLM.name, ownedPort<- **thisModule**.resolveTemp(BLM, 'port')), port : MMWSDL!Port(name<- 'Service'+BLM.name.toString().concat('Port'), ownedSOAPAddress<- **thisModule**.resolveTemp(BLM,'soapAddress')), soapAddress : MMWSDL!SOAPAddress(location<-'')}
R3: "The logical business service corresponds to several elements of the WSDL model, namely. 1. It relates to the concept element (request) of the WSDL. 2. It corresponds to the concept element (response) of WSDL.	**rule** BLSToWSDLelem { **from** bls : MMLogicalFactory!BLS **to** element : MMWSDL!Element (name<- bls.name, ownedXMLType<-bls. ownedParameter), OutputElement : MMWSDL!Element (name<- bls.name.toString().concat('Response'), ownedXMLType<-bls. ownedReturnValue), message : MMWSDL!Message(

(*continued*)

Table 9. (*continued*)

3. It corresponds to the message (request) of the WSDL. 4. It corresponds to the WSDL message (response). 5. It refers to the WSDL concept of operation. 6. It refers to the SOAPoperation concept of WSDL. Note: The SoapAction and style meta-attribute does not correspond to any meta-attribute of the logical factory metamodel, but must be filled in when modeling the WSDL."	name<- bls.name.toString().concat('Query'), ownedPart<-bls. ownedParameter->collect(f | **thisModule**.resolveTemp(f, 'part'))), messageOutput : MMWSDL!Message(name<- bls.name.toString().concat('Response'), ownedPart <-**thisModule**.resolveTemp(bls. ownedReturnValue, 'partResponse')), operation : MMWSDL!Operation(name<- bls.name), SOAPoperation : MMWSDL!SOAPoperation (soapAction<- '', style<- '')}
R4: "The BLS parameter corresponds to two elements of the WSDL model, namely. 1. It corresponds to the XMLType element.	**rule** ParamToXMLTYPE { **from** param : MMLogicalFactory!Parameter **to** xmlType : MMWSDL!XMLType (name<- param.name.toString().toLower(), XMLType<-''),
2. It corresponds to the Part element."	part : MMWSDL!Part(name<- param.name.toString().toLower())}
R5: "The return value of the BLS corresponds to two elements of the WSDL model, namely the following: 1. It corresponds to the XMLType element. 2. It corresponds to the Part element."	**rule** ValRetToElement { **from** retVal : MMLogicalFactory!ReturnValue **to** xmlTypeResponse : MMWSDL!XMLType (name<-retVal.name.toString().toLower().concat('Response'), XMLType<-''), partResponse : MMWSDL!Part(name<- retVal.name.toString().toLower().concat('Response'))}

Table 10. Elements used by WSDL for web service description.

Element	Description
Type	This element provides the definition of data types for the description of message exchanges
Message	This element describes all the data transmitted during the operation
Port Type	This element refers to the collection of abstract operations. Each abstract operation imports an input message and an output message
Binding	This element describes how a set of abstract operations, called "port type" is linked to a port according to a real protocol
Port	This element allows the implementation of the PortType, taking into account the Binding, including SOAPBinding and SOAPOperations
Service	A set of network endpoints called "ports" to determine the location of the service

4.2 Proposed Methodology for the M2T Approach

The initial problem of this article is based on the logical service automatically localized from eLEL, which cannot be exploited in the code skeleton of an object-oriented application. Consequently, the process of automatic articulation of the aspects of the Praxeme methodology stops at the logical aspect. In order to overcome this obstacle, our strategy consists of automatically translating the logical components obtained from the ReLEL natural language oriented requirements model into Praxeme software components using the M2T approach. The logical components used in this approach are those derived from the semantic aspect of Praxeme. This section will present two different methods for obtaining the software aspect of Praxeme. The first approach consists in automatically generating code skeletons of an object-oriented application from the Praxeme logic model obtained in Sect. 1.1. Then, the second approach is based on the automatic generation of WSDL documents from the WSDL model obtained in Sect. 1.1.

The two approaches are identical, as they use the logical components automatically derived from the intentional aspect specified by ReLEL and the UML class diagram of the semantic aspect of Praxeme. However, the difference lies in the choice of technology taken from the technical aspect of Praxeme. The first method, called "Bottom-up", uses Java technology for the implementation of the software aspect of Praxeme. We have presented an approach called 'translationist' which directly translates the Java file (code) of the software aspect from the logical components classified as PIM in MDA [17]. We have added in the Acceleo template engine the Java API that simplifies the generation of WSDL document from the produced class. Table 11 summarizes the basic rules for translating the logic factory model into Java code skeleton. The logical model is the source model in the translation.

Table 11. The logical factory rule of translation into Java code skeleton.

Natural language transformation rule	Translation rule in Acceleo
R1: "The business logic machine (BLM) of the logical aspect becomes a Java class of the Praxeme software aspect."	[for (machine : BLM | ownedBLM)] [file (machine.name.concat ('.java'), false, 'UTF-8')] [comment default class constructor /] public class [machine.name] {} [/file] [/for]
R2: "The business logic service (BLS) of the logical aspect becomes a method of a Java class of the software aspect of Praxeme." Note: This rule only presents an extract of the generation of getters in Java for a type symbol of a BLS of the Praxeme logic model.	[for (service : BLS | ownedBLS)] [comment generation of getters /] [if (service.name.contains ('get'))] [for (return : ReturnValue | ownedReturnValue)] [comment generate getters for type symbol /] [if (return.ownedTypeReturnValue.name='Type_Symbol')] [for (type_symbol : Type_BLM| ownedTypeReturnValue)] public [type_symbol.referenceBLM.name /] [service.name /](){return [return.name.toLower()/] ; }[/for][/if][/for][/if][/for]
R3: "The parameter of a BLS of the logical aspect becomes a variable of a Java class of the Praxeme software aspect." R4: "The type of a parameter of the BLS of the logical aspect becomes a type of an instance variable of a Java class."	[for (param : Parameter | ownedBLS. ownedParam)] [if (param.ownedTypeParameter.name='Type_Symbol')] [for (type_symbol : Type_BLM| param. ownedTypeParameter)] private [type_symbol.referenceBLM.name /] [param.name.toLower()/]; [/for] [/if] [if (param. ownedTypeParameter.name ='Type_simple')] [for (type_simple : Type_primitive| ownedTypeParameter)] private [type_simple.type.toString().replaceAll('class', '') /] [param.name.toLower() /]; [/for][/if][/for]
R5: "The return value of a	[for (service : BLS | ownedBLS)] [if (service.name.contains('get'))]

BLS translates to the return value of a Java class."
R6: "The type of the return value of a BLS becomes the type of the return value of a method of a Java class."
	[for (return : ReturnValue | ownedReturnValue)]
	[if (return.ownedTypeReturnValue.name='Type_simple')] [for (type_simple :Type_primitive | ownedTypeReturnValue)]
	public [type_simple.type.toString().replaceAll('class', '') /] [service.name /](){
	return [return.name.toLower() /];
	}[/for][/if][/for][/if] [/for]

R6: "The parameter of a BLS is mapped into a parameter of a Java class method."
R7: "The type of a BLS parameter becomes the type of a Java class method."
	[if (service.name.contains('set'))]
	[for (param : Parameter | ownedParam)]
	[if (param. ownedTypeParameter.name='Type_Symbol')]
	[for (type_symbol : Type_Symbol | ownedTypeParameter)]
	public void [service.name/]([type_symbol.referenceBLM.name/] [param.name.toLower()/]){
	this.[param.name.toLower() /] = [param.name.toLower() /];
	}[/for][/if][/for][/if]

The second approach uses the WSDL model obtained from the logical model to translate the WSDL document. Indeed, our approach consists in writing the syntax of a WSDL document with Acceleo and specifying the values to be used from the WSDL model generated. The syntax [variable_name/] in the WSDL code represents the values to use contained in the WSDL model (PSM). The following code program illustrates the extractions with Acceleo of the elements used by WSDL described in Table 10.

```
  [template public generateElement(aDefinition : Defini-
tion)]
  [comment @main/]
  [file (aDefinition.name.concat('.wsdl'), false, 'UTF-
8')]
  <?xml version="1.0" encoding="UTF-8"?>
      <wsdl:definitions
        xmlns:SOAP-
ENV="http://schemas.xmlsoap.org/soap/envelope/"
        xmlns:xsd="http://www.w3.org/2001/XMLSchema"
        xmlns:xsi="http://www.w3.org/2001/XMLSchema-
instance"
        xmlns:SOAP-
ENC="http://schemas.xmlsoap.org/soap/encoding/"

xmlns:soap="http://schemas.xmlsoap.org/wsdl/soap/"
        xmlns:wsdl="http://schemas.xmlsoap.org/wsdl/"
        xmlns="http://schemas.xmlsoap.org/wsdl/"
        name="[aDefinition.name/]"
        targetNamespace="[aDefinition.targetNamespace/]"
        xmlns:tns="[aDefinition.targetNamespace/]">
```

```
      <wsdl:types>
            <xsd:schema                                    target-
Namespace="[aDefinition.targetNamespace/]">

            <xsd:import                                    names-
pace="http://schemas.xmlsoap.org/soap/encoding/"/>
            <xsd:import                                    names-
pace="http://schemas.xmlsoap.org/wsdl/"/>
                      [for  (element  :  Element  |  aDefini-
tion.ownedElement)]
                            [if        (element.ownedXMLType-
>isEmpty()=true)]
                              <xsd:element
name="[element.name/]">
                                    <xsd:complexType>

<xsd:sequence></xsd:sequence>
                                <xsd:complexType>
                              </xsd:element>
                            [/if]
                          [if      (element.ownedXMLType      -
>isEmpty()=false)]
                              <xsd:element
name="[element.name/]">
                               <xsd:complexType>
                                      <xsd:sequence>
                              [for  (xmlType  :  XMLType  |
ownedXMLType)]
  <xsd:element                           name="[xmlType.name/]"
type="[xmlType.XMLType/]"></xsd:element>
                              [/for]
                                      </xsd:sequence>
                                 </xsd:complexType>
                              </xsd:element>
                          [/if]
                       [/for]
               </xsd:schema>
            </wsdl:types>
   [for (message : Message | aDefinition.ownedMessage)]

               <wsdl:message name="[ message.name/]">
              [for (part : Part | ownedPart)]
                 [if (part.name.contains('')=true)]
                             <wsdl:part  name="[  part.name/]"
element="tns:[part.referedElement.name /]"/>
```

```
                [/if]
            [/for]
            </wsdl:message>
  [/for]
  [for (portType : PortType | aDefinition.ownedPortType)]
            <wsdl:portType name="[ portType.name/]">
              [for   (operation   :   Operation   |   port-
Type.ownedOperation)]
                <wsdl:operation       name="[       opera-
tion.name/]">
                    <wsdl:input                         mes-
sage="tns:[operation.Request.name /]"></wsdl:input>
                    <wsdl:output                        mes-
sage="tns:[operation.Response.name /]"></wsdl:output>
                </wsdl:operation>
              [/for]
          </wsdl:portType>
   [/for]
   [for (binding : Binding | aDefinition.ownedBinding)]

      <wsdl:binding        name="[binding.name         /]"
type="tns:[binding.type.name /]">
              <soap:binding              style="document"
transport="http://schemas.xmlsoap.org/soap/http"/>
                  [for  (soapOp  :  SOAPoperation  |  bind-
ing.ownedSOAPoperation)]
                  <wsdl:operation
name="[soapOp.operationName.name/]">
                      <soap:operation               soapAc-
tion="[aDefinition.targetNamespace/]    ServiceCityOpera-
tion[soapOp.operationName.name/]"    style="[soapOp.style
/]"/>
                      <wsdl:input>
                          <soap:body        use="encoded"
namespace="[aDefinition.targetNamespace/]"         encod-
ingStyle="http://schemas.xmlsoap.org/soap/encoding/" />
                      </wsdl:input>
                      <wsdl:output>
                          <soap:body        use="encoded"
namespace="[aDefinition.targetNamespace/]"         encod-
ingStyle="http://schemas.xmlsoap.org/soap/encoding/" />
                      </wsdl:output>
                  </wsdl:operation>
                  [/for]
          </wsdl:binding>
```

```
      [/for]
      [for    (service    :    Service    |    aDefini-
tion.ownedService)]
      <wsdl:service name="[ service.name /]">
            [for (port : Port | service.ownedPort)]
                  <wsdl:port name="[ port.name /]" bind-
ing="tns:[ port.binding.name/]" >
                        <soap:address    location="[    ser-
vice.ownedPort.ownedSOAPAddress.location /]"/>
                  </wsdl:port>
            [/for]
         </wsdl:service>
      [/for]
   </wsdl:definitions>
   [/file]
   [/template]
```

5 Experimentation

The experiment we conducted was oriented towards the process of travel booking for a transport agency located in Madagascar [6, 8]. Indeed, the agency offers customers the opportunity to easily reach two cities in Madagascar by means of a land trip. Using the process of building the ReLEL model presented in the article by Rapatsalahy [6], we obtained as a result of step 1 (description of the source of information), step 2 (construction of the universe of discourse) and step 3 (identification of candidate terms) twenty-four ReLEL symbols including two of subject type, six of object type, eleven of verb type and five of state type. Table 12 represents step 3 of the ReLEL construction process [6].

Table 12. List of terms by classification.

Type	Candidate Terms	Number of candidate terms
Subject	Agency, customer	2
Object	Travel, reservation, car, city, passenger, luggage	6
Verb	Create a trip(s), view a trip(s), make a reservation, validate a reservation, cancel an unpaid reservation, update the status of a paid reservation, create a digital version of a paid reservation, email a reservation ticket, print a reservation ticket, validate registration, issue a registration ticket	11
State	Opening a reservation, refusing a reservation, closed reservation, unconfirmed reservation, confirmed reservation, cancelled reservation	5

In this paper, we have presented only the concept "city" for the process of transformation from logic aspect to software aspect among the candidate terms illustrated in Table 12.

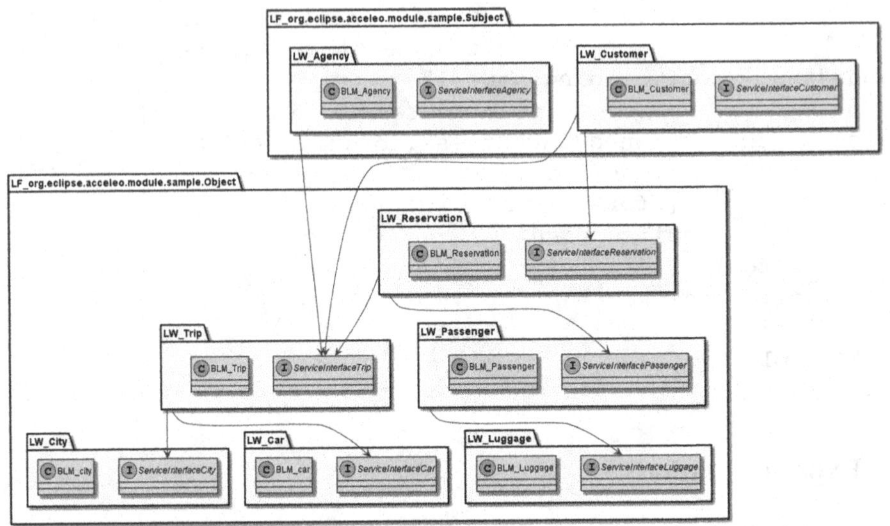

Fig. 5. Logic model in concrete form of the transport agency's travel reservation

After executing the transformation rules described in Tables 5, 6, 7 of this article, finally we automatically obtained the model of the logical factory represented in Fig. 5 above. Only the components of the logical model such as the factory, the workshop, the logical machine and the service interface are illustrated in Fig. 5. The relations between the logical factory of the "business" stratum are dynamic, based mainly on the service call. Indeed, it offers neither interface nor service, which allows it to simplify the architectural design, by concentrating the architectural decisions on the intermediate unit of the logical factory. Certainly, the encapsulation rule chosen for our architecture (Fig. 5) imposes to hide the machines inside the workshops. In return, our workshops offer an interface in which they gather the public services of their machines. Thus, the access to the service of a machine is done via the interface services known outside the workshop in order to keep the principle of encapsulation of the machines. Then, after the execution of the two approaches for the transformation of the logical model named city into a WSDL document, finally, in this paper we obtained a web service software component of the travel reservation "ServiceCity.wsdl" from the software aspect of the Praxeme methodology (Fig. 6).

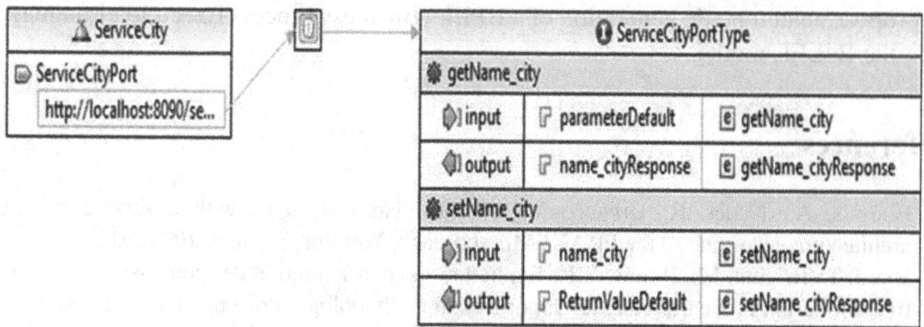

Fig. 6. Web service component (City.wsdl)

6 Conclusion

In this article, we have presented a strategy that consists of instantiating the ReLEL natural language oriented requirements model in the methodology for the software development process noted Praxeme. Certainly we have discarded the eLEL requirements model from the hypothesis to specify the intentional aspect of Praxeme and replace it with ReLEL which is at the same time a model that represents the conceptual information corresponding to each term of the domain, unifies the language of the domain, and specifies the requirements [8]. Since the initial problem of this article is based solely on the business logic services of the logical aspect of Praxeme, therefore, the new method specifically involves all aspects of the logical model, which are derived from the semantic and intentional aspect of Praxeme.

The logical aspect of Praxeme models the service architecture (SOA). It ensures the flexibility of an enterprise's information system with respect to its changing needs. Of course, the logical components (logical factory, logical business machine, logical business service) derived from the Praxeme intentional and semantic models are the most preferable for identifying Praxeme software components (packages, classes, methods and wsdl). Thus, in Sect. 4 of this paper, we presented an MDA-based approach that consists in automating the software development process from the intentional aspect specified by ReLEL to the Praxeme software aspect. In this way, the processes are composed of a series of model-to-model (M2M) transformations, followed by the translation of the model into text (M2T). The M2M transformation series encompasses the derivation of the intentional aspect specified by ReLEL into the semantic aspect (UML class diagram and transition state machine), logical aspect (logical factory model) and software aspect (WSDL model) of Praxeme. The M2T translation series first incorporates the direct translation of the logical model (logical aspect) into Java code skeletons (software aspect) and then the WSDL model (software aspect) into Praxeme's WSDL document (software aspect). Therefore, we can deduce that the approach proposed in this paper allows solving the problem related to the logical modeling in Praxeme obtained from the near-natural language model [7]. However, our approach does not yet explore the pragmatic part of the enterprise in Praxeme, and does not subsequently allow the modeling of the business process of the latter. Thus, as a perspective of this research work, we propose an automatic generation of a BPEL (Business Process Execution Language) from the ReLEL model.

References

1. Boussis, A., Nader, F.: Urbanization of information systems with a service oriented architecture according to the PRAXEME approach. Web Inf. Technol. **102** (2012)
2. Biard, T., Brigant, M., Bourey, J.P.: Explicitation et structuration des connaissances pour la transformation de l'entreprise: les apports de la méthodologie Praxeme. CIGI (2013)
3. Vauquier, D.: Modus la méthodologie PRAXEME, Guide général. Praxeme Institute (2006)
4. Vauquier, D.: Modus la méthodologie PRAXEME, Guide de l'aspect logique. Praxeme Institute (2007)
5. Lamyae, S., Abdennebi, T.: Overall design approach for urbanized information systems: application of the method Praxeme. In: 2014 Third IEEE International Colloquium in Information Science and Technology (CIST), Tetouan, Morocco, pp. 18–23. IEEE (2014)
6. Rapatsalahy, M.A., Razafindramintsa, J.L., Mahatody, T., Ilie, S., Razafindrakoto, R.N.: Restructuring extended Lexical elaborate language. In: 23rd International System Theory Control and Computing (ICSTCC), Sinaia, Romania, pp. 266–272 (2019)
7. Razafindramintsa, J.L., Mahatody, T., Simionescu, S.M., Razafimandimby, J.P.: Logical services automatic location from eLEL. In: Proceedings of the 21st International Conference on System Theory Control and Computing (ICSTCC), Sinaia, Romania, pp. 849–854 (2017)
8. Rapatsalahy, A.M., Razafimahatratra, H., Mahatody, T., Ilie, M., Ilie, S., Razafindrakoto, R.N.: Derivation of logical aspects in Praxeme from ReLEL models. In: ENASE, pp. 413–420 (2021)
9. Biard, T., Bigand, M., Bourey, J.P.: Explicitation et structraration des connaissances pour la transformation de l'entreprise: les apports de la méthode Praxeme. In: Congrès International de Génie Industriel (2013)
10. Leite, J.C.S.P., Franco, A.P.M.: A strategy for conceptual model acquisition. In: Proceedings of the IEEE International Symposium on Requirements Engineering, pp. 243–246. IEEE (1993)
11. Razafindramintsa, J.L., Mahatody, T., Razafimandimby, J.P.: Elaborate lexicon extended language with a lot of conceptual information. airXiv e-prints, arXiv-1601 (2016)
12. Hinkelmann, K.: SBVR-Semantic of Business Vocabulary and Business Rules (2008)
13. Sayao, M., de Carvalho, G.R.: Lexicon construction for information systems. Inteligencia Artificial. Revista Iberoamericana d'Inteligencia Artificial **11**(36), 35–42 (2007)
14. Razafindramintsa, J.L., Mahatody, T., Becheru, A., Razafimandimby, J.P.: Semantic aspect derivation of the Praxeme methodology from the elaborate extended language. In: 2016 20th International Conference on System Theory, Control and Computing (ICSTCC), pp. 842–847. IEEE (2007)
15. Niu, N., Easterbrook, S.: Extracting and modeling product line functional requirements. In: 2008 16th IEEE International Requirements Engineering Conference, pp. 155–164. IEEE (2008)
16. Valipour, M.H., AmirZafari, B., Maleki, K.N., Daneshpour, N.: A brief survey of software architecture concepts and service oriented architecture. In: 2nd IEEE International Conference on Computer Science and Information Technology, pp. 34–38. IEEE (2009)
17. Benouda, H., Azizi, M., Esbai, R., Moussaoui, M.: Modeling and code generation of Android applications using acceleo. Int. J. Softw. Eng. Appl. **10**(3), 83–94 (2015)

Stakeholder-Centric Clustering Methods for Conflict Resolution in the Requirements Engineering Process

Ishaya Gambo[1,2(✉)] and Kuldar Taveter[1]

[1] Institute of Computer Science, University of Tartu, Tartu, Estonia
{ishaya.gambo,kuldar.taveter}@ut.ee

[2] Department of Computer Science and Engineering, Obafemi Awolowo University, Ile-Ife, Nigeria

Abstract. This paper describes the development and evaluation of a framework that combines expert-based and clustering methods for resolving conflicts in requirements elicited from stakeholders. The purpose of the framework was to identify and resolve conflicts among expectations by multiple stakeholders that often arise during the requirements elicitation phase. By means of qualitative and quantitative research approaches, face-to-face oral interviews, quantitative surveys, brainstorming sessions, and focus groups, scenarios were generated with stakeholders of a given problem domain. Our approach was implemented within an interactive system that empirically supports the adequacy of our framework with the involvements of experts and other stakeholders of the chosen problem domain. In addition, we presented a dataset of requirements with their weight scales that formed the basis for resolving conflicting views by stakeholders by applying scientific criteria. The framework was validated in a real-life case study. The results demonstrated 85.71% of correctly clustered instances of requirements, based on which the experts agreed that the interactive system was good enough for resolving conflicting subjective views in requirements analysis. The research performed has the two-fold threat to validity, which suggests (i) the need to adequately capture and harmoniously represent the views by different stakeholders in a multicultural and multidisciplinary domain and (ii) the need to validate the framework in other real life case studies in different domains. The research performed has a high potential for reducing software development costs and saving time at the early stage of the development of software products.

Keywords: Requirements engineering · Stakeholders · Conflict resolution · Clustering algorithm · Delphi method · Software engineering

1 Introduction

In requirements engineering (RE), the involvement of stakeholders is crucial for determining the requirements necessary to build a software-intensive system. As has been observed in [50] and [6], the quality of the system requirements improves when the stakeholders collaboratively interact in defining the overall goals of the system. However, managing different views, perspectives, desires, and goals by stakeholders in such

R. Ali et al. (Eds.): ENASE 2021, CCIS 1556, pp. 183–210, 2022.
https://doi.org/10.1007/978-3-030-96648-5_9

a collaborative setting requires dealing with conflicting interests [33]. On one hand, conflicts between stakeholders' views harness positive aspects of the problem domain at hand and should therefore be identified and resolved rather than suppressed [20,61,72]. In this context, identifying and resolving the conflicts can positively impact the application domain and helps to increase the economic value of the system to be designed for stakeholders' satisfaction [32].

On the other hand, unresolved conflicts make stakeholders lose confidence in accepting the technology that has been developed. Failing to care for the needs of stakeholders, especially in a conflicting situation, often leads to inconsistencies in system specifications and the rejection of software and technology [30,55]. This can lead to dissatisfaction by stakeholders, waste of invested resources, and ultimately to system failures. Therefore, to achieve mutual understanding between stakeholders, satisfy their needs, and avoid conflicts, it is necessary to devise a framework that would help to resolve issues of misunderstanding between the stakeholders.

In the context of this paper, we strongly agree that eliciting conflicting requirements for software product development is always expected [74]. Conflicts between requirements enable to analyze and discuss further various perspectives of the stakeholders, which have been revealed by the conflicts [33]. As has been described in [32] and [3], conflicting requirements reflect the disagreement between two or more viewpoints by different stakeholders on some decisions or values wished for a software product to be designed. For example, a stakeholder's interest in a development project is a potential candidate for conflict when such interest is frustrated by another interest [7]. Conflicts of this nature can go beyond the normal limit, which might eventually be too big to be reasonable or acceptable. Also, conflicts of this kind can lead to a strong and painful bitterness one feels in a conflicting situation, which potentially can hinder mutual satisfaction and understanding among stakeholders. When this happens, there are bound to be divisions and separation, which will eventually make negotiations difficult [67]. This can lead to poor specification of requirements and, subsequently, system failures.

Moreover, the problem of conflict management is further aggravated by the iterative nature of some popular development methodologies used in the software industry. For instance, agile software engineering (SE) methodologies [58] require changes and elaboration of a requirements specification repeatedly along with the iterations of an agile SE process [21]. As an extension of what was reported by Gambo and Taveter in [32] and [33], in this paper we further articulate the views described on identifying and resolving conflicts in RE by establishing a conflict resolution scheme. An important contribution of this paper is putting forward an analytic process model that supports conflict resolution through requirements negotiation. The analytic process model is required to determine the outcome of the decisions to be made about the requirements to be implemented during the SE process.

The research work reported in this paper aims to improve the resolution of conflicts in requirements elicited from different stakeholders. We have developed a framework for resolving conflicts and evaluated its adequacy in a real life case study. We have validated our approach in the healthcare domain by considering the Pharmacy Department at the Obafemi Awolowo University Teaching Hospital Complex (OAUTHC). Our main consideration for choosing this case study was that today's healthcare environment arguably provides a "perfect storm" of opportunities for conflict resolution because of the multidisciplinary team and multicultural nature of this problem domain. In the case study, we considered for conflict resolution requirements by many diverse stakeholders.

We have organized the remaining part of this paper as follows. In Sect. 2, we provide the background and motivation for the research work. In Sect. 3, we review and identify gaps in the RE literature addressing conflict resolution. In Sect. 4, we discuss the research methodology to be employed. In particular, we discuss the data collection process, work out the process of conflict identification, and formulate the framework for conflict resolution. Section 5 describes the conflict resolution system implemented by us that provides a tool for putting the framework formulated by us into practice. In Sect. 6, we describe the empirical analysis. The validation of the framework is explained in Sect. 7, and the results are presented and discussed in Sects. 8 and 9. In Sect. 10, we analyze the threats to validity. Finally, the conclusions are presented and future work is outlined in Sect. 11.

2 Background and Motivation

Conflict resolution is a universal phenomenon with different research strands within software engineering (SE), management science, international relations, psychology and design science. Problems revolving around resolving conflicts in these disciplines have been a subject of investigation over the years [15], focusing on mutual understanding and satisfaction by stakeholders. In this context, stakeholders can either be the individuals, groups, or organizations that affect or are affected by a system [28]. A common approach to resolving conflicts in different disciplines is through negotiation [32], especially in SE during the RE process.

The adoption of the RE process in the SE community contributes to the development of high-quality software systems [5]. However, the RE process deals with humans [51], whose needs are virtually insatiable, making conflicts inevitable. Also, RE is naturally collaborative [17] and involves various stakeholders and activities to produce the correct, complete, and consistent requirements specifications. Such collaborative nature of RE involving many stakeholders often makes conflicts unavoidable. Because of conflicts involving a large number of diverse stakeholders, requirements engineers face several difficulties when deciding about the priorities and order of implementing the requirements [2,31]. Involvement of the stakeholders in RE is essential for decision-making, as their different preferences are dependent on their levels of understanding, experiences, and knowledge of the problem domain [84].

On the other hand, requirements are the vital objectives that need to be precise and unambiguous for the resulting software to be consistent in behavior. Still, requirements are mostly inclined to troubles of disputes, inconsistencies, the collision of concerns, disparity, and disagreement amongst the stakeholders [2,42]. These challenges in requirements often lead to system failures [75] and product dissatisfaction if not correctly managed. In particular, inconsistencies often emerge when stakeholders express multiple disagreeing viewpoints during the requirements elicitation and analysis phase of a SE process [64]. Therefore conflicts always emerge as nearly unavoidable because the stakeholders seek to achieve mismatching goals [12]. It is essential to have requirements specification that has resolved conflicts or contradictions amongst the stakeholders to obtain a failure-free system [9].

As a continuation and extension of the work presented in [32] and [33], our concern is five-fold in this paper. First, we seek to understand and establish how to deal with conflicts in requirements by stakeholders in the RE process, especially during the elicitation and analysis phases. Secondly, we want to know how conflicts as a problem affect software development in a multidisciplinary domain development project. Thirdly, we seek to determine how conflict arising from stakeholders' requirements can be resolved to avoid software system failure. Fourthly, we seek to uncover the challenges of existing techniques to resolve conflicting stakeholders' requirements during RE. Finally, we seek to learn what suitable technique(s) exist to help fill the gaps in conflict resolution to ensure an improved RE process and stakeholders' continuous satisfaction. Specifically, we have addressed these concerns in Sects. 3, 4, 5, 6, 7, 8, and 9 by answering the main research question: **How can we resolve conflicts arising from requirements elicited from different stakeholders in a given problem domain to avoid a failure of the resulting software-intensive system?** This question is answered analytically in Sect. 4 and empirically in Sects. 5 and 6 of this paper.

3 Related Work

The RE community has studied the issue of conflicts from a different perspective [23], covering different types and the phases in the RE process where conflicts manifest [63]. Many of these studies primarily support the continuous input from the various stakeholders (e.g., [38,55]). Overall, Bendjenna et al. [9] explained the importance of dealing with conflicts in requirements by stakeholders during the RE process to obtain a consistent system in meeting its objective(s). For that, common objectives by different stakeholders are recognized to be essential [49].

While Aldekhail et al. [3] reported other literature related to conflicts in RE, Grünbacher and Seyff [35] observed the significant part of conflicts in RE that manifest themselves, especially within the current methods used for developing software systems. Also, many researchers have noted that SE is collaborative (e.g., [19,54,62]) and requires the usage of different tools and techniques and participation by stakeholders. In particular, conflicts become inevitable whenever stakeholders have different expectations for a system [12]. Studies have shown that conflicts in SE practices are common [63], and the RE process is the most suitable part of a SE process for addressing conflicting viewpoints and expectations [9,79]. Conflicts left unattended in a real-life development project tend to escalate [52] and negatively affect the system to be developed. Notably, existing methods do not address practical and inclusive ways of resolving conflicts.

Further, the extent of research in RE devoted to conflicting requirements indicates that conflict resolution requires proper decision-making because unresolved conflicts will always have a strong negative effect on software product success and customer satisfaction [34]. Previous work on conflicts in RE focused on identifying and resolving requirements in general terms [47]. For example, Barchiesi et al. [7] observed that conflicts are resolved through negotiations between human participants [66]. Nevertheless, the negotiation approach could not provide the expected satisfaction for stakeholders [57]. In Easterbrook [22], the usage of the computer-supported negotiation system

(Synoptic) was proposed. However, it could not guarantee absolute satisfaction for the stakeholders. Boehm et al. [10] introduced the Win-Win technique to solve risks and reconcile uncertainties through a negotiation approach. Still, the approach suffers from some setbacks in selecting a resolution plan and scalability.

Several other authors have proposed resolving conflicts in requirements using other techniques (e.g., [11,14,24,25,63,79,82,87]. Still, inconsistencies and contradictions [36] in stakeholders' views of the system to be developed often arise. These problems hinder the mutual satisfaction of stakeholders and result in poor requirements specifications and faulty systems. This points to the need for a more stakeholder-centric analytical approach that supports conflict resolution through requirements negotiation and prioritization. The desired approach would enable requirements engineers to obtain a consensus among stakeholders.

In addition, some work in conflict resolution has focused on conflicts in particular kinds of requirements and systems, such as conflicts among non-functional requirements [11,25,41,59,68]; conflicts in pervasive computing systems [46]; compliance requirements [53]; requirements classification [86], web application requirements [78]; contextual requirements [4]; requirements in aspect-oriented RE [13,69]; requirements in goal-oriented RE [33,38,43,55,79], and so on.

For instance, van Lamsweerde et al. [79] used a formal and heuristical approach to identify conflicts between requirements by multiple stakeholders specified as goals. The method by van Lamsweerde et al. [79] borders with matching these goals with existing domain-specific divergence patterns, which was based on previous experiences in conflict detection. However, this approach includes some bias in the process of conflict identification, which makes the approach inefficient in a situation where mutual agreement among stakeholders is pertinent [39].

Additionally, the technique by van Lamsweerde et al. [79] only uncovers conflicts. It cannot differentiate the contradictions in the different stakeholders' specifications. The argumentation approach by Jureta et al. [43] supports integration of claims into the goal model. For that, the stakeholders decide on acceptable criteria and can convert the requirements to argument-based models. This approach by Jureta et al. [43] intends to document stakeholders' decision-making processes to generate the specifications without resolving conflicts. Notably, other researchers [81] suggested various frameworks that have not been implemented and experimented with in real-life case studies.

In Table 1, we provide a summary of nine other related works and uncover some strengths and weaknesses based on seven criteria: (i) modeling conflicts in elicited requirements, (ii) ability to identify conflict, (iii) ability to generate a resolution scheme, (iv) ability to make a resolution selection, (v) involvement of stakeholders, (vi) ability to evaluate for consensus, and (vii) scalability..

Differently, in our research, we introduce a streamlined approach for describing the views by the stakeholders of a system to be developed and reconciling the conflicting views and use the framework for conflict identification and resolution by engaging the stakeholders extensively in the process. We achieve this by combining expert-based and clustering approaches. As the literature reflects, the clustering approach by Veerappa and Leiter has been used to group the stakeholders' requirements into clusters. The goal is to make relevant decisions on the similarities to gain insight into the stakeholders'

Table 1. Strength and limitations of existing approaches to conflict resolution in RE.

Criteria for resolution	[10]	[27]	[79]	[56]	[24]	[85]	[78]	[55]	[38]	ReqCCR (our tool)
Modelling conflicts in elicited requirements	✓	✓	✓	✓	✓	✓	✓	✓	✓	✓
Ability to identify conflict	✓	✓	×	✓	✓	✓	✓	✓	✓	✓
Ability to generate a resolution plan	Partially	×	×	✓	✓	Partially	×	Partially	×	✓
Ability to make a resolution selection	×	×	×	×	×	×	×	Partially	×	✓
Experts and/or other stakeholders involvement	Partially	×	×	×	×	✓	Partially	Partially	✓	✓
Ability to evaluate for consensus	Partially	×	×	×	×	Partially	×	×	×	✓
Scalability	×	×	×	×	×	×	Partially	×	×	✓

preferences while explaining the relationships between different requirements. In RE, clustering has been used to improve the quality of the system's requirements [48,89] and requirements reuse [8,48]. Clustering as an unsupervised machine learning approach is remarkable and can improve the entire RE methodologies, especially with the recent emergence of explainability and freedom from discrimination as new requirements [83].

4 Methodological Approach

We addressed the study through qualitative and quantitative approaches in the case study research [88]. The philosophy behind our approach contributes to the theories about the collection, analysis, and further processing of data about the phenomenon being studied [16]. In this regard, we based our research on the positivist (quantitative) and interpretivist (qualitative) philosophies by employing expert-based and clustering techniques for conflict resolution in RE.

The positivist (quantitative) aspect considers the phenomenon that is measurable by using statistical instruments. This is complemented by the interpretivist approach that helps to understand the phenomenon without searching for determinism or universal laws [65] and supports the interpretation of outcomes based on the context, participants, and resources. The intepretivist (qualitative) approach relates to the interpretivist school of thought about resolving conflicts that arise from requirements expressed by different stakeholders. In our research, the qualitative approach allowed for a number of alternative interpretations of reality that jointly accommodate the scientific knowledge behind conflict resolution.

We used the statistical instruments rooted in the Delphi method [44] and the clustering technique for measuring the similarity of requirements. While the Delphi technique supports setting priorities and gaining consensus (agreement) on an issue [44], the clustering approach offers the potential to tackle how to consequently and proficiently coordinate large numbers of requests from stakeholders and organize the resulting requirements into a coherent structure.

We considered requirements elicitation from different stakeholders as a "warfare" process because every stakeholder has his/her views of the same system being designed and is often passionate about her/his understanding of the system. We modified the Delphi technique [44] for filtering and ranking requirements and reducing duplication. Also, we engaged experts to resolve the conflicting requirements. The experts who were engaged in the modified Delphi process were the pharmacists. They were selected based on their number of years of experience. They had the same background and training, but they had different values that make conflicts between their viewpoints inevitable as humans.

4.1 Framework for Resolution

Our framework is a unified process that recognizes the importance of communication between the stakeholders during requirements elicitation. It comprises streamlined methods for describing the stakeholders' views of a system being designed through an expert-oriented approach - the Delphi method [44]. The framework we have described is shown in Fig. 1. This framework for conflict resolution suggests a process flow that is iterative and incremental. It offers an evolutionary feel crucial in modern SE processes [32].

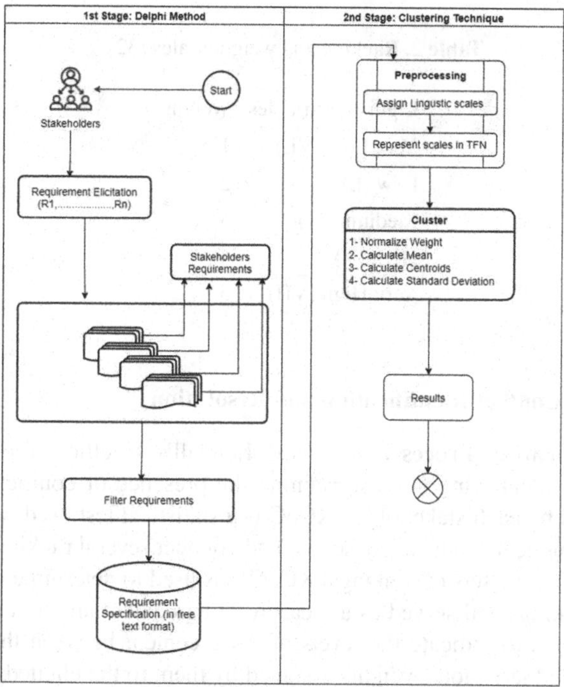

Fig. 1. A description of the framework for resolution (Modified from [32]).

As Fig. 1 reflects, the framework consists of two stages. At the first stage, the modified Delphi method is used in two iterations. In the initial iteration, requirements are elicited from the stakeholders using qualitative interviews, stakeholder analysis, brainstorming sessions, focus group approach, and scenario generation. The next iteration at the first stage involves filtering the lists of the elicited requirements by generating a master list of requirements. At this point, the selected experts are involved in the process, where their opinions and the expectations extracted from the interviews are captured to produce the master list. With the application of the Delphi method, it was possible to obtain consensus amongst the lists of elicited requirements and produce the final list of requirements for clustering.

After producing the list of user requirements, the second stage of the framework (in Fig. 1) is identifying conflicts and applying the clustering approach. First, we prioritized the requirements based on the linguistic evaluations by the stakeholders. As is shown in Table 2, we used the ranking scales as variables to capture the ranking scales for each stakeholder on each requirement evaluated[1]. Also, since conflicts can be viewed as uncertainties, the fuzzy logic approach reported in [1] and [30] was followed. Thus, we obtained the ranking scale of preference weights for requirements prioritized by different stakeholders on each requirement in the second iteration[2]. We explain in Subsect. 4.2 how our conflict resolution framework (in Fig. 1) was used to identify and resolve conflicts between requirements.

Table 2. Ranking and weight scales [32].

Liguistic variables	Weight
Very Low (VL)	1
Low (L)	2
Medium (M)	3
High (H)	4
Very High (VH)	5

4.2 Process of Conflict Identification and Resolution

Conflict Identification Process. We used Kendall's Coefficient of Concordance (KCoC) [45] for identifying and ascertaining the presence of conflicts based on the weights assigned by each stakeholder. KCoC is a statistical test used within the modified Delphi technique to evaluate consensus and conduct several rankings for N objects or individuals. Given k sets of rankings, KCoC was used to determine the associations among these rankings and served as a measure of agreement among the stakeholders. Thus, KCoC aimed to indicate the levels of disagreement between the stakeholders' views considering the various weights assigned by them to the elicited sets of requirements. We denote KCoC as W and define it as follows:

Definition 1: Let us assume that m stakeholders assign weights to k requirements that are ordered from 1 to k. Let r_{ij} denote the rating the stakeholder j gives to the requirement i. For each requirement i, let $R_i = \sum_{j=1}^{r_{ij}}$ and let $\overline{R}$ be the mean of the R_i, and let R be the squared deviation [70], that is:

[1] https://doi.org/10.5281/zenodo.4603841.

[2] https://doi.org/10.5281/zenodo.4603824.

$$R = \sum_{i=1}^{k} *(R_i - \overline{R})^2 \tag{1}$$

Now W is defined by:

$$W = \frac{12R}{m^2(k^3 - k)} \tag{2}$$

For each stakeholder j

$$\sum_{i=1}^{k} r_{ij} = 1 + 2 + ... + k = \frac{k(k+1)}{2} \tag{3}$$

Therefore, the mean of the Ri is:

$$\overline{R} = \frac{1}{k}\sum_{i=1}^{k} R_i = \frac{1}{k}\sum_{i=1}^{m}\sum_{j=1}^{k} r_{ij} = \frac{1}{k}\sum_{j=1}^{m}\sum_{i=1}^{k} r_{ij} = \frac{1}{k}\sum_{j=1}^{m}\frac{k(k+1)}{2} = \frac{m(k+1)}{2} \tag{4}$$

On the other hand, if W is:

$$W = \frac{12S^2}{m^2(k^3 - k)} - \frac{3(k+1)}{k-1} \tag{5}$$

where

$$S^2 = \sum_{i=1}^{k} *Ri^2 \tag{6}$$

Based on the Wilcoxon Rank Sum Test in [70], if all the stakeholders are in a complete agreement (that is, they give the same rating to each of the requirements), then

$$S^2 = \sum_{i=1}^{k} *Ri^2 = \sum_{i=1}^{k} *(mj)^2 = m^2 * \sum_{i=1}^{k} *j^2 \tag{7}$$

But

$$\sum_{i=1}^{k} *j^2 = \frac{k(k+1)(2k+1)}{6} \tag{8}$$

and therefore

$$W = \frac{12S^2}{m^2(k^3-k)} - \frac{3(k+1)}{k-1} = \frac{12m^2k(k+1)(2k+1)}{6m^2k(k-1)(k+1)} - \frac{3(k+1)}{k-1} = \frac{2(2k+1)}{k-1} - \frac{3(k+1)}{k-1} = 1 \tag{9}$$

In the opposite case, if all the values of Ri are the same (that is, if the stakeholders are in a complete disagreement), then by definition 1, $W = 0$. Most often, $0 \leq W \leq 1$. We used Algorithm 1 [32] to identify the presence of conflicts. When computing the value of W, we arranged the dataset into a kxN table. Each row represents the weights assigned by a particular stakeholder to N requirements. After that, each column of the table was summed up (Ri) and divided by k to find the average rank Ri. The resulting average ranks were then summed and divided by k to obtain the mean value of the $Ri's$.

We expressed each of the average ranks as a deviation from the grand mean. Thus, we computed W, as is shown in Eq. (10) [32]:

$$W = \frac{\sum_{i=1}^{N}(\overline{Ri} - \overline{R})^2}{N(N^2 - 1)/12} \tag{10}$$

where K is the number of sets of rankings, i.e., the number of stakeholders; N is the number of requirements ranked; Ri is the average weight assigned to the ith requirement; and R is the average (or grand mean) of the weights assigned across all requirements.

Algorithm 1. The algorithm for conflict identification [31].

Input: k : *number of stakeholders (integer)*; $D[row][col]$: *data set in form of* $k * n$; n : *number of requirements (integer)*; *Ri average of the weigth*; *R average of all objects*

Output: W

```
for (int i=0, i<k, i++) do
    for (int j=0, j<n, j++) do
        r_ij = j * (j + 1)/2;
        enter D[i][j];
    end for
    R_i = r_ij
    R̄+ = Ri;
    R = (Ri = Ri)^2
    W = R/(n(n^2 − 1)/2);
    if W=0 then
        There are conflicting expectations
    else if W=1 then
        No conflicts
    end if
    Returnmessage
end for
```

In Eq. (10), $N(N^2 - 1)/12$ is the maximum possible sum of the squared deviations. That value would hold if there was a seamless understanding among the k rankings, and the average rankings were 1,2, . . ., N. If $W = 0$, it means that there are conflicting expectations based on the subjective weights assigned by each stakeholder, i.e., there is a conflict. If $W = 1$, it means that the stakeholders agree about the weights they assigned to each requirement, i.e., there is no conflict. Values between 0 and 1 are approximated to the values 0 and 1 to represent the variability ratio for evaluating consensus [45]. In our case, the KCoC was calculated to be $0.000115598 \approx 0.00$, which by approximation is 0.

Conflict Resolution Process. In our research work, the K-Means clustering algorithm established the framework for resolving conflicts by grouping the datasets of requirements based on the assigned weights into classes of similar requirements called clusters. The weights assigned to the requirements $Ri \ldots Rn$ by each stakeholder Si represent the attributes. At the same time, each stakeholder represents an instance of a class (cluster) as specified in the dataset. The K-Means algorithm is described as Algorithm 2.

We used the clustering approach to establish a scheme for conflict resolution. Two major activities of the clustering approach - data preprocessing and data clustering - were used to resolve conflicts. We preprocessed the dataset and used the K-Means clustering algorithm [73] to divide the requirements into clusters. The K-Means algorithm calculates distances between each point of the dataset containing the instances and attributes and the center by utilizing the Euclidean distance measure [40,73]. Also, the K-Means algorithm automatically normalizes numerical attributes in the process of computing the Euclidean distance [73].

We used the K-Means clustering algorithm to obtain the clusters and identify the most desirable user requirements. The algorithm takes the number of clusters K as input, generates the initial clusters from the dataset, and computes the average of each individual cluster in the dataset to determine the relative closeness degrees and consistency indexes of the requirements contained by the cluster. Also, the K-Means algorithm assigns each individual record in the dataset to one of the initial clusters using the Euclidean Distance Measure [40]. The individual record is then re-assigned to the most similar cluster in the dataset. After that, the averages of all of the most similar clusters are recomputed. The K-Means algorithm is iterative and ensures the establishment of stable clusters [37]. With the K-Means clustering algorithm, we were able to formulate the framework for conflict resolution. The framework enabled identifying the centers of agreements to support decision-making on the lists of requirements by different stakeholders.

Algorithm 2. The K-Means algorithm for clustering [31].

```
Input: k: number of clusters
Output: the set of clusters
for (int i=0, i<k, i++) do                         ▷ iteration until ii from 0 to k
    for (int j=0, j<n, j++) do
        Enter D[i][j]
        random_value=rand(1tok + 1)      ▷ calculate the random value of object(s) entered
                                                   ▷ initial cluster centers
        for (int k=0, k<random_value, k++) do      ▷ k is the no. of clusters
            dist = square ((k − i)^2 + (k − j)^2;  ▷ determine which k (clusters) is closer
            dist = sq
            if dist=j then
                sum +=i
            end if
        end for
        sum_cluster+=sum
    end for
    return sum_cluster
end for
```

5 System Implementation

We implemented an interactive system to empirically prove the adequacy of our framework on a 64-bit Windows 10 Enterprise Operating System (OS) with an Intel(R)

Core™ i5-8250U CPU @ 1.60 GHz processor and 16 GB RAM. The interactive system called Requirement Clustering for Conflict Resolution (ReqCCR) assumed relative weights of requirements provided by the stakeholders as input to generate a list of prioritized requirements. The sample data set used for clustering was based on the "stakeholders' ranked dataset" available in a spreadsheet CSV format (requirement-datasetN.csv)[3].

As such, for each element in the dataset, the Euclidean distance between individual requirements and clusters was computed, as was explained in Sect. 4. Table 3 shows the normal distribution of the first 25 requirements with their corresponding minimum and maximum values, the mean, and standard deviation (*stdev*). The distribution presents the data in its normalized form, allowing it to be scaled to fall within a small specified range for clustering. The purpose of normalizing the dataset is to prevent variables with the most significant values from dominating the measure. Again, normalization before clustering was required to determine the Euclidian distance sensitive to differences in the magnitude or scales of the attributes [18]. During the clustering process, we defined the total number of clusters "K" as 5. This number was decided based on the five Ranking Scales used as labels. In general, the K-Means algorithm was quite sensitive to how clusters were initially assigned. Clustering by the K-means algorithm gave us 5 clusters, as shown in Fig. 2, 3, 4, 5 and 6. The results of clustering include 101 requirements in each cluster. The K-Means clustering algorithm split the requirements Ri… Rn into k clusters in which each requirement belongs to the cluster with the nearest mean.

Table 3. Normal distribution of requirements after preprocessing.

RiD	R1	R2	R3	R4	R5	R6	R7	R8	R9	R10	R11	R12	R13
Min	1	1	1	1	1	1	2	2	1	1	1	1	1
Max	5	5	5	5	5	5	5	5	5	5	5	5	5
Centroids	4.167	3.667	4.5	3.786	4.405	3.571	4.429	4.5	4.071	3.69	4	3.738	3.452
Stdev	1.208	1.391	0.994	1,138	1.149	1.252	0.77	0.834	1.156	1.316	1.23	1.17	1.4

RiD	R14	R15	R16	R17	R18	R19	R20	R21	R22	R23	R24	R25
Min	1	1	1	3	2	1	2	2	2	1	2	1
Max	5	5	5	5	5	5	5	5	5	5	5	5
Centroids	3.405	3.095	4.024	4.405	4.024	3.905	4.119	4.238	4.5	4.143	4.333	4.167
Stdev	1.326	1.376	1.137	0.798	0.95	1.165	1.017	1.031	0.773	1.117	0.816	0.853

RID	Centroids	Stdev	RID	Centroids	Stdev	RID	Centroids	Stdev	RID	Centroids	Stdev	RID	Centroids	Stdev
R1	4.00	0.89	R22	4.17	0.75	R43	2.67	0.82	R64	3.50	0.84	R85	3.67	0.52
R2	3.50	1.64	R23	3.67	1.51	R44	3.83	0.75	R65	3.17	1.47	R86	4.00	0.89
R3	4.67	0.52	R24	3.83	0.98	R45	3.33	0.52	R66	3.50	0.84	R87	3.33	0.82
R4	3.17	0.98	R25	4.00	0.63	R46	3.50	0.84	R67	3.17	0.98	R88	3.83	0.75
R5	4.50	0.55	R26	3.33	1.03	R47	2.83	0.98	R68	3.50	1.05	R89	4.67	0.52
R6	2.83	1.33	R27	3.83	0.98	R48	3.83	0.75	R69	2.67	1.03	R90	3.83	0.75
R7	4.00	0.63	R28	3.33	0.52	R49	3.17	0.98	R70	3.17	1.47	R91	3.50	0.84
R8	4.33	0.52	R29	3.50	1.05	R50	3.00	0.89	R71	2.83	0.75	R92	3.17	0.75
R9	4.17	0.75	R30	3.33	1.03	R51	2.67	1.63	R72	3.17	1.47	R93	4.17	0.98
R10	3.67	0.82	R31	3.17	1.33	R52	3.00	0.89	R73	3.00	1.41	R94	3.50	0.55
R11	3.83	0.41	R32	3.17	0.75	R53	3.33	1.03	R74	2.83	0.75	R95	3.50	0.55
R12	3.33	1.03	R33	3.50	0.84	R54	2.83	1.17	R75	2.67	1.37	R96	3.83	0.41
R13	3.33	1.03	R34	3.50	1.05	R55	3.17	1.33	R76	3.67	1.37	R97	3.83	0.98
R14	3.17	1.47	R35	3.50	0.55	R56	3.33	1.51	R77	3.50	1.05	R98	3.67	0.82
R15	3.00	0.89	R36	3.17	0.75	R57	3.17	1.33	R78	3.83	0.41	R99	3.67	0.52
R16	4.17	0.75	R37	3.17	1.17	R58	3.50	0.55	R79	3.00	0.89	R100	3.83	0.75
R17	4.17	0.75	R38	3.67	0.52	R59	3.33	1.03	R80	3.67	0.52	R101	4.00	0.89
R18	3.50	1.05	R39	3.67	1.21	R60	3.00	0.89	R81	3.83	1.17	-	-	-
R19	4.00	0.89	R40	3.67	0.82	R61	3.50	1.05	R82	3.67	1.51	-	-	-
R20	3.50	1.05	R41	3.50	1.52	R62	3.50	1.05	R83	3.67	1.37	-	-	-
R21	3.67	1.03	R42	3.67	0.82	R63	3.17	1.17	R84	3.17	1.47	-	-	-

Fig. 2. Cluster 1.

[3] https://doi.org/10.5281/zenodo.4603824.

RID	Centroids	Stdev	RID	Centroids	Stdev	RID	Centroids	Stdev	RID	Centroids	Stdev	RID	Centroids	Stdev
R1	5.00	0.00	R22	2.50	0.71	R43	2.00	0.00	R64	2.00	0.00	R85	2.50	0.71
R2	2.00	0.00	R23	2.50	0.71	R44	2.50	0.71	R65	3.00	1.41	R86	3.00	1.41
R3	2.00	1.41	R24	2.50	0.71	R45	2.50	0.71	R66	2.50	0.71	R87	2.50	0.71
R4	2.50	2.12	R25	2.00	1.41	R46	2.00	0.00	R67	2.00	1.41	R88	3.00	1.41
R5	3.50	2.12	R26	2.00	1.41	R47	2.50	0.71	R68	2.50	2.12	R89	1.50	0.71
R6	2.50	2.12	R27	2.00	0.00	R48	2.00	0.00	R69	2.00	1.41	R90	1.50	0.71
R7	2.50	0.71	R28	2.00	1.41	R49	2.00	0.00	R70	2.50	2.12	R91	2.00	0.00
R8	2.00	0.00	R29	2.50	2.12	R50	2.00	1.41	R71	2.50	0.71	R92	2.50	0.71
R9	1.50	0.71	R30	2.50	0.71	R51	2.00	1.41	R72	3.00	1.41	R93	2.50	0.71
R10	1.50	0.71	R31	2.50	0.71	R52	2.00	0.00	R73	2.50	0.71	R94	2.50	0.71
R11	2.00	0.00	R32	2.50	0.71	R53	1.50	0.71	R74	2.50	0.71	R95	2.00	1.41
R12	2.00	0.00	R33	2.00	0.00	R54	2.00	1.41	R75	2.50	0.71	R96	2.00	1.41
R13	2.00	1.41	R34	2.00	0.00	R55	1.50	0.71	R76	2.50	0.71	R97	2.00	1.41
R14	2.00	1.41	R35	2.50	0.71	R56	2.50	0.71	R77	2.50	0.71	R98	2.00	1.41
R15	1.50	0.71	R36	3.00	1.41	R57	1.00	0.00	R78	2.50	2.12	R99	2.50	0.71
R16	1.50	0.71	R37	1.50	0.71	R58	2.50	0.71	R79	2.00	1.41	R100	2.50	0.71
R17	3.00	0.00	R38	2.50	0.71	R59	2.00	0.00	R80	2.00	1.41	R101	3.00	0.00
R18	3.00	0.00	R39	1.50	0.71	R60	2.50	0.71	R81	2.50	0.71	-	-	-
R19	1.50	0.71	R40	2.00	1.41	R61	2.00	0.00	R82	2.50	0.71	-	-	-
R20	2.00	0.00	R41	1.50	0.71	R62	2.00	0.00	R83	3.50	0.71	-	-	-
R21	2.00	0.00	R42	2.00	0.00	R63	2.00	0.00	R84	2.50	0.71	-	-	-

Fig. 3. Cluster 2.

RID	Centroids	Stdev	RID	Centroids	Stdev	RID	Centroids	Stdev	RID	Centroids	Stdev	RID	Centroids	Stdev
R1	4.82	0.40	R22	4.91	0.30	R43	3.91	1.14	R64	4.73	0.47	R85	4.82	0.40
R2	4.55	1.21	R23	4.82	0.40	R44	4.55	0.52	R65	4.82	0.40	R86	4.82	0.40
R3	4.91	0.30	R24	4.82	0.40	R45	4.73	0.47	R66	4.73	0.47	R87	4.64	0.67
R4	4.36	1.21	R25	4.45	0.69	R46	4.82	0.40	R67	4.82	0.40	R88	4.91	0.30
R5	5.00	0.00	R26	4.27	0.90	R47	4.73	0.47	R68	4.91	0.30	R89	5.00	0.00
R6	4.27	0.79	R27	4.09	1.22	R48	4.73	0.47	R69	4.82	0.40	R90	5.00	0.00
R7	4.82	0.60	R28	4.00	1.18	R49	4.64	0.50	R70	4.82	0.60	R91	4.73	0.65
R8	5.00	0.00	R29	4.36	0.92	R50	4.55	0.52	R71	4.82	0.60	R92	5.00	0.00
R9	4.55	1.21	R30	4.18	0.98	R51	4.73	0.47	R72	4.45	1.04	R93	4.91	0.30
R10	4.73	0.47	R31	4.36	0.92	R52	4.91	0.30	R73	4.64	1.21	R94	4.91	0.30
R11	4.82	0.40	R32	4.55	0.93	R53	4.91	0.30	R74	4.91	0.30	R95	4.82	0.40
R12	4.00	1.18	R33	4.36	1.21	R54	4.82	0.40	R75	4.82	0.40	R96	4.82	0.40
R13	3.82	1.33	R34	4.64	0.67	R55	4.82	0.40	R76	5.00	0.00	R97	4.82	0.40
R14	4.27	0.90	R35	4.27	1.10	R56	4.82	0.40	R77	4.91	0.30	R98	4.82	0.40
R15	3.82	1.17	R36	3.73	1.62	R57	4.73	0.65	R78	5.00	0.00	R99	4.82	0.40
R16	4.73	0.65	R37	4.45	0.93	R58	4.91	0.30	R79	4.82	0.40	R100	4.82	0.40
R17	4.91	0.30	R38	4.00	1.61	R59	4.91	0.30	R80	4.91	0.30	R101	4.91	0.30
R18	4.45	0.69	R39	3.82	1.54	R60	4.91	0.30	R81	4.64	0.67	-	-	-
R19	4.64	0.67	R40	3.55	1.69	R61	4.73	0.47	R82	4.91	0.30	-	-	-
R20	4.73	0.47	R41	3.82	1.66	R62	4.82	0.40	R83	4.64	0.67	-	-	-
R21	4.82	0.60	R42	3.82	1.47	R63	4.82	0.40	R84	4.82	0.40	-	-	-

Fig. 4. Cluster 3.

RID	Centroids	Stdev	RID	Centroids	Stdev	RID	Centroids	Stdev	RID	Centroids	Stdev	RID	Centroids	Stdev
R1	3.84	1.39	R22	4.53	0.70	R43	3.63	1.07	R64	4.32	0.58	R85	4.63	0.50
R2	3.42	1.22	R23	3.89	1.10	R44	4.37	0.60	R65	4.32	0.67	R86	4.47	0.61
R3	4.42	1.07	R24	4.42	0.69	R45	4.11	0.99	R66	4.00	0.75	R87	4.32	0.58
R4	3.63	0.96	R25	4.26	0.73	R46	3.74	0.87	R67	4.26	0.81	R88	4.42	0.84
R5	4.21	1.27	R26	3.95	0.97	R47	4.26	0.81	R68	4.21	0.86	R89	4.68	0.75
R6	3.79	1.03	R27	4.32	0.95	R48	4.58	0.51	R69	4.00	1.00	R90	4.58	0.51
R7	4.53	0.61	R28	3.58	1.17	R49	4.11	0.74	R70	4.05	0.78	R91	4.21	0.71
R8	4.53	0.70	R29	3.68	0.82	R50	4.16	1.01	R71	4.16	0.69	R92	4.16	0.76
R9	3.89	0.99	R30	3.74	1.19	R51	4.32	0.67	R72	4.00	0.82	R93	4.63	0.68
R10	3.63	1.26	R31	4.00	0.88	R52	4.58	0.51	R73	4.26	1.10	R94	4.58	0.77
R11	4.05	1.18	R32	3.95	1.08	R53	4.32	0.58	R74	4.21	0.86	R95	4.53	0.70
R12	3.95	1.03	R33	3.95	0.91	R54	4.53	0.61	R75	4.21	0.86	R96	4.32	0.82
R13	3.47	1.50	R34	3.74	1.10	R55	4.16	0.76	R76	4.37	0.68	R97	4.37	0.76
R14	3.26	1.15	R35	3.58	1.07	R56	4.32	0.82	R77	4.26	0.65	R98	4.16	1.17
R15	3.05	1.39	R36	3.63	1.16	R57	4.16	0.76	R78	4.16	0.69	R99	4.21	1.03
R16	4.00	0.94	R37	4.16	1.01	R58	4.21	0.71	R79	4.16	0.76	R100	4.37	1.07
R17	4.42	0.77	R38	4.21	0.79	R59	4.00	0.82	R80	4.21	0.71	R101	4.53	0.77
R18	4.05	0.97	R39	3.89	0.99	R60	4.32	0.82	R81	4.21	0.71	-	-	-
R19	3.89	1.05	R40	3.37	1.26	R61	4.42	0.51	R82	4.63	0.60	-	-	-
R20	4.21	0.86	R41	3.37	1.07	R62	4.42	0.51	R83	4.47	0.84	-	-	-
R21	4.32	0.82	R42	3.26	0.93	R63	4.42	0.51	R84	4.32	0.75	-	-	-

Fig. 5. Cluster 4.

6 Empirical Analysis

The research has a mixed approach, as was discussed earlier in Sect. 4. We used these approaches in the case study of RE for the Pharmacy Information Systems to be developed for OAUTHC. Specifically, the case study approach [88] was adopted for elicitation and analysis purposes. Interviews, scenario generation, and document analysis were used for the case study approach.

RID	Centroids	Stdev	RID	Centroids	Stdev	RID	Centroids	Stdev	RID	Centroids	Stdev	RID	Centroids	Stdev
R1	3.75	1.89	R22	4.75	0.50	R43	1.75	0.96	R64	3.75	1.89	R85	2.75	1.71
R2	3.50	1.73	R23	5.00	0.00	R44	4.25	0.50	R65	3.50	1.73	R86	2.75	1.71
R3	4.75	0.50	R24	4.25	0.50	R45	4.00	0.82	R66	4.00	1.41	R87	3.50	1.00
R4	4.50	0.58	R25	4.25	0.50	R46	4.00	0.82	R67	3.50	1.91	R88	3.50	1.91
R5	4.00	2.00	R26	3.75	1.26	R47	2.75	0.96	R68	4.50	1.00	R89	4.75	0.50
R6	2.25	1.50	R27	4.00	1.41	R48	4.50	0.58	R69	3.75	1.89	R90	4.25	0.96
R7	4.50	0.58	R28	4.75	0.50	R49	4.50	1.00	R70	4.75	0.50	R91	2.00	2.00
R8	4.50	1.00	R29	3.50	1.73	R50	4.75	0.50	R71	2.50	1.91	R92	3.50	1.91
R9	4.75	0.50	R30	3.00	1.83	R51	4.75	0.50	R72	3.25	1.71	R93	4.25	1.50
R10	2.25	1.50	R31	3.00	1.41	R52	5.00	0.00	R73	4.00	2.00	R94	3.00	1.83
R11	2.75	2.06	R32	2.50	1.73	R53	4.75	0.50	R74	3.00	1.41	R95	2.25	1.89
R12	3.50	1.73	R33	2.50	1.29	R54	4.75	0.50	R75	2.50	1.91	R96	4.50	1.00
R13	3.25	1.71	R34	3.00	1.83	R55	4.25	1.50	R76	3.00	1.83	R97	4.50	1.00
R14	2.75	2.06	R35	1.75	0.50	R56	3.25	2.06	R77	3.00	1.83	R98	4.00	1.41
R15	2.25	1.89	R36	1.50	0.58	R57	3.25	2.06	R78	3.50	1.73	R99	2.50	1.91
R16	3.25	1.71	R37	2.75	1.50	R58	4.00	1.41	R79	2.75	2.06	R100	2.50	1.91
R17	4.00	1.15	R38	2.25	1.89	R59	2.75	1.71	R80	3.75	1.89	R101	4.00	0.82
R18	4.00	1.15	R39	2.00	0.82	R60	4.25	0.96	R81	1.75	1.50	-	-	-
R19	3.00	1.41	R40	1.25	0.50	R61	3.50	1.73	R82	2.75	2.06	-	-	-
R20	4.00	1.41	R41	1.25	0.50	R62	3.75	1.26	R83	3.00	1.63	-	-	-
R21	4.25	1.50	R42	1.25	0.50	R63	4.50	1.00	R84	3.50	1.00	-	-	-

Fig. 6. Cluster 5.

The interview process, which follows the guidelines provided in [88] and [16], entailed speaking directly with the stakeholders involved and asking them questions about their specific needs. These needs are relevant to the pharmacy information services provided at the OAUTHC. The interview started with predefined questions, and in the process, as lots of different critical issues arose, open discussion was granted on the expectations by the participants about the system to be designed. Thirty staff members from ten sub-units of the Pharmacy Department participated in the study[4]. After the interviews, the first author conducted a mini-workshop session with heads of sub-units to synthesize all the lists of requirements into a master list of requirements.

6.1 Analysis

The analysis of clusters required the examination of the cluster centroids [26]. These centroids are the clustering factors and the typical values of all the objects in a given cluster [60]. The clustered results (see Fig. 2, 3, 4, 5 and 6) show how the requirements are assigned to the different clusters formed, and the corresponding centroids and *stdev* values. Figure 7 represents the statistics on the number and percentage of instances assigned to different clusters. As Fig. 7 shows, cluster 1, 2, 3, 4 and 5 has 14%, 5%, 26%, 45%, and 10%, of the instances. The cluster centroids are the mean vectors for each cluster that are used to characterize the clusters.

[4] https://doi.org/10.5281/zenodo.4603848.

The execution of Algorithm 2 considered the means (averages) of feature values and their *stdev* values. Each cluster is defined by the mean, forming its center and *stdev*, center and perimeter or radius. The *stdev* value for each requirement in a cluster indicates how tightly the given clustered requirement is located around the centroid of the cluster's dataset. We used the "mean of mean" to assess how the values are spread either above or below the mean. We hypothesize that a high *stdev* value implies that the data is not tightly clustered and is therefore less reliable and consistent. In contrast, a low *stdev* value indicates that the data is clustered tightly around the mean, making it more reliable and consistent.

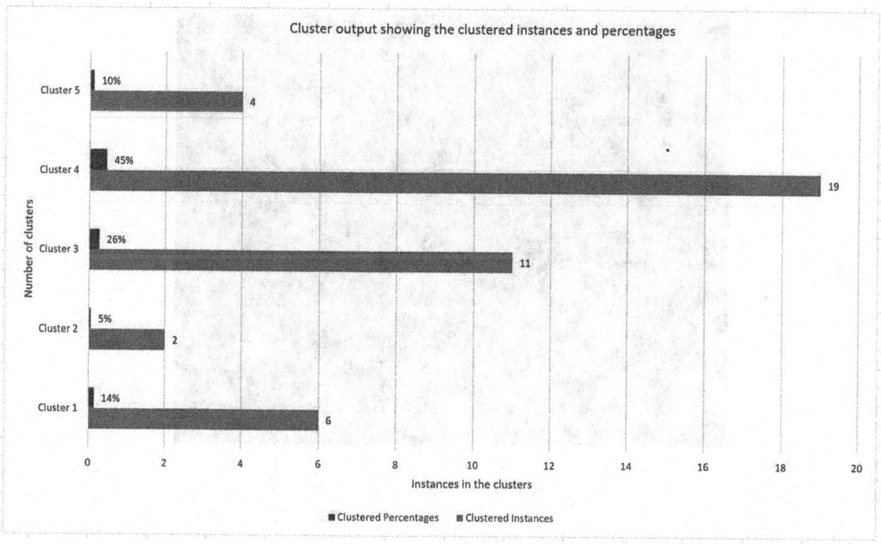

Fig. 7. Cluster output showing the clustered instances and percentages.

6.2 The Implication of Empirical Analysis of Cluster Output

Algorithm 2 divided the instances of the elicited requirements into five clusters. Each instance belongs to one and only one cluster. The five clusters (see Fig. 2, 3, 4, 5 and 6) represent the responses by the stakeholders based on the weight they assigned to each requirement. Figure 8 shows the visualized cluster assignments indicating clustered datasets and the classes assigned to each cluster [32]. The x-axis of Fig. 8 denotes the clusters, and the y-axis contains the number of instances in each cluster. Figure 9 shows a scattered chart comparing a selection of centroids of each cluster, indicating centroids of each cluster as separate points. As has been depicted in Fig. 9, clusters 3 and 4 have the highest values of centroids, as is indicated by the green triangle (△) and the purple cross shapes (×), respectively. The centroids of cluster 4 are closer to each other, and cluster 4 has the highest number of clustered instances, as Fig. 7 indicates. The centroids of cluster 2 indicated by the red rectangle (▭) shapes are far from each other. As Fig. 9 reflects, on the x-axis is the number of instances while the y-axis represents the clusters. Figure 10 shows the trend of the percentage that centroids of each cluster have contributed over time during the K-Means iteration process to the ordered categorization of the clusters. On the x-axis is the number of instances, while the y-axis represents the percentages of the cluster centroids.

6.3 Decision on Resolution Selection of Clusters

We applied the following scientific criteria as conditions to decide on the final results:

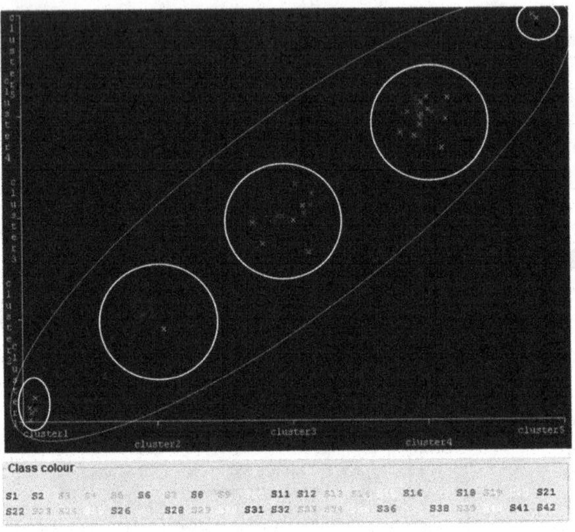

Fig. 8. Visualised cluster assignments [32].

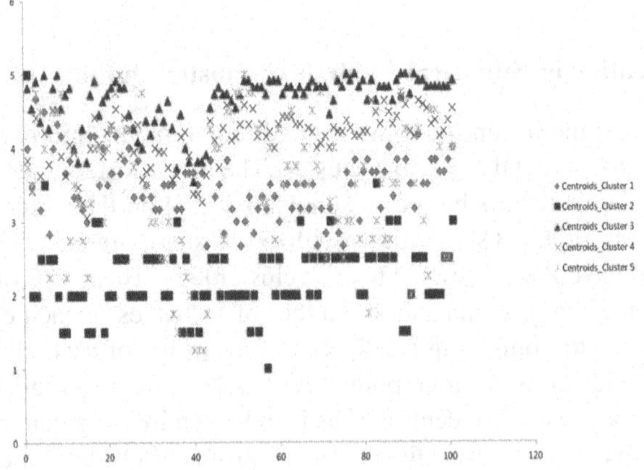

Fig. 9. A scattered chart comparing clustered centroids [32].

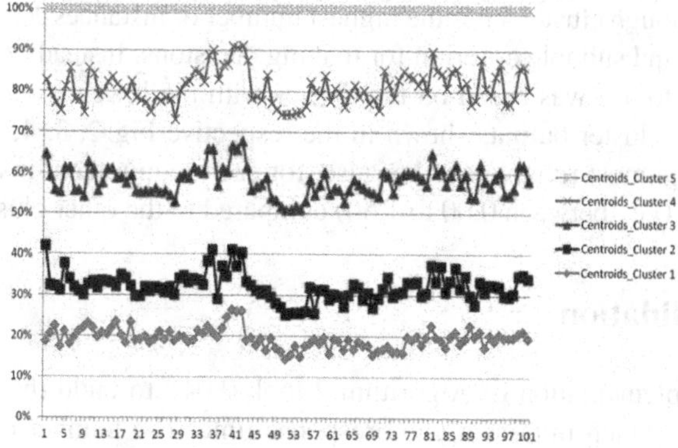

Fig. 10. Percentages of cluster centroids [32].

(a) By inspecting the *stdev* value to eliminate clusters with relatively high *stdev* values. In the context of our research, the *stdev* value measures how well the stakeholders agree with each other. The lower the *stdev* value, the stronger the agreement level. A low *stdev* value implies that most of the requirements' instances are exceptionally near to the centroids, while a high *stdev* value implies that the instances are spread out [73]. The *stdev* value for each instance in a cluster determines how dispersed (spread out) the data is from the cluster's centroid. Thus, the *stdev* value establishes the centroid that gives a meaningful representation of the dataset. For example, the *stdev* value 0 would mean that every instance is exactly equal to the centroid. The closer the *stdev* is to 0, the more reliable the centroid is. Also, the *stdev* value close to 0 indicates that there is very little volatility in the sample.

(b) By computing the average of the *stdev* value for each cluster to determine the cluster with the highest and lowest *stdev* value. As a result, the average *stdev* values for the clusters 1, 2, 3, 4 and 5 are respectively 0.95, 0.78, 0.61, 0.86 and 1.31. Thus, the cluster with the highest *stdev* value is cluster 5, while the cluster with the lowest *stdev* value is cluster 3. Also, by inspection, 81.19% of all the attributes with the lowest *stdev* value are in cluster 3, while 18.81% of all the attributes with the lowest *stdev* value are in the other clusters (i.e., 1, 2, 4, and 5).

(c) By inspecting the number of instances assigned to each cluster. As shown in Fig. 7, clusters 1, 2, and 4 have a few instances allocated to them, making this cluster inappropriate for any meaningful decision. Clusters 3 and 4 have 11 and 19 instances allocated to them, respectively.

Against the scientific criteria described in the three preceding paragraphs (a), (b), and (c), the decision on the final cluster output was made. As a result, by comparing the average *stdev* value of each cluster with the corresponding average centroid value of the cluster, cluster 3 appeared to be the most reliable one. We observed that 82 out of the 101 requirements in cluster 3 have the lowest *stdev* value within the five clusters. In comparison, the remaining 19 requirements have the lowest *stdev* value within clusters 1, 2, 4, and 5.

Secondly, although cluster 4 has the highest number of instances assigned, this is not the most reliable and suitable criterion for making decisions. Instead of that, a decision on which cluster to use was based on the cluster with the lowest average *stdev* value. As a result of the cluster outputs shown in the respective Fig. 2, 3, 4, 5 and 6, cluster 3 appears to be the most reliable one because, for each requirement instance, the *stdev* value is very low (i.e., between 0.00 to 1.50) compared to the other clusters.

7 Model Validation

The software implementation of Algorithm 2 took 0.04 s to build the model with the complete dataset, which implies a good response time. The number of iterations performed was 5, and the sum of squared errors was 223.61. This sum of squared errors is a measure that is specific to K-Means. The squared error is the squared Euclidean distance of the requirement instance from the closest cluster center. The confusion matrix in Fig. 11 summarises our model validation results. The confusion matrix in Fig. 11 contains information about the actual and predicted classifications used to measure the model performance [32].

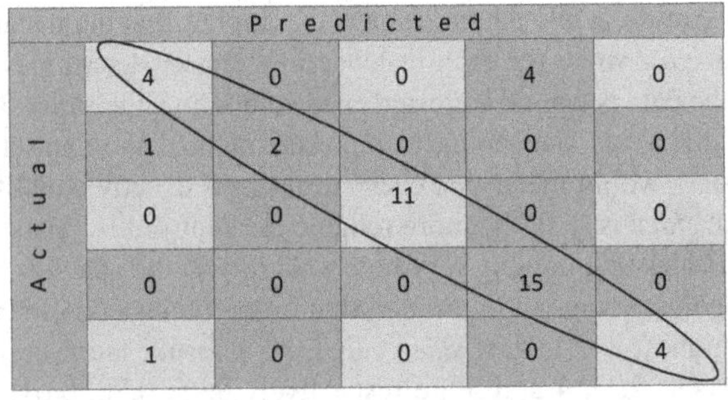

Fig. 11. Confusion matrix of K-Means clustering.

We performed sensitivity analysis and determined the confidence level to evaluate the completeness and consistency of the model for the given data in the matrix. In Table 4, the confusion matrix shown in Fig. 11 is summarized by presenting the numbers of predicted and actual requirements instances. Based on the data included by Table 4, we performed the sensitivity analysis (recall), determined the confidence level (precision), and computed the F-score and overall accuracy. The sensitivity analysis, also known as recall, defines the proportion of the actual positive cases correctly identified. The confidence level, also known as the precision, is the proportion of the positive cases that have been correctly identified. The F-score is the degree of the test's accuracy

Table 4. Confusion matrix showing predicted and actual number of instances.

Clusters	Predicted instances	Number of actual instances
Cluster 1	4	8
Cluster 2	2	3
Cluster 3	11	11
Cluster 4	15	15
Cluster 5	4	5

to determine the harmonic mean of the recall and precision for each cluster for which the recall and precision have been calculated. This means that the F-score conveys the balance between the precision P and recall R. The accuracy determines the overall correctness of the classifier after prediction [29]. As Gambo and Taveter [32] observed, the accuracy helped to determine whether the resolution resulting from the model reflected the opinions by the stakeholders. The equations that were respectively used for calculating sensitivity, confidence, F-score, and accuracy are presented as the formulae 11, 12, 13, and 14 below:

$$Sensitivity(RecallR) = \frac{TP}{TP + FN} \tag{11}$$

$$Confidence(PrecisionP) = \frac{TP}{TP + FP} \tag{12}$$

$$F - Score = 2 * \frac{P * R}{P + R} \tag{13}$$

$$Accuracy = \frac{TP + TN}{TP + TN + FP + FN} \tag{14}$$

As included by Eqs. 11, 12, 13, and 14, TP is the number of true positives; FN is the number of false negatives; FP is the number of false positives; TN is the number of true negatives.

8 Results

Figure 12 shows the results of the model evaluation. As revealed by Fig. 12, clusters 3 and 4 had 100% recall, while clusters 1, 2 and 5 had 50%, 66.7%, and 80% recalls, respectively. This means that all of the positive cases correctly identified by the model belong to clusters 3 and 4. Additionally, the model indicated 100% precision for clusters 2, 3, and 5, respectively, while clusters 1 and 4 had 66.7% and 78.95% precision. The F-score showed the harmonic means of precision and recall to be 0.57, 0.80, 1.00, 0.88, and 0.89 for the respective clusters 1, 2, 3, 4, and 5.

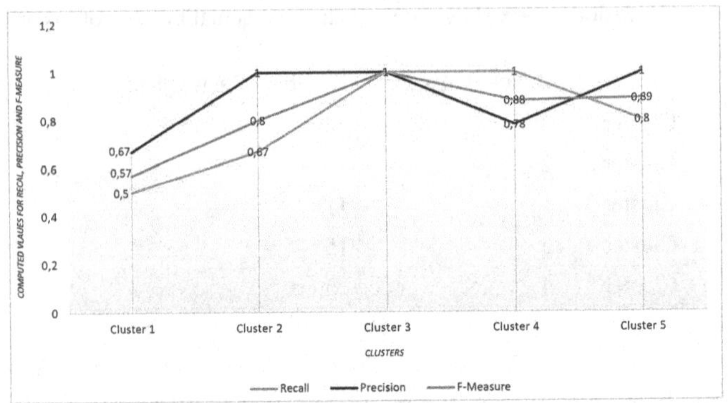

Fig. 12. Results of the model evaluation.

The F-score of cluster 3 – with the value of 1.00 (100%) – is the most effective and reliable one. In other words, the implementation of Algorithm 2 correctly clustered all the requirement instances that initially belonged to cluster 3 to the same cluster. The result of the F-score value remarkably indicates that all the requirement instances belonging to cluster 3 were correctly clustered. Consequently, inspecting and comparing both the recall and precision proves that cluster 3 has the highest percentage of positive cases correctly identified and the highest predicted number of positive cases that turned out to be correct. This outcome justifies the reason why cluster 3 is the most reliable one for the final conflict resolution.

With the choice of cluster 3 for the final resolution, this result demonstrated that the model is complete and consistent. The total value of false negative (FN) requirement instances defines the number of incorrectly clustered instances, which is 6.0 (14.29%).

Overall, the framework for resolving conflicts we have presented in this paper achieved the accuracy of 85.71%. Consequently, this approach can cater for as many requirements as needed for any SE project. It can be adapted to solve a wide variety of decision-making and selection problems about the order of implementing requirements.

9 Discussion

Given the requirements' dataset with 42 stakeholders as instances and 101 requirements as attributes, the value of Kendall's Coefficient of Concordance W calculated by using Eq. 10 was $0.000115598 \approx 0.00$. The resulting value of W indicated some level of disagreement between the stakeholders' subjective views. This means there are conflicts in the expectations by the stakeholders based on the weights assigned by them to individual requirements.

The framework we presented in Sect. 4 classifies ranked requirements by calculating for each requirement centroids and *stdev* values. This suggests that software engineers can utilize our framework to decide the most and least preferred requirements to support software release planning and avoid breaches of contracts, agreements, and trust [32].

After the clustering analysis, cluster 3 emerged as the final solution based on the scientific criteria outlined in Sect. 6.3 and the statistical evidence shown with the F-score value. Remarkably, the F-score for each cluster captures the properties of recall and precision by combining them as a single measure. The F-score also provided both the recall and precision with the same weight. This means both measures are balanced in importance, resulting in the harmonic mean consisting of two factors. For that, high precision and recall always result in a high F-score, as has been obtained in cluster 3. In addition the F-score takes care of imbalanced classes in the dataset of requirements.

The final solution in Fig. 13 indicates the conflict resolution by the K-Means algorithm presented in the order of priorities assigned to all of the requirements. As Fig. 13 shows, 77 requirements had a "very high" priority, corresponding to 76.24% of the entire set of requirements. On the other hand, 24 requirements had "high" priority, corresponding to 23.76% of the entire set of requirements. The evaluation of the model for completeness and consistency indicated 100% recall and precision of the final solution (cluster 3) and 85.7% accuracy of the resulting model.

Theoretically, our research confirmed that there is no perfect system. However, with 14.29% of incorrectly clustered instances, the experts agreed that the results were good enough for resolving the conflicting subjective views arising during requirements analysis.

Consequently, our research offers an improvement for the requirements engineering stage of SE. Our research results also demonstrate that the framework can accommodate for large sets of requirements by multiple stakeholders by resolving conflicts between these requirements with a very high precision level.

10 Threats to Validity

We identified two kinds of threats to validity, as described in [32]:

RID	Cent-roids	*Stdev*	Resolved Weights	RID	Cent-roids	*Stdev*	Resolved Weights	RID	Cent-roids	*Stdev*	Resolved Weights	RID	Cent-roids	*Stdev*	Resolved Weights
R5	5.00	0.00	VH	**R11**	4.82	0.40	VH	**R10**	4.73	0.47	VH	**R18**	4.45	0.69	H
R8	5.00	0.00	VH	**R21**	4.82	0.60	VH	**R16**	4.73	0.65	VH	**R25**	4.45	0.69	H
R76	5.00	0.00	VH	**R23**	4.82	0.40	VH	**R20**	4.73	0.47	VH	**R37**	4.45	0.93	H
R78	5.00	0.00	VH	**R24**	4.82	0.40	VH	**R45**	4.73	0.47	VH	**R4**	4.36	1.21	H
R89	5.00	0.00	VH	**R46**	4.82	0.40	VH	**R47**	4.73	0.47	VH	**R29**	4.36	0.92	H
R90	5.00	0.00	VH	**R54**	4.82	0.40	VH	**R48**	4.73	0.47	VH	**R31**	4.36	0.92	H
R92	5.00	0.00	VH	**R55**	4.82	0.40	VH	**R51**	4.73	0.47	VH	**R33**	4.36	1.21	H
R3	4.91	0.30	VH	**R56**	4.82	0.40	VH	**R57**	4.73	0.65	VH	**R14**	4.27	0.90	H
R17	4.91	0.30	VH	**R62**	4.82	0.40	VH	**R61**	4.73	0.47	VH	**R6**	4.27	0.79	H
R22	4.91	0.30	VH	**R63**	4.82	0.40	VH	**R64**	4.73	0.47	VH	**R26**	4.27	0.90	H
R52	4.91	0.30	VH	**R65**	4.82	0.40	VH	**R66**	4.73	0.47	VH	**R35**	4.27	1.10	H
R53	4.91	0.30	VH	**R67**	4.82	0.40	VH	**R91**	4.73	0.65	VH	**R30**	4.18	0.98	H
R58	4.91	0.30	VH	**R69**	4.82	0.40	VH	**R19**	4.64	0.67	VH	**R27**	4.09	1.22	H
R59	4.91	0.30	VH	**R70**	4.82	0.60	VH	**R34**	4.64	0.67	VH	**R12**	4.00	1.18	H
R60	4.91	0.30	VH	**R71**	4.82	0.60	VH	**R49**	4.64	0.50	VH	**R28**	4.00	1.18	H
R68	4.91	0.30	VH	**R75**	4.82	0.40	VH	**R73**	4.64	1.21	VH	**R38**	4.00	1.61	H
R74	4.91	0.30	VH	**R79**	4.82	0.40	VH	**R81**	4.64	0.67	VH	**R43**	3.91	1.14	H
R77	4.91	0.30	VH	**R84**	4.82	0.40	VH	**R83**	4.64	0.67	VH	**R13**	3.82	1.33	H
R80	4.91	0.30	VH	**R85**	4.82	0.40	VH	**R87**	4.64	0.67	VH	**R15**	3.82	1.17	H
R82	4.91	0.30	VH	**R86**	4.82	0.40	VH	**R2**	4.55	1.21	VH	**R39**	3.82	1.54	H
R88	4.91	0.30	VH	**R95**	4.82	0.40	VH	**R9**	4.55	1.21	VH	**R41**	3.82	1.66	H
R93	4.91	0.30	VH	**R96**	4.82	0.40	VH	**R32**	4.55	0.93	VH	**R42**	3.82	1.47	H
R94	4.91	0.30	VH	**R97**	4.82	0.40	VH	**R44**	4.55	0.52	VH	**R36**	3.73	1.62	H
R101	4.91	0.30	VH	**R98**	4.82	0.40	VH	**R50**	4.55	0.52	VH	**R40**	3.55	1.69	H
R1	4.82	0.40	VH	**R99**	4.82	0.40	VH	**R72**	4.45	1.04	VH	-	-	-	-
R7	4.82	0.60	VH	**R100**	4.82	0.40	VH	-	-	-	-	-	-	-	-

Fig. 13. Prioritized and resolved weights.

The first is internal validity, which involves eliciting, analyzing, and understanding the stakeholders' views while identifying the existence of conflicts. To mitigate this threat, we involved experts - pharmacists - in the process prescribed by the proposed conflict resolution framework. These experts have many years of experience in the problem domain. Remarkably, these experts have common backgrounds and training. They can coherently explain the views by different stakeholders to avoid the exclusion of view(s) and obtain consensus [32].

An additional threat to internal validity is the presentation and acceptance of our results. To mitigate this threat, we demonstrated the interactive system to the experts of the problem domain. We showcased the scientific process inherent in the solution to justify the conflict resolution procedure. Since the experts involved in our case study were scientifically inclined, they agreed with the results.

The second threat to validity is external validity. A threat to external validity is that the developed framework is yet to be validated in other problem domains within and outside the healthcare domain. Also, even while our research was conducted in the healthcare domain, the research was confined to only a subset of this problem domain. However, we anticipate that the overall results of our case study can be repeated to identify and resolve conflicts in a different problem domain where a large number of stakeholders is involved. Besides, we have explained and demonstrated our approach to some software engineers. They have provided positive feedback indicating that the framework proposed by us is required to determine the order of the requirements to be implemented during the software engineering process [30].

11 Conclusions and Future Work

The paper describes a framework for conflict identification and resolution spanning from requirements elicitation to requirements analysis. The framework consists of expert-based and clustering techniques for conflict resolution. The approach proposed by us constitutes a significant step that supports making crucial decisions about the software-intensive system to be developed, increasing the value offered by the system to its end users. In this paper, we present technical details of the framework, describe a software tool supporting the ideas, and describe the validation of the framework and the tool in the healthcare domain.

We emphasize that an important part of our approach consists of engaging stakeholders extensively in the conflict resolution process. Moreover, the whole Delphi process employed by the framework is stakeholder-centric because of the involvement by experts. Considering this, experts and other stakeholders participated fully in devising a unified conflict resolution scheme for the framework. In addition, the Delphi process ensured the reliability of various ideas explored and the generation of suitable information for decision-making. During this process, we introduced the ranking scale for prioritizing the specification of requirements. According to the ranking scale, the level of acceptability of requirements specified by each stakeholder was determined with the help of linguistic variables. The linguistic variables were used to capture the priority of each stakeholder on each requirement.

In addition, the clustering approach consisting of an unsupervised machine learning algorithm established the basis for achieving the resolution plan. The clustering technique organized various requirements into clusters so that the requirements inside a given cluster are more similar to each other than to the requirements belonging to the other clusters. In particular, it was possible with the clustering approach to characterize the dataset of requirements according to their weight scales suitable for analysis and prediction. For that purpose, we followed fuzzy logic [1,30] to establish pairwise comparisons of criteria and alternatives by means of ranking scales. This resulted in a data matrix that could be applied for clustering. The research performed by us showed that the clustering approach in RE can improve the quality of the resulting requirements and contributes to requirements reuse [8,89].

From the point of view of conflict management in RE, our research revealed two crucial features [32]. The first feature is the ability to cater for a large volume of requirements in a multi-stakeholder and multicultural setting. The second feature is the ability to successfully make clearcut decisions based on acceptable scientific criteria to minimize conflicts between prioritized sets of requirements expressed by the stakeholders. Importantly, these two features can considerably reduce software development costs and save time at the early stage of developing software products.

The results of this study suggest that the algorithm we implemented resolved the issues of scalability and computational complexity by providing a reliable conflict resolution. It can be implied that the stakeholders had some level of understanding of the choice of requirements needed for the Pharmacy Information System at the OAUTHC. The research results indicated that requirements engineers were able to resolve conflicts by means of our framework. Notably, the stakeholders participating in the case study agreed with the framework proposed by us. The research work also pointed out that there is no perfect system for resolving conflicts in requirements.

With respect to the future work, we suggest combining our strategy and tool with other methods and tools for data mining and analysis, such as the one proposed in [90], especially for dealing with large sets of requirements and many stakeholders in real life projects. By doing this, the scalability of our framework can be evaluated in different problem domains.

Additionally, we consider the need to conduct further research work in conflict management in the RE community to address conflicts in goal-oriented RE (GORE). For example, a pragmatic view about the need for better conflict management in GORE for sociotechnical systems (STS) is presented in [32]. This view is the first step that requires further investigation, especially considering the goals presented by the stakeholders, representing their needs and intentions. Interestingly, it is recommended to investigate conflicts in the agile agent-oriented modeling (AAOM) methodology for designing STS [71,76,77]. Within the AAOM methodology, it is also crucial to consider addressing some of the psychological problems stakeholders have in dealing with their collective and individual goals. In particular, we plan to continue the work reported in [74] about discovering and reconciling conflicts between emotional or affective requirements, which have been rendered as emotional goals attached to functional goals in a goal tree.

Acknowledgment. The authors would like to thank all the experts at the Pharmacy Department of the OAUTHC who provided invaluable input to the framework for resolution. The research work reported in this paper has received funding from the European Social Fund via the IT Academy programme and from the Mobilitas Pluss Postdoctoral Research grant MOBJD343 by the Estonian Research Agency awarded to the first author.

References

1. Achimugu, P., Selamat, A., Ibrahim, R.: A clustering based technique for large scale prioritization during requirements elicitation. In: Herawan, T., Ghazali, R., Deris, M.M. (eds.) Recent Advances on Soft Computing and Data Mining. AISC, vol. 287, pp. 623–632. Springer, Cham (2014). https://doi.org/10.1007/978-3-319-07692-8_59
2. Ahmad, S.: Negotiation in the requirements elicitation and analysis process. In: 19th Australian Conference on Software Engineering (ASWEC 2008), pp. 683–689. IEEE (2008)
3. Aldekhail, M., Chikh, A., Ziani, D.: Software requirements conflict identification: review and recommendations. Int. J. Adv. Comput. Sci. Appl. (IJACSA) **7**(10), 326 (2016)
4. Ali, R., Dalpiaz, F., Giorgini, P.: Reasoning with contextual requirements: detecting inconsistency and conflicts. Inf. Softw. Technol. **55**(1), 35–57 (2013)
5. Alshazly, A.A., Elfatatry, A.M., Abougabal, M.S.: Detecting defects in software requirements specification. Alex. Eng. J. **53**(3), 513–527 (2014)
6. Azadegan, A., Cheng, X., Niederman, F., Yin, G.: Collaborative requirements elicitation in facilitated collaboration: report from a case study. In: 2013 46th Hawaii International Conference on System Sciences, pp. 569–578. IEEE (2013)
7. Barchiesi, M.A., Costa, R., Greco, M.: Enhancing conflict resolution through an AHP-based methodology. Int. J. Manag. Decis. Mak. **13**(1), 17–41 (2014)
8. Benavides, D., Cortés, A.R., Trinidad, P., Segura, S.: A survey on the automated analyses of feature models. In: JISBD, pp. 367–376 (2006)
9. Bendjenna, H., Charrel, P., Zarour, N.: Using AHP method to resolve conflicts between nonfunctional concerns. In: International Conference on Education, Applied Sciences and Management (ICEASM 2012), pp. 26–27 (2012)
10. Boehm, B., Bose, P., Horowitz, E., Lee, M.J.: Software requirements negotiation and renegotiation aids: a theory-w based spiral approach. In: 1995 17th International Conference on Software Engineering, p. 243. IEEE (1995)
11. Boehm, B., In, H.: Identifying quality-requirement conflicts. IEEE Softw. **13**(2), 25–35 (1996)
12. Boehm, B., Port, D., Al-Said, M.: Avoiding the software model-clash spiderweb. Computer **33**(11), 120–122 (2000)
13. Brito, I.S., Moreira, A., Ribeiro, R.A., Araújo, J.: Handling conflicts in aspect-oriented requirements engineering. In: Moreira, A., Chitchyan, R., Araújo, J., Rashid, A. (eds.) Aspect-Oriented Requirements Engineering, pp. 225–241. Springer, Heidelberg (2013). https://doi.org/10.1007/978-3-642-38640-4_12
14. Butt, W.H., Amjad, S., Azam, F.: Requirement conflicts resolution: using requirement filtering and analysis. In: Murgante, B., Gervasi, O., Iglesias, A., Taniar, D., Apduhan, B.O. (eds.) ICCSA 2011. LNCS, vol. 6786, pp. 383–397. Springer, Heidelberg (2011). https://doi.org/10.1007/978-3-642-21934-4_31
15. Capra, L., Emmerich, W., Mascolo, C.: A micro-economic approach to conflict resolution in mobile computing. ACM SIGSOFT Softw. Eng. Notes **27**(6), 31–40 (2002)
16. Coolican, H.: Research Methods and Statistics in Psychology. Psychology Press (2017)

17. Damian, D., Izquierdo, L., Singer, J., Kwan, I.: Awareness in the wild: why communication breakdowns occur. In: International Conference on Global Software Engineering (ICGSE 2007), pp. 81–90. IEEE (2007)
18. De Souto, M.C., De Araujo, D.S., Costa, I.G., Soares, R.G., Ludermir, T.B., Schliep, A.: Comparative study on normalization procedures for cluster analysis of gene expression datasets. In: 2008 IEEE International Joint Conference on Neural Networks (IEEE World Congress on Computational Intelligence), pp. 2792–2798. IEEE (2008)
19. Derntl, M., Renzel, D., Nicolaescu, P., Koren, I., Klamma, R.: Distributed software engineering in collaborative research projects. In: 2015 IEEE 10th International Conference on Global Software Engineering, pp. 105–109. IEEE (2015)
20. Deutsch, M.: The Resolution of Conflict: Constructive and Destructive Processes. Yale University Press (1973)
21. van Dijk, R.: Determining the suitability of agile methods for a software project. In: 15th Twente Student Conference on IT (2011)
22. Easterbrook, S.: Handling conflict between domain descriptions with computer-supported negotiation. Knowl. Acquis. **3**(3), 255–289 (1991)
23. Easterbrook, S.: Resolving requirements conflicts with computer-supported negotiation. Requirements Eng. Soc. Tech. Issues **1**, 41–65 (1994)
24. Egyed, A.: Fixing inconsistencies in UML design models. In: 29th International Conference on Software Engineering (ICSE 2007), pp. 292–301. IEEE (2007)
25. Egyed, A., Grunbacher, P.: Identifying requirements conflicts and cooperation: how quality attributes and automated traceability can help. IEEE Softw. **21**(6), 50–58 (2004)
26. Faber, V.: Clustering and the continuous k-means algorithm. Los Alamos Sci. **22**(138144.21), 67 (1994)
27. Finkelstein, A., Kramer, J., Nuseibeh, B., Finkelstein, L., Goedicke, M.: Viewpoints: a framework for integrating multiple perspectives in system development. Int. J. Softw. Eng. Knowl. Eng. **2**(01), 31–57 (1992)
28. Freeman, R.E.: Strategic Management: A Stakeholder Approach. Cambridge University Press (2010)
29. Gambo, I., Adjicheboutou, A., Ikono, R., Iroju, O., Yange, S.: An investigative process model for predicting information difusion on social media: Information system perspective. Ife J. Technol. **27**(1), 47–59 (2020)
30. Gambo, I., Ikono, R., Achimugu, P., Soriyan, A.: An integrated framework for prioritizing software specifications in requirements engineering. Requir. Eng. **12**(1), 33–46 (2018)
31. Gambo, I.P., Ikono, R., Iroju, O.G., Omodunbi, T.O., Zohoun, O.K.: Hybridized ranking model for prioritizing functional software requirements. Int. J. Softw. Innov. **9**(4), 1–31 (2021). https://doi.org/10.4018/IJSI.289167
32. Gambo, I., Taveter, K.: Identifying and resolving conflicts in requirements by stakeholders: a clustering approach. In: ENASE, pp. 158–169 (2021)
33. Gambo, I., Taveter, K.: A pragmatic view on resolving conflicts in goal-oriented requirements engineering for socio-technical systems. In : Proceedings of the 16th International Conference on Software Technologies, pp. 333–341 (2021). https://doi.org/10.5220/0010605703330341
34. Gobeli, D.H., Koenig, H.F., Bechinger, I.: Managing conflict in software development teams: a multilevel analysis. J. Product Innov. Manag. **15**(5), 423–435 (1998)
35. Grünbacher, P., Seyff, N.: Requirements negotiation. In: Aurum, A., Wohlin, C. (eds.) Engineering and Managing Software Requirements, pp. 143–162. Springer, Heidelberg (2005). https://doi.org/10.1007/3-540-28244-0_7
36. Hadar, I., Zamansky, A., Berry, D.M.: The inconsistency between theory and practice in managing inconsistency in requirements engineering. Empir. Softw. Eng. **24**(6), 3972–4005 (2019). https://doi.org/10.1007/s10664-019-09718-5

37. Haraty, R.A., Dimishkieh, M., Masud, M.: An enhanced k-means clustering algorithm for pattern discovery in healthcare data. Int. J. Distrib. Sens. Netw. **11**(6), 615740 (2015)
38. Hassan, T., Hussain, M.Z., Hasan, M.Z., Ullah, Z., Qamar, N.: Quantitative based mechanism for resolving goals conflicts in goal oriented requirement engineering. In: Bajwa, I.S., Kamareddine, F., Costa, A. (eds.) INTAP 2018. CCIS, vol. 932, pp. 822–831. Springer, Singapore (2019). https://doi.org/10.1007/978-981-13-6052-7_71
39. Hassine, J., Amyot, D.: An empirical approach toward the resolution of conflicts in goal-oriented models. Softw. Syst. Model. **16**(1), 279–306 (2015). https://doi.org/10.1007/s10270-015-0460-6
40. Hennig, C., Meila, M., Murtagh, F., Rocci, R.: Handbook of Cluster Analysis. CRC Press (2015)
41. In, H., Olson, D., Rodgers, T.: A requirements negotiation model based on multi-criteria analysis. In: Proceedings Fifth IEEE International Symposium on Requirements Engineering, pp. 312–313. IEEE (2001)
42. In, H., Roy, S.: Visualization issues for software requirements negotiation. In: 25th Annual International Computer Software and Applications Conference. COMPSAC 2001, pp. 10–15. IEEE (2001)
43. Jureta, I.J., Faulkner, S., Schobbens, P.Y.: Clear justification of modeling decisions for goal-oriented requirements engineering. Requirements Eng. **13**(2), 87 (2008)
44. Keeney, S., McKenna, H., Hasson, F.: The Delphi Technique in Nursing and Health Research. Wiley, Hoboken (2011)
45. Kendall, M.G., Smith, B.B.: The problem of m rankings. Ann. Math. Stat. **10**(3), 275–287 (1939)
46. Khaled, O.M., Hosny, H.M., Shalan, M.: Exploiting requirements engineering to resolve conflicts in pervasive computing systems. In: Damiani, E., Spanoudakis, G., Maciaszek, L. (eds.) ENASE 2017. CCIS, vol. 866, pp. 93–115. Springer, Cham (2018). https://doi.org/10.1007/978-3-319-94135-6_5
47. Kim, M., Park, S., Sugumaran, V., Yang, H.: Managing requirements conflicts in software product lines: a goal and scenario based approach. Data Knowl. Eng. **61**(3), 417–432 (2007)
48. Lim, W.C.: Effects of reuse on quality, productivity, and economics. IEEE Softw. **11**(5), 23–30 (1994)
49. Litvak, C., Antonelli, L., Rossi, G., Gigante, N.: Improving the identification of conflicts in collaborative requirements engineering. In: 2018 International Conference on Computational Science and Computational Intelligence (CSCI), pp. 872–877. IEEE (2018)
50. Lutz, R., Schäfer, S., Diehl, S.: Using mobile devices for collaborative requirements engineering. In: Proceedings of the 27th IEEE/ACM International Conference on Automated Software Engineering, pp. 298–301 (2012)
51. Maalej, W., Thurimella, A.K.: Towards a research agenda for recommendation systems in requirements engineering. In: 2009 Second International Workshop on Managing Requirements Knowledge, pp. 32–39. IEEE (2009)
52. Matthiesen, S.B., Aasen, E., Holst, G., Wie, K., Einarsen, S.: The escalation of conflict: a case study of bullying at work. Int. J. Manag. Decis. Mak. **4**(1), 96–112 (2003)
53. Maxwell, J.C., Antón, A.I., Swire, P.: A legal cross-references taxonomy for identifying conflicting software requirements. In: 2011 IEEE 19th International Requirements Engineering Conference, pp. 197–206. IEEE (2011)
54. Mistrík, I., Grundy, J., Van der Hoek, A., Whitehead, J.: Collaborative software engineering: challenges and prospects. In: Mistrík, I., Grundy, J., Hoek, A., Whitehead, J. (eds.) Collaborative Software Engineering, pp. 389–403. Springer, Heidelberg (2010). https://doi.org/10.1007/978-3-642-10294-3_19

55. Murukannaiah, P.K., Kalia, A.K., Telangy, P.R., Singh, M.P.: Resolving goal conflicts via argumentation-based analysis of competing hypotheses. In: 2015 IEEE 23rd International Requirements Engineering Conference (RE), pp. 156–165. IEEE (2015)
56. Nentwich, C., Emmerich, W., Finkelsteiin, A., Ellmer, E.: Flexible consistency checking. ACM Trans. Softw. Eng. Methodol. (TOSEM) **12**(1), 28–63 (2003)
57. Nuseibeh, B., Easterbrook, S.: Requirements engineering: a roadmap. In: Proceedings of the Conference on the Future of Software Engineering, pp. 35–46 (2000)
58. Version One: 9th annual state of agile survey. Survey (2015). Accessed Online 15
59. Poort, E.R., de With, P.: Resolving requirement conflicts through non-functional decomposition. In: Proceedings of the Fourth Working IEEE/IFIP Conference on Software Architecture (WICSA 2004), pp. 145–154. IEEE (2004)
60. Punj, G., Stewart, D.W.: Cluster analysis in marketing research: review and suggestions for application. J. Mark. Res. **20**(2), 134–148 (1983)
61. Robbins, S.: Organisational Behaviour, Concepts, Controversies and Applications, p. 599. Prentice Hall Inc., New York (1989)
62. Robillard, P.N., Robillard, M.P.: Types of collaborative work in software engineering. J. Syst. Softw. **53**(3), 219–224 (2000)
63. Robinson, W.N., Pawlowski, S.D., Volkov, V.: Requirements interaction management. ACM Comput. Surv. (CSUR) **35**(2), 132–190 (2003)
64. Rodrigues, O., Garcez, A.A., Russo, A.: Reasoning about requirements evolution using clustered belief revision. In: Bazzan, A.L.C., Labidi, S. (eds.) SBIA 2004. LNCS (LNAI), vol. 3171, pp. 41–51. Springer, Heidelberg (2004). https://doi.org/10.1007/978-3-540-28645-5_5
65. Rombach, H.D., Basili, V.R., Selby, R.W.: Experimental Software Engineering Issues: Critical Assessment and Future Directions. International Workshop, Dagstuhl Castle, Germany, 14–18 September 1992. Proceedings, vol. 706. Springer, Heidelberg (1993)
66. Ross, S., Fang, L., Hipel, K.W.: A case-based reasoning system for conflict resolution: design and implementation. Eng. Appl. Artif. Intell. **15**(3–4), 369–383 (2002)
67. Saaty, T.L.: The analytic hierarchy process in conflict management. Int. J. Conflict Manag. (1990)
68. Sadana, V., Liu, X.F.: Analysis of conflicts among non-functional requirements using integrated analysis of functional and non-functional requirements. In: 31st Annual International Computer Software and Applications Conference (COMPSAC 2007), vol. 1, pp. 215–218. IEEE (2007)
69. Sardinha, A., Chitchyan, R., Weston, N., Greenwood, P., Rashid, A.: EA-analyzer: automating conflict detection in aspect-oriented requirements. In: 2009 IEEE/ACM International Conference on Automated Software Engineering, pp. 530–534. IEEE (2009)
70. Siegel, S.: Nonparametric statistics for the behavioral sciences (1956)
71. Sterling, L., Taveter, K.: The Art of Agent-Oriented Modeling. MIT Press, Cambridge (2009)
72. Strauss, A.L.: Negotiations: Varieties, Contexts, Processes, and Social Order, vol. 1. Jossey-Bass San Francisco (1978)
73. Tan, P.N., Steinbach, M., Kumar, V.: Data mining cluster analysis: basic concepts and algorithms. In: Introduction to Data Mining, pp. 487–533 (2013)
74. Taveter, K., Sterling, L., Pedell, S., Burrows, R., Taveter, E.M.: A method for eliciting and representing emotional requirements: two case studies in e-healthcare. In: 2019 IEEE 27th International Requirements Engineering Conference Workshops (REW), pp. 100–105. IEEE (2019)
75. Taylor, P.S., Greer, D., Coleman, G., McDaid, K., Keenan, F.: Preparing small software companies for tailored agile method adoption: minimally intrusive risk assessment. Softw. Process Improv. Pract. **13**(5), 421–437 (2008)
76. Tenso, T., Norta, A., Vorontsova, I.: Evaluating a novel agile requirements engineering method: a case study. In: ENASE, pp. 156–163 (2016)

77. Tenso, T., Taveter, K.: Requirements engineering with agent-oriented models. In: ENASE, pp. 254–259 (2013)
78. Urbieta, M., Escalona, M.J., Robles Luna, E., Rossi, G.: Detecting conflicts and inconsistencies in web application requirements. In: Harth, A., Koch, N. (eds.) ICWE 2011. LNCS, vol. 7059, pp. 278–288. Springer, Heidelberg (2012). https://doi.org/10.1007/978-3-642-27997-3_27
79. Van Lamsweerde, A., Darimont, R., Letier, E.: Managing conflicts in goal-driven requirements engineering. IEEE Trans. Softw.Eng. **24**(11), 908–926 (1998)
80. Veerappa, V., Letier, E.: Clustering stakeholders for requirements decision making. In: Berry, D., Franch, X. (eds.) REFSQ 2011. LNCS, vol. 6606, pp. 202–208. Springer, Heidelberg (2011). https://doi.org/10.1007/978-3-642-19858-8_20
81. Viana, T., Zisman, A., Bandara, A.K.: Identifying conflicting requirements in systems of systems. In: 2017 IEEE 25th International Requirements Engineering Conference (RE), pp. 436–441. IEEE (2017)
82. Vieira, F., Brito, I., Moreira, A.: Using multi-criteria analysis to handle conflicts during composition. In: Workshop on Early Aspects, 5th International Conference on Aspect-Oriented Software Development (AOSD 2006) (2006)
83. Vogelsang, A., Borg, M.: Requirements engineering for machine learning: perspectives from data scientists. In: 2019 IEEE 27th International Requirements Engineering Conference Workshops (REW), pp. 245–251. IEEE (2019)
84. Wang, X.T., Xiong, W.: An integrated linguistic-based group decision-making approach for quality function deployment. Expert Syst. Appl. **38**(12), 14428–14438 (2011)
85. Yang, D., Wu, D., Koolmanojwong, S., Brown, A.W., Boehm, B.W.: WikiWinWin: a wiki based system for collaborative requirements negotiation. In: Proceedings of the 41st Annual Hawaii International Conference on System Sciences (HICSS 2008), p. 24. IEEE (2008)
86. Yang, H., Kim, M., Park, S., Sugumaran, V.: A process and tool support for managing activity and resource conflicts based on requirements classification. In: Montoyo, A., Muńoz, R., Métais, E. (eds.) NLDB 2005. LNCS, vol. 3513, pp. 114–125. Springer, Heidelberg (2005). https://doi.org/10.1007/11428817_11
87. Yen, J., Tiao, W.A.: A systematic tradeoff analysis for conflicting imprecise requirements. In: Proceedings of ISRE 1997: 3rd IEEE International Symposium on Requirements Engineering, pp. 87–96. IEEE (1997)
88. Yin, R.K., et al.: Case study research and applications: design and methods (2018)
89. Zhang, W., Mei, H., Zhao, H.: Feature-driven requirement dependency analysis and high-level software design. Requirements Eng. **11**(3), 205–220 (2006)
90. Iqbal, T., Khan, M., Taveter, K., Seyff, N.: Mining reddit as a new source for software requirements. In: 2021 IEEE 29th International Requirements Engineering Conference (RE), pp. 128–138. IEEE, 20 September 2021

Challenges and Novel Approaches to Systems and Software Engineering (SSE)

CitrusGenome: Applying User Centered Design for Evaluating the Usability of Genomic User Interfaces

Alberto García S.[1(✉)], Carlos Iñiguez-Jarrín[2], Oscar Pastor Lopez[1], Daniel Gonzalez-Ibea[3], Estela Pérez-Román[3], Carles Borredà[3], Javier Terol[3], Victoria Ibanez[3], and Manuel Talón[3]

[1] PROS Research Center, VRAIN Research Institute, Universitat Politècnica de València, Camí de Vera, s/n, 46022 València, Spain
{algarsi3,anleopa,opastor}@vrain.upv.es

[2] Escuela Politécnica Nacional, Quito, Ecuador
carlos.iniguez@epn.edu.ec

[3] Centro de Genómica, Instituto Valenciano de Investigaciones Agrarias (IVIA), Moncada, Valencia, Spain

Abstract. Several tools have been developed to extract knowledge from the vast amount of data in genomics. The success of the knowledge extraction process depends to arge extent on how easy to learn and use are the tools for bioinformaticians. User interface design is neglected frequently in the genomic tool development process. As a result, user interfaces contain usability problems that make knowledge extraction a complex task. User-Centered Design (UCD) is a design approach that can be applied to improve the usability of interfaces. A fundamental principle of UCD is to design the UI based on users' knowledge, their needs, objectives, and tasks to ensure that the resulting user interface meets the real user needs. We apply the UCD approach to design, evaluate and improve CitrusGenome, a tool that enables bioinformaticians to extract knowledge from genomic data. Following the UCD process, we first conduct user research to define user needs by applying UCD techniques such as interviews and task analysis. Then, we design a user interface that meets those user needs by using GenomIUm. GenomIUm is a systematic method that guides the design process of user interfaces in the genomic domain. We have performed two UCD iterations and, after each iteration, the user interfaces were validated by bioinformaticians. Some usability problems were found in each iteration. Therefore, we refined the user interface by solving the usability problems and incorporating such solutions into the final design. Finally, bioinformaticians using the refined user interface reported a reduction in the complexity of extracting knowledge from genomic data. We conclude that UCD techniques, together with GenomIUm, can be a useful strategy to design user interfaces that are easier to learn and use in the genomic domain.

Keywords: Genomics · User-centred design · User interface · GenomIUm

R. Ali et al. (Eds.): ENASE 2021, CCIS 1556, pp. 213–240, 2022.
https://doi.org/10.1007/978-3-030-96648-5_10

1 Introduction

Amongst one of the biggest challenges of the century is to get a deep understanding of genomics [22]. A so complex domain, which contains hundreds of dynamic variables, requires immense efforts to study it. The amount of genomic data that is publicly available has increased considerably over the last decades [8]. This is mainly explained by the reduction in the costs of sequencing genome data [15] and the increase in the speed of sequencing thanks to Next Generation Sequencing (NGS) technologies [9]. However, being able to generate such an amount of data has originated a series of issues that require special attention. The result of these issues is that extracting knowledge in the genomic domain is complex, tedious, slow, and prone to error.

User-centered design (UCD) can be a convenient solution to improve knowledge extraction in the genomic domain. UCD is a product design approach that grounds its design process in information about who will use the product. It is widely recognized that bioinformatics resources suffer from serious usability problems [14]. Applying UCD can significantly improve the usability of bioinformatics tools, making knowledge extraction more efficient and effective. Although successfully applied in other domains, UCD has been little used in the genomic domain because of its specific particularities. Applying UCD in this domain is complex and requires overcoming several additional challenges.

This work extends our previous work, where we applied UCD techniques to develop a bioinformatics tool that improves domain knowledge extraction processes [21]. The tool has been developed in a real-world use case along with the collaboration of the *Instituto Valenciano de Investigaciones Agrarias (IVIA)* [29,30], an agri-food research institute whose work focuses on improving productivity and sustainability of the citrus agricultural activity. We focused on identifying their key tasks and how to improve them by defining the most convenient User Interfaces (UIs) in terms of usability. The tool has been developed using GenomIUm [10], a UCD-based framework that provides i) a method to design and implement big data UIs, and ii) a catalog of User Interface design patterns to support the process. Sections 3 and 4 detail our previous work.

The new contributions of this work are the following: i) to validate the first version of the UI of CitrusGenome by performing a usability evaluation with users, which allowed us to identify a set of usability problems; and ii) to generate the second version of the UI of CitrusGenome by solving the usability problems identified in the first version.

The rest of the paper is structured as follows: Sect. 2 discusses the state of the art regarding the use of UCD in the genomic domain. Section 3 studies the use case to be improved by identifying the problems to address (i.e., the lack of automation and how to visualize the data). Section 4 presents how these problems are addressed by applying GenomIUm to generate the needed bioinformatics tool. Section 5 validates our proposed solution, identifies a set of usability problems, and generates a new version of the UI in order to solve them. Lastly, Sect. 6 discusses conclusions and proposes future work.

2 State of the Art

The ultimate goal of UI design is to produce *usable* UIs that are both easy to use and easy to learn. These UIs should allow users to perform their tasks and achieve their goals efficiently [19]. However, in complex domains such as bioinformatics, this goal is poorly addressed, and there is a growing concern that current approaches are inadequate for this kind of domain [5]. Javahery et al. highlight that the complexity of the UIs of bioinformatics resources is higher when they are compared to the interfaces of websites that people use daily [14]. In line with that, Carpenter et al. suggest that usability should be a more highly valued goal to increase the adoption of bioinformatics tools [4].

Understanding how users work becomes vital to provide usable UIs in such a complex domain. Understanding what tasks they perform and what workflows they follow allows UI designers to better adapt the tools to the specific needs of domain experts. Svanæs et al. state that genomics tool UIs should take into account not only the user's needs but also its particular context as a manner of providing more usable solutions [25]. Stevens et al. conducted a set of surveys of bioinformatics tasks resulting in a task classification to assess the quality of query systems [23]. Tran et al. performed a cross-sectional study of bioinformatics tasks that were documented and proposed as potentially desirable system features in bioinformatics tools [27]. Rutherford et al. examined how large DNA sequences are studied and navigated by users to improve the usability of DNA-sequencing navigating tools [20]. All these works provided a better understanding of the unmet needs of genomic domain users.

There has been an explosion in the number of available bioinformatics tools in the last decades. A good example is OMICtools, which provides a catalog of more than 20.000 web-accessible bioinformatics tools [7]. A common point among those tools is that their developers tend not to focus on their interfaces or usability aspects [18]. The designed UIs do not consider the user's perspective and requirements as the starting point of the design process [1]. Consequently, most of the users of these tools find it hard to access the information and too frequently struggle to find valuable information for their research. They accept tools with poor usability because they use them freely, though these tools do not always provide what they need [18]. A usability testing of bioinformatics tools conducted by Bolchini et al. [3] reported that usability issues that affect the efficiency and effectiveness of bioinformatics work. Several reasons seem to be the underlying cause of not focusing on bioinformatics tool UIs and their usability aspects [5, 16, 18]:

- Bioinformatics has historically relied on command-line tools and using UCD requires a "cultural shift".
- Bioinformatics data that have to be presented are complex and highly interconnected. Additional technical and scalability constraints have to be considered. Besides, it is a constantly evolving subject whose rules usually have plenty of exceptions.
- Using UCD techniques generates an initial delay in the design process and measuring the impact of applying these techniques is too difficult. UCD techniques improve scientific discovery processes, but "discovery" is an intangible metric and therefore difficult to measure.

- The prior knowledge that is needed to adequately carry out UCD techniques in this domain (human-computer interaction, bioinformatics and computing) creates a gap between domain users and developers.
- The usability validation, crucial to provide successful solutions [12], needs to be carried out by skilled UI designers, which is not always possible.

These reasons make the design process of user-friendly UI difficult. Apart from that, authors tend to give more importance to the novelty of the developed tool lessening down usability and UI aspects. In other words, it is the novelty of the tool its most valued aspect rather than its associated UCD work[18]. In summary, usability and UI aspects have been frequently ignored historically.

However, more recent bioinformatics projects are considering UCD when designing and developing their UIs. A scenario-based visualization tool to support epidemiological research called ADVISES was developed using UCD methods [24]. They used prototyping and storyboarding techniques to analyze user tasks and their domain mental model. The EB-eye search service was redesigned following UCD principles [28]. Several user interviews were conducted to gather the initial information and requirements before developing the search service. After developing it, one-to-one usability testing sessions were performed to collect user feedback. The Enzyme Portal was developed after performing a series of user workshops and interviews to identify user needs [16]. Afterward, they tested multiple prototypes until finding an optimal design in terms of navigation and functionality.

In conclusion, having the user as the primary source of information of the UI design and development processes results in multiple benefits [18]. The users will be more likely to use a tool if they guide the design process. Having greater access to the data will increase users' scientific discoveries. Overall, UCD supports the development of high-quality bioinformatics resources that ease users' work and better adapt to their specific needs.

3 Problem Statement

The reported use case consists of applying UCD techniques to develop a bioinformatics tool to aid in performing a specific analysis process regarding genomic citrus plant (variety) improvement. This analysis consists of establishing genotype-phenotype relationships, in other words, the observable traits in the varieties (phenotype) caused by the genetic code (genotype). For instance, which variations in the genetic code make a variety drought resistant? Consequently, it is crucial to prioritize (i.e., identify and select) which variations have an impact on the phenotype under study correctly. We focus on the prioritization of genetic variations that might have a notorious impact on plant phenotypes. This analysis is a problematic and inefficient process that involves several manual tasks. These tasks are complex, slow to perform, and prone to human failures. The tasks can be grouped into:

Task 1: Select Variety Groups. There are tens of sequenced citrus varieties, and it is arduous to work with multiple of them because of the large amount of data that is contained on each of them. In order to work with the varieties, bioinformaticians have to select and group them based on specific phenotypes. Two groups are created, one group contains varieties that highly express a phenotype of interest, and the other group contains varieties that do not express it. For instance, a phenotype of interest is the sweetness of the fruits that a set of sequenced varieties produce.

Task 2: Compare Groups. There are a plethora of variables to consider when filtering the data. Domain experts have to reduce the existing amount of genomic data by applying several conditions as a previous step before comparing the groups of varieties. For instance, by establishing a quality data threshold or by selecting a specific genomic region. Also, they need a report of the applied filters to manage them. Considering the filter conditions, the groups of varieties have to be compared in order to extract their differences at a genotype level (i.e., genetic variations). Although applying a single filter or performing simple set operations (e.g., data intersection or subtraction) are challenging but feasible tasks, chaining multiple filters or performing more complex operations are not possible. The complexity and the cost of the data filtering task increase dramatically as the number of varieties involved increases.

Task 3: Visualize. The amount of data obtained after performing Task 2 can become unmanageable, and the bioinformaticians require to fluidly examine them to identify potential genetic variations of interest. By "examine" we mean to i) show how the data are distributed based on specific criteria and ii) interact with the data by showing or hiding data columns and performing data.

The generated knowledge is *highly valuable* because it allows modifying citrus varieties to potentially increase or decrease the expression levels of phenotypes of interest. However, because of the complexity of the process reported above, extracting knowledge is complex and requires considerable effort. The UI design process focused on automating the process and decreasing its complexity so that bioinformaticians can extract knowledge more easily. To accomplish this goal, the three tasks identified above become the starting point to apply our UCD-oriented solution.

4 Proposed Solution

Our proposed solution consists of developing a bioinformatics tool, whose UIs have been designed following a UCD approach. UCD puts the user in the center of the design process to ensure that the resulting UI meets their real needs and interactions. From a general perspective, UCD can be summarized into two main activities: user research and solution production. In the first activity, we have researched our domain expert users by applying UCD techniques such as user observation and task analysis. Observing them while performing the prioritization of genetic variations process is a crucial activity to identify problems related to the data manipulation, detail the high-level tasks identified in the problem statement, and determine which UIs should be designed. In the second activity, we have designed the UIs by using the UI design patterns that better address the data manipulation-related problems identified in the previous activity.

4.1 User Research

Domain users have been characterized through several interviews and observing how they work. Identifying and analyzing the tasks involved in the prioritization of genetic variations allowed us to understand both the user mental model (i.e. how they think the variation prioritization process works) and the domain under study. The gathered information has been consolidated in a task model of the envisioned system defined by using Concur Task Trees (CTT) notation [17] as shown in Fig. 1. CTT notation allows to represent the tasks with a chronological and hierarchical structure. Figure 1.1 is the main CTT whilst the "Define filters" and "Examine variation distribution" tasks are detailed in Figs. 1.2 and 1.3 respectively for reasons of space. The task model contains the three high-level tasks defined in Sect. 3 (i.e. select variety groups, compare groups and visualize) decomposed in lower-level tasks.

The **first task**, select variety groups task, consists of defining the two groups of varieties to be compared. Each citrus variety has a set of genetic variations from which some of them are unique and some are shared with other varieties. The system shows the list of available sequenced citrus varieties. Then, the user selects the varieties of interest and adds them to the groups.

The **second task**, compare groups task, consists of two lower-level tasks: define filters and perform comparison. In the first one, the conditions to filter the genetic variations are defined (Fig. 1.2). Up to eight filters can be defined from which six are mandatory:

1. Variation type (mandatory, unique): Two types of genetic variations can be compared, namely, Single Nucleotide Polymorphism (SNP) and insertion/deletion (indel). On the one hand, SNPs are changes in the genetic code that only affect one nitrogenous base (A, C, G or T). For example, a variation that changes a C for a T at a given position. On the other hand, indels are genetic variations where the length of the genetic code is altered, either by addition, deletion or both.
2. Set flexibility criteria (mandatory, unique): This filter refers to how restrictive is to accept a variation based on its frequency of appearance among the varieties of a group. By default, only genetic variations that appear in every variety of a group are accepted. However, in some cases this might be too restrictive. The "flexibility" has to do with the ability to filter genetic variations that exist in a subset of the varieties of a group. Such subset is defined by indicating a minimum and maximum threshold of varieties to be considered. There are multiple reasons to do that: working with large groups of varieties, genetic variations wrongly identified in the sequencing process, varieties exhibiting a common phenotype caused by different genetic variations, etc.
3. Quality (mandatory, unique): Because of technological limitations in the sequencing process, genetic variations are complemented with a set of quality indicators that show how reliable they are. This filter allows specifying the quality threshold to accept genetic variations.
4. Annotation impact (mandatory, multiple): Genetic variations are annotated with software to predict their effect and impact at a genomic level [6]. This filter allows specifying the impact and effect under which a variation is accepted. Genetic variations are classified by how significant they are. A variation will be much more relevant if it is predicted to alter a protein's functionality in a disruptive way (high impact).
5. Genome regions (mandatory): Genetic variations can be located in specific types of regions (intergenic regions, genes, exons, introns, etc.) with unique functionality.

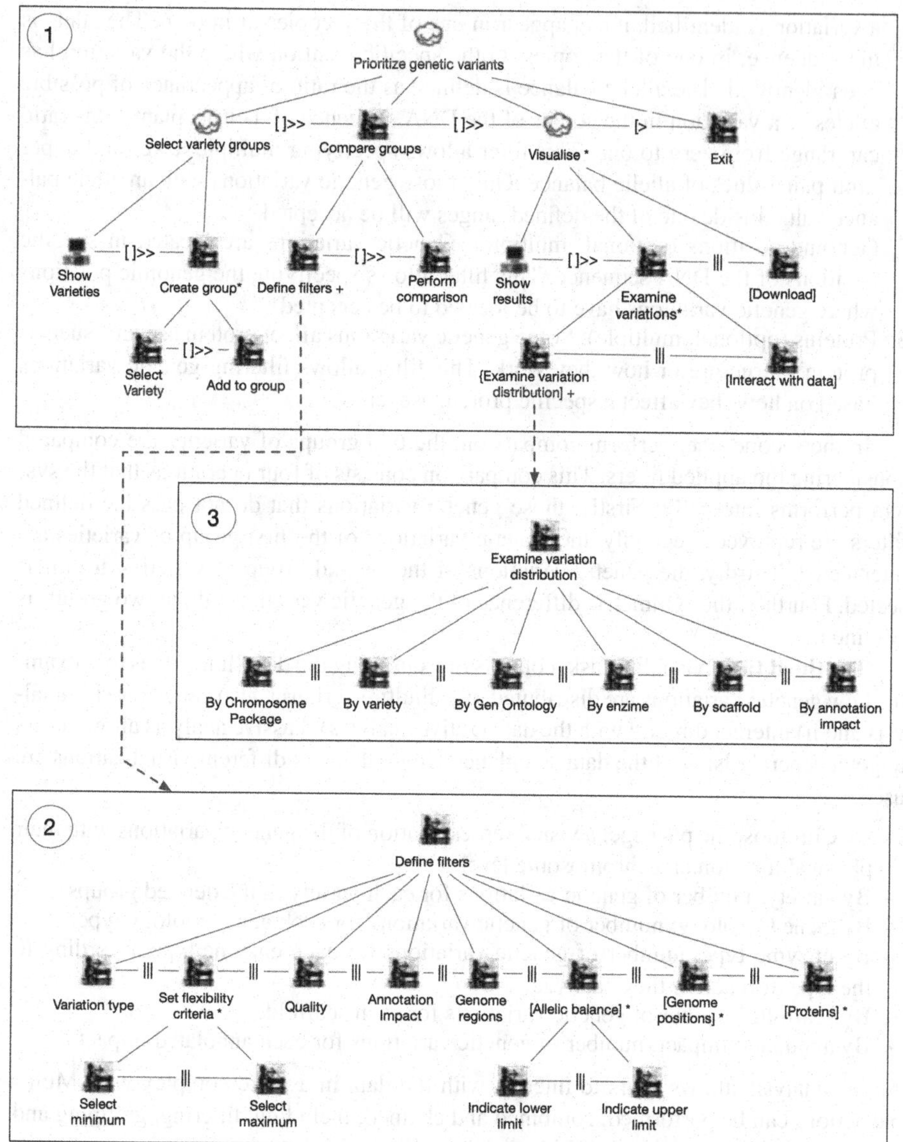

Fig. 1. Task analysis. Source: [21].

This filter allows specifying the genomic regions where genetic variations have to be located to be accepted.

6. Allelic balance (optional, multiple): The analyzed citrus plants are diploid (i.e. their cells has paired chromosomes[1]) so they have two copies of the DNA sequence. When

[1] https://www.genome.gov/genetics-glossary/Diploid.

a variation is identified, it can appear in one of these copies or in both. The allele is the sequence, in one of the copies, in the specific position where the variation has been identified. The allelic balance is defined as the ratio of appearance of possible alleles of a variation in the copies of the DNA sequence of a citrus plant. This ratio can range from zero to one. This filter allows specifying multiple lower and upper limit pair values of allelic balance. Only those genetic variations with an allele balance value inside one of the defined ranges will be accepted.
7. Genome positions (optional, multiple): Genetic variations are located in specific positions of the DNA sequence. This filter allows specifying the genomic positions where genetic variations have to be located to be accepted.
8. Proteins (optional, multiple): Some genetic variations affect protein aspects, such as protein's structure or how they work. This filter allows filtering genetic variations based on how they affect a specific protein aspect.

In the second one, perform comparison, the two groups of varieties are compared considering the applied filters. This comparison consists of four operations that the system performs internally: Firstly, those genetic variations that do not pass the defined filters are removed. Secondly, the genetic variations of the first group of varieties are intersected. Thirdly, the genetic variations of the second group of varieties are intersected. Fourthly, the symmetric difference of the genetic variations of the two groups is obtained.

The **third task**, visualize task, consists of examining the data. It involves to i) examine how genetic variations are distributed over multiple criteria, also called passive analysis and ii) interact directly with the data (active analysis). Passive analysis allows users to get a general vision of the data at a glance. To do that, six different visualizations are used:

- By Chromosome package: a visual representation of the genetic variations with their physical location at a chromosome level.
- By variety: number of genetic variations for each variety in the defined groups.
- By Gene Ontology: number of genetic variations for each gene ontology type.
- By enzyme type: number of genetic variations for each enzyme type according to the type of reaction they catalyze.
- By scaffold: number of genetic variations for each scaffold.
- By annotated impact: number of genetic variations for each annotated impact.

Active analysis allows users to interact with the data in a more complex way. Multiple actions can be performed, combined and chained, including: filtering, grouping and aggregating data, showing and hiding data attributes and performing pivoting operations. Interaction with data can be performed by filtering, grouping and aggregating operations that can be combined and chained.

The characterization of these tasks becomes a foundation that guides the design decisions to generate the UIs that will improve and facilitate the genetic analysis process.

4.2 User Interface Design

So far, we have identified the tasks involved in genomic analysis. Now, our attention focuses on translating those tasks into a tangible UI design. To do that, we focus on developing a key artifact of the design activity: the *conceptual design* (CD) of the UI, which captures the structure and flow of the UI. To define the CD, we have applied a method called *GenomIUm* that has been developed in previous work [10] (see Fig. 2). It is based on Pattern Oriented Design (POD) approach [13] and aims to assist designers in creating the CD of genomics UIs.

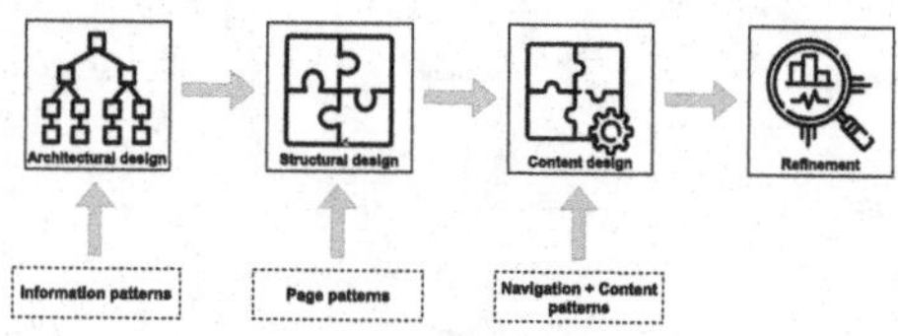

Fig. 2. GenomIUm phases. Source: [21].

GenomIUm takes advantage of the two main characteristics of POD by providing i) a systematic design process and ii) a catalog of interconnected patterns that support the systematic process.

The systematic design process consists of four steps:

1. Architectural Design: This step consists on defining the UIs that will make up the system and their navigation flow. This step is supported by information architecture patterns, which describe system-wide solutions that organize the content to be displayed by defining high-level presentation units and how they are linked.
2. Structural Design: This steps focuses on establishing the internal structure of each of the UIs defined in the previous step. This step is supported by page patterns, which describe the internal structure (i.e. sectors) of presentation units.
3. Content Design: This step consists of selecting the specific content elements that conform the internal structure of each UI defined in the previous step. This step is supported by navigation and content patterns, which describe the content elements that compose sectors. Each pattern allows users to perform a specific identified task.
4. Refinement: Each design pattern provides a general UI design solution. This step consists of adapting such a general design solution by indicating the visual details of the selected patterns in the previous step according to the specific particularities of the data that is involved in the genomic analysis.

The process is iterative in nature and designers can repeat the steps several times until the CD meets the user needs.

The catalog is structured in several pattern categories, one for each step of the design process and it covers general design problems (i.e. navigation or interface distribution) as well as specific design problems (i.e. visualizing the complete set of chromosomes of a species). Designers can exploit the pattern relationships to create complete or partial UI designs.

The process and its pattern catalog cover the design of the UIs of a complete genomic application. In the following paragraphs, we describe the CD resulting from applying GenomiUm in a joint work with bioinformaticians. Figure 3 shows the designed UI after performing the GenomIUm method.

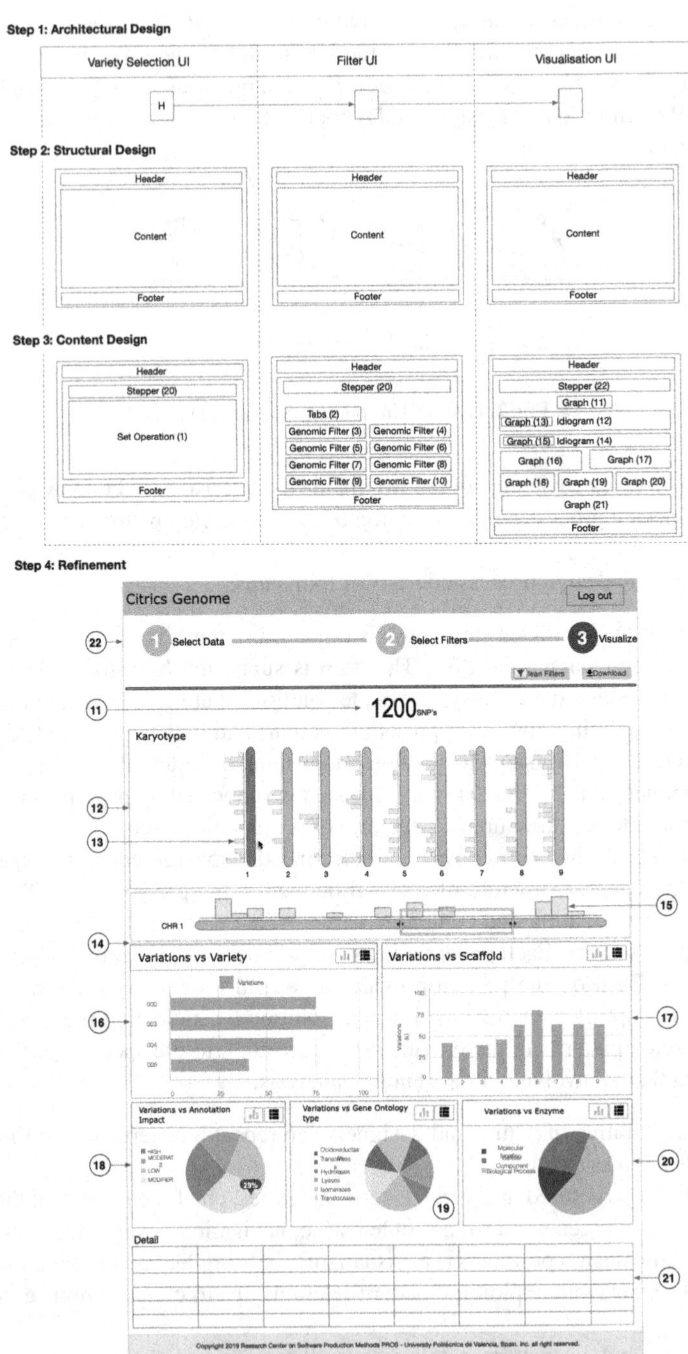

Fig. 3. UI design through the GenomIUm method. Source: [21].

In Step 1, *Architectural design*, three UIs have been defined based on the tasks analysis (Fig. 1): *Variety Selection UI* for the "Select variety groups" task, *Filter UI* for the "Apply Filters" task and *Visualization UI* for the "Visualize" task. Bioinformaticians performed several UCD activities to guide the definition of the UIs. As an example, Fig. 4 shows them performing a card sorting session. The defined UIs are connected through the "Sequential" pattern (the UI with the "H" letter indicates the initial UI). This pattern is used when a complex task can be divided into more simple tasks that are performed in a sequential order. It guides bioinformaticians through the three UIs to carry out the "prioritize genetic variations" process.

Fig. 4. Geneticists and designers working together in a Card Sorting Session. Source: [21].

In Step 2, Structural design, the sectors of the UIs have been designed using the "Conceptual Framework" pattern. This pattern suggests that the UIs should share the same layout. The defined layout consists of three sectors: a heading, a body and a footer.

In step 3, *Content design*, the design patterns that compose each UI have been selected. Most of them pertain to the "Genomic Patterns" category, which addresses how to show and interact with genomic-related content. Table 1 describes the selected patterns for each UI.

In Step 4, *Refinement*, the selected patterns have been adapted to the specific particularities of the data to be displayed as well as the identified task that they solve. Step 4 in Fig. 3 shows the refined *Visualization UI*. Only the refinement of the Visualization UI will be addressed due to space limitations. The resulting Visualization UI gives the reader a clear idea of how the refinement process works.

The corresponding CD of the three UIs have been iteratively validated by bioinformaticians who provided valuable feedback to improve the UI designs. The refined CDs

Table 1. UI patterns used in the Conceptual Design of the UIs. Source: [21].

Id	Pattern	Applied to
Variety selection UI		
1	Set Operation	Define genomic data groups and compare them
Filter UI		
2	Tabs	Separate the content into sections that can be accessed using a flat navigation [26]
3	Genetic Filter	Filter the variations by their type
4	Genetic Filter	Filter the variations by their frequency of appearance
5	Genetic Filter	Filter the variations by their quality
6	Genetic Filter	Filter the variations by their annotated impact
7	Genetic Filter	Filter the variations by their genomic region
8	Genetic Filter	Filter the variations by their allelic balance
9	Genetic Filter	Filter the variations by their position
10	Genetic Filter	Filter the variations by their effect over protein aspects
Visualization UI		
11	Chart	Show the number of genetic variations identified
12	Ideogram	Show the chromosome set
13	Chart	Show the distribution of genetic variations on each chromosome of the chromosome set
14	Ideogram	Show the detail of the selected chromosome in pattern 3
15	Chart	Show the distribution of genetic variations along the selected chromosome
16	Chart	Show the genetic variations distribution by varieties
17	Chart	Show the genetic variations distribution by scaffolds
18	Chart	Show the genetic variations distribution by Impact Annotation
19	Chart	Show the genetic variations distribution by Gene Ontology type
20	Chart	Show the genetic variations distribution by Enzyme type
21	Hidden Column	List the genetic variations involved in the overview visualizations (patterns 2 to 11)
Present in the three UIs		
22	Stepper	Guide users through the genetic analysis process

have been implemented with standard web technologies. More specifically, we designed the UI using the Angular framework[2], and utilized a set of open source libraries to

[2] https://angular.io/.

implement the UI paterns (i.e., angular2-charts.js[3], ideogram.js[4], and agGrid[5]). These libraries offer angular-specific implementations that allows to include them in the project easily. Table 2 indicates the framework or library that implement each of the selected UI patterns.

Table 2. Frameworks and libraries used to implements the UI patterns used in the Conceptual Design of the UIs. Source: [21].

Id(s)	Pattern	Implemented with	License
Variety selection UI			
1	Set Operation	Angular	MIT
Filter UI			
2	Tabs	Angular	MIT
3, 4, 5, 6, 7, 8, 9, 10	Genetic Filter	Angular	MIT
Visualization UI			
11	Chart	Angular	MIT
12, 14	Ideogram	Ideogram.js	CC0 1.0 Universal
13, 15, 16, 17, 18, 19, 20	Chart	angular2-chartjs	MIT
21	Hidden Column	agGrid	MIT
Present in the three UIs			
22	Stepper	Angular	MIT

Figure 5 illustrates the final implementation of the Visualization UI. Each pattern has been labelled according to the CD of the step four in Fig. 3.

5 Validation

To validate the CitrusGenome tool, we focused on evaluating how easy is for the users to find the information for performing the genomic analysis.

To do that, we defined a typical genomic analysis problem whose goal is *to identify a set of genetic variations with the potential to cause premature fruit abscission (PFA)*. PFA occurs when citrus trees have more fruits than they can maintain, causing some of these fruits to be degraded. PFA is a biological process of interest in the agricultural field because high PFA results in small amounts of high-quality fruits while low PFA results in large amounts of lower-quality fruits [2]. Therefore, achieving an optimal level of PFA is crucial.

From the genomic analysis problem, we then defined three questions to be tested. They become the Research Questions (RQs) of the validation study.

[3] https://github.com/emn178/angular2-chartjs.
[4] https://github.com/eweitz/ideogram.
[5] https://github.com/ag-grid/ag-grid.

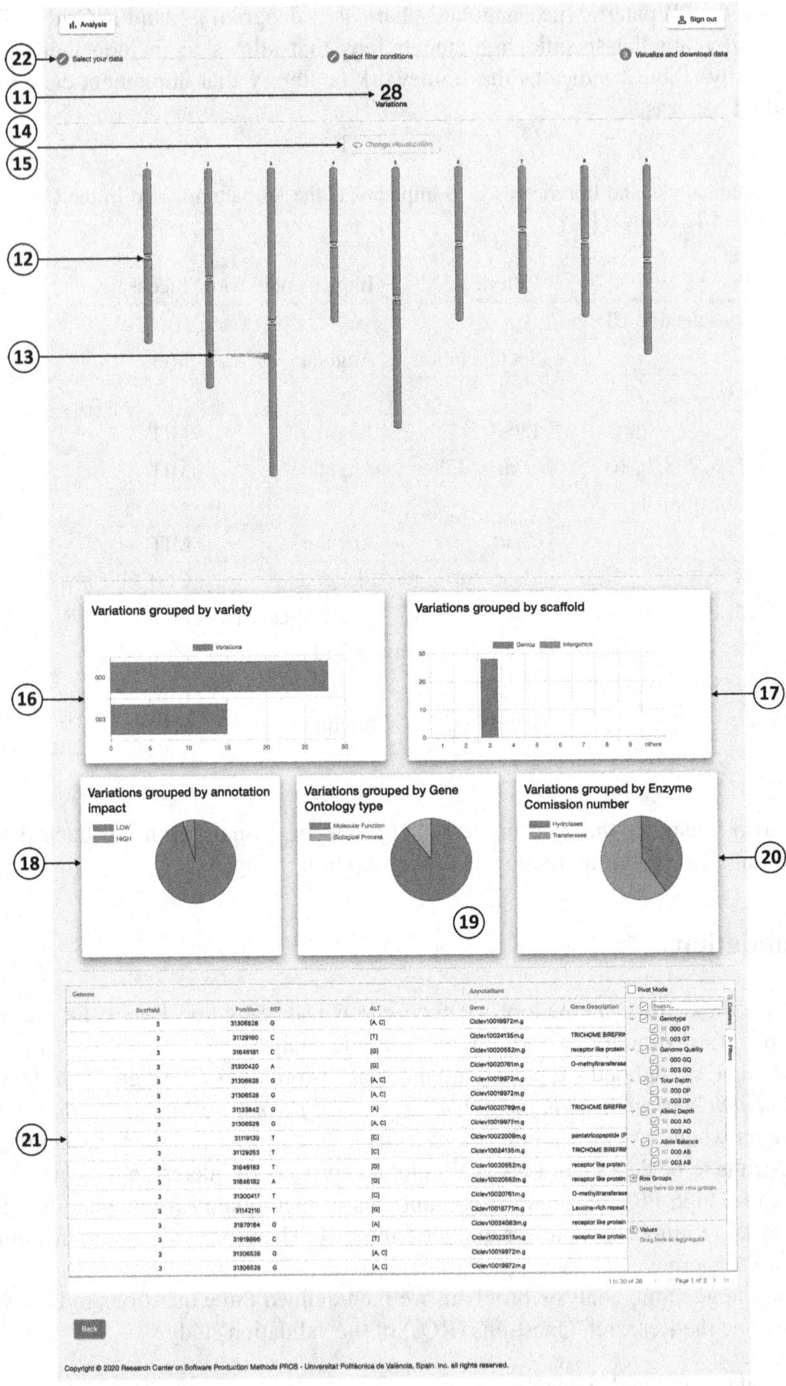

Fig. 5. Implementation of Visualisation UI. Source: [21].

RQ 1—Will the participants be able to select the data that is involved in the genomic analysis?
RQ 2—Will the participants be able to set the filters required to refine the data?
RQ 3—Will the participants be able to identify variants that are potentially responsible for PFA?

5.1 Method

The participants involved in the validation were five bioinformaticians from the IVIA research institute. Two of them are part of the IVIA staff as senior researchers, and they had no previous experience using the tool. Another two of them are Ph.D students that work as analysts, one of them had little previous experience using the tool while the other one did not have any experience at all. The last participant is a Ph.D student analyst with considerably previous experience using the tool (see Table 3).

Table 3. Information of the participants that validated UI of the tool.

Id	Experience	Educational level	Tool experience
1	Senior	Ph.D	None
2	Senior	Ph.D	None
3	Medium	Ph.D. Student	Significant
4	Junior	Ph.D. Student	Little
5	Junior	Ph.D. Student	None

The validation consisted of 28 tasks (See the tasks in Appendix A) to test the RQs written above, and it was performed in a virtual way by using the Zoom video conference platform because of the restrictions derived from COVID-19 pandemia. Each virtual session involved one participant with the user role, and one of us with the evaluator role. The evaluator guided the user by explaining the task to be done and asking him/her for speaking aloud about the actions or decisions made during the test.

The sessions were recorded and stored in a shared repository in order to review and analyze the comments made by participants. We divided the review and analyze process into two stages. In the first stage, we met with the participants individually to review the correspondent recorded session and get their feedback. In the second stage, we performed a focus group to discuss how easy or difficult was for them to use the CitrusGenome tool.

5.2 Results

In this section, we describe how the participants performed the tasks related to each RQ. Then, based on the difficulties that the participants had to complete the tasks, we identified a set of usability problems.

Set of tasks related to RQ1: Will the participants be able to select the data that is involved in the genomic analysis?

All the participants completed the tasks related to RQ1, and, in general, they reported a favorable opinion about the data selection. They pointed out that the drag-and-drop mechanism was intuitive and more sophisticated compared to other tools they use. However, participants 4 and 5 had some difficulties finding two varieties. The reason for this is that the varieties are shown in the UI of CitrusGenome using their common name and internal code, but participants 4 and 5 are used to work with the scientific name of the variety. Besides, participant 1 mentioned that displaying the cultivar[6] of the varieties would enhance the process by adding relevant information.

Thus, the varieties information that is shown in the UI should include the scientific name and the cultivar. Participants 1 and 2 described potential cases where such information is necessary: i) some researchers do not know the internal code of all of the citrus varieties; and ii) the same variety can be sequenced multiple times, so the common name is not always enough to identify the variety of interest (here, the cultivar can help to select the correct one).

From the discussions of this set of tasks, we have defined the following usability problem:

- **Usability Problem 1:** The participant wants to know additional information (the cultivar and the scientific name) of the citrus varieties when creating the groups in the first step of the analysis.

Set of tasks related to RQ2: Will the participants be able to set the filters required to refine the data?

All the participants completed the tasks related to RQ2, but those participants with previous experience using the tool (i.e., participants 3 and 4) completed the tasks faster than the rest of the participants. All the participants agreed that the way in which the filters are designed is intuitive, and they had no problem setting them.

Participants emphasized the ease with which they set the filters. In the opinion of participants 4 and 5, the biological concept of flexibility (Sect. 4.1 describes this concept and the task to configure it) is complex to understand, but they indicated that the UI helped understanding this concept.

In general, all the participants pointed out that the filters give researchers the ability to do analyses with a high degree of modularity and flexibility. However, senior participants (i.e., participants 1 and 2) mentioned searching in promoter regions as a desirable feature because they are gaining attention in recent academic works. This feature was not of interest when we carried out the "research user" stage of the UCD process, and the subsequent first version of the prototype did not include such a feature. However, this interest has changed. This is an example of the continuous evolution of the domain, which requires updating genomics tools continuously.

From the discussion of this set of tasks, we have defined the following usability problems:

- **Usability Problem 2:** The participant wants to search in promoter regions of the DNA, but the option is not available.

[6] A cultivar is defined as a group of selected plants that share common characteristics.

- **Usability Problem 3:** The participant wants to search in the promoter region of a specific gene, but the option is not available.

Set of tasks related to RQ3: Will the participants be able to identify variants that are potentially responsible for PFA?

The tasks related to RQ3 are more complex and time-consuming when compared to the tasks of RQ1 and RQ2. The reason is that these tasks require the user to analyze the data resulting from the comparison exercise. With regards to this, all of the participants mentioned that the charts displayed eased their work. While the participants with some experience using the tool (i.e., participants 3 and 4) mentioned that the grid (see number 21 of Fig. 5) provided them with a very useful and flexible tool, the rest of the participants (i.e., participants 1, 2, and 5) indicated that some of the features of the grid were difficult to use at first. All of the participants were able to complete the tasks except participant 5. This was because there is not an explicit representation of the varieties that compose each group, and participant 5 did not know to which varieties correspond the codes displayed in the grid. As a result, this participant could not complete the following tasks: Tasks 14 to 18 and Task 26 to 28. Besides, participant 4 struggled to complete the tasks that participant 5 could not complete. In this case, the reason was that recalling to which group of the analysis (i.e., group A and group B) each variety belongs leads to a significant mental workload to this participant. Thus, the participants agreed that this situation should be somehow remedied.

From this set of tasks, we have defined the following usability problems:

- **Usability Problem 4:** The participant wants to see at a glance which varieties compose each group of the analysis.
- **Usability Problem 5:** The participant struggles differentiating between varieties of group A and varieties of group B in the following columns of the grid: Genotype, Genotype Quality, Total Depth, Allelic Depth, and Allelic Balance.

In addition to these results, the users provided us with four comments that were not directly related to the research questions but considered relevant:

Comment 1—The participants missed a home page from which to navigate to perform the analysis. Having a home page has become a *de facto* standard, and they think that CitrusGenome should have one. From this comment, we have defined the following usability problem:
  - **Usability Problem 6:** The tool lacks a home page.

Comment 2—After having configured the filters of the analysis, the participants more experienced in the genomics field (i.e., participants 1, 2, and 3) realized that a relevant feature was missing. Having information on the quality of the sequencing process for citrus varieties before setting up the analysis filters can be very helpful. They stated that this information should be displayed grouped by variety and genotype. Also, this information could help to configure certain filters, such as the allele balance one, with more confidence. From this comment, we have defined the following usability problem:
  - **Usability Problem 7:** Before starting the analysis, the participant wants to know the values of the mean value of the GQ and DP attributes of the variants of the citrus varieties based on the value of the GT attribute.

Comment 3—Novel participants (i.e., 1, 2, 4, and 5) expressed that a getting started page with a detailed description of the steps of the analysis would ease the first use of the tool. From this comment, we have defined the following usability problem:

- **Usability Problem 8:** Novel participants may struggle when using the tool for the first time.

Comment 4—Participants aim to be able to study the results at anytime. They also want to be able to switch between the visualization of different analyses to compare the results. However, they can only visualize the result of an analysis when it is completed. From this comment, we have defined the following usability problem:

- **Usability Problem 9:** The participants want to be able to visualize analyses at anytime, but it can only be seen once.

5.3 Discussion and Design Solutions

Considering the results from the validation with the user, our team (i.e., the evaluators) met to evaluate the results and identify the severity level of each usability problem. The severity level allows us to prioritize our effort in designing and implementing a potential solution to this problem.

To define the severity level, we used the severity rating scale of five degrees proposed by Nielsen [11]: 0 (it is not a usability problem), 1 (it is a cosmetic problem and can be solved in overtime of the project), 2: Minor usability problem (its resolution should be given in low priority), 3: Major usability problem (the problem needs to be solved and is given high priority), and 4: Usability catastrophe (the problem must be solved before the project is launched). Table 4 shows the list of usability problems together with their severity levels.

Of the nine usability problems that we have identified, problem 9 was scored with severity level 4, which means that this problem represents a usability threat and should be solved with the highest priority. Five problems (2, 3, 4, 5, 8) were considered major usability problems and were scored with severity level 3. This level is the second highest one, and it means that they should be solved with high priority. Problems 1 and 7 were considered minor usability problems, so they were scored with severity level 2. The priority level of these problems is low. Finally, problem 6, which is related to the lack of the home page, was considered a cosmetic problem and got the lowest priority.

The order in which the problems were solved followed the priority level assigned, from the highest to the lowest. We have defined and implemented a solution that solve each usability problem. Table 4 shows a match between the usability problems reported above and the corresponding design solution ("Design solution" column).

Design solution 1: update the card that contains variety information in the first step of the analysis.

In the previous version of the CitrusGenome UI, each variety was represented using the common name and the internal code attributes (see Fig. 6). However, this representation proved to be insufficient to meet the requirements of the participants, and we have updated it. In the current version of the UI, we have added two new attributes (see Fig. 7). The first attribute is the scientific name of the variety, which is shown below the common name in a smaller font size. The second attribute is the cultivar of the variety.

Design solution 2: Allow users to search in promoter regions of the DNA

Table 4. Improvements that have been considered as usability problems to be addressed in the second iteration of the DCU.

Id	Usability problem	Severity	Design solution
1	The participant wants to know additional information (the cultivar, the common name, and the scientific name) of the citrus varieties when creating the groups in the first step of the analysis	2	Update the card that contains variety information in the first step of the analysis to include the needed data (see Fig. 7)
2	The participant wants to search in promoter regions of the DNA, but the option is not available	3	Allow users to search in promoter regions of the DNA (see Fig. 9)
3	The participant wants to search in the promoter region of a specific gene, but the option is not available	3	Allow users to search in the promoter region of a specific gene (see Fig. 11)
4	The participant wants to see at a glance which varieties compose each group of the analysis	3	Two new chart components, one per variety group, have been implemented to display the required information (see Fig. 12)
5	The participant struggles differentiating between varieties of group A and varieties of group B in the following columns of the grid: Genotype, Genome Quality, Total Depth, Allelic Depth, and Allelic Balance	3	The values of these columns have been grouped into two columns, namely, Group A and Group B (see Fig. 14)
6	The tool lacks a home page	1	Create a *home* page (See Fig. 15)
7	Before starting the analysis, the participant wants to know the mean value of the GQ and DP attributes of the variants of the citrus varieties based on the value of the GT attribute	2	Create a page displaying the required information (see Fig. 16)
8	Novel participants may struggle when using the tool for the first time	3	Create a *getting started* page (See Fig. 15)
9	The participant wants to be able to visualize analyses at anytime, but it can only be seen once	4	Allows users to visualize analyses at anytime by providing them with a page to retrieve analyses. Each analysis is identified by a unique identifier that is given to the user when he starts the analysis (see Fig. 17)

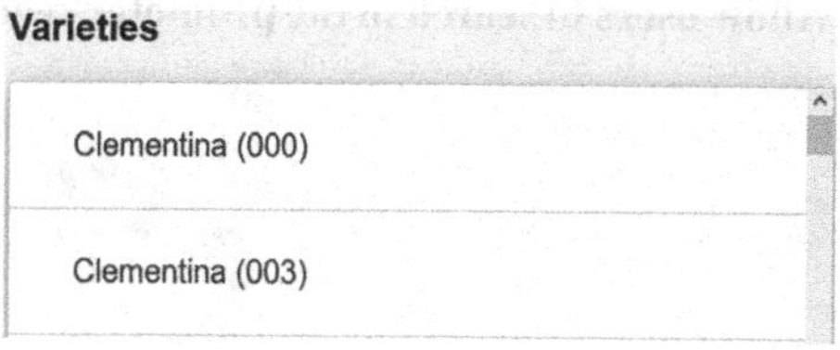

Fig. 6. Previous version of the card containing variety information, causing usability problem 1.

Fig. 7. New version of the card containing variety information to solve usability problem 1.

Fig. 8. Previous version of the menu lacking promoter regions, causing usability problem 2.

The *genome regions* filter is configured using a drop-down menu. There were eight options in the drop-down menu of the previous version of the CitrusGenome UI (see Fig. 8). In the current version of the UI, we have included another option, namely, *promoter*, so that the user can search for variations in these regions (see Fig. 9).

Fig. 9. New version of the menu including promoter regions, solving usability problem 2.

Design solution 3: Allow users to search in the promoter region of a specific gene

Fig. 10. Previous version of the menu lacking the promoter region of a specific gene, causing usability problem 3.

The *genome positions* filter allows users to search for variations in specific positions of the DNA such as a gene or its introns, and it is configured using a drop-down menu, to select the type of region (e.g., gene, intron, exon, etc.), and a free text search service to identify the specific element. There were eight options in the drop-down menu of the previous version of the CitrusGenome UI (see Fig. 10). In the current version of the UI, we have included another option, namely, *promoter*, so that the user can search for variations in the promoter of a specific gene (see Fig. 11).

Add regions

Sequence regions | Sequence feature regions | Sequence regions related to protein elements

Exon

5' UTR

3' UTR

CDS

Promoter

Fig. 11. New version of the menu including the promoter region of a specific gene, solving usability problem 3.

Design solution 4: implement chart components to display the required information

In the previous version of the UI, there was no easy way to see which varieties compose each group. In the current version of the UI, we have implemented two cards, one per group, in order to display which varieties compose each group (see Fig. 12). We used chip components[7] to represent each variety.

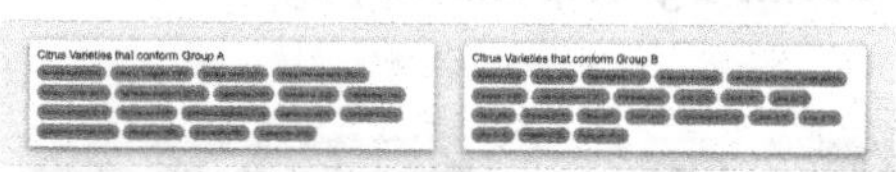

Fig. 12. New charts including the varieties of group A and group B in the analysis, solving usability problem 4.

Design solution 5: group the values of these columns into two new columns

Genotype							
003 GT	134 GT	000 GT	016 GT	324 GT	323 GT	321 GT	015 GT
0/1	0/1	0/1					
							0/1
						1/2	
0/1	0/1	0/1					

Fig. 13. Previous version of the data grid, causing usability problem 5.

[7] https://material.io/components/chips.

In the previous version of the UI, the grid displayed the following variety-specific information of variants: genotype, genome quality, total depth, allelic depth, and allelic balance. As Fig. 13 shows, each attribute is divided into multiple columns, one per variety, and it is not possible to identify which varieties pertain to each group of the analysis. This usability problem is related to the "Recognition rather than recall" Nielsen's Heuristic[8], which states that user should not have to remember information from one part of the interface to another, but recognize it. To solve this usability problem, we grouped these columns to make group composition explicit (see Fig. 14), allowing the user to easily recognize the group at which each variety belongs.

Genotype							
Group A			Group B				
003 GT	134 GT	000 GT	016 GT	324 GT	323 GT	321 GT	015 GT
0/1	0/1	0/1					
							0/1
						1/2	
0/1	0/1	0/1					

Fig. 14. New version of the data grid, solving usability problem 5.

Design solution 6: Create a *home* page

In the previous version of the UI, there was no home page. In the current version of the UI, we have implemented a home page (see Fig. 15).

Design solution 7: Create a page displaying the required information

In the previous version of the UI, users could not know the mean value of the GQ and DP attributes of the variants. These values have great importance because they can alter the result of the analyses. Therefore, we implemented a page to display the mean value of the GQ and DP attributes of the variants based on the GT attribute and the variety (see Fig. 16).

Design solution 8: Create a *getting started* page

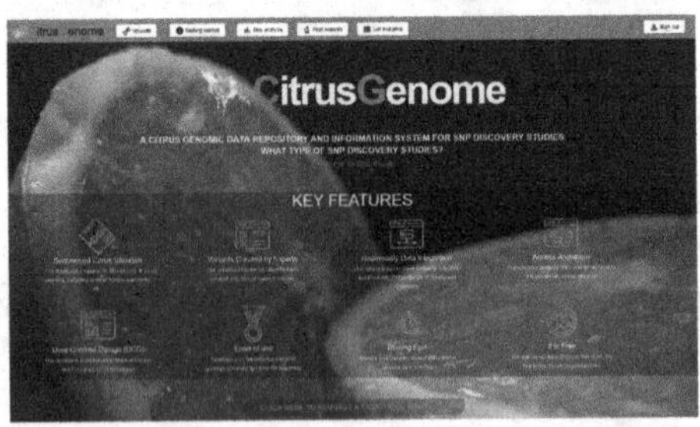

Fig. 15. Screenshot of the home page created to solve usability problem 6.

[8] https://www.nngroup.com/articles/ten-usability-heuristics/.

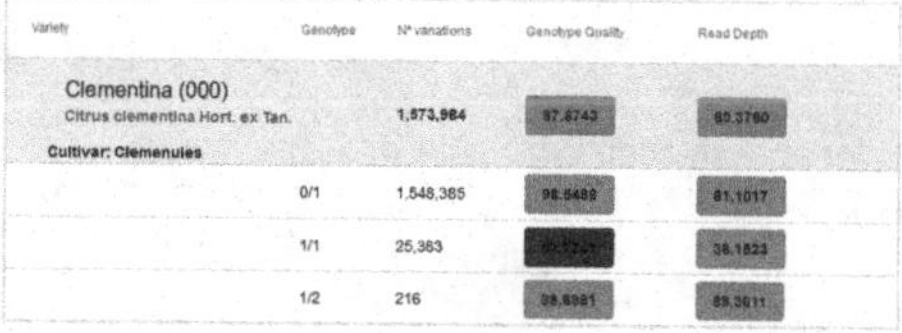

Fig. 16. Screenshot of the page displaying the information needed to solve usability problem 7.

In the previous version of the UI, novel users indicated that a *getting started* page could increase the adoption of the tool and ease its usage. In the current version of the UI, we have created a *getting started* page (see Fig. 17) that describes each step of the analysis in detail.

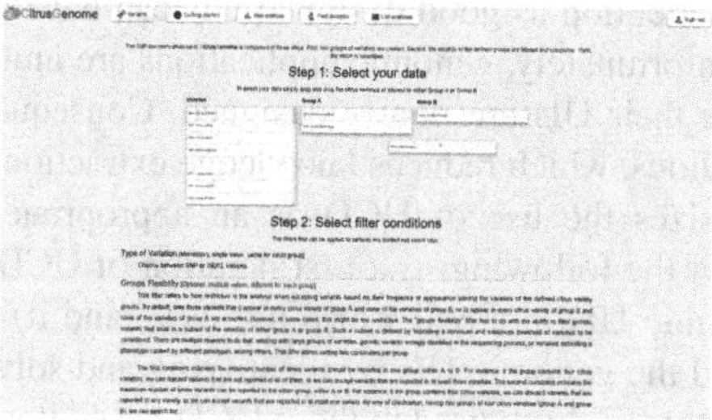

Fig. 17. Screenshot of the getting started page created to solve usability problem 8.

Design solution 9: Allow users to visualize analyses at anytime

The main problem that we have identified is that the result of the analysis can not be visualized if the user leaves the page. Participants indicated to us that it was crucial to be able to access the result of the analyses at any time. They reported several reasons to justify the importance of this usability problem: i) users may need to re-evaluate the result of past analyses; ii) a common use case is to perform a set of analyses and jump from one to another to compare the results; and iii) both technical and human failures can cause the user to leave the page unintentionally.

In the current version of the UI, we have implemented two new pages. In the third step of the analysis, the user receives a code to identify the analysis result instead of visualizing it directly (see Fig. 18). The second page contains a text input where the user writes the unique identifier the analysis whose result is to be visualized (see Fig. 19). If the identifier corresponds to an analysis, the result is then visualized, and the user can work with it.

Fig. 18. The message displaying the unique identifier of the analysis, solving usability problem 9.

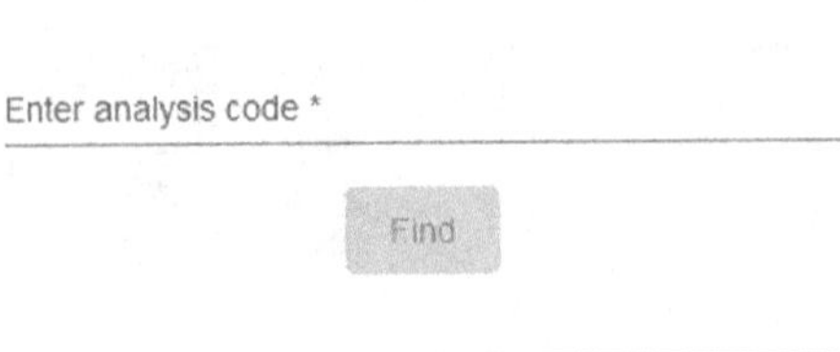

Fig. 19. The page to introduce the identifier of the analysis to visualize it, solving usability problem 9.

6 Conclusions

UIs are crucial to manage data and extract knowledge from it. Its design and development require proper attention as good designed UIs can have a huge impact in performing these tasks. Unfortunately, genomic applications are unintuitive, complex and overly verbose because their UIs are poorly designed. Consequently, learning to use them is difficult and tedious, which reduces knowledge extraction from genomic data.

This paper emphasizes the use of UCD as an appropriate approach to design genomic UIs. We report the following: i) a first iteration of UCD, where we designed and implemented genomic UIs in a real-world use case, and ii) a second iteration of UCD, where we refined the genomic UIs by identifying and solving a set of usability problems. The method that we have used in these UCD-based iterations is GenomIUm. The GenomIUm method is both conceptual model-based and pattern-oriented. This method incorporates both general patterns (i.e., design patterns whose definition is not limited to a specific context) and domain-specific patterns (i.e., design patterns whose definition is specific to the genomic context).

As we have mentioned above, our works consisted of two UCD iteration. The first iteration focused on analyzing the tasks involved in genomic analysis, conceptualizing the UI by selecting and adapting design patterns, and generating a first version of the UI as a functional prototype to be evaluated by users (i.e., bioinformaticians). The second iteration focused on identifying usability problems as a result of the user evaluation of the first version. We then proposed a set of design solutions to solve the identified usability problems. Finally, we refined the UI design by incorporating such design solutions, which are more adjusted to the real needs of the users.

Complementing UCD techniques with the support of a pattern-based method (i.e., GenomIUm) to design UIs provided us with a systematic way to generate easy-to-use UIs in the genomics field. While UCD techniques allow us to research the users, and to specify the actual user tasks, the pattern-based method guides the design and implementation of the UI based on the user tasks. Besides, composing UIs with widely used design patterns makes them familiar and, consequently, easier for bioinformaticians to use.

Bioinformaticians reported being satisfied with the designed UI in the first interaction because the CitrusGenome platform improved how users performed their knowledge extraction and data management processes. The reasons for this improvement can be summarized into four statements:

1. Automation of the analysis process.
2. Intuitive, easy, and guided process
3. Effortless management of large amounts of data.
4. No need for high computer skills to perform the analysis process.

However, the design solutions that were proposed and implemented to refine the first version of the UI enhanced the ability of users to find the information and, consequently, provided bioinformaticians with a better user experience.

Future work includes the following: as the UCD methodology states, conducting continuous design-evaluation iterations in order to refine the UIs of CitrusGenome to the current and future needs of its users; to incorporate new patterns in the GenomIUm catalog in order to cover a wider range of interactions in the genomics domain; and to extend the tool to other agri-food domains the IVIA is currently working with, such as the rice genome.

Acknowledgements. The authors would like to thank the members of the PROS Research Center Genome group for fruitful discussions regarding the application of Conceptual Modeling in the medical field. This work has been developed with the financial support of the Spanish State Research Agency and the Generalitat Valenciana under the projects TIN2016-80811-P, PROMETEO/2018/176, and INNEST/2021/57 and co-financed with ERDF. Work at IVIA is funding by the Ministerio de Ciencia, Innovación y Universidades (Spain) trough grant RTI2018-097790-R-100 and by the Instituto Valenciano de Investigaciones Agrarias (Spain), through grants 51915 and 52002.

A Appendix A: Tasks

We have divided the problem in three steps: 1) select the working data, 2) set the filter conditions, and 3) analyze the data. These steps correspond to the three UIs that we have designed and implemented.

Select the Working Data: this step consists of creating the two groups under study, the varieties of the first group (group A) have high levels of PFA, and the varieties of the second group (group B) have low levels of PFA. The first step is divided into two tasks:

- Task 1: Create group A with 17 varieties of citrus with high levels of PFA.
- Task 2: Create group B with 12 varieties of citrus with low levels of PFA.

Set the Filter Conditions: this step consists of setting the different criteria used to perform the analysis. Only those variants that fulfill the criteria will be visualized. The second step is divided into 8 tasks:

- Task 3: Accept Single Nucleotide Polymorphism (SNP) variations.
- Task 4: Accept variations that appear in every variety of group A and at most in four varieties of group B.
- Task 5: Accept variations that appear in every variety of group B and at most in four varieties of group A.
- Task 6: Accept variations with every GQ and DP values.
- Task 7: Accept variations annotated with high, moderate, or low impacts.

- Task 8: Accept variations with an allele balance value between 0.45 and 1 in all the varieties.
- Task 9: Accept variations that are located inside gene sequences.
- Task 10: Accept variations located between the 28,000,000 and 36,400,000 positions of chromosome 2.

Analyze the Data: this step consists of visualizing the accepted variations and get insight from these data. The third step is divided into X tasks. Each task consists of answering a knowledge question using the data available:

- Task 11: How many variations have been accepted?
- Task 12: What group has more variations?
- Task 13: What variety has more variations?
- Task 14: Which varieties compose group A and group B?
- Task 15: How many variations with a 0/1 genotype have been accepted in group A?
- Task 16: How many variations with a 0/1 genotype have been accepted in group B?
- Task 17: How many variations with a 1/1 genotype have been accepted in group A?
- Task 18: How many variations with a 1/1 genotype have been accepted in group B?
- Task 19: How many high impact annotations have been identified?
- Task 20: How many cellular component annotations have been identified?
- Task 21: What is the most common group of enzymes affected by the accepted variations?
- Task 22: What are the 3 genes with the most variations?
- Task 23: What are the 3 genes with the most high impact annotations?
- Task 24: What is the enzyme type with the most variations?
- Task 25: What is the pathway type with the most variations?
- Task 26: What are the biological processes affected by variations annotated with a high impact, with a 0/1 genotype in group A, and 1/1 genotype in group B?
- Task 27: How many variations have low Genotype Quality values in group A?
- Task 28: How many variations have low Genotype Quality values in group B?

References

1. Al-Ageel, N., Al-Wabil, A., Badr, G., AlOmar, N.: Human factors in the design and evaluation of bioinformatics tools. Procedia Manuf. **3**, 2003–2010 (2015). https://doi.org/10.1016/j.promfg.2015.07.247. https://www.sciencedirect.com/science/article/pii/S2351978915002486
2. Bangerth, F.: Abscission and thinning of young fruit and their regulation by plant hormones and bioregulators. Plant Growth Regul. **31**(1), 43–59 (2000). https://doi.org/10.1023/A:1006398513703
3. Bolchini, D., Finkelstein, A., Perrone, V., Nagl, S.: Better bioinformatics through usability analysis. Bioinformatics **25**(3), 406–412 (2009). https://doi.org/10.1093/bioinformatics/btn633. http://www.ncbi.nlm.nih.gov/pubmed/19073592. https://academic.oup.com/bioinformatics/article-lookup/doi/10.1093/bioinformatics/btn633
4. Carpenter, A.E., Kamentsky, L., Eliceiri, K.W.: A call for bioimaging software usability (2012). https://doi.org/10.1038/nmeth.2073

5. Chilana, P.K., Wobbrock, J.O., Ko, A.J.: Understanding usability practices in complex domains. In: Conference on Human Factors in Computing Systems - Proceedings, vol. 4, pp. 2337–2346. ACM Press, New York (2010). https://doi.org/10.1145/1753326.1753678. http://portal.acm.org/citation.cfm?doid=1753326.1753678
6. Cingolani, P., et al.: A program for annotating and predicting the effects of single nucleotide polymorphisms, SnpEff: SNPs in the genome of drosophila melanogaster strain w1118; iso-2; iso-3. Fly **6**(2), 80–92 (2012)
7. Clément, L., et al.: A data-supported history of bioinformatics tools. arXiv preprint arXiv:1807.06808 (2018)
8. Galperin, M.Y.: The molecular biology database collection: 2008 update. Nucleic Acids Res. **36**(Suppl. 1), D2 (2008). https://doi.org/10.1093/nar/gkm1037
9. Goodwin, S., McPherson, J.D., McCombie, W.R.: Coming of age: ten years of next-generation sequencing technologies. Nat. Rev. Genet. **17**(6), 333–351 (2016). https://doi.org/10.1038/nrg.2016.49
10. Iñiguez-Jarrin, C.: GenomIUm: a pattern based method for designing user interfaces for genomic data access. Ph.D. thesis, Universitat Politècnica de València (2019)
11. Jakob, N.: Severity Ratings for Usability Problems: Article by Jakob Nielsen (1994). https://www.nngroup.com/articles/how-to-rate-the-severity-of-usability-problems/
12. Jaspers, M.W.: A comparison of usability methods for testing interactive health technologies: methodological aspects and empirical evidence. Int. J. Med. Inform. **78**(5), 340–353 (2009). https://doi.org/10.1016/j.ijmedinf.2008.10.002
13. Javahery, H., Seffah, A.: A model for usability pattern-oriented design. In: Proceedings of the First International Workshop on Task Models and Diagrams for User Interface Design, TAMODIA 2002, pp. 104–110. INFOREC Publishing House Bucharest (2002). http://dl.acm.org/citation.cfm?id=646617.697237
14. Javahery, H., Seffah, A., Radhakrishnan, T.: Beyond power: making bioinformatics tools user-centered. Commun. ACM **47**(11), 58–63 (2004). https://doi.org/10.1145/1029496.1029527. http://doi.acm.org/10.1145/1029496.1029527
15. Mardis, E.R.: A decade's perspective on DNA sequencing technology. Nature **470**(7333), 198–203 (2011). https://doi.org/10.1038/nature09796
16. de Matos, P., et al.: The Enzyme portal: a case study in applying user-centred design methods in bioinformatics. BMC Bioinform. **14** (2013). https://doi.org/10.1186/1471-2105-14-103
17. Paternò, F.: ConcurTaskTrees: an engineered notation for task models. In: The Handbook of Task Analysis for Human-Computer Interaction, pp. 483–503 (2003)
18. Pavelin, K., Cham, J.A., de Matos, P., Brooksbank, C., Cameron, G., Steinbeck, C.: Bioinformatics meets user-centred design: a perspective. PLoS Comput. Biol. **8**(7), e1002554 (2012). https://doi.org/10.1371/journal.pcbi.1002554. http://dx.plos.org/10.1371/journal.pcbi.1002554
19. Rimmer, J.: Improving software environments through usability and interaction design (2004). https://doi.org/10.1080/01405110310001639050
20. Rutherford, P., Abell, W., Churcher, C., McKinnon, A., McCallum, J.: Usability of navigation tools for browsing genetic sequences. In: Conferences in Research and Practice in Information Technology Series, vol. 106, pp. 33–41 (2010). http://researcharchive.lincoln.ac.nz/handle/10182/4484
21. García, A., et al.: Applying user centred design to improve the design of genomic user interfaces. In: Proceedings of the 16th International Conference on Evaluation of Novel Approaches to Software Engineering - ENASE, pp. 25–35. INSTICC, SciTePress (2021). https://doi.org/10.5220/0010187800250035
22. Stephens, Z.D., et al.: Big data: astronomical or genomical? PLoS Biol. **13**(7) (2015). https://doi.org/10.1371/journal.pbio.1002195

23. Stevens, R., Goble, C., Baker, P., Brass, A.: A classification of tasks in bioinformatics. Bioinformatics **17**(2), 180–188 (2001). https://doi.org/10.1093/bioinformatics/17.2.180. http://www.ncbi.nlm.nih.gov/pubmed/11238075
24. Sutcliffe, A., et al.: User engagement by user-centred design in e-Health. In: Philosophical Transactions of the Royal Society A: Mathematical, Physical and Engineering Sciences, vol. 368, pp. 4209–4224. Royal Society (2010). https://doi.org/10.1098/rsta.2010.0141
25. Svanæs, D., Das, A., Alsos, O.A.: The contextual nature of usability and its relevance to medical informatics. In: Studies in Health Technology and Informatics, vol. 136, pp. 541–546 (2008). https://pubmed.ncbi.nlm.nih.gov/18487787/
26. Toxboe, A.: User Interface Design Pattern Library (2007). http://ui-patterns.com/
27. Tran, D., Dubay, C., Gorman, P., Hersh, W.: Applying task analysis to describe and facilitate bioinformatics tasks. In: Studies in Health Technology and Informatics, vol. 107, pp. 818–822 (2004). https://doi.org/10.3233/978-1-60750-949-3-818. https://www.ncbi.nlm.nih.gov/pubmed/15360926
28. Valentin, F., Squizzato, S., Goujon, M., McWilliam, H., Paern, J., Lopez, R.: Fast and efficient searching of biological data resources-using EB-eye. Briefings Bioinform. **11**(4), 375–384 (2010). https://doi.org/10.1093/bib/bbp065. https://pubmed.ncbi.nlm.nih.gov/20150321/
29. Wu, G.A., et al.: Sequencing of diverse mandarin, pummelo and orange genomes reveals complex history of admixture during citrus domestication. Nat. Biotechnol. **32**(7), 656–662 (2014). https://doi.org/10.1038/nbt.2906
30. Wu, G.A., et al.: Genomics of the origin and evolution of Citrus. Nature **554**(7692), 311–316 (2018). https://doi.org/10.1038/nature25447

Addressing the Influence of End User Human Aspects on Software Engineering

John Grundy(✉), Ingo Mueller, Anuradha Madugalla, Hourieh Khalajzadeh, Humphrey O. Obie, Jennifer McIntosh, and Tanjila Kanij

HumaniSE Lab, Faculty of IT, Monash University, Melbourne, Australia
{john.grundy,ingo.mueller,anu.madugalla,hourieh.khalajzadeh, humphrey.obie,jenny.mcintosh,tanjila.kanij}@monash.edu
https://www.monash.edu/it/humanise-lab

Abstract. We outline some of the key challenges in supporting diverse human aspects of end users in software engineering. This includes examples of age, gender, physical and mental challenges, human values, personality, emotions, language and culture. We review key related work from a range of disciplines, and propose an initial taxonomy of end user human aspects that need careful consideration throughout the software engineering life cycle. Finally we outline a research road map of key areas requiring further investigation and work.

Keywords: Human aspects of end users · Taxonomy · Living lab · Stakeholders · Personas · Modelling · Design · Defect reporting

1 Introduction

Software is designed and built to solve human challenges in almost every domain [27]. However, we continually hear about many issues with current software relating to its poor fit with its target end users. This results in hard-to-use software that does not meet the user's needs and causes frustration, economic cost, inefficiencies, not fit-for-purpose solutions, and even dangerous and life-threatening situations. Many of these problems can be traced to a lack of understanding and incorporation during software engineering of end user human aspects. Humans are diverse and present software designers and builders with diverse challenges, including but not limited to different age, gender, culture, language, language proficiency, socio-economic status, physical and mental challenges, personality, emotional reaction to technology, engagement, and many others [29,30].

In this paper we present an initial taxonomy of end user human aspects that impact software usage and hence design, implementation, testing, defect reporting and correction and ultimately its requirements and processes, methods and tools needed for development. Providing a taxonomy of human centric aspects in software engineering helps not only to classify human-centric aspects, but also provides a language to use when describing human aspects [63]. Taxonomies are used in science to define, group and rank by similar characteristics, and by doing this we will generate a scientific nomenclature that can be used to explore and address human centric aspects relevant to the industry.

R. Ali et al. (Eds.): ENASE 2021, CCIS 1556, pp. 241–264, 2022.
https://doi.org/10.1007/978-3-030-96648-5_11

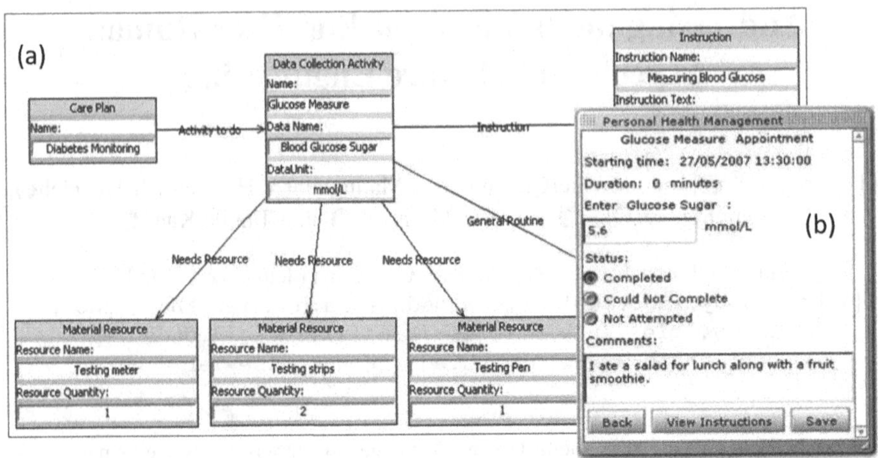

Fig. 1. A clinician-oriented Domain-specific Visual Language for care plan modelling and generating eHealth app (from [41]).

Our aim is to better characterise these diverse end user aspects and their impact on software development, with some examples from our recent work addressing some of these. We begin with a motivating example in Sect. 2 and review of key related work in Sect. 3. We follow this by introducing our initial taxonomy of end user human aspects needing careful consideration during software engineering in Sect. 4. In Sects. 5 to 10 we discuss a range of our recent work to try and address some of these human aspects during different software engineering tasks. In Sect. 11 we outline a research roadmap needed to continue to advance this area, and summarise this paper in Sect. 12.

2 Motivation

Motivating Example. Figure 1 shows an example model-driven engineering tool that takes a high level visual care plan model (a) and uses this to generate a fully functional eHealth app to implement the care plan (b) [41]. While in theory this is a good idea, the tool fails to account for the fact that end users of the app are generally elderly, many have English as a second language, they are unfamiliar with much of the health and technology terminology used, come from different cultures with differing concepts of and approaches to health and illness, many users have diverse physical and mental challenges that impact using the app, the app is boring for many to use, and many users worry about their data privacy and transparency of recommendations the app makes to them. The resultant app is unusable for many target end users, illustrating the problem of failing to consider diverse end user human aspects, individually and in combination, during development.

Developer Survey and Interviews. We wanted to gain a better understanding of current developer approaches to addressing such diverse end users' human aspects, key

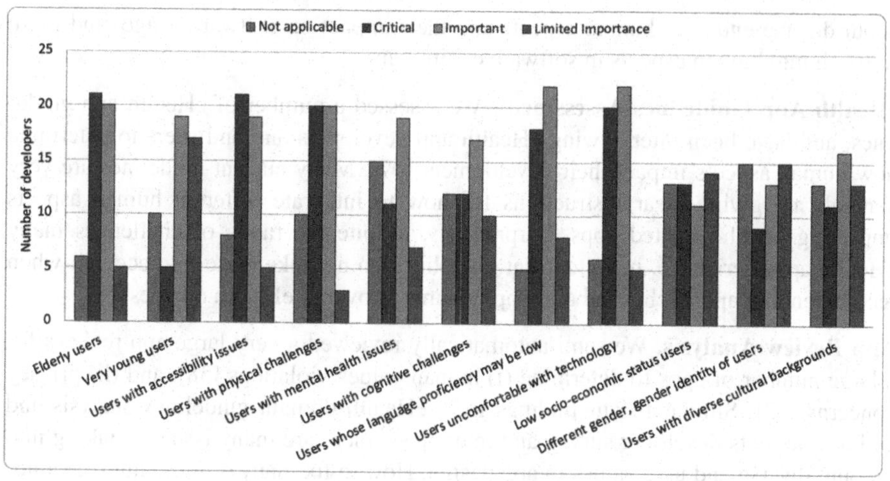

Fig. 2. End user human aspects survey respondents judge to be critical (or not) in their work (from [30]).

open challenge areas in this domain, and determine key focus areas for researching new techniques and tools to address these, both in general and specifically for eHealth app development [30,67]. We conducted a detailed survey, answered by 61 developers and managers, and then interviewed a further 12 developers in detail. We wanted to better understand how these diverse end user human aspect issues are understood and addressed from a software engineering perspective. Figure 2 summarises our respondents' ratings of some of the end user human aspects they encountered in their work.

Some of the key reasons given by respondents why they find these end user human aspects challenging to address included: the broad range of the end user human differences that exist and have to be catered for; the different languages and range of comfort with technology of different user groups; different problem solving styles of many end user groups; complexity of user interfaces in many application domains; and differences in terminology used, digital literacy and the need to carefully consider text and icon usage for many target end users.

We asked developers what would help them to improve development of their software to better address some of these diverse end user human aspects. Examples reported included: better requirements capture and human aspect modelling support; providing developers with better guidelines and practices to follow to address diverse end user human aspects; better design frameworks and tooling to address a greater range of end user human aspects; development tools that automatically prompt and advise on missing end user human aspect issues in designs and implementations; simpler interfaces in software for many end user groups; more live testing with representative end users, including better participant recruitment approaches ensuring more diverse end users are included; better defect reporting to enable end users to more easily identify, describe and report problems with their software; the need for better development processes to improve target end user involvement; a need for better education of software engineers about diverse end user human aspects and their impact on software usage; and more research into human aspects in software engineering.

eHealth App Guidelines Assessment. We assessed a number of eHealth app guidelines, and have been interviewing eHealth app developers and end users to determine how human aspects impact their development [67]. Many current guidelines are very general, not giving clear instructions for how to integrate different human aspects impacting health-oriented apps. Surprisingly, despite the range of challenges many eHealth app users have, many current guidelines do not take these into account when recommending approaches to build app features or overall eHealth app design.

App Review Analysis. We semi-automatically reviewed a very large app reviews for a large number of apps to determine (i) human values violations [58], and (ii) privacy concerns [32]. Similar to our findings from eHealth domain guidelines analysis and end user aspects developer survey and interviews, there are many issues in taking into account diverse end user values in app design. How to fix many of these human values issues is still unclear.

3 Related Work

Human aspects impacting software design, implementation and evaluation have been studied for many years. Work of particular note has occurred in the disciplines of business, ergonomics, and human-computer interaction (HCI). Several taxonomies and classifications have been created as part of these efforts [4,56,57,66,71]. However, we argue that these taxonomies have shortcomings that limit their applicability for practical software development activities:

1. they focus on problem-solving rather than comprehension of diverse human needs and empathising with the people behind these needs and expectations;
2. they predominantly centre on the formal representation and modelling of software features derived from human needs - often at a higher level of abstraction - thus bypassing the people and their natural characteristics, skills, abilities, strengths, weaknesses, etc.; and
3. they lack comprehensiveness.

We argue that these shortcomings result in a lack of support that developers require for critical activities, not only during requirements elicitation and capture but also software design and testing.

Morris and Stauffer [56] developed a taxonomy of keywords that is aimed at helping with requirements elicitation activities by providing a systematic structure for user/customer interviews. It is deliberately kept short in order to allow its application under tight time-to-market deadlines. The elements of the taxonomy refer to features of computer systems rather than human aspects. Each keyword is presented at a higher level of abstractions (e.g. 'control', 'display', 'form'), thus potentially providing barriers between the developers and users who are not familiar with this terminology and way of thinking.

Saurin and Patriarca [4] specifically focus their taxonomy on interaction (human-to-human as well as human-to-machine) in socio-technical systems. The 'nature of the agent' taxonomy category is a generic placeholder for collecting information about human aspects but it does not provide support for systematically and comprehensively cover such aspects.

Longo et al. [47] propose a taxonomy of human factors to enable the systematic capture of cognitive and physical abilities and psychological attitudes of industrial workers. The taxonomy comprises very detailed sub categories such as attention, comprehension, knowledge, memory functions, musculoskeletal health, neurological health, motion, perception (including sight, sound, and touch) to name a few. The categories are certainly human-centric, however the entire taxonomy does not link them back to people. Moreover, the large number of 50 sub categories may potentially make this taxonomy hard to operationalise.

Singh et al. [71] discuss a taxonomy to capture usability requirements for telehealth systems. The scope of the taxonomy is tailored towards addressing concrete usability and accessibility needs. However, the categories of the taxonomy are structured based on abstract terms such as 'natural input' and 'guided instructions'. The taxonomy is designed from a system perspective and does not centre on people and their needs *per se*. Furthermore, the categories of the taxonomy are accompanied by long descriptions. This may indicate that additional training is required to work with this taxonomy and individual categories may be interpreted and applied differently by developers.

Seneler et al. [66] propose a technology adoption taxonomy aimed at supporting developers to identify key properties of user interfaces that promote the adoption of a technological solution. The motivations behind this taxonomy are usability and accessibility aspects and several categories relate to human aspects such as 'user characteristics & mental and emotional states'. Each category has a number of sub categories that are aimed at helping to systematically document information about human users. However, the set of sub categories is incomplete, for example they do not cover physical aspects and needs.

Mosqueira-Rey et al. [57] propose two taxonomies. Firstly, a usability taxonomy organised in abstract categories, e.g. knowability, operability, safety, efficiency. Secondly, a context-of-use taxonomy with three main categories named 'user', 'task' and 'environment'. Both taxonomies remain at an abstract level. Human values, needs and characteristics are not in focus.

Our approach does not overcome all shortcomings of these existing taxonomies. However, we believe that by making the end user human central and focusing on taxonomy categories that reflect human values, needs and characteristics, we provide developers with knowledge and tools to better understand the needs of diverse users and consequently to develop more inclusive software.

4 A Preliminary Taxonomy – End User Human Aspects and Software Engineering

In previous work we have developed taxonomies to better structure and understand different domains in software engineering. This included a new synthesized taxonomy for usability defect report classification [79] and human aspects impacting software

Table 1. Personal characteristics of end users and their impact on software usage and engineering.

Human aspect	Impact/Issues to consider
Age	Impact of age on usage and/or age bias in design of software systems. People of differing ages e.g. young vs older may have quite different expectations, challenges and reactions to software which need to be carefully designed into solutions [52]
Gender	Impact of gender bias towards software end users. Not just terminology/words used, but unconscious biases including treatment, assumptions about users and software usage [75]. Several prominent mainstream articles and books have highlighted the gender bias in e.g. apps and smart technologies [73]
Ethnicity	Ethnic bias against some end users, assumptions about users from different ethnic backgrounds, biased training sets etc. [68,77]
Personality	Researchers have studied personality impact on programming, testing, design, requirements engineering and maintenance, which has shown to have impact on developer performance [19]. Much less researched to date has been on impact of personality of different end users
Emotions	Different people react differently to technology solutions from an emotional perspective [23]. Impact of emotional reactions, effective and cognitive states on use of software, perception of software. Some react positively, while others negatively, to the exact same solution, which can dramatically impact the acceptance and usage of the software
Engagement	No one wants to use boring or disengaging software; this is especially important for software for behaviour change e.g. diet, fitness eHealth apps, finances etc., and also for games in general [43]
Physical or mental challenges	Impact of wide range of physical challenges on end users e.g. colour-blind, sight challenges, hearing, coordination, stroke, obesity, cardiac, infection, etc. [38]. Impact of mental challenges e.g. due to injury or illness
Cognitive style	Impact of different problem-solving approaches e.g. neuro-atypical users
Preferences	The users own personal preferences, whatever their particular demographics - all else may be the same, but individual users might have different personal preferences for some aspects of their software

engineers involved in the requirements engineering process [33]. We want to develop a similar taxonomy of human aspects impacting end users of software, and/or how human aspects of end users impact the engineering of software [29]. We started by dividing human characteristics into three groups: 1. personal demographic characteristics (Table 1); 2. skill or expertise-based characteristics (Table 2); and 3. group-based characteristics (Table 3).

Table 2. Skill, experiential or environmental-influenced characteristics of end users and their impact on software usage and engineering.

Human aspect	Impact/Issues to consider
Spoken Language	Impact of spoken and written language assumptions on software end users. Does the software support users who need different read/spoken languages? Are translations accurate? Are requirements multi-lingual [40]
Socio-economic status	Different end users may have very different access to technology, living and work environments etc. [31,74]. Can they afford the latest handset to run an app on? Does their internet connection support expectations of high bandwidth?
Language proficiency	Impact of language complexity, jargon, dialogue on users
Education	Impact of different end user educational attainment, range of technology and domain-specific skills developed [10]
Comfort with technology	Many end user groups are much less comfortable using technology solutions than the software engineers that develop them [61]
Location	Where an end user is may impact their software usage, including the different environments the software is used in, rural vs urban living, different software regulations, etc. [78]
Religious beliefs	End users have wide variety of different beliefs and practices, some greatly impacting their use of software in different parts of their living and work
Human values	Set of human values important to individuals, teams, organisations, end users, societies [58]. Includes but not limited to values including inclusive, transparent, creative, authoritative, belonging, secure, security, family, tradition, devout, polite, open, obedient, loyal, forgiving, social justice, protecting environment, privacy, ...
Skill level	Personal (vs team) experience in a work domain that impacts software usage

Table 1 summarises some key ***personal, demographic*** characteristics of end users that (i) may impact their usage of software and (ii) need to be taken into consideration by software engineers to ensure software meets that characteristics, different to other end user groups. It is understood that people can have multiple combinations of these characteristics.

Table 2 summarises some end user human aspects that are ***context driven***, due to external influences such as upbringing, training, experience or other influences. Many of these aspects change over time unlike characteristics in Table 1 which may also change e.g. due to ageing or illness, but generally remain more or less the same over one's lifetime.

Table 3. Group or multiple human characteristics of end users and their impact on software usage and engineering.

Human aspect	Impact/Issues to consider
Culture	Different cultural practices, assumptions, behaviours, accepted and unaccepted practices, biases against particular users of software [5,6,77]
Geographic location	Where end users are located geographically may impact them and a range of software systems significantly [78]
Team climate	Working in a team environment means end users need to interact with others and may be impacted by other individuals, group, organisational and even societal differences [46]
Family environment and Martial status, Child status, Caring responsibilities	Impact of various living arrangements that differ from person to person and family unit to family unit. Potential for bias against different arrangements or simply not sufficiently taking into account differences [42]
Work status	Impact of having no work, being under-employed, working in preferred vs non-preferred job, income, and other work-related differences [50]
Collaboration, Communication style	Living and working with others requires communication and collaboration skills, many of which need to be adequately and appropriately supported in software systems
Organisational or Societal values	Related to personal human values above, collective group/organisational/societal values differences that impact end users and their software usage

Table 3 summarises end user human characteristics that result from ***social contexts and interactions***, including living and working with other people. Some may change over time as social interactions and contexts change, while some have a life-long influence.

In following sections we give some examples of our recent work addressing some of these human aspects of end users in the context of software engineering. For each we briefly describe the end user human aspect, discuss issues software engineers face in addressing the human aspect, and briefly describe the research we are undertaking to try and assist them. We then summarise key outstanding issues we have found and present the outline of a research roadmap to address these.

5 Age

5.1 Design for Differently-Aged Users

There is an increase in the average age of internet users, with 73% of United States adults over the age of 64 accessing the internet according to the internet usage report

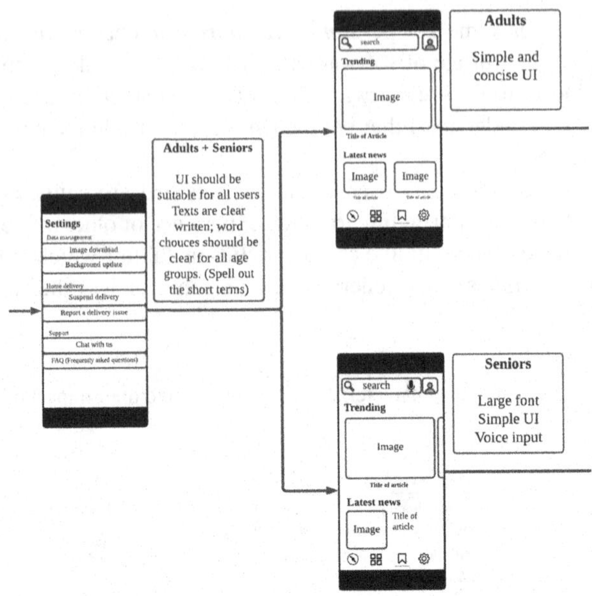

Fig. 3. Example of branching (from [39]).

from Pew Research centre [62]. Web-browsing behaviour differs between various age groups according to a study by Joyce and Nielsen in 2019 [35]. Elderly users may face issues such as screen readability due to visual impairment associated with ageing [35]. Young people also report age-specific preferences. Despite developers and designers are mainly being younger [60], teenagers also complain about poor visual designs, such as font size, background colour and layout of certain websites.

Based on the findings by Masood et al., younger children also commonly have problems working with mobile applications, such as the system status not being apparent for them, having a hard time working out what to do next, and not remembering which page or button was accessed earlier [49]. They recommend that children-oriented software needs to more clearly show the current state of the page, and sometimes the child users may need some guidance to do the next step. Moreover, the buttons and menus need to be simple enough and buttons and menu links should be easily identified as being clickable while menu headings and titles as being not clickable. A Fingerprint app [59] is used to describe how to design the software user interface for the children. This work discusses four key points for the vision element regarding kids – integer vision effect, functional area design, icon and button design, and font design. The work of Michaels and Boyatzis et al. discusses colour preferences of children users as well as the effect of colour on children's emotions [13,54].

5.2 AgeMag: Countering Age Bias in eCommerce Software

Boll et al. provide a set of user interface design guidelines for people between 55 to 75 years old [12]. Based on their studies with older users, most reported that the icons were too small, and that double-clicking a small button was a problem for older people. Moreover, they found that the menu needed to be put in conventional positions to make consistent in the software.

We had similar findings in our study exploring age bias in eCommerce software. We found age bias in the design and presentation of eCommerce websites. Elderly people had a lot of difficulty navigating their way around eCommerce websites as the interface was difficult to see (small font) and visually confusing (too cluttered). Older people had trouble navigating back and forth through the website and could not easily locate what they were looking for. Often they had to ask for help, and were likely to give up rather than try to resolve a problem. Interestingly, there was a clear delineation between the elderly or 'Silent Generation' (born between 1928 and 1945), and the 'younger generations' (born before 1945) when using eCommerce, suggesting people in their 60s and even early 70s had less difficulty in using eCommerce.

From our results, we developed an 'AgeMag' to evaluate eCommerce applications for age bias. The AgeMag had two personas - an 'elderly user persona' and a 'general user persona' - which were used to conduct a cognitive walk-through of eCommerce websites. The cognitive walk-through involves using the personas as if they are real people, to identify where they might struggle to use the website, and how the design and interface of the website might be adapted to make it more usable. Given many people have been forced to rely on eCommerce for their necessities during the pandemic, this is a simple way to evaluate eCommerce for age bias and adapt the design of eCommerce websites for elderly people, many of whom are using eCommerce for the first time [52].

Designing emotion-oriented software has been the focus of some researchers [23]. A goal model for a smart home device was created by analysing the emotions of older people to helps developers to understand the expectations of an older adult. The model included different emotions for the elderly people to help get the elderly people to accept the device and feel like this is what they need. Curumsing et al. demonstrate a case study of an emergency alarm system for elderly people [24]. They suggested a few important factors in designing the framework and also keeping the interest of the elderly people. These include designing solutions in a way that is easy to use and cost-effective.

These studies reflect the fact that users' age should be taken into account when designing software applications. Age-related considerations need to be taken into the account from the early stages of software development, i.e. modelling and design of the software. There are many existing modelling frameworks, most do not currently support modelling the age of end users and providing different design solutions for different age groups and needs of end users [39]. We developed a set of extensions to the commonly used wire-frame modelling approach to incorporate different designs for child, adult and senior end users in [39]. The modelling approach was evaluated with developers and a prototype news app was developed using our approach with a range of differently aged end users. Further work includes incorporating other human-centric aspects into the extended wire-frame model e.g. gender, culture, language, and trying the same model extension approach in other modelling frameworks, such as user stories, use cases, and sequence diagrams. Figure 3 shows an example of such an extended wire-frame design. This shows multiple "pathways" suitable to different aged users planned for in the application under design.

6 Gender

Gender is another important human aspect of the end user. After a comprehensive review of literature Burnett et al. [16] concluded that there are five facets where people differ based on gender. Those include: motivation, information processing style, computer self-efficacy, risk aversion and tinkering. They incorporate the facets into persona descriptions of users and propose a cognitive walk-through approach of usability inspection on problem solving software. They developed a tool called GenderMag based on the approach [16]. They reported several application of GenderMag tool to successfully identify gender inclusiveness issues in problem solving software [15].

In our study of understanding the characteristic, challenges and goals of domestic workers in Bangladesh, in order to design digital solution for them, we found that there are 1.8 million domestic workers in Dhaka and around 90% of them are female. The research project is in progress and with the focus groups already conducted we have already identified some gender-based characteristics such as motivation behind using digital solutions. We plan to use these requirements to inform future domestic work recruitment, management and payment solutions with these requirements. In addition, many works have low educational attainment, come from rural areas, and often share smart phones among several, introducing several other important human aspects to the design process.

7 Physical Challenges

7.1 Adaptable User Interfaces for Diverse End Users

At a time where User Interfaces (UI) are becoming increasingly complex, it is no longer sufficient to develop a single UI for all users with a 'one size fits all' approach. As a solution, designers can aim to cater all diverse users with a single design, but this will lead to compromises due to conflicting user requirements. Therefore, in most software design, usability is generally designed for the majority of users with homogeneous characteristics, often neglecting those in need of special features and support. These users who need special features can be users with vision impairments, cognitive impairments, aging population as well as users from socially and culturally diverse backgrounds.

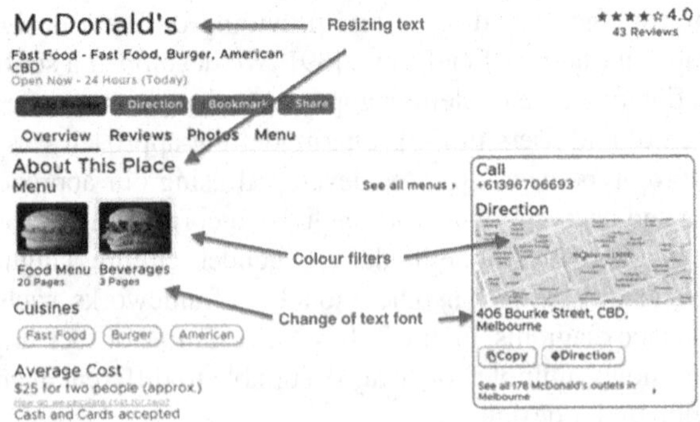

Fig. 4. Adaptive Zomato – text size increased, colour changed (from [48]).

Our solution to this problem is to develop an *Adaptable UI*, which allows users to tailor the UI components to their individual needs [48]. To achieve this, we developed a framework with an adaptable user interface component library. We implemented it with the open-source web development platform, Flutter, which is increasingly becoming famous among web developers. Our framework supported the following three adaptable features:

1. adaptive colour themes: Pre-defined colour vision and custom colour themes;
2. adaptive image settings: Allowed selecting image colour filters to apply on all images; and
3. adaptive font settings: changeable text colour, size, font type.

We rebuilt the popular Zomato website using our framework and provided the adaptive feature via an accessibility menu. In this prototype, to represent the diverse users, we chose users with colour blindness, low vision and dyslexia. We evaluated the rebuilt Zomato in a user study, based on W3C guidelines for accessibility [76]. Due to COVID-19 restrictions, we adopted a Persona based evaluation method, where each participant was assigned a Persona with a vision impairment and this impairment was simulated via browser plugins during the study. Figure 4 shows an example of our adaptive Zomato app in use.

All participants found the functionality provided by the adaptive features helpful for their simulated vision deficiency, enabling them to view certain elements of the website easier. Our evaluation indicated that the adaptable version of Zomato outperformed the original Zomato website in all anticipated sections from the W3C guidelines. Therefore, we recommend web developers to explore the use of such adaptable widgets via a framework similar to ours as this would assist them to cater for the diverse user needs with a less workload.

7.2 Improving Human-Centric Software Defect Evaluation, Reporting and Fixing

Customarily, *defect reporting* exists in most applications and web sites to enable end-users to report issues and for developers to receive actionable feedback. However, the impact of "human-centric" issues - such as age, gender, language, culture, physical and mental challenges, and socio-economic status - is often overlooked in defect reporting. Therefore, most defect reporting tools lack focus on human-centric features to enable a challenged user (eg: a vision impaired user) to adequately navigate and report defects. Furthermore, most defect reporting tools lack sufficient defect report structuring, reporting guidance, and do not emphasize the perceived severity of the defect to developers. Due to these usability issues, sometimes diverse end-users are unable to report defects effectively and thus developers find it difficult to understand and fix the reported defect.

In our research, we aimed to understand the issues faced by diverse end-users in reporting defects and developers issues in understanding them via a novel human-centred defect reporting tool prototype [36]. Our research contained two stages. In the first stage, we developed a simple prototype of a defect reporting tool and developed Personas to represent diverse end users with vision, hearing, motor and reading impairments. Using these Personas, we conducted cognitive walk-throughs on four chosen applications (Grab, a university Moodle, Snapchat and Skype) and requested participants to report any human centric issues via the prototype. Based on this, we identified a list of potential improvements that could be introduced to a human-centric defect reporting tool. In the next stage, we re-implemented the prototype tool by addressing most of the identified improvements and conducted a second cognitive walk-through. In this walk-through, we evaluated the end users' ability to report a defect as well as developers' ability to understand the reported defect, using Personas of both end users and developers. Figure 5 shows an example of some of the defect reporting app screens we prototyped.

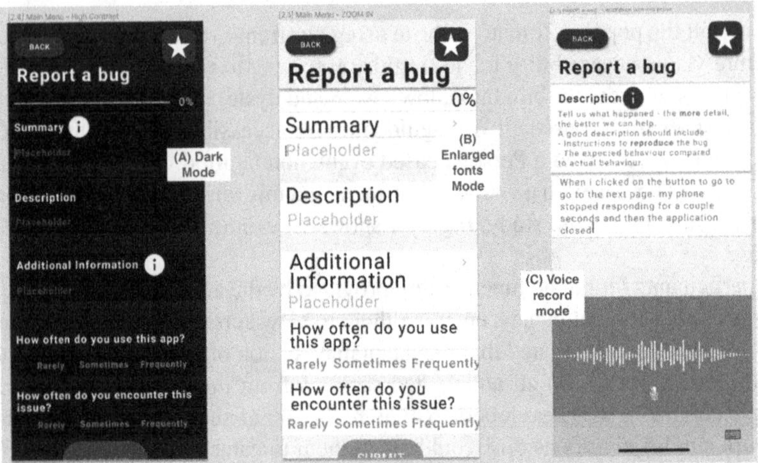

Fig. 5. Human-centric defect reporting prototype with Additional accessibility controls turned on (from [36]).

Based on both these stages, we developed a set of guidelines to improve the usability of defect reporting for diverse end users and to increase the useful information provided to developers. Additionally, we identified three major factors that can assist developers in human-centric defect evaluation and resolution: 1) Educating users about defect reporting and educating developers about Personas of different users and their diverse challenges 2) Capturing the frequency of the application use and defect encountering frequency does not affect the developers perceived severity of the issue 3) Increasing the amount of extra information collected about a defect, while taking appropriate steps to prevent the over complication of defect reports, is effective. We recommend developers and defect reporting tool designers to adopt these guidelines and findings to generate more human-centric defect reporting tools.

8 Human Values

Human values such as tradition, helpfulness, freedom, creativity, etc. are a critical human aspect and should be considered in the design, development, and deployment of software systems. Human values are the guiding principles for what people consider to be important in life [22] and these affect the choices and decisions that they make including technological choices. Because human values serve as a vehicle for expressing need [26], they should be properly articulated and captured in the requirements gathering process. Moreover, human values also determine behaviour and attitude [65], thus users' and other stakeholders' values should be embodied in the interaction models of the software systems – showing how their interaction with the system reflects and supports their values (or at the least not violate their values).

Human values, if they are not properly captured and integrated throughout the entire software development process, can have deleterious consequences, not only on direct stakeholders such as companies and end-users but also on indirect stakeholders and society as a whole. Recent media has shown some of these violations of human values and their associated negative consequences, e.g., Robodebt - an inaccurate automated debt recovery tool that distressed thousands of Australians [51], Facebook Cambridge Analytica scandal - privacy and tool for social manipulation and undermining of democratic processes [17], Amazon algorithms terminating contracts of package delivery drivers [72].

We have carried out some work in mining values requirements and detecting violations of human values from app reviews [58]. App reviews provide useful information such as critiques, bug reports, feature requests from a user perspective, and have been mined to support change requirements for future software updates and evolution. We analysed 22,119 app reviews from the Google Play store using natural language processing (NLP) techniques to understand potential values violation as reported by users. We analysed reviews from 12 apps chosen to cover different audiences and age groups, with different expectations and interactions with technology. We based our NLP values violations detection approach on the widely accepted Schwartz theory of basic human values. The results of our analysis showed that 26.5% of the 22,119 app reviews contained user-perceived violations of human values. In terms of the broader values categories, *benevolence* and *self-direction* were the most violated values categories while *tradition* and *conformity* were the least violated values categories. Moreover, looking into the finer details of specific values items showed that *helpfulness, pleasure,* and *curiosity* ranked amongst the topmost violated value items while *obedience* and *influential* were the least violated values items.

Our results show that values requirements can be mined from app reviews. Nonetheless, we note that app reviews mining is still a reactive approach that happens post-factum, and we recommend proactive approaches such as participatory design and the direct engagement of and elicitation of values requirements from all stakeholders involved in the software project. Furthermore, careful consideration of stakeholders' specific domain context in the design of values elicitation protocols should be made - thus effectively capturing human values as an important human aspect.

9 Emotions

Different end users may react to the same software application in quite different ways, in terms of their "emotional response" [23]. For example, in an in-home aging user support solution, a "smart home" software solution can be perceived in quite different ways by different elderly end users and their carers. For example, one person may find the presence of sensors and voice-enabled interaction induces a feeling of safety, care, security, and reduces feelings of isolation. Another end user may find the exact same software solution overly controlling, inducing feelings of lack of control, invasive, and even threatening to their self-worth and liberty. This will lead to very different experiences, acceptance and take-up of the solution. Very different configuration of the solution – or adoption of a totally different solution – may be needed to satisfy the range of diverse end user emotional reactions.

We used extensions to a goal-directed requirements modelling language [55] in a case study of designing and building a smart home for elderly [23]. An example of an extended goal-directed requirements model is shown in Fig. 6. This allows requirements engineers to reason about potential emotional reactions of stakeholders, positive and negative, look to address these in design solutions, and evaluate whether these are adequately addressed in testing.

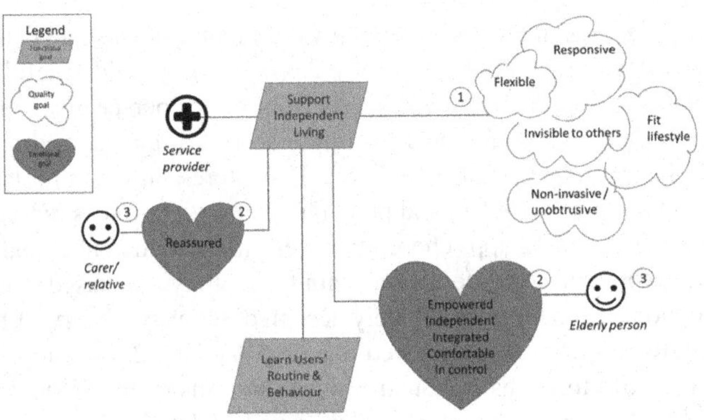

Fig. 6. An Emotion-oriented domain-specific visual language (from [29]).

10 Language and Culture

Socio-cultural context and language preferences are important human aspects that influence end users' interaction with software. In our on going research project with domestic workers and fisher-folk in Bangladesh [2], we identified that user interface and voice instructions in the software developed for them needs to be in "Bangla". English language literacy of the target end users are low, therefor in order to make the software interface usable by them the communication language used in the software needs to be "Bangla" - only language they are proficient in. We have found that, due to socio-cultural context, mobile phones are often shared among family members, as such designing of personalized user interface needs to consider "plural" end users.

In another on going project of identifying interrelationship among different factors influencing online shopping, we have found the influencing factors are related very differently for Australian and Chinese online consumers. For Chinese consumers, their demographic characteristics influence how web aesthetics is perceived, on the other hand, for Australian online consumers demographic characteristics have connection with web aesthetics, however both demographic characteristics and web aesthetics influence their overall shopping experience. This can be related to "Indulgence Vs Reatraint" dimension of Hoftesde cross culture theory [34]. According to this dimension indulgence society tends to enjoy life and free gratification of human desires while restraint society tends to restrain one's desire to abide by social norm (Fig. 7).

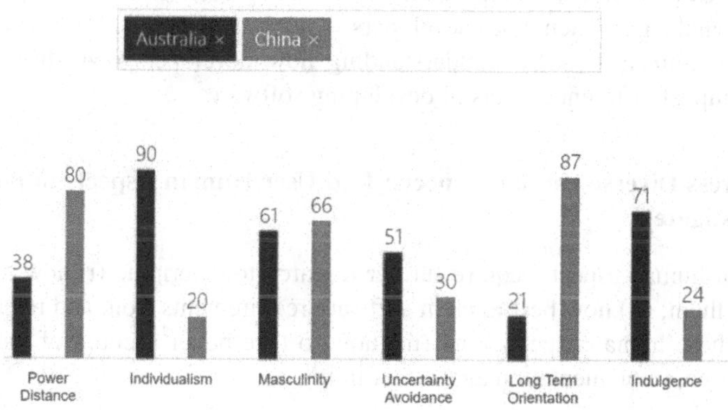

Fig. 7. Comparing Australia and China by Hofstede's cross-culture theory (from [1]).

In our smart parking development project [45], we identified several personas with a variety of differing human aspects impacting their usage of the smart parking app. Several of these factors we have highlighted in previous sections – age, gender, emotional frustrations with current solutions. Other key differences included language proficiency – both primary spoken language and also level of read language ability. We needed to provide users the ability to ask for the app to display text in their preferred spoken/read language, and to request simplified descriptions of tasks to perform. Similar to the human-centric defect reporting app and adaptive user interface widgets projects, we also encountered users with dyslexia who wanted different fonts be used and reduced text label usage.

11 Research Roadmap

To further investigate a range of end user human aspects impacting software engineering, we propose a number of research directions below. Some of these we are currently working on. Some extend previous work, and some we think are promising directions for the research and practice communities to explore. These fall into several research themes:

- End user human aspects – better understanding the nature of human aspects
- Engagement of stakeholders – better engaging diverse stakeholders throughout development
- Requirements capture – eliciting, modelling and reasoning about requirements relating to diverse end users of software
- Understanding end users – helping developers to better empathise with, appreciate challenges of and address diverse end user human characteristics and challenges using software
- Design support – providing developers with better techniques and tools for design and implementation of software to address diverse end user human characteristics and challenges
- End user empowerment – helping end users take greater control of their software solutions and engagement with developers
- Developer human aspects – understanding how developers own diverse human aspects impact different aspects of developing software

11.1 Address Diverse Human Aspects: End User Human Aspects to Further Investigate

A number of human aspects require further research to determine (i) how to describe and discuss them; (ii) how best to elicit software requirements from and regarding end users with these human aspects; and (iii) how to take better account of them during software design, implementation and defect fixing:

- personality – while a lot of SE research has investigated personality impact on software engineers, little to date has focused on how different end user personalities impact software usage;
- ethnicity – AI-based software biases have been highlighted in recent times. How to better address these has been subject to recent work, but more work is required.
- engagement – how to understand diverse end user preferences and needs around their engagement with their software requires more research.
- cognitive style – limited understanding of how different cognitive styles can and should be taken account of during software development exists. To date this has main focused on children or elderly with specific cognitive challenges.
- socio-economic status – and its impact on access to and use of software is still not well understood. Addressing the growing digital divide is critical.
- human values – and taking account of different end user values has become an area of increasing interest in recent years. The impact of different values on software design is still poorly understood.
- culture – understanding diverse end user culture, incorporating cultural values into software, and fixing culture-related defects is also poorly understood.
- family environment – diverse non-work living environments and its impact on software design and usage by end users also requires further study.
- organisational values – and their impact on teams and individuals complements individual human values research.

As noted in several of our projects, humans have multiple characteristics. It is largely unknown in many domains and in general how these interplay to influence software usage i.e. which is the most important characteristic to consider, or how different characteristics interact in different ways for different people and have a major influence on their software experience. Studying various combinations of human aspects is of course very difficult as there are an almost infinite set of combinations. In addition, one's own experiences, current state of physical or mental health, family, team or organisational usage context, and other variables might themselves have a major influence on what makes a "good" or "bad" software design for a particular user.

11.2 Address Engagement of Stakeholders: Co-creation Living Lab

We have begun to explore the "Living Lab" approach to co-creating software requirements and designs with end users [29]. The idea is to better involve end users, and indeed all stakeholders whether eventual end users or not, throughout the software development process as equals with software engineers. Living lab approaches have been used in a variety of domains but most particularly for eHealth software and smart living software domains, but not usually from a software engineering perspective. We would like to explore the use of such an approach on software engineering processes, techniques and tools. The attraction of this approach is the concept of co-creation with diverse stakeholders that fully takes their varied human characteristics into account during requirements and design, and treat them as equal co-creators of the solutions.

11.3 Address Engagement of Stakeholders and Better Requirements: Stakeholder Identification

Not all stakeholders of a software system are end users. How different stakeholders e.g. sponsors, managers, affected people who do not directly operate or interact with the software used by others, etc. are impacted by their own human aspects is a potentially important area for further study and translation to practice. Using living lab and other techniques, we would like to develop better guidelines for identifying and having dialogue with diverse software stakeholders, taking better account of their human aspects as well as those of direct end users during its development.

11.4 Address Better Requirements and Understanding Diverse End Users: Diverse Personas

Software is increasingly used by more diverse users. How to convey this diversity, their differing needs, differing experiences with the same software, and how to ensure peoples' differing needs are met is still unclear. One approach we have used in several projects is developing a range of personas to represent diverse end user demographics, goals, and frustrations with current solutions. Some of these have used data-driven techniques to help construct the personas, such as app reviews highlighting key unmet needs [45]. We have been compiling persona examples for diverse end users, particularly the elderly and children, reported in a variety of literature to inform development for these user groups [3, 8, 44, 70].

11.5 Address Better Understanding Diverse End Users: Modelling Human Aspects

Human aspects of end users are sometimes captured during requirements engineering and design phases of software development. However, we currently lack suitable approaches to formally model these in models and then reason about completeness, correctness and whether addressed in software solutions [39]. We have been developing preliminary extensions to a number of models – including iStar, wire-frame designs, goal-based requirements, user stories and others – to try and support better capture, reasoning and use of differing end user characteristics [23,39,45].

11.6 Address Better Understanding Diverse End Users and Better Designs: Design Support for End User Human Aspects

As well as better identifying diverse end user needs during requirements engineering, developers need to be better supported to recognise, appreciate, understand and design for these diverse end users during their design and implementation tasks. Some end users have different problem solving styles, depending on gender, age, cognitive style, personality, etc. [19,21,75]. Accessibility has been long studied and design approaches to address developed for many end user challenges. However, many of these approaches are as yet not well known or well supported in software design tools, platforms and APIs [7]. Adaptive interfaces have been trialled to address platform differences, but also to a lesser degree end user differences [48].

11.7 Address Better Designs and End User Empowerment: End User Development

End user development offers the promise of end users being able to develop, or at least reconfigure, their software solutions to suit their individual preferences and needs. Many approaches have been tried, from programming by example to low code/no code pre-packaged solutions to (more or less) configurable applications [11,14]. While software is too complex in general for end users to develop solutions, in controlled settings giving end users the ability to (re)configure software solutions may greatly improve their experiences and efficiency and effectiveness of the software. This includes reconfiguring user interface layout and flow [48], specifying rules and constraints around data, data integration support from diverse sources [9], configuring domain-specific applications [28], and integration of multiple disparate solutions [18].

11.8 Address End User Empowerment and Better Understanding Diverse End Users: Human-Centric Defect Reporting and Fixing

We carried out a preliminary investigation of improving “human-centric defect reporting”, including developing a set of human-centric defect reporting interfaces and a set of personas to represent different defect reporters [36]. This highlighted a number of unsolved and under-researched to date issues in defect reporting, understanding, diagnosing and fixing. Examples of further research to carry out include understanding if personas representing end user defect reporters help developers to understand, diagnose and fix human-centric defects; how industry teams currently handle such defect reports; whether different users have different challenges reporting defects with their software; and whether software domain, company culture and developer human characteristics impact human-centric defect fixing.

11.9 Address Developer Human Aspects: Understand Impact of Developers' Own Diverse Human Aspects

While end users are naturally diverse in terms of their human aspects for many software domains – banking, education, home automation, business etc. – software developers are far less diverse and often very different to their end users [64,69]. Most software developers are relatively wealthy, highly educated, have high language proficiency, most are male, and most relatively young [69]. Many of the end users and stakeholders they develop software for are often quite different to this profile, particularly in software domains. Assisting developers to appreciate, understand, empathise with and ultimately design and build software more suited to people very different to them remains a challenge for the software engineering discipline. A greater diversity of software engineers and better education about the challenges of supporting diverse end users are claimed by various studies to improve this situation [20,25,53,64]. However, how a variety of developer human aspect differences impact software engineering in general and particular phases of software development is still largely unclear [25,33,37].

12 Summary

End users of a software application have many different "human characteristics". Some have been studied extensively in psychology, human-computer interaction, management and other disciplines, if not Software Engineering researchers. We have presented a preliminary taxonomy of some of these human aspects and some key related work done to date, predominantly in other disciplines. Some of the areas that we have been studying how they impact software engineers and their work include age, gender, physical and mental challenges, emotions, culture and language. Many however are as yet unclear in terms of their impact on software engineering, how well they are accommodated by software teams, and how combinations of human differences impact software engineering and software products. Some areas we see as how potential for further research include some under-researched human aspects; improving stakeholder identification and engagement via living lab co-creation approaches; further use of diverse personas in software engineering; better modelling and design support for diverse human characteristics and challenges; end user development allowing end users to tailor their solutions to their own needs; and improved human-centric defect reporting. Understanding how developers own diverse human aspects impact software engineering and interplay with their end user human aspects is also a rich area for continued work.

Acknowledgements. Parts of this work has been supported by ARC Discovery Projects DP200100020, DP170101932 and DP140102185, Industry Transformation Research Hub IH170100013, and ARC Laureate Fellowship FL190100035.

References

1. Compare countries - hofstede insights (2021). https://www.hofstede-insights.com/product/compare-countries/
2. Participatory research and ownership with technology, information and change (protic) ii. https://www.monash.edu/it/hcc/dedt/projects/participatory-research-and-ownership-with-technology,-information-and-change-protic-ii
3. Abd Malik, S., Azuddin, M.: Mobile technology for older people: Use of personas. In: 2013 International Conference on Research and Innovation in Information Systems (ICRIIS), pp. 97–101. IEEE (2013)
4. Abreu Saurin, T., Patriarca, R.: A taxonomy of interactions in socio-technical systems: a functional perspective **82**, 102980 (2020)
5. Alkaabi, A., Maple, C.: Cultural impact on user authentication systems **4**(4), 323–343 (2013)
6. Alsanoosy, T., Spichkova, M., Harland, J.: Cultural influence on requirements engineering activities: a systematic literature review and analysis. Requirements Eng. **25**(3), 339–362 (2019). https://doi.org/10.1007/s00766-019-00326-9
7. Alshayban, A., Ahmed, I., Malek, S.: Accessibility issues in android apps: state of affairs, sentiments, and ways forward. In: 2020 IEEE/ACM 42nd International Conference on Software Engineering (ICSE), pp. 1323–1334. IEEE (2020)
8. Antle, A.N.: Child-based personas: need, ability and experience. Cogn. Technol. Work **10**(2), 155–166 (2008). https://doi.org/10.1007/s10111-007-0071-2
9. Avazpour, I., Grundy, J., Zhu, L.: Engineering complex data integration, harmonization and visualization systems **16**, 100103 (2019)
10. Ball, K., Mouchacca, J., Jackson, M.: The feasibility and appeal of mobile 'apps' for supporting healthy food purchasing and consumption among socioeconomically disadvantaged women: a pilot study. Health Promot. J. Austr. **25**(2), 79–82 (2014)
11. Barricelli, B.R., Cassano, F., Fogli, D., Piccinno, A.: End-user development, end-user programming and end-user software engineering: a systematic mapping study **149**, 101–137 (2019)
12. Boll, F., Brune, P.: User interfaces with a touch of grey?-towards a specific UI design for people in the transition age **63**, 511–516 (2015)
13. Boyatzis, C.J., Varghese, R.: Children's emotional associations with colors **155**(1), 77–85 (1994)
14. Brich, J., Walch, M., Rietzler, M., Weber, M., Schaub, F.: Exploring end user programming needs in home automation. ACM Trans. Comput.-Human Interact. (TOCHI) **24**(2), 1–35 (2017)
15. Burnett, M., Peters, A., Hill, C., Elarief, N.: Finding gender-inclusiveness software issues with GenderMag: a field investigation, pp. 2586–2598. Association for Computing Machinery, New York (2016). https://doi.org/10.1145/2858036.2858274
16. Burnett, M., et al.: GenderMag: a method for evaluating software's gender inclusiveness. Interact. Comput. **28**(6), 760–787 (2016). https://doi.org/10.1093/iwc/iwv046
17. Cadwallader, C., Graham-Harrison, E.: Revealed: 50 million facebook profiles harvested for cambridge analytica in major data breach. https://www.theguardian.com/news/2018/mar/17/cambridge-analytica-facebook-influence-us-election
18. Cappiello, C., Matera, M., Picozzi, M.: End-user development of mobile mashups. In: Marcus, A. (ed.) DUXU 2013. LNCS, vol. 8015, pp. 641–650. Springer, Heidelberg (2013). https://doi.org/10.1007/978-3-642-39253-5_71
19. Capretz, L.F., Ahmed, F.: Making sense of software development and personality types **12**(1), 6–13 (2010)

20. Capretz, L.F., Ahmed, F.: Why do we need personality diversity in software engineering? **35**(2), 1–11 (2010)
21. Charness, N.: Aging and problem-solving performance, pp. 225–259 (1985)
22. Cheng, A.S., Fleischmann, K.R.: Developing a meta-inventory of human values. In: ASIS&T, vol. 47 (2010)
23. Curumsing, M.K., Fernando, N., Abdelrazek, M., Vasa, R., Mouzakis, K., Grundy, J.: Emotion-oriented requirements engineering: a case study in developing a smart home system for the elderly **147**, 215–229 (2019)
24. Curumsing, M.K., Lopez-Lorca, A., Miller, T., Sterling, L., Vasa, R.: Viewpoint modelling with emotions: a case study **4**(2), 25–53 (2015)
25. Gila, A.R., Jaafa, J., Omar, M., Tunio, M.Z.: Impact of personality and gender diversity on software development teams' performance. In: 2014 International Conference on Computer, Communications, and Control Technology (I4CT), pp. 261–265. IEEE (2014)
26. Gouveia, V.V., Milfont, T.L., Guerra, V.M.: Functional theory of human values: testing its content and structure hypotheses **60** (2014)
27. Grundy, J.: Human-centric software engineering for next generation cloud-and edge-based smart living applications. In: 2020 20th IEEE/ACM International Symposium on Cluster, Cloud and Internet Computing (CCGRID), pp. 1–10. IEEE (2020)
28. Grundy, J., Abdelrazek, M., Curumsing, M.K.: Vision: improved development of mobile ehealth applications. In: 2018 IEEE/ACM 5th International Conference on Mobile Software Engineering and Systems (MOBILESoft), pp. 219–223. IEEE (2018)
29. Grundy, J., Khalajzadeh, H., McIntosh, J., Kanij, T., Mueller, I.: HumaniSE: approaches to achieve more human-centric software engineering. In: Ali, R., Kaindl, H., Maciaszek, L.A. (eds.) ENASE 2020. CCIS, vol. 1375, pp. 444–468. Springer, Cham (2021). https://doi.org/10.1007/978-3-030-70006-5_18
30. Grundy, J.C.: Impact of end user human aspects on software engineering. In: 2021 International Conference on Evaluation of Novel Approaches to Software Engineering (ENASE2021), pp. 9–20 (2021)
31. Grundy, J., Grundy, J.: A survey of Australian human services agency software usage. J. Technol. Hum. Serv. **31**(1), 84–94 (2013)
32. Haggag, O., Haggag, S., Grundy, J., Abdelrazek, M.: Covid-19 vs social media apps: does privacy really matter? In: 2021 IEEE/ACM 43rd International Conference on Software Engineering: Software Engineering in Society (ICSE-SEIS), pp. 48–57. IEEE (2021)
33. Hidellaarachchi, D., Grundy, J., Hoda, R., Madampe, K.: The effects of human aspects on the requirements engineering process: a systematic literature review (2021)
34. Hofstede, G., Hofstede, G.J., Minkov, M.: Cultures and Organizations - Software of the Mind: Intercultural Cooperation and its Importance for Survival, 3rd edn. McGraw-Hill, London (2010)
35. Hussain, A., Abd Razak, M.N.F., Mkpojiogu, E.O., Hamdi, M.M.F.: UX evaluation of video streaming application with teenage users, **9**(2–11), 129–131 (2017)
36. Huynh, K., et al.: Improving human-centric software defect evaluation, reporting, and fixing. In: 2021 IEEE International Conference on Computers, Software, and Applications Conference (COMPSAC2021), 12–16 July 2021. IEEE (2021)
37. Izquierdo, D., Huesman, N., Serebrenik, A., Robles, G.: OpenStack gender diversity report. IEEE Softw. **36**(1), 28–33 (2018)
38. Jefferson, L., Harvey, R.: Accommodating color blind computer users. In: Proceedings of 8th International ACM SIGACCESS Conference on Computers and Accessibility, pp. 40–47 (2006)
39. Jim, A.Y., et al.: Improving the modelling of human-centric aspects of software systems: a case study of modelling end user age in wirefame designs. In: ENASE, pp. 68–79 (2021)

40. Kamalrudin, M., Grundy, J., Hosking, J.: MaramaAI: tool support for capturing and managing consistency of multi-lingual requirements. In: 2012 Proceedings of the 27th IEEE/ACM International Conference on Automated Software Engineering, pp. 326–329. IEEE (2012)
41. Khambati, A., Grundy, J., Warren, J., Hosking, J.: Model-driven development of mobile personal health care applications. In: 2008 23rd IEEE/ACM International Conference on Automated Software Engineering, pp. 467–470. IEEE (2008)
42. Kim, H., Powell, M.P., Bhuyan, S.S.: Seeking medical information using mobile apps and the internet: are family caregivers different from the general public? J. Med. Syst. **41**(3), 38 (2017). https://doi.org/10.1007/s10916-017-0684-9
43. Kumar, J.: Gamification at work: designing engaging business software. In: Marcus, A. (ed.) DUXU 2013. LNCS, vol. 8013, pp. 528–537. Springer, Heidelberg (2013). https://doi.org/10.1007/978-3-642-39241-2_58
44. LeRouge, C., Ma, J., Sneha, S., Tolle, K.: User profiles and personas in the design and development of consumer health technologies. Int. J. Med. Inform. **82**(11), e251–e268 (2013)
45. Li, C., et al.: A human-centric approach to building a smarter and better parking application. In: 2021 IEEE International Conference on Computers, Software, and Applications Conference (COMPSAC2021), 12–16 July 2021. IEEE (2021)
46. Liang, H., Xue, Y.L., Ke, W., Wei, K.K., et al.: Understanding the influence of team climate on it use **11**(8), 2 (2010)
47. Longo, F., Nicoletti, L., Padovano, A.: Modeling workers' behavior: a human factors taxonomy and a fuzzy analysis in the case of industrial accidents **69**, 29–47 (2019)
48. Luy, C., et al.: A toolkit for building adaptive user interfaces for vision-impaired users. In: 2021 IEEE Symposium on Visual Languages and Human-centric Computing (VLHCC2021), 10–13 October, St Louis, USA. IEEE (2021)
49. Masood, M., Thigambaram, M.: The usability of mobile applications for pre-schoolers **197**, 1818–1826 (2015)
50. Mata-Greve, F., et al.: Mental health and the perceived usability of digital mental health tools among essential workers and people unemployed due to Covid-19: cross-sectional survey study. JMIR Mental Health **8**(8), e28360 (2021)
51. McDonald, C.: IT 'professionals' are to blame for robodebt - what happened to ethics? https://ia.acs.org.au/article/2020/it-professionals-are-to-blame-for-robodebt.html
52. McIntosh, J., et al.: Evaluating age bias in e-commerce. In: 2021 IEEE/ACM 13th International Conference on Cooperative and Human Aspects of Software Engineering (CHASE), pp. 31–40. IEEE (2021)
53. Menezes, Á., Prikladnicki, R.: Diversity in software engineering. In: Proceedings of 11th International Workshop on Cooperative and Human Aspects of Software Engineering, pp. 45–48 (2018)
54. Michaels, G.M.: Colour preference according to age **35**, 79–87 (1924)
55. Miller, T., Pedell, S., Lopez-Lorca, A.A., Mendoza, A., Sterling, L., Keirnan, A.: Emotion-led modelling for people-oriented requirements engineering: the case study of emergency systems **105**, 54–71 (2015)
56. Morris, L.J., Stauffer, L.A.: A design taxonomy for eliciting customer requirements **27**(1), 557–560 (1994). 16th Annual Conf. on Computers and Industrial Engineering
57. Mosqueira-Rey, E., Alonso-Ríos, D., Moret-Bonillo, V.: Usability taxonomy and context-of-use taxonomy for usability analysis. In: 2009 IEEE International Conference on Systems, Man and Cybernetics, pp. 812–817 (2009)
58. Obie, H.O., et al.: A first look at human values-violation in app reviews. In: 2021 IEEE/ACM 43rd International Conference on Software Engineering: Software Engineering in Society (ICSE-SEIS), pp. 29–38. IEEE (2021)

59. Pan, X.: Research of Iphone application UI design based on children cognition feature. In: 2010 IEEE 11th International Conference on Computer-Aided Industrial Design & Conceptual Design, vol. 1, pp. 293–296. IEEE (2010)
60. Parker Software: Key considerations for making age-friendly software (2019)
61. Perry, K., Shearer, E., Sylvers, P., Carlile, J., Felker, B.: mhealth 101: an introductory guide for mobile apps in clinical practice. J. Technol. Behav. Sci. **4**(2), 162–169 (2019). https://doi.org/10.1007/s41347-019-00108-8
62. Pew Research Center: Internet, Science & Tec: Internet/broadband fact sheet (2019)
63. Ralph, P.: Toward methodological guidelines for process theories and taxonomies in software engineering **45**(7), 712–735 (2018)
64. Rodríguez-Pérez, G., Nadri, R., Nagappan, M.: Perceived diversity in software engineering: a systematic literature review. Empir. Softw. Eng. **26**(5), 1–38 (2021). https://doi.org/10.1007/s10664-021-09992-2
65. Rokeach, M.: The Nature of Human Values (1973)
66. Seneler, C.O., Basoglu, N., Daim, T.U.: A taxonomy for technology adoption: a human computer interaction perspective. In: PICMET '08 - 2008 Portland International Conference on Management of Engineering Technology, pp. 2208–2219 (2008)
67. Shamsujjoha, M., Grundy, J., Li, L., Khalajzadeh, H., Lu, Q.: Human-centric issues in ehealth app development and usage: A preliminary assessment. In: 2021 IEEE International Conference on Software Analysis, Evolution and Reengineering (SANER), pp. 506–510. IEEE (2021)
68. Silva, S., Kenney, M.: Algorithms, platforms, and ethnic bias **62**(11), 37–39 (2019)
69. Silveira, K.K., Prikladnicki, R.: A systematic mapping study of diversity in software engineering: a perspective from the agile methodologies. In: 2019 IEEE/ACM 12th International Workshop on Cooperative and Human Aspects of Software Engineering (CHASE), pp. 7–10. IEEE (2019)
70. Sim, G., et al.: Child-generated personas to aid design across cultures. In: Lamas, D., Loizides, F., Nacke, L., Petrie, H., Winckler, M., Zaphiris, P. (eds.) INTERACT 2019. LNCS, vol. 11748, pp. 112–131. Springer, Cham (2019). https://doi.org/10.1007/978-3-030-29387-1_7
71. Singh, J., Lutteroth, C., Wünsche, B.C.: Taxonomy of usability requirements for home telehealth systems. In: Proceedings of 11th International Conference NZ ACM Special Interest Group on Human-Computer Interaction, CHINZ '10, pp. 29–32. ACM (2010)
72. Soper, S.: Fired by bot at amazon: 'it's you against the machine'. https://www.bloomberg.com/news/features/2021-06-28/fired-by-bot-amazon-turns-to-machine-managers-and-workers-are-losing-out?sref=EJ3iffSv
73. Strengers, Y., Kennedy, J.: The Smart Wife: Why Siri, Alexa, and Other Smart Home Devices Need a Feminist Reboot. MIT Press, Cambridge (2020)
74. Vangeepuram, N., et al.: Smartphone ownership and perspectives on health apps among a vulnerable population in East Harlem, New York. Mhealth, 4 (2018)
75. Vorvoreanu, M., Zhang, L., Huang, Y.H., Hilderbrand, C., Steine-Hanson, Z., Burnett, M.: From gender biases to gender-inclusive design: an empirical investigation. In: Proceedings of 2019 CHI Conference on Human Factors in Computing Systems, pp. 1–14 (2019)
76. (WAI), W.W.A.I.: W3c accessibility standards overview. https://www.w3.org/WAI/standards-guidelines/

77. Xu, T., White, J., Kalkan, S., Gunes, H.: Investigating bias and fairness in facial expression recognition. In: Bartoli, A., Fusiello, A. (eds.) ECCV 2020. LNCS, vol. 12540, pp. 506–523. Springer, Cham (2020). https://doi.org/10.1007/978-3-030-65414-6_35
78. Yan, P., Schroeder, R.: Variations in the adoption and use of mobile social apps in everyday lives in urban and rural China. Mobile Media Commun. **8**(3), 318–341 (2020)
79. Yusop, N.S.M., Grundy, J., Schneider, J.G., Vasa, R.: A revised open source usability defect classification taxonomy **128**, 106396 (2020)

Gender Classification Models and Feature Impact for Social Media Author Profiling

Paloma Piot-Perez-Abadin(✉), Patricia Martin-Rodilla, and Javier Parapar

IRLab, CITIC Research Centre, Universidade de Coruña, A Coruña, Spain
{paloma.piot,patricia.martin.rodilla,javier.parapar}@udc.es

Abstract. Automatic profiling models infer demographic characteristics of social network users from their generated content or interactions. Due to its use in business (targeted advertising, market studies...), automatic user profiling from social networks has become a popular task. Users' demographic data is also crucial information for more socially concerning tasks, such as automatic early detection of mental disorders. For this type of users' analysis task, it has been demonstrated that the way users employ language is an essential indicator that contributes to the effectiveness of the models. For this reason, we also believe that considering the usage of the language from both psycho-linguistic and semantic characteristics it is useful for detecting variables such as gender, age, and user's origin. A proper selection of features will be critical for the performance of retrieval, classification, and decision-making software systems, a proper selection of features will be critical. In this work, we shall discuss gender classification as a part of the automated profiling task. We present an experimental analysis of the performance of existing gender classification models for automated profiling based on external corpus and baselines. We also investigate the role of linguistic characteristics in the model's classification accuracy and their impact on each gender. Following that analysis, we have developed a feature set for gender classification models in social networks that outperforms existing benchmarks in terms of accuracy.

Keywords: Gender classification · Author profiling · Feature relevance · Social media

1 Introduction

Automatic author profiling is a research area that has gained some relevance in recent years. It focuses on inferring social-demographic information about the author or user of a certain application or software service [3]. The huge number of prospective applications in critical industries like security, marketing, forensics, e-commerce, and the detection of false profiles, among others, explains the rising number of research in author profiling [36].

Recent author profiling initiatives have included the creation of shared tasks and corpora for assessing author profiling, focusing on using the user's written texts as relevant data for the demographic profile construction. Existing author profiling models

R. Ali et al. (Eds.): ENASE 2021, CCIS 1556, pp. 265–287, 2022.
https://doi.org/10.1007/978-3-030-96648-5_12

demonstrate that the language used in social network communications is a very important demographic indicator, identifying gender, age and user's origin based on psycholinguistic and semantic characteristics. These features are crucial for retrieval, classification, and decision-making software systems.

Gender classification is an essential component of the demographic profile since it is a part of the existing corpora and common responsibilities for author profiling. Current classification models include a large number of characteristics regarding the users' behaviour and their linguistic style in written texts (as well as other semantic factors) which increase the complexity and effort spent designing and executing gender classification models. On the other hand, some authors have begun to examine this area, calling for more "corpora benchmarks to develop and evaluate techniques for author profiling" [12] and focusing on the classification model design as a time-consuming task that requires some time-saving efforts and comparative analysis.

An experimental analysis of the performance of existing gender classification models is presented in this research. For our study, we have used external corpora and baselines from well-known author profiling shared tasks. The findings enabled us to discover linguistic and semantic characteristics that are particularly relevant in gender classification models derived from social networks, resulting in a feature-combined gender classification model that outperforms existing baselines in terms of accuracy.

In our previous work published in Piot-Perez-Abadin et al. [33] we have already shown the different experiments that we have run, which classifier has proved to achieve a better result and the feature importance for the best classifier. Now, in this work, we are extending our analysis and, as a result, presenting an exhaustive interpretation model by gender, identifying which features are indicatives for each gender category.

Moreover, we have incorporated new external datasets available for gender profiling. The reason for incorporating these new data sources is double. On the one hand, we have used them following the previous experiments reported for training purposes. Our aim was to try to increase the accuracy and study whether, in all cases, more training data is associated with a better result. On the other hand, we have performed an initial validation of the interpretation model presented, using a subset of the new data source involved as an external reference source for this validation.

The paper's background is given in Sect. 2, which includes works and real-world applications on author profiling, particular examples in gender categorisation from social networks, and demands in terms of feature studies and their linguistic basis and assessing the ethics in profiling, showing our awareness. Section 3 presents the use of external data. Section 4 describes the experimental analysis design, which includes the baselines used and the experimental procedure. The experiment findings and the final model are detailed in Sect. 5. Section 6 presents the model interpretation from the algorithm that achieved the best result. Section 7 exposes an initial validation, showing our findings when validating our initial model in external corpora, and examines the final findings. Section 8 draws some judgements regarding application potential and suggests future research.

2 Background

When specific organisations and services are interested in automatic profiling algorithms, it is customary to integrate automatic profiling software in marketing analysis and decision-making processes. The major objective is to understand their present users or potential market to refocus their advertising efforts and to assess their customers' opinions on products or services.

We can find some more user-centred research in a different large group of applications, where automatic profiling algorithms allow a forensic analysis at a behavioural and psycho-linguistic level of the author or user of a certain application or software service, such as blogs [29], social networks [2,32], etc. This approach has been beneficial in detecting early risk of specific behaviours (e.g. cyberbullying [10], hate speech [8], etc.) and certain mental disorders (depression [21,22], bipolar disorder [38], anorexia [20], etc.).

We may classify existing approaches based on the primary source of information. To begin with, we may discover in this field numerous researches and applications, already in production, that employ pictures or audiovisual content as a major source for automated profiling [25,41]. These images or videos are from a user's post on a social network, blog, or the internet, or can be part of a more private repository as confidential material, such as medical repositories. The classification algorithms, such as Support Vector Machines (SVM) [28] or Convolutional Neural Network (CNN), have shown to be successful [17] in this sort of approach.

Another method is to employ the user's behaviour, emotions, and decisions made through software systems as a data source. This method is commonly used in author profiling from social media or in applications related to online service usage. In general, the behaviour-based approach tends to include behavioural variables (visited pages, links, connection times, purchases made, colour-based studies, and so on) [1,2,32] as information for author profiling (e.g. age or gender classification), with findings of about 0.60 in terms of accuracy. Behavioural factors are frequently coupled with semantic and psycho-linguistic variables based on the study of the user's textual remarks (posts on social networks, reviews of services, etc.) to improve these findings, necessitating feature identification with a high linguistic foundation. Recent author profiling sharing tasks and studies have looked at lexical, grammatical or discursive components [27,30] as author profiling traits, even in multilingual environments [12].

As a result, the natural language employed in the social network publications is relevant for the automated profiling task. The most current findings show classification models with an accuracy of above 0.70 [16] for some aspects of the author's profile (mostly age and gender). Vasilev [39] conducts a thorough examination of these systems in the context of Reddit, achieving an accuracy of 0.85 utilising controlled subreddits as sources, demonstrating the potential of the hybrid behavioural and linguistic combination for automatic profiling from social networks.

To get over 0.70 accuracy rates, many of these success instances, particularly semantic and psycho-linguistic aspects, require a large number of characteristics in their classification models. Some researchers have already raised concerns about the overwhelming number of features used in automatic profiling classification systems, making designing classification models for these systems very time-consuming. Researchers have suggested special experiments to minimise the number of features in the models [1].

This paper focuses on gender classification as a specific feature for automatic profiling, taking into account the potential of automatic profiling systems based on semantic and linguistic features and the need for experimental studies on existing classification models to reduce their complexity. Gender is used as a differentiating aspect in treating and detecting early risk signals in mental disorders, making gender a critical piece of information in a user's demographic profile for these social network apps.

2.1 Ethics in Profiling

When executing any personal profiling effort, it is necessary to assess ethics and discuss possible implications of the methodology chosen and the results achieved. Commonly, this is a major issue when building the corpus or sets of data, because this should be collected under legal and ethical compliance. Moreover, it should be built inclusively. Specifically, in the gender classification task, this means that it should reflect both genders equally, avoiding advantaging the prevailing one (male).

In these experiments, we haven't built our corpus, as we have used PAN datasets, and all the experiments fulfil the legal and ethical issues [31].

Nevertheless, we must keep in mind that when analysing and profiling information, we must be committed to legal and ethical compliance [35]. On a personal level, within professions, and at the operational level, ethical principles and values serve as a guide to behaviour. Profiling hurts when excluding, providing false leads, pointing to wrong individuals, and damaging the personal life of a citizen. In this work, we have approached the gender profiling task with the final goal of early risk detection of mental disorders, keeping in mind the ethics in profiling.

The sections that follow detail the experimental design used to investigate the features involved in gender classification in a variety of author profiling tasks, as well as their importance in the proposed classification models. Following that, we present a gender classification model that reduces characteristics depending on the relevance discovered, increasing accuracy.

3 Datasets

PAN[1] initiatives, with shared tasks editions between 2013 and 2020, are the most well-known efforts on author profiling. Our experimental investigation used three distinct datasets that incorporate gender information from PAN as external corpora. Specifically, we have selected from the competition "PAN Author Profiling 2019", "PAN Celebrity Profiling 2019" and "PAN Celebrity Profiling 2020" datasets, both in English. We have chosen these datasets since they were the most recent available datasets at the time of our experiment design. All PAN datasets are available in their website[2].

There are two components in the first dataset: a training dataset and a test dataset. Because the major aim of the job was to determine if the author of Twitter information

[1] https://pan.webis.de/.

[2] https://pan.webis.de/shared-tasks.html.

was a person or a bot user, and in the event of a human, it was required to infer the user's gender, both are formed of bots and individuals. As a result, the bots have been filtered out of our repository. Each dataset was employed in the appropriate phase of our research.

The second dataset only contains training data from Twitter. In this instance, the goal of the shared task is to predict celebrity traits based on their Twitter publications history. In terms of celebrity gender, we had to filter out only 18 "nonbinary" users (as we modelled gender only in male/female situations for our applications). Only in the training phases of our experiments, we did use the second dataset.

The third dataset contains validation data from Twitter. This task aims to predict celebrity traits from their followers' history. But, there was an extra dataset with the celebrity history (the one we have used). We have used this dataset to validate our model and find out if the most important features of the trained model are fulfilled in this data source.

The next subsections detail in depth both datasets in terms of volume and internal characteristics.

3.1 "PAN Author Profiling 2019" Dataset

"PAN Author Profiling 2019" dataset[3] comes from the "Bots and Gender Profiling 2019" PAN shared task. The objective of this task was: "Given a Twitter feed, determine whether its author is a bot or a human. In the case of human, identify their gender".

We have decided to use this dataset because it is a well-balanced collection of social media texts that hasn't been cleaned. The interactive social media nature of the data is also better suited to our goals. In addition, this dataset contains text streams with temporal continuity in the writings. This enables the development of linguistic phenomena in the writers' contributions that are likely to be important as characteristics in our gender classification research.

Each user is represented by a `.xml` file in the dataset. Each file has an `author` tag, which includes a `documents` tag holding a list of 100 `document` each representing one Tweet. The gender label for each author is contained in the `truth.txt` master file of this dataset. Examples of the input data can be seen in Table 1.

We came up with a balanced sample of 2060 individuals after preprocessing the data: 1030 female users and 1030 male users. (See Table 2).

3.2 "PAN Celebrity Profiling 2019" Dataset

"PAN Celebrity Profiling 2019" dataset[4] comes from the "Celebrity Profiling 2019" PAN task. The goal of this task was: "Given a celebrity's Twitter feed, determine its owner's age, fame, gender, and occupation".

We have decided to use this dataset for the same reasons as described in the "PAN Author Profiling 2019" dataset, and, besides, it contains a large number of user profiles and an average of 2000 Tweets per user. Thus, it will adequately complement the author's competition dataset.

[3] https://pan.webis.de/data.html.

[4] https://pan.webis.de/data.html.

Table 1. "Author Profiling 2019" dataset. Published in Piot-Perez-Abadin et al. [33].

	author_id	gender
0	ccbe6914a203b899882	male
1	a3b93437a32dba31def	male
2	a1655b4b89e7f4a76a9	male
3	de3eee10fbac25fe396	male
4	2a61915c1cd27b842ee	male
...	...	...
2055	f92806b515385388c83	female
2056	a820cb38384e19a3043	female
2057	f17345aeea69b649063	female
2058	f334e25ccf9a18f1eb2	female
2059	b2eb427fb56beace062	female

Table 2. "Author Profiling 2019" dataset users by gender. Published in Piot-Perez-Abadin et al. [33].

	Total
male	1030
female	1030

The available data is split into two files: the `feed` file, which contains the author id and a list of all Tweets for each user, and the `labels` file, which holds the author id and the value for each trait. Fame, occupation, birth year, and gender are the traits of this dataset. All variables except gender were ignored in this investigation. See Table 3 for input data examples.

We ended up with an imbalanced dataset after preparing the data, with twice as many male users than female users. (See Table 4).

Table 3. "PAN Celebrity Profiling 2019" dataset. Published in Piot-Perez-Abadin et al. [33].

	author_id	gender
0	3849	male
1	957	female
2	14388	female
3	7446	male
4	1107	female
...	...	...
14494	33530	female
14495	29315	male
14496	36954	male
14497	4554	male
14498	4512	male

Table 4. "PAN Celebrity Profiling 2019" dataset users per gender. Published in Piot-Perez-Abadin et al. [33]

	Total
male	10409
female	4072
nonbinary	18

3.3 "PAN Celebrity Profiling 2020" Dataset

"PAN Celebrity Profiling 2020" dataset[5] comes from the "Celebrity Profiling 2020" PAN task. This task may look similar to their equally named from 2019, but the goal is different. In 2020 the aim changed to "Develop a piece of software which predicts three demographics of a celebrity from the text of their followers: occupation, age, and gender".

Though our study aims to predict the gender from the celebrity own posts, this PAN task provided a celebrity feed dataset for additional study. Therefore we have made use of this dataset to enrich our training data.

As mentioned in the previous subsections, this dataset will complement our training data, but, it might be that we could encounter some barriers, as the previous datasets are from 2019. This one from 2020, and some linguistic differences can be reflected in one year of difference.

The available data is given in the same format as the "PAN Celebrity Profiling 2019" dataset. Two files, the `feed` file, enclosing the author id and the feed list, and the `labels` file, which is formed by the author id and the traits values. All variables but gender were ignored in this study. See Table 5 for input data examples.

Table 5. "PAN Celebrity Profiling 2020" dataset.

	author_id	gender
0	1	male
1	2	male
2	3	female
3	4	male
4	5	male
...	...	...
1915	1916	male
1916	1917	male
1917	1918	male
1918	1919	male
1919	1920	female

5 https://pan.webis.de/clef20/pan20-web/celebrity-profiling.html.

Table 6. "PAN Celebrity Profiling 2020" dataset users per gender.

	Total
male	1072
female	848

We have ended up with an almost balanced dataset after preparing the data, with 200 more male users than female users. (See Table 6).

These are the datasets that best suit our demands due to the intricacy of the work and the study's aims. As a result, we have chosen to employ them in our research. Furthermore, these sets would allow us to compare our findings to a clear baseline.

4 Design of Experiments

4.1 Workflow

Our research is divided into two parts. First, a performance study of the most commonly used gender classification models is performed on the external chosen datasets, monitoring each feature contained in each classification model in terms of its significance and impacts on the evaluated model. Each model's accuracy [26] will be used as a performance metric, with the accuracy of the given models being measured. This phase yields findings in two directions: 1) which classification algorithms offer the best gender results, and 2) which of the semantic and linguistic features included in the model have more relevance in the model, i.e., which of them contribute more to the reported accuracy.

Once we have the most relevant features, we can go on to the second phase of assessment, which involves creating a model that contains the most important features and employing gender classification algorithms that provide better results. This model may be used as a basic model for gender categorisation in automated profiling with a considerable decrease in characteristics.

The experiments in both phases follow the same workflow design, which is based on a traditional classification algorithm experimentation method with two primary processes: training and testing. Both the train and test procedures include a preprocessing step in which the raw data is converted into a data frame and a feature engineering stage in which the features are extracted from the corpus.

Splitting the dataset into a train and a test subset to train our models is the next step in the training process. Cross-validation is used, and the resultant classification model is the outcome.

The test phase comprises the classification models to forecast previously unknown data and determines their accuracy. Figure 1 depicts the workflow that was followed in each experiment.

4.2 Data Preprocessing

The procedure depicted in Fig. 1 is replicated by each combination of gender classification algorithm + classification model features.

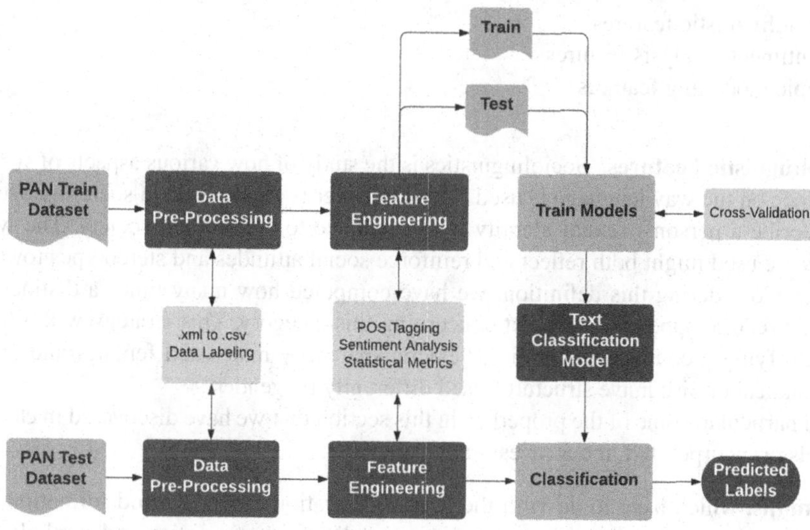

Fig. 1. Gender classification task workflow. Published in Piot-Perez-Abadin et al. [33].

We first have converted the various documents into a homogeneous set before doing feature engineering on the data. We have combined each `.xml` file into one file and have translated it to a `.csv` file for the "PAN Author Profiling 2019". In the case of "PAN Celebrity Profiling 2019", we have merged both `.json` files and have transformed it into a `.csv` file.

The final `.csv` file consists of an `id` column, a `text` column enclosing all messages (our corpus), and a `gender` column (what we want to predict).

Even though it is typical to perform more exhaustive preprocessing steps and data cleaning, including Stemming, Lemming, and eliminating stop words [13], these operations might suppose in the total or partial elimination of words that form our classifier input data and might imply a counterproductive action [40]. Stemming or Lemming would imply a loss of potentially important information for the classification task, just as eliminating stop words and special characters would imply a loss of substance and precision since the corpus would be considerably shortened. Therefore, we have opted not to perform any extra preprocessing procedures.

4.3 Feature Engineering

The fundamental idea behind feature engineering is to extract features from a corpus using domain expertise. These characteristics were utilised to discover a common pattern among different writers. The main objective of this research is to determine what types of characteristics are included in existing gender categorisation models and their significance and impacts on the model. For this aim, we have split the discovered features, as well as some additional features that we have added, into three groups depending on the intrinsic nature of the information involved:

1. Sociolinguistic features
2. Sentiment Analysis features
3. Topic modelling features

Sociolinguistic Features. Sociolinguistics is the study of how various aspects of social influence on the way language is used [9,34]. Gender is a term used in sociolinguistics to describe a person's sexual identity with reference to culture and society. The way words are used might both reflect and reinforce social attitudes and stereotypes toward gender. Considering this definition, we have computed how many times a distinctive stylistic feature appears in the text concerning this category. This strategy will aid us in identifying a common generalised lexicon shared by males and females and infer grammatical or discursive structures used differently by gender.

In particular, some of the properties in this section that we have discovered in earlier models or incorporated in our investigations include:

- **Emojis**, which have to do with the lexical derivation and new word formation, as well as the semantics and neurolinguistics implications of emotion and symbols.
- **Punctuation marks**, as well as **word and text length**, are related to syntax and speech analysis.
- Features as **repeated alphabets**, **readability**, and **cosine similarity** are perceived as pragmatic features, as well as **URLs** and **hashtags**. Those two last features are, at the same time, personal-temporal-space references.
- **Self-referentiality** -I, me, my- is a feature that is often given to stop words, so it is not recorded. Yet, it has a significant sociolinguistic impact on the classification job.
- **Part-of-Speech (POS)** evidence in the form of POS Tags marks sociolinguistic traits if we take into account the syntax, but also linked to speech and discourse analysis, as well as grammar. This group encloses adjectives, adverbs, conjunctions, determiners, interjections, nouns, pronouns, symbols, verbs, and so on.
- **Readability** is a metric that shows how difficult a text in English is to comprehend. It is defined by Flesch-Kincaid reading ease, where a higher score indicates that the paragraph is simpler to read [11]. This score is calculated using the following formula:

$$206.835 - 1.015\left(\frac{\text{total words}}{\text{total sentences}}\right) - 84.6\left(\frac{\text{total syllables}}{\text{total words}}\right) \tag{1}$$

Table 7 provides an overview of the sociolinguistic features investigated and analysed. On a technical level, we have extracted and performed this feature analysis from the datasets information using regular expressions, *pandas*, and libraries like *scikit-learn*[6], *NLTK*[7], *spaCy*[8], *pyphen*[9] and *Emoji*[10].

[6] https://scikit-learn.org/stable/.
[7] https://www.nltk.org/.
[8] https://spacy.io/.
[9] https://pyphen.org/.
[10] https://github.com/carpedm20/emoji/.

Table 7. Sociolinguistic features described. Published in Piot-Perez-Abadin et al. [33].

Feature names	Feature description
Emojis use	Emojis use ratio per user's documents
Special characters	Special characters ratio per user's documents
Punctuation marks	Punctuation marks ratio per user's documents
URLs, hashtag	Separately URLs and hashtags ratio per user
Tokens	Words ratio per user's documents
Words and text length	Mean word length and text length
POS Tags	Part-of-speech tagging: ratio per user's documents
Repeated alphabets	Repeated alphabets ratio per user's documents
Self-referentiality	Ratio of sentences referring to itself
Readability	Metric for how easily a reader can comprehend a written text
Cosine similarity	Measure of similarity between two documents

Sentiment Analysis. Sentiment analysis is the field of study that analyses people's opinions, views, sentiments, emotions, and other feelings as expressed in written language [18,19]. We generally try to figure out whether a piece of writing is positive, negative, or neutral throughout this process.

To extract the compound and neutral scores for each document in the corpus, we have used the *NLTK* sentiment analysis analyser. Sentiment analysis aids in the comprehension of the author's experiences and can be distinguished between males and females. As a result, sentiment analysis information is a characteristic to consider in gender classification models.

Topic Modelling. Latent Dirichlet Allocation (LDA) is a topic model proposed by David Blei et al. [6] used to classify text in a document referring to a particular topic. It is an unsupervised generative statistical model that uses Dirichlet distributions to create a topic per document and words per topic model.

LDA is often used to extract and discover automatically hidden patterns in a corpus. This feature can aid in the modelling of topic-topic relationships for each gender category.

This is the methodology we have used for topic modelling. This method was used to retrieve the twenty most important topics, each specified by twenty words and comprising (twenty) features in our gender categorisation research. The numerals 0 to 19 reflect these characteristics. These topics are represented in Fig. 2 by the properties labelled with numbers ranging from 0 to 19.

4.4 Classification Algorithms and Experimental Configurations

We have looked at a variety of classifiers and, because gender recognition is a binary classification job, we have considered a variety of methods using the algorithms below. To achieve the best performance with our models, we have performed a grid search to hyper-parameter tune our experiments. Finally, we have used the following methods and settings in our tests:

- ***Random Forest***, is implemented using the default configuration of `sklearn` of this algorithm, except the estimators, which we have set to 500. We have opted to use Random Forest to learn a non-linear decision boundary and aim to get greater accuracy scores than using a linear-based algorithm, because this is a sophisticated undertaking [15].
- ***Adaptive Boosting***, with Decision Tree as a base estimator, 500 estimators, algorithm SAMME, maximum depth 9. The fundamental concept underlying boosting algorithms is to train predictors in a sequential manner. Each one attempts to rectify the faults of the one before it in each iteration, such that the next classifier is constructed based on the preceding one's classification error. After seeing how well AdaBoost performed in the bot detection challenge at the PAN competition, we decided to give it a shot in the gender classification task [5].
- ***LightGBM***, set with 500 iterations, maximum depth 7, learning rate 0.15, GBDT boosting, metric binary logloss, min data in leaf 600, bagging fraction 0.8, feature fraction 0.8. We have decided to use LightGBM since it is a gradient boosting framework that uses tree-based learning techniques. It is one of the algorithms that is winning classification competitions because of its focus on the accuracy of outcomes [14].

5 Experiments

We conducted a series of experiments to determine which classifier is the most successful for the gender profiling job, assessing its precision to determine which is the most appropriate.

We have used the "PAN Author Profiling 2019" train dataset and the "PAN Celebrity Profiling 2019" dataset to train the model. The accuracy of the model on the "PAN Author Profiling 2019" test dataset was used to determine our categorisation findings.

The outcomes of our experiments are shown in Table 8. Each row indicates the features combination and the algorithm employed, while each column represents the dataset used to train each experiment. We have represented the "PAN Author Profiling 2019" train dataset as "Author" and "PAN Celebrity Profiling 2019" as "Celebrity". The combination of both is "Author + Celebrity". Furthermore, our models were validated using the "PAN Author Profiling 2019" test dataset. Therefore the accuracy is based on this dataset.

We have tested our models in terms of feature combination following these experiments setups: 1) considering initial sociolinguistic traits but no topic information, 2) having all of the initial features + adding topic modelling data, 3) removing features that have no bearing on the data -in Fig. 2, the ones with zero coefficient-, 4) deleting the less important features -in Fig. 2, those with a coefficient less than 20 are eliminated- and 5) significant features in the first half -in Fig. 2, those having a coefficient greater than 50 are kept-.

Regarding classification algorithms, we have trained Random Forest, Ada Boost using Decision Tree as a base estimator and LightGBM; with the aforementioned

Table 8. Gender classification accuracy. Published in Piot-Perez-Abadin et al. [33].

Model + features	Author	Celebrity	Author + Celebrity
All features and topics			
RandomForestClassifier	0.6030	0.5470	0.7174
AdaBoostClassifier	0.5538	0.5114	0.7470
LightGBM	0.5818	0.6121	**0.7735**
All features without topics			
RandomForestClassifier	0.6621	0.5174	0.6780
AdaBoostClassifier	0.6523	0.5197	0.6780
LightGBM	0.6598	0.5795	0.7152
Without less important features			
RandomForestClassifier	0.6720	0.5303	0.6985
AdaBoostClassifier	0.6598	0.5083	0.7258
LightGBM	0.6803	0.5068	**0.7561**
Top half important features			
RandomForestClassifier	0.6530	0.5523	0.6583
AdaBoostClassifier	0.6545	0.5871	0.6795
LightGBM	0.6538	0.5985	0.7008

parameter setup. Table 8 shows the accuracy results for 1, 2, 4 and 5 feature configurations (combination 3 had the same accuracy as 2).

When comparing the results, we have found that utilising the LightGBM learning algorithm with LDA topics and maintaining all features was the best approach. We acquired an accuracy of **0.7735** which we can compare to the classification accuracy in the "PAN Author Profiling 2019" task, because we have verified our models with the test dataset given by PAN. Our accuracy results are not among the best in the PAN competition because we chose to focus on primary linguistic features; however, we have demonstrated that this approach produces good results (nearly 4 out of 5 are correctly classified), and that combining this approach with word and char n-grams can result in an excellent classifier.

It's also worth mentioning that combining both datasets yields a better result because the model can generalise more effectively. Thus, the result in the unseen data is slightly better than in the other studies.

We have carried some additional experiments using the third mentioned dataset "PAN Celebrity Profiling 2020". We have decided to try the best-acquired result (LightGBM, accuracy 0.7735) and see what changes.

We have stuck to the same parameter configuration, but in this case, we had to add an additional parameter: `scale_pos_weight: 0.125` to deal with the unbalanced dataset. We had to add this parameter now, because we had added even more male users, making the training data more unbalanced than in the previous experiments.

After training the three datasets, applying 10-fold cross-validation, and testing our model with the "PAN Author Profiling 2019" test dataset, we reached an accuracy of

0.5947. We can see that the accuracy achieved at the "PAN Celebrity 2020" task is much lower than the achieved at the "PAN Author Profiling 2019" task. This could be because of the source data, and could be one reason that explains why our result is worse when incorporating this dataset. Moreover, as mentioned before, this dataset is from 2020, and the others are from 2019. Therefore, it is possible that some linguistic traits changed in one year of period, making our model get worse.

6 Model Interpretation

This section presents a model interpretation of the LightGBM algorithm, trained with the "PAN Author Profiling 2019" and "PAN Celebrity Profiling 2019" datasets. We have decided to introduce and explain the model that yields the best accuracy in our experiments.

6.1 Feature Importance

It is interesting to note that the executed trials also allow us to analyse every single characteristic and its significance and effects on each model. Moreover, we can also examine the impact of each feature on each gender category. Taking this into account, Fig. 2 depicts the relevance of each feature in the classification model with higher accuracy (LightGBM). The feature importance helps us estimate how much each feature has contributed to the model's prediction. The graph was plotted making use of SHAP `summary_plot` function.

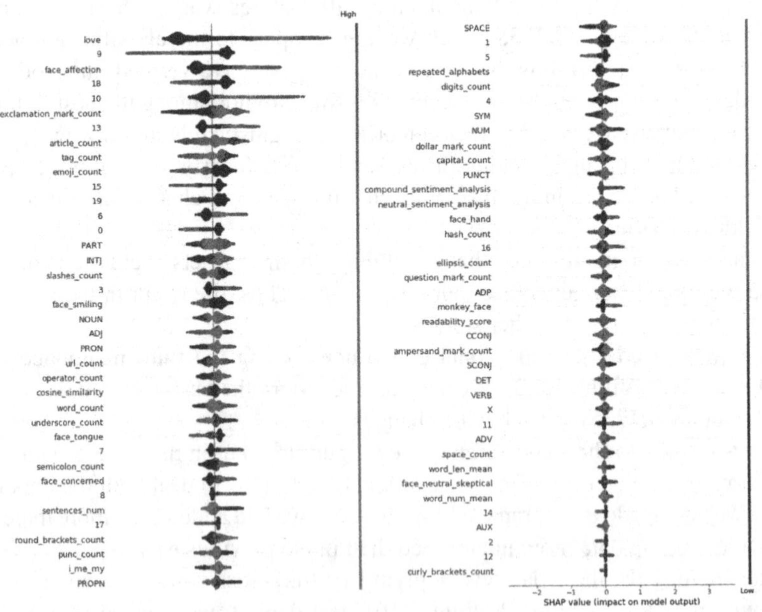

Fig. 2. Results on feature relevance.

The most important features in the classification model analysed are *Love Emojis*, *Face Affection Emojis*, *Exclamation Marks*, and *Articles*, together with four of the topic models. This feature relevance measure represents the number of times a feature is employed in a model; the greater the value, the more important the feature.

We can find features like *Cosine Similarity*, *Self-Referentiality*, *Readability*, *Numbers*, *Interjections*, and *Adjectives* among the half more relevant features.

Although *Determiners*, *Monkey Emojis*, *Word Ratio*, and *Word Length Mean* have a minor impact, their contribution is nevertheless significant because the classifier becomes worse when they are removed. These features appear to be of minor importance in classifier models, yet deleting them may result in a fall in the model's accuracy.

6.2 Feature Impact

One of the most common recurring problems of machine learning is that it works like a black box. However, it is possible to explain the algorithm prediction based on its kind. Taking into account that LightGBM has a decision tree structure, it makes it intrinsically interpretable. Therefore, it is straightforward to understand the relationship between the features and the model's prediction.

It is vital to understand and provide insights into the model, and in most cases, a single metric, such as accuracy, does not give a complete description of the task.

In the last few years, a technique called SHapely Additive exPlanations (SHAP) started to get more attention. SHAP provides a unified framework for the analysis of explanation models [24]. Important values are generally assigned to each input feature

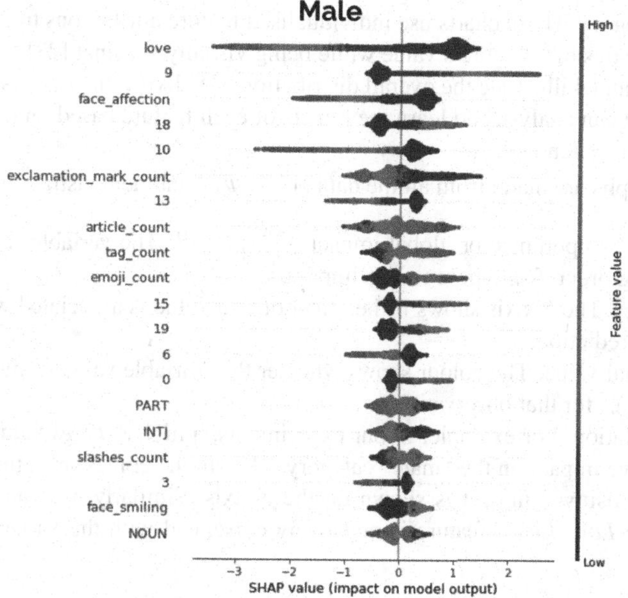

Fig. 3. Feature impact on males.

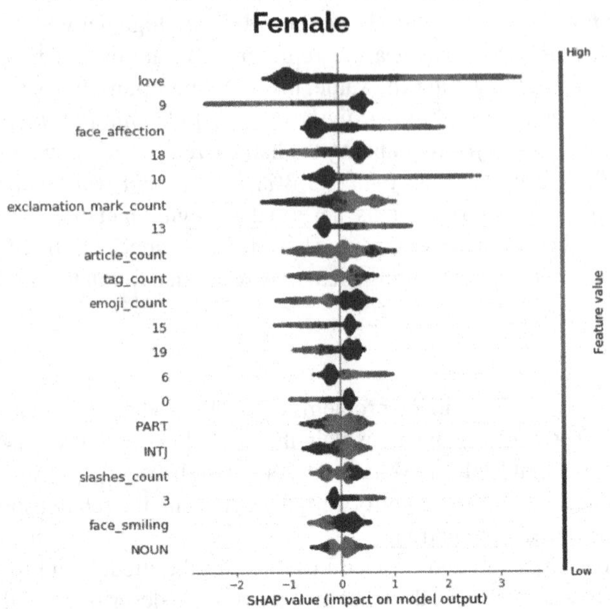

Fig. 4. Feature impact on females.

to comprehend predictions using tree ensemble techniques like gradient boosting. To interpret our best model, we have generated two SHAP Summary Plots, one for each predicted category. These charts use individualised feature attributions to express all of the characteristics of a feature's value while being visually succinct [23].

Figures 3 and 4 illustrate the overall distribution of SHAP values across all features. Therefore, we can analyse and learn the effects of each feature based on the prediction category (male or female).

These graphs are made from all the data points $\Phi_i^{(j)}$ and demonstrate:

- The feature importance or global impact $\sum_{j=1}^{N} |\Phi_i^{(j)}|$. The variables are ranked in descending order, from more to less important.
- The impact. The X-axis shows if the effect of that value is associated with a higher or lower prediction.
- The original value. The colour shows whether that variable value is high (in red) or low (in blue) for that observation.
- The correlation. For example, in our experiments, a high *Articles* value has a high and positive impact on the "male" category. The "high" comes from the red colour, and the "positive" impact is shown on the X-axis. Similarly, we can say that for males, the *Love Emoji* feature is negatively correlated with the variable target for males.

Therefore, for males, when analysing the *articles* feature, the higher the value, the model tends to classify the data as "male". On the other hand, in the case of the *Love Emoji* feature, the lower the value, the model tends to classify the profile as "male".

So, we can confirm that males use somewhat more *Articles*, *Tags* -can be interpreted as Twitter Hashtags- and *Emojis* in general and *Smiley-face Emojis* and *Tongue-face Emojis* in particular. In addition, a greater use of *Slashes*, *Adjectives*, *Underscores*, *Number of Sentences*, *Punctuation Marks* -including *Ellipsis*, *Question Marks* and *Curly Brackets*-, *Proper Names* -which include person names, brands, etc.-, *Digits* and *Dollar Marks* -we may say that males use more money reference than females-, *Capital Letters*, *Subordinating conjunction* -e.g. if, while, that, etc. - *Determiners* and *Long Words*, the model tends to classify the profile as "male".

This output confirms previous works where it has been concluded that the use of *Articles*, *Long Words*, and *Smiley-face Emojis* are male indicative [4,37]. This work has also reached the same conclusions and extends these sociolinguistic traits with more features.

In the case of females, *Love*, *Affection-face*, *Concern-face*, *Hand*, *Monkey* and *Neutral-Skeptical-face Emojis*, among *Exclamation Marks*, *Particles* -e.g.'s, not, etc.-, *Interjections*, *Nouns*, *Pronouns*, *URLs*, *Operators* -e.g. +, =, -, *, etc.-, *Cosine Similarity* -female social media texts are more similar among them than male ones-, *Number of Words*, *Semicolons*, *Round brackets*, *Self-Referentiality* -e.g. I, me, my-, *Repeated Alphabets*, *Symbols* -e.g. $, %, §, ©, etc.-, *Coordinating conjunctions* -e.g. and, or, but, etc.-, *Ampersands* and *Other Characteristics* -e.g. asdhgjaf, qwruiasj, aknsdkj, etc.- are traits that indicate that the profile is a "female".

Regarding the extracted topics, the labelled topics "9" and "18" are strong indicators of being male. These topics are formed by the following words:

Topic 9:

```
0.036*"mate" + 0.009*"lad" + 0.008*"england" +
0.007*"rugby" + 0.006*"pal" + 0.004*"league" +
0.004*"massive" + 0.004*"hahaha" + 0.003*"cheers" +
0.003*"golf" + 0.003*"world_cup" + 0.003*"arsenal" +
0.003*"squad" + 0.003*"quality" + 0.003*"ha" +
0.003*"liverpool" + 0.003*"cup" + 0.002*"chelsea" +
0.002*"sort" + 0.002*"decent"
```

Topic 18:

```
0.009*"tho" + 0.009*"shit" + 0.008*"yea" + 0.007*"ai" +
0.007*"smh" + 0.006*"lmao" + 0.006*"hahaha" + 0.006*"bout" +
0.006*"yo" + 0.006*"fam" + 0.006*"dont" + 0.005*"fuck" +
0.004*"lil" + 0.004*"homie" + 0.004*"em" + 0.004*"bruh" +
0.004*"ppl" + 0.004*"thats" + 0.004*"cuz" + 0.004*"wit"
```

On the other hand, for women, the more prevalent topics for women are the number "10" and the number "13". Each of these is formed by:

Topic 10:

```
0.007*"athlete" + 0.007*"australia" + 0.005*"olympics" +
0.005*"olympic" + 0.004*"women" + 0.004*"sydney" +
```

```
0.004*"australian" + 0.004*"rio" + 0.004*"swim" +
0.004*"bike" + 0.003*"cricket" + 0.003*"medal" +
0.003*"melbourne" + 0.003*"aussie" + 0.003*"champ" +
0.003*"compete" + 0.003*"world_cup" + 0.003*"hockey" +
0.003*"tennis" + 0.003*"nz"
```

Topic 13:

```
0.018*"xx" + 0.008*"xxx" + 0.007*"favourite" +
0.005*"mum" + 0.004*"mate" + 0.004*"gorgeous" +
0.004*"thankyou" + 0.004*"fab" + 0.003*"ha" +
0.003*"ah" + 0.003*"bloody" + 0.003*"fabulous" +
0.002*"gig" + 0.002*"cheers" + 0.002*"bbc" +
0.002*"loving" + 0.002*"manchester" + 0.002*"massive" +
0.002*"cheer_mate" + 0.002*"exeter"
```

Previous works have already identified that *Sequence of Exclamation Marks*, *Love Emojis*, *Repeated Alphabets*, *Conjunctions* and *Pronouns* are female indicative [4,37]. Our work has also concluded this and offers a quite more extensive list of sociolinguistic features by gender. Moreover, *Auxiliary Verbs* have been associated with female profiles [4], but our work doesn't clearly conclude this feature. Our result shows that both males and females use *Auxiliary Verbs* with the same frequency.

Occasionally, research yields conflicting findings. Our study reports that males use more *Emojis* than females as the output of other works like [4,37] do. But other studies have found that females use more *Emojis* [7]. These discrepancies could be because the way people express themselves on social media depends on the context, demographics, year, domain, etc. In our case, we have explored the sociolinguistic traits in Twitter during 2019.

7 Initial Validation and Discussion

As presented in the previous section, for males, the three top features are *Articles*, *Tags* and *Emojis* in general. On the other hand, for females, we can find that *Love Emojis*, *Face affection Emojis*, and *Exclamation Marks* are the linguistic features that have a greater impact on the classification. In this section, we are studying if, for the dataset "PAN Celebrity Profiling 2020", these features are also a male and female indicator.

We have made use of SHAP `summary_plot` function in order to find the impact of the selected feature on each gender category. In this case, we have removed all the features but the six we want to study.

We can see in Fig. 5 that for females, these three features are still a strong female indicative, but for males, only *Tags* and *Emojis* in general help classifying the author to be male. The *Articles* feature for this dataset is female indicative.

Firstly, it is important to highlight that, while combining both author and celebrity datasets yields a higher accuracy model, it is feasible that combining similar sources to generate a larger amount of training data could improve the presented results. Nevertheless, combining the 2020's dataset, we were unable to improve the result. This could

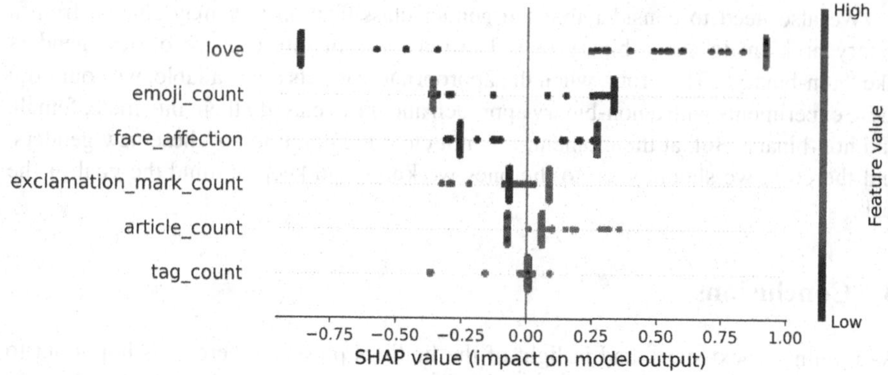

Fig. 5. Feature impact on Celebrity 20 dataset.

be because the linguistic differences on social media (Twitter) have changed from 2019 to 2020.

As a result, when compared to certain previously published results on gender classification PAN tasks[11], our work and the resulting models show some gains in accuracy. This research has demonstrated how linguistic features such as sentiment analysis and topic modelling play a vital part in author profiling gender classification.

Another intriguing impact observed in the experiments is that, despite the presence of almost non-relevant features in the models, eliminating some characteristics with extremely low relevance coefficients reduces accuracy. This means that each of the features we have calculated implies somehow an effect (i.e. positive or negative effects on the gender classification model). This circumstance explains the prior tendency of adding features to classification models until they reach the massive number of characteristics described in scientific literature. However, we must consider the true cost of designing and implementing these models with so many features.

Consequently, this study provides quantitative data on feature relevance, allowing us to investigate the impact of deleting features from certain classification combinations. The accuracies achieved 1) for the best algorithm -LightGBM- in the case of the complete model (with all characteristics) and 2) for that algorithm -LightGBM- in the case of the efficient model (without fewer essential features) are not that far apart, as shown in Table 8.

These findings open up the possibility of debating in which cases and for which software systems a slightly higher accuracy is required in the case of gender classification, but with a much higher design and execution time-consuming model (due to the large number of features), or whether we can apply the efficient model, with fewer features, without compromising the gender classification of the software systems. Although there is still work to be done to enhance accuracy for models with fewer characteristics, the time and effort saved in terms of design and execution can exceed the benefits in many cases.

[11] https://pan.webis.de/data.html.

We also need to consider that the gender classification task may change from a binary problem to a non-binary one. The reason is mainly because of new genders like "non-binary". Therefore, when the appropriate datasets are available, we could run these experiments with a non-binary approach and try to classify them into male, female and non-binary. But, at the moment, it is not clear the definition of these new genders, and therefore we should stick to the ones we know and keep in mind the goal of the task.

8 Conclusions

As imminent next steps, and in light of the findings presented here, it is important to generalise more the original datasets utilised as data sources. And combining datasets from the same year, with the study on how features changed from one year to another. We aim to perform the same battery of tests with other datasets containing gender information to enhance the generalisation of our findings as we have better results combining datasets.

Similar research on particular elements of author profiling tasks, such as age or socio-economic factors (income level, etc.) classification and inference, is also planned in the future. Due to the non-binary nature of the classification problem, these investigations provide unique problems when compared to gender classification. As a result, the number of alternative techniques and features for these models is even higher than for binary classification issues, making these studies useful in addressing the problem of a large number of features in the models.

We might employ a more linguistic-based approach, such as n-grams or n-chars models, to solve these problems. Incorporating these strategies might aid us in achieving better results. Also, meanwhile using a word embedding method may enhance the models; we have chosen to focus on the primary features.

Finally, we intend to test the classification models with the greatest performance (highest accuracy with fewer features) with real-world systems that currently execute author profiling, both for gender and for the rest of the automated profiling aspects. These experiments will allow us to compare efficient models to the ones that are already in use (with a greater number of features), determining if it is worthwhile to deploy less time-consuming models (with fewer features) into production to get similar accuracy results. As a result, we can determine which types of applications benefit from the efficient model and which applications, on the other hand, benefit from the time-consuming approach.

Acknowledgements. This work was supported by projects RTI2018-093336-B-C21, RTI2018-09333 6-B-C22 (Ministerio de Ciencia e Innvovación & ERDF) and the financial support supplied by the Consellería de Educación, Universidade e Formación Profesional (accreditation 2019-2022 ED431G/01, ED431B 2019/03) and the European Regional Development Fund, which acknowledges the CITIC Research Center in ICT of the University of A Coruña as a Research Center of the Galician University System.

References

1. Alowibdi, J.S., Buy, U.A., Yu, P.: Empirical evaluation of profile characteristics for gender classification on twitter. In: 2013 12th International Conference on Machine Learning and Applications, vol. 1, pp. 365–369 (2013)
2. Alowibdi, J.S., Buy, U.A., Yu, P.: Language independent gender classification on twitter. In: Proceedings of the 2013 IEEE/ACM International Conference on Advances in Social Networks Analysis and Mining, ASONAM '13, pp. 739–743. Association for Computing Machinery, New York (2013)
3. Álvarez-Carmona, M.A., López-Monroy, A.P., Montes-y-Gómez, M., Villaseñor-Pineda, L., Meza, I.: Evaluating topic-based representations for author profiling in social media. In: Montes-y-Gómez, M., Escalante, H.J., Segura, A., Murillo, J.D. (eds.) IBERAMIA 2016. LNCS (LNAI), vol. 10022, pp. 151–162. Springer, Cham (2016). https://doi.org/10.1007/978-3-319-47955-2_13
4. Argamon, S., Koppel, M., Pennebaker, J.W., Schler, J.: Mining the blogosphere: age, gender, and the varieties of self-expression. First Monday 12 (2007)
5. Bacciu, A., Morgia, M.L., Mei, A., Nemmi, E.N., Neri, V., Stefa, J.: Bot and gender detection of twitter accounts using distortion and LSA notebook for PAN at CLEF 2019. CEUR Workshop Proceedings 2380 (2019)
6. Blei, D.M., Ng, A.Y., Jordan, M.I.: Latent Dirichlet allocation. J. Mach. Learn. Res. **3**(4–5), 993–1022 (2003)
7. Burger, J.D., Henderson, J., Kim, G., Zarrella, G.: Discriminating gender on Twitter. In: Proceedings of the 2011 Conference on Empirical Methods in Natural Language Processing, pp. 1301–1309. Association for Computational Linguistics, Edinburgh (2011). https://aclanthology.org/D11-1120
8. Chopra, S., Sawhney, R., Mathur, P., Ratn Shah, R.: Hindi-English hate speech detection: author profiling, debiasing, and practical perspectives. In: Proceedings of the AAAI Conference on Artificial Intelligence (2020)
9. Coates, J.: Women, Men and Language: A Sociolinguistic Account of Gender Differences in Language, 3rd edn, pp. 1–245. Taylor and Francis (2015)
10. Dadvar, M., Jong, F.D., Ordelman, R., Trieschnigg, D.: Improved cyberbullying detection using gender information. In: Proceedings of the Twelfth Dutch-Belgian Information Retrieval Workshop (DIR 2012). University of Ghent (2012)
11. Ease, F.R.: Flesch-Kincaid readability test (2009)
12. Fatima, M., Hasan, K., Anwar, S., Nawab, R.M.A.: Multilingual author profiling on facebook. Inf. Process. Manag. **53**(4), 886–904 (2017)
13. Joo, Y., Hwang, I.: Author profiling on social media: an ensemble learning model using various features notebook for PAN at CLEF 2019. In: CEUR Workshop Proceedings (2019)
14. Ke, G., et al.: LightGBM: a highly efficient gradient boosting decision tree. In: Guyon, I., et al. (eds.) Advances in Neural Information Processing Systems, vol. 30, pp. 3146–3154. Curran Associates, Inc. (2017). https://proceedings.neurips.cc/paper/2017/file/6449f44a102fde848669bdd9eb6b76fa-Paper.pdf
15. Kirasich, K., Smith, T., Sadler, B.: Random forest vs logistic regression: binary classification for heterogeneous datasets. SMU Data Sci. Rev. **1**, 9 (2018)
16. Koppel, M., Argamon, S., Shimoni, A.R.: Automatically categorizing written texts by author gender. Liter. Linguist. Comput. **17**(4), 401–412 (2002)
17. Levi, G., Hassner, T.: Age and gender classification using convolutional neural networks. In: Proceedings of the IEEE Conference on Computer Vision and Pattern Recognition (CVPR) Workshops (2015)

18. Liu, B.: Sentiment analysis and subjectivity. In: Handbook of Natural Language Processing, Second Edition (2010)
19. Liu, B.: Sentiment analysis and opinion mining. Synth. Lect. Human Lang. Technol. **5**(1), 1–184 (2012)
20. Losada, D.E., Crestani, F., Parapar, J.: eRISK 2017: CLEF lab on early risk prediction on the internet: experimental foundations. In: Jones, G.J.F., et al. (eds.) CLEF 2017. LNCS, vol. 10456, pp. 346–360. Springer, Cham (2017). https://doi.org/10.1007/978-3-319-65813-1_30
21. Losada, D.E., Crestani, F., Parapar, J.: Overview of eRisk: early risk prediction on the internet. In: Bellot, P., et al. (eds.) CLEF 2018. LNCS, vol. 11018, pp. 343–361. Springer, Cham (2018). https://doi.org/10.1007/978-3-319-98932-7_30
22. Losada, D.E., Crestani, F., Parapar, J.: Overview of eRisk 2019 early risk prediction on the internet. In: Crestani, F., et al. (eds.) CLEF 2019. LNCS, vol. 11696, pp. 340–357. Springer, Cham (2019). https://doi.org/10.1007/978-3-030-28577-7_27
23. Lundberg, S.M., Erion, G., Lee, S.I.: Consistent individualized feature attribution for tree ensembles. ArXiv abs/1802.03888 (2018)
24. Lundberg, S.M., Lee, S.I.: A unified approach to interpreting model predictions. In: Advances in Neural Information Processing Systems (2017)
25. Makinen, E., Raisamo, R.: Evaluation of gender classification methods with automatically detected and aligned faces. IEEE Trans. Pattern Anal. Mach. Intell. **30**(3), 541–547 (2008)
26. Metz, C.E.: Basic principles of ROC analysis. Seminars in Nuclear Medicine (1978)
27. Miller, Z., Dickinson, B., Hu, W.: Gender prediction on twitter using stream algorithms with n-gram character features. Int. J. Intell. Sci. **02**(04), 143–148 (2012)
28. Moghaddam, B., Yang, M.H.: Gender classification with support vector machines. In: Proceedings Fourth IEEE International Conference on Automatic Face and Gesture Recognition (Cat. No. PR00580), pp. 306–311 (2000)
29. Mukherjee, A., Liu, B.: Improving gender classification of blog authors. In: Proceedings of the 2010 Conference on Empirical Methods in Natural Language Processing, pp. 207–217. Association for Computational Linguistics, Cambridge (2010). https://www.aclweb.org/anthology/D10-1021
30. Ortega-Mendoza, R.M., Franco-Arcega, A., López-Monroy, A.P., Montes-y-Gómez, M.: I, me, mine: the role of personal phrases in author profiling. In: Fuhr, N., et al. (eds.) CLEF 2016. LNCS, vol. 9822, pp. 110–122. Springer, Cham (2016). https://doi.org/10.1007/978-3-319-44564-9_9
31. Pardo, F.M.R., Rosso, P.: Overview of the 7th author profiling task at PAN 2019: bots and gender profiling in twitter. In: Cappellato, L., Ferro, N., Losada, D.E., Müller, H. (eds.) Working Notes of CLEF 2019 - Conference and Labs of the Evaluation Forum, Lugano, Switzerland, 9–12 September 2019. CEUR Workshop Proceedings, vol. 2380. CEUR-WS.org (2019). http://ceur-ws.org/Vol-2380/paper_263.pdf
32. Peersman, C., Daelemans, W., Van Vaerenbergh, L.: Predicting age and gender in online social networks. In: Proceedings of the 3rd International Workshop on Search and Mining User-Generated Contents, SMUC '11, pp. 37–44. Association for Computing Machinery, New York (2011)
33. Piot-Perez-Abadin., P., Martin-Rodilla., P., Parapar., J.: Experimental analysis of the relevance of features and effects on gender classification models for social media author profiling. In: Proceedings of the 16th International Conference on Evaluation of Novel Approaches to Software Engineering - ENASE, pp. 103–113. INSTICC, SciTePress (2021)
34. Rajend, M., Swann, J., Deumert, A., Leap, W.: Introducing Sociolinguistics. Edinburgh University Press, Edinburgh (2009)
35. Rangel, F., Rosso, P.: On the implications of the general data protection regulation on the organisation of evaluation tasks. Language and Law= Linguagem e Direito (2019)

36. Rangel, F., et al.: Overview of the 2nd author profiling task at pan 2014. In: CEUR Workshop Proceedings, vol. 1180, pp. 898–927. CEUR Workshop Proceedings (2014)
37. Schwartz, H.A., et al.: Personality, gender, and age in the language of social media: the open-vocabulary approach. PLoS ONE **8**, e73791 (2013)
38. Sekulic, I., Gjurković, M., Šnajder, J.: Not just depressed: bipolar disorder prediction on reddit. In: Proceedings of the 9th Workshop on Computational Approaches to Subjectivity, Sentiment and Social Media Analysis, pp. 72–78. Association for Computational Linguistics, Brussels (2018). https://www.aclweb.org/anthology/W18-6211
39. Vasilev, E.: Inferring gender of Reddit users. Bachelor thesis, GESIS - Leibniz Institute for the Social Sciences (2018)
40. Weren, E.R.D., Kauer, A.U., Mizusaki, L., Moreira, V.P., Oliveira, J.P.M.D., Wives, L.K.: Examining multiple features for author profiling. J. Inf. Data Manag. **5**, 266 (2014)
41. Leng, X., Wang, Y.: Improving generalization for gender classification. In: 2008 15th IEEE International Conference on Image Processing, pp. 1656–1659 (2008)

Agile Mindset Adoption in Student Team Projects

Simona Motogna, Dan Mircea Suciu, and Arthur-Jozsef Molnar(✉)

Faculty of Mathematics and Computer Science, Babeş-Bolyai University, Cluj-Napoca, Romania
{simona.motogna,dan.suciu,arthur.molnar}@ubbcluj.ro
http://www.cs.ubbcluj.ro

Abstract. Developing and maintaining complex software systems requires both technical expertise as well as soft skills such as teamwork and good communication abilities. These become even more important as the size and geographical distribution of teams grow. The adoption of Agile development methodologies further emphasizes interaction, collaboration and adaptability to change, all with the purpose of prioritizing working software. Organizations of higher education have acknowledged this by incorporating capstone or team projects as part of their curricula. Our exploratory study reports the experience of 47 teams of 3rd year Computer Science students, each tasked with developing a medium-sized software application as part of a Team Project course. We focus our work on the issues reported by student teams planning to take up Agile values and practices. We report the most important challenges faced during application development and present them from both the students' and their mentors' perspectives. We show that soft skills remain an important component of adopting an Agile mindset when teaching collaborative software engineering. We provide an open source replication package that allows repeating or extending our investigation.

Keywords: Software engineering education · Soft skills · Agile software development · Project · Empirical study

1 Introduction

Industry and society both expect students graduating from Universities to possess relevant professional skills that enable them to take up a productive role in a modern work environment. Generally, these 'professional skills' encompass hard skills and soft skills. The former denotes scientific and technical proficiency that enables graduates to develop complex software applications. The latter one denotes a complementary set of skills that enable professionals to work in a team environment where communication, collaboration and teamwork are essential, which we find to be the case when developing real-life applications [1]. The realization of the importance soft skills in modern software development, especially with the acknowledgement and adoption of Agile methodologies, have lead to the introduction of project-based coursework that provides students the opportunity to work in a collaborative environment that includes an important soft skills component.

R. Ali et al. (Eds.): ENASE 2021, CCIS 1556, pp. 288–305, 2022.
https://doi.org/10.1007/978-3-030-96648-5_13

The present paper follows our precursor study [13] that detailed the most important results of an exploratory study carried out in the context of implementing a project-based course. Its three most important characteristics were the development of real-life systems, feedback from mentors working in the local IT industry and several workshops focused on the adoption of soft skills and an Agile mindset. The course was available to third year Computer Science students at the Babeş-Bolyai University. Students were expected to already posses a strong technical background with proficiency in several programming languages and associated popular frameworks and libraries. While most University courses were geared towards the development and evaluation of hard skills, the "Team Projects" course aimed to challenge students to overcome the challenges specific to working in a team and provide them with a solid, experience-driven foundation regarding the importance of soft skills and the advantages of Agile methods. Furthermore, the presence of mentors from the IT industry strengthens the collaboration between the University and local companies and helps provide students with a fresh perspective on their progress.

The main goal of the present work was to obtain an improved understanding of the students' perception on the importance of soft skills and the way Agile methods could be leveraged in a more complex project. In addition to our previous work [13], we complemented our detailed examination regarding the accumulation of hard and soft skills with an evaluation of the importance and the impact made by adopting an Agile mindset. We used both student and mentor feedback together with the final project evaluation that was carried out by teaching staff experienced in the development of complex software systems. We published the questionnaires used for both students and mentors, together with all replies in order to enable replicating or extending our study [12].

Our current work further details our initial efforts [13] and follows the best practices outlined in [14]. We present some key aspects of software projects in education in Sect. 2, emphasizing the role played by adopting an Agile mindset. We detail our methodology in Sect. 3, where we present our research questions, data collection and analysis processes. Our main observations are discussed in Sect. 4, while the threats to our study's validity are discussed in Sect. 5. Finally, we put our work into context using Sect. 6, with Sect. 7 dedicated to presenting our conclusions and future work ideas.

2 Key Elements of Software Engineering Projects

2.1 Agile Mindset and Software Development

In the last 20 years, Agile methodologies and frameworks for project management have gained importance in almost all segments of the software industry. In general, the Agile mindset has emerged as a popular iterative and incremental project management approach and it focuses on collaboration, communication and interdependent teamwork. At the same time, there is less focus on detailed initial plans, the significant improvement coming from what project team members learn through experience.

The main goal of Agile methodologies is to build high quality software applications, being focused on satisfying customers and end users needs. This is a difficult goal to achieve since the requirements for a software project often change while implementation is still in progress. Such changes are not desirable because they invalidate existing plans. However, requirements are likely to change as the customer and potential users interact with the software application only after its deployment.

In 2001 the Agile Manifesto [2] was written by 17 consultants in software development, most of them already using at that moment some lightweight project management methodologies like Scrum, eXtreme Programming, Feature Driven Development or Crystal. The Manifesto defines the core values and principles of the Agile mindset and emphasizes the most significant differences between Agile and traditional approaches by valuing:

- Individuals and interactions over processes and tools
- Working software over comprehensive documentation
- Customer collaboration over contract negotiation
- Responding to change over following a plan.

Moreover, individuals and interpersonal communication between stakeholders are in the center of attention and most Agile software development processes that support the above values are incremental and iterative.

2.2 *Team Project* Course Description

In education, an Agile mindset is adopted in two ways. On one side, Agile practices are introduced as part of software engineering courses, making students implement them in developing real software applications. On the other side, learning and teaching practices are adapted to follow Agile values and principles, improving learning outcomes.

Both directions were followed in implementing the *Team Project* course. As part of the third year of study, students in *Computer Science* and *Mathematics and Computer Science* educational tracks are required to develop a software system of their choice, working in project teams of 10 members(on average), during the first semester of their third academic year. The number of teams formed in each year depends on student enrollment and organization, but usually it is between 45 and 50. The course is 14 weeks long and takes place from October to January.

Starting from 2017, with the purpose to improve collaboration between team members and to heighten the quality of the delivered product, we integrated experienced mentors from the local software industry. Each student team is assigned such a mentor who helps them organize, collaborate and embrace the Agile mindset, no matter which was the development methodology selected by the team at project onset. Whenever it is needed, the mentor also plays the role of the customer (or the role of Product Owner, if the chosen methodology is Scrum), in order to give the team a better perspective of how a final user would see their solution. Usually, each mentor is assigned to coordinate two or three teams of students.

As software project themes selected for implementation usually there are internship or volunteer management tools, learning management systems, educational quizzes, e-commerce solutions, video games and systems for the management of personal finances.

In parallel with the development of their software projects, enrolled students attend four different half-day workshops. Two of these workshops are focused on solution development and product mindset (*Agile Software Development* and *Entrepreneurship*) while the other two target soft skills (*Communication* and *Presentation skills*).

The *Agile Software Development* workshop discusses the Agile mindset (values, principles and way of thinking in an Agile context) and two important Agile methodologies: Scrum and Kanban. Most of the teams have already selected their development methodology when attending this workshop, based on their mentor's suggestion. Still, during the workshop they have the opportunity to better understand the relevance of the Agile approach in building valuable software projects and discover new practices to implement within their effort.

At the end of the 14-week semester, a demo day is organized in which each team presents the result of their work in a 15-min live demonstration session. This is carried out in front of a faculty committee composed of senior teaching staff specialized in software engineering, who assign a grade to each of the teams. Within each team, student grades are decided by the mentors, based on each team member's contribution and such that the average of team member grades fits the grade assigned to the team by the teaching staff.

The distinctive characteristics of the course are:

- *Project based*: the software system to be developed represents the kernel of the course and also the main evaluation criterion.
- *Real-life*: the system solves a real-life problem, and real-life project management is simulated as the team is supervised by a mentor, who is an experienced professional from partner software companies.
- *Teamwork*: students organize teams internally according to their choice and work in the same team for the entire duration of the semester.
- *Evidence based*: all performed activities correspond to set milestones and must be documented.
- *Freedom of Choice*: students are encouraged and have to decide both the software methodology and the technology stack, including programming languages, application architecture, employed frameworks and tools for project management and version control.

Learning objectives are focused on practical competencies acquired by students, which include the knowledge and skills necessary to implement and follow through an Agile software development process, adapting the life cycle of a software project to an Agile context and improving team communication and collaboration skills. The data used in this study corresponds to the academic year 2019–2020, when 492 students, forming 47 teams and 15 mentors were involved. The semester was not affected by the subsequent pandemic-related restrictions.

3 Research Methodology

3.1 Research Objectives

We adopted the Goal-Question-Metric approach as defined in [15] as our study's guiding methodology. The main objective was to carry out a "qualitative investigation of the students' perception regarding the adoption of Agile practices in team projects". We projected the objective into three main research questions, some of which were further divided into more fine grained ones, as follows:

RQ1: *How do students adopt an Agile mindset in their working process?* Agile methodologies imply different practices related to software development and a successful adoption of Agile values, principles and practices depends on changing traditional practices. As a consequence, we planned to investigate: ***RQ1.1:*** *How are Agile values and principles adopted by students?* and ***RQ1.2:*** *Which Agile practices are implemented by students in their working processes?*
RQ2: *What were the main challenges that students had to deal with?* We aimed to analyse which were the main challenges, both technical and soft skills related, as described by the students themselves. These answers can offer important feedback in order to improve course content and project management during the semester.
RQ3: *How did students manage the adoption of Agile practices?* We wanted to evaluate the degree of Agile practices adoption, in order to have a better picture of what kind of Agile practices students have learned, both from their own self assessment and their mentors perspective. We divided this question into the following two sub-questions: ***RQ3.1:*** *How did students evaluate their own process of learning Agile practices?* and ***RQ3.2:*** *How did mentors evaluate the adoption of Agile practices?*

Qualitative analysis based on open coding was applied to data collected from students in order to provide answers to these research questions. We also collected mentor feedback through surveys. Data collection and data analysis is described in the following sections.

3.2 Data Collection

The data for this research was collected within the academic year 2019–2020, in the form of surveys that were completed by 47 student teams and questionnaires that were completed by 8 of the mentors. The questionnaires, responses from students and mentors are available within a replication package [12].

Student Surveys. A survey was designed consisting of four questions, as depicted in Fig. 1, which was then used to generate data for the corresponding four perspectives. Each team was expected to discuss the feedback internally and the team leader then submitted the result; one response per team was registered, based on agreement of opinions between team members. The survey also collected data about team name, project name and a short description of the project. All answer fields were free text, and students were encouraged to provide detailed information.

Mentor Feedback. Practitioners from partner companies who acted as mentors for the teams were asked to fill in a questionnaire at the end of the semester, after the projects were evaluated. The questions targeted student performance, challenges within the team and major outcomes of the course, as recommended in [8].

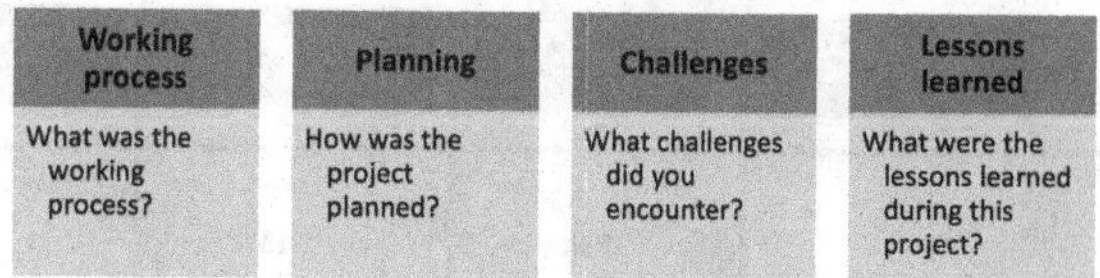

Fig. 1. Structure of the survey.

3.3 Data Analysis

As our data collection strategy consisted of administering a survey comprised of a set of four questions with the answers provided in the form of free text without restrictions of length, we decided that the most suitable qualitative analysis method was open coding [4,6]. The steps corresponding to the open coding process are represented in Fig. 2. 47 out of the 49 teams provided answers for the four questions (see Fig. 1), each question being considered as a perspective in our analysis. For this study, the perspective associated to "Planning" did not provide meaningful information, so we did not take it into consideration in the present work. For each question, two of the authors performed the initial two steps of coding. The process is depicted in Fig. 2, where the steps are marked in circles, and the considered number of initial, respectively merged topics are represented in rectangles. Step 1 consisted in detecting the keywords and establishing the labels, while step 2 involved determining the topics, which means that the topics have been classified according to labels based on their semantics. The third author had the role of the third independent coder performing the task of merging these labels as step 3. These results were then discussed between the authors and a consensus was reached between initial topics, merged topics and labels for each perspective.

An entire document analysis was performed, examining each response and paragraph in detail, which enabled breaking the data into discrete ideas, actions and experiences. During the coding process we focused on:

- Identifying labels: based on terminology from software development and project management practices as described in the literature [2];
- Determining initial topics: based on text processing to eliminate duplicates and ambiguities;
- Merging topics - in order to construct more general concepts. For example, student responses mentioned "task distribution", "task prioritization", "task management", which were all merged to "task management" as being the most comprehensive topic.

The results for each perspective are presented in the following tables, containing labels, topics and suggestive examples from students responses. The student quotes are anonymized and indexed in order to support easy access as follows: T4.WR represents the response given by team 4 to the working process (W) question, labelled with roles (R).

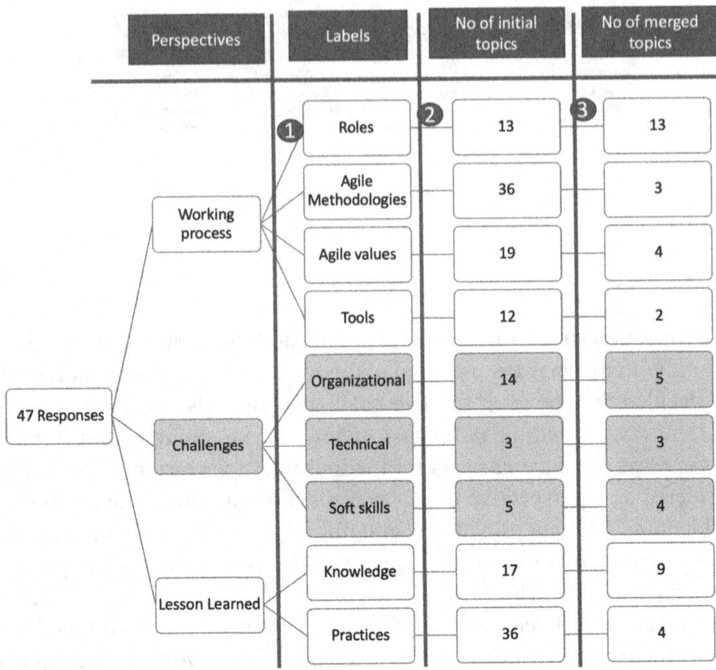

Fig. 2. Open coding process: the steps of the process appear as rounded indexes, and the numbers in rectangles represent the count of initial topics, respectively merged topics.

4 Answers to RQs

RQ1: *How do Students Adopt an Agile Mindset in Their Working Process?* We wanted to make a clear distinction between the roles, practices and tools that were used by the project teams and the values and principles that stayed behind them. This is the reason why we created two subsequent research questions: one referring to the Agile values that were followed by the project teams (*RQ1.1 How are Agile values and principles adopted by students?*) and another one that took into account the implementation of a particular Agile methodology (*RQ1.2 Which Agile practices are implemented by students in their working processes?*)

Table 1 summarizes the labels, topics and examples corresponding to the working process perspective. Four main concepts were inferred as a result of applying open coding in this part of the survey: the habits and artifacts that are linked with Agile values, the applied development methodology, the roles assigned to team members, and tools that were used by the teams.

RQ1.1: *How are Agile Values and Principles Adopted by Students?* 32 teams explicitly declared that they approached their projects in an Agile way. However, there is an important distinction between doing Agile (meaning implementing specific Agile practices, methodologies or frameworks) and being Agile (meaning embracing the Agile values and principles as they were described in the Agile Manifesto). In this respect, we analyzed the answers from the last perspective, identifying those situations where we found discrepancies between the intention and the outcome in Agile adoption.

A careful investigation revealed that in some cases, even if the students declared to have an Agile approach, their responses actually described a waterfall way of thinking. As an example, upfront design was adopted by four teams and this comes in contradiction with building emergent designs in an incremental and iterative way: *"the first couple of weeks was mostly dedicated to the engineering of the layers and architecture"* (T5.WM) or *"but in the end [of the first project stage] we had our almost complete structure and plan"* (T18.WM). The last example also contradicts the fourth value of the Agile Manifesto, since it refers to building a complete up-front plan in the beginning of the project.

As we observed when we analyzed the roles played by students in their teams, more than half of project teams stated that they divided the team into backend and frontend sub-teams, each sub-team working on its assigned tasks. This has a negative impact in following the first value of the Agile Manifesto, where the collaboration and interaction between all team members is considered very important. The application of this value often drives to cross-functional and self -organized teams with team members working together during the project lifecycle and not being divided based on their technical abilities.

Moreover, this way to organize the team in frontend, backend and sometimes in database and testing sub-teams leads to focus on finishing horizontal slices of software project features, while the second value of the Agile Manifesto recommendation is to focus on finishing vertical working slices of the project.

Given that students used free text for responses we divide our findings based on the relation with the aforementioned values of the Agile Manifesto.

V1. Individuals and Interactions over Processes and Tools: We identified a number of eight teams that exposed self-organizing procedures in their working process: *"brainstorming"*, *"efficient organization"*, *"interact"* (T37.WV), *"We held daily meetings"* (T22.WV) *"several times a week, we discussed what we did, what we will do and what problems we encountered"* (T24.WV). We appreciated the desire of teams to learn, as training was labeled in seven team answers (*"first ticket was associated to different learning activities"*, T17.WV) and mentoring (*"We scheduled workshops, where some of our more experienced colleagues held training sessions for the rest of the team"*, T14.WV). One team was identified as having dysfunctional teamwork (*"I'll tried... but the team mates mostly ignored me"*, T43.WV), while another team emphasized the importance of a friendly environment (*"gave feedback and tried to keep the atmosphere as friendly as possible"*, T24.WV).

V2. Working Software over Comprehensive Documentation: We observed that eight teams declared they measured their progress counting the number of working features built (*"we've clearly stated... which features needed to be implemented"*, T26.WV), and three other teams explicitly mentioned that the implemented process was followed in order to build intermediary working software (*"[the process] focuses on the goal of delivering working software frequently"*, T27.WV, *"...the implementation of small modules/functionalities and then we thoroughly tested them, building-up on working* *software"*, T33.WV). Only three teams mentioned documentation as a specific activity in their team (*"we allocated a little more time to research, documentation and concept"*, T33.WV), all of them referring to technical documentation. We deduced that customer documentation (user manual) was usually developed at the final stages of application development, just before presenting it in front of the faculty committee.

V3. Customer Collaboration over Contract Negotiation: Our analysis did not reveal strong connections between student team approaches and the third value of the Agile Manifesto. This happened mainly because the project theme was selected by the students themselves, so very often they played both the development and customer roles. Therefore, there was no clear distinction between the development tasks and customer collaboration activities, the customer satisfaction being mentioned just in those few cases when the mentor played the customer role. Only one team mentioned Minimum Viable Product, thinking of what could be the smallest set of features to bring value to the final customer (*"build the process of the app in such a way that we can have a MVP as soon as possible"*, T34.WV).

V4. Responding to Change over Following a Plan: As revealed by student responses, in most of the cases activities were oriented on iterations (or sprints), tasks or features. A number of 11 teams used sprint-driven planning (*"we aimed to have at the end of each sprint a working version of the software"*, T28.WV, *"At the beginning of the sprints we had planning sessions", T18.WV*), seven teams made task oriented planning (*"we created and choose the tasks each of us would have to do"*, T5.WV), while six teams had feature oriented planning: *"Though we didn't succeed in implementing all the features we talked about at the beginning"* (T32.WV). Two student teams expected that they will face some changes in requirements during the project lifecycle (*"...to be able to change the requirements then when the situation demands it"*, T50.WV), and one team declared that the requirements were pretty unclear at the beginning of the project (*"we did not know in advance exactly what we want to implement"*, T3.WV).

RQ1.2: Which Agile Practices Are Implemented by Students in Their Working Processes? **Methodologies:** Agile methodologies were adopted by most teams, as 15 teams mentioned Agile (*"As an organization methodology I used Agile", T16.WM*), 10 others mentioned Scrum, respectively 5 mentioned Kanban, and 2 teams used Feature Driven Development. Other teams adopted an iterative way of developing software but they did not explicitly mention the methodology used (*"we split our available time for development in sprints"*, T4.WM). One team decided to use a custom tailored methodology (*"we defined our own Agile methodology"*, T20.WM).

Roles: 26 teams stated that they divided the team into backend and frontend subteams (*"the tasks were divided... into backend and frontend tasks", T4.WR, "to allow parallel development on backend and frontend", T38.WR*), 10 teams had an assigned role for testing (*"members responsible with testing"*, T30.WR), while six teams acknowledged the role of the Scrum master: *"each subteam had its own Scrum master", T36.WR*. A set of other roles were mentioned, either functional or non-functional, including IT support, documentation, or team leader.

Tools: Teams used several tools as part of project implementation. They can be classified in tools for source control such as Github, GitLab or Bitbucket and task management tools such as Trello or Discord.

Table 1. Labels for "Working process" (open coding redone based on [13]).

Label	Topics	Examples
Agile Values (label WV)	Stand-up, feedback, self organize, communication, frequent releases, documentation, incremental, reviews, continuous delivery, iterations, sprints, deadlines	*"gave feedback and tried to keep the atmosphere as friendly as possible", "we allocated a little more time to research, documentation and concept", "We have learned to make constructive reviews and learn from the feedback we receive", "respecting our client's requirements", "We went back and forth with several idea proposals"*
Agile Methodologies (label: WM)	Scrum, Kanban, Feature driven development	*"The methodology used in development, that was implemented by the team is Feature-Driven Development", "As a methodology we tried to be Agile by applying a Scrum process", "We went with a Kanban way"*
Roles (identified roles in the team) (label: WR)	Backend/frontend, project manager, product owner, requirements engineer, devops, testing, IT support, technical leader, documentation, reviewer, team leader, scrum master, AI	*"X took responsibility for the backend", "groups that worked on different tasks: mobile application, backend development, testing, documentation"*
Tools (label: WT)	Source control tools and task management tools	*"Github", "GitLab", "BitBucket", "Discord"*

RQ2: *What Were the Main Challenges That Students Had to Deal With?* The challenges that students faced and tried to overcome can be grouped into three main types: organizational, technical and related to soft skills, as shown in Table 2. In order to have the full picture, we incorporated mentor feedback, illustrated in Table 3, into our analysis.

Organizational Challenges: 16 teams considered the hardest challenge to be task management (*"Challenge: create and detail tasks to be easily understood", T2.CO*) or time management (*"one challenge was intense work in last days to finish project", T10.CO*). Summarizing, either tasks or time have put pressure on project development for approximately 68% of the teams. Eight teams faced technology choice as the main challenge: *"main issues was to decide which tools and frameworks to use" (T14.CO).*

TechnicalChallenges: More than half of the teams (53%) dealt with technical problems, in some part due to lack of technical knowledge (*"a more messy challenge was learning new frameworks and libraries on the go", T2.CT*), or due to incorrect project management (*"Our challenge arose when, after starting our implementation, we frequently needed to change the DB schema and relations, thus indirectly forcing everyone to do the same updates"*, T28.CT).

Soft Skills Challenges: the extent of each team member's involvement was the main problem for 10 of the teams: *"Being able to motivate everyone to work consciously and constantly" (T5.CS).* Five teams were confronted with communication problems: *"biggest challenges that we encountered were communication with the team members, ... and the communication with the mentor"* (T18.CS).

Table 2. Labels for "Challenges" [13].

Label	Topics	Examples
Organizational (label: CO)	Time management, task management, teamwork, collaboration, technology choice	*"synchronizing as a team and working together", "decide which tools and frameworks to use", "finish everything before the deadline"*
Technical (label: CT)	Technical skills, effective collaboration, over-engineering	*"learn to use the technologies", "how to combine what we worked on", "over-engineering in some places"*
Soft skills (label: CS)	Involvement, communication, collaboration, teamwork	*"Being able to motivate everyone to work consciously and constantly", "it was way harder for everyone to keep in touch with everyone", "organizing and coordinating"*

Table 3. Mentor feedback on 10 common issues in team projects and the relevant Agile values that are influenced. Scores recorded on a 1 (not likely at all) to 5 (very likely) scale, including standard deviation (σ) (adapted from [13]).

Challenge	Values	Mean	σ
Lack of engagement from team members	V1	3.62	1.30
Student task knowledge and assumption	V4	3.50	0.53
Miscommunication within the team	V1	3.25	1.03
Problems with time management	V4	3.25	0.88
Team leader dictates what team members do	V1	2.87	1.24
Lack of technical expertise	–	2.87	1.12
Dividing the work among team members	V1, V2	2.50	1.41
Work is carried out by one or two team members	V1	2.37	1.3
Conflicts among team members	V1	2.37	1.4
No one wants to act as team leader	V1	2.12	1.45

One team declared that they had no challenges worth mentioning, and that the ones that appeared were easily solved, while two other teams (T12, T24) did not complete this part of the survey.

Mentor Feedback: Table 3 shows the mentor's answers regarding some of the most common challenges in the team projects [8]. The most significant highlighted challenge was the lack of engagement from team members, for which mentors reported a mean score of 3.62, with 3 out of 8 respondents attributing it the maximum value on a 5-point scale. Another significant issue regarded communication and the assumption of project roles and tasks within teams. We note the low value of the standard deviation ($\sigma = 0.53$), which shows agreement among the mentors. Mentor feedback was mostly positive regarding the existence of team conflicts, or for the presumed case of students not wanting to assume coordination responsibilities. In most cases, we observe a value of $\sigma \geq 1$, which shows that the prevalence of issues still varied among the teams.

We were also interested in a cross-sectional exploration of challenges as perceived by students versus mentors. In this regard, our answer to *RQ2* shows alignment between

Table 4. Labels for "Lessons learned" [13].

Label	Topics	Examples
Acquired knowledge	Teamwork, technical skills, communication, estimation, collaboration, code review, SCRUM, time management, version control system, task management	*"We learned ... teamwork and the ability to support and help each other", "We have learned to make constructive reviews and learn from the feedback we receive", "We learned mostly about the efficiency of the SCRUM methodology, about teamwork and time management"*
Good practices	Communication, motivation, teamwork, project management	*"Communication is Key", "we have learnt is how hard it is to motivate people, and to manage a team of 9 people", "task management is crucial"*

student and mentor perception. On one hand, challenges were an important motivator of progress; we believe that agreement between student and mentor perceptions represents an important indicator of effective communication and team progress.

Most of the common challenges identified by mentors were connected with the first value of the Agile Manifesto. At the same time, the third value was not represented in this list most probably because the teams themselves played both the customer and developer roles, so the communication and interaction with the customer were not approached in an explicit manner. In addition, there was the challenge regarding the lack of technical expertise that had no direct connection with any of the Agile values.

***RQ3:** How Did Students Manage the Adoption of Agile Practices?* Students had the freedom to employ a project development methodology of their own choice. Issues related to planning, working process and lessons learned were reported in detail within our precursor work [13]. The present paper is specifically focused on the process and experience of adopting Agile methodologies. 32 out of the 47 participating teams stated that they approached their project in an Agile way. We focused our evaluation on them. We employed the free text feedback from the student and mentor questionnaires together with the results of the open coding process. However, as already reported in our answer to *RQ1.1*, we did note a few discrepancies. Several teams stated using an Agile approach but instead described a waterfall process. As such, we expected most teams to show a partial adoption of Agile practices, limited to those that students were familiar with or felt they better suited the project. This provides an opportunity to understand the students' perception of the importance and suitability of Agile practices and provide more focused training that covers areas of uncertainty. We provide our answer to *RQ3* by first evaluating the students' own feedback, followed by that of the mentors, who also reported on the progress teams achieved during the semester.

***RQ3.1:** How Did Students Evaluate Their Own Process of Learning Agile Practices?* We used the student responses to our questionnaire to identify the Agile practices employed by each team, and use Fig. 3 to represent our findings. Out of the 47 teams that

	Roles			Ceremonies / Practices									Artifacts		
	PO	TM	SM	CS	CP	CR	CD	PS	PP	Pok	Cde	FDD	TB	US	B
T2	X		X						X				X		
T3					X						X				
T4								X					X		
T5													X		
T6		X											X		
T8															
T9															
T10		X						X							
T11				X	X	X	X				X		X		
T12		X													
T13								X							
T14		X													
T15		X						X							
T16				X				X					X		
T17								X					X		
T18		X	X	X	X			X					X	X	
T19		X									X		X		
T20		X													
T21													X		
T22		X		X	X		X	X							X
T24			X	X	X	X		X					X		
T25		X						X					X		
T26	X	X	X					X		X				X	
T27				X				X				X	X		
T28					X			X					X		
T29			X		X			X		X			X		
T30		X	X										X		
T31							X	X					X		
T32		X	X	X		X		X					X		
T33		X						X							
T34		X				X		X							
T35		X											X		
T36		X		X									X		
T37		X											X		
T38		X											X		
T39							X	X					X		
T40			X												
T41		X						X							
T42		X													
T43															
T44		X										X			
T45		X	X	X	X			X					X		
T46											X		X		
T47											X		X		
T48		X	X	X			X	X					X		
T49		X		X			X	X							
T50		X		X		X	X	X						X	

Fig. 3. Agile Practices used by the student teams (Roles: PO - Product Owner, SM - Scrum Master, TM - Team member (self organizing team), Ceremonies/Practices: CS - standup ceremony, CP - planning ceremony, CD - demo/review ceremony, CR - retrospective ceremony, PS - Sprint/Iteration, PP - PairProgramming, Pok - Planning Poker, CDe - Continuous delivery, FDD - Feature Driven Development practices, Artifacts: TB - taskboard, US - user stories, B - backlog); teams T1, T7 and T23 did not respond to our questionnaire.

responded to our questionnaire, 32 specifically mentioned using Agile. Our analysis of the student responses however identified Agile practices being used by 44 teams, representing 93% of the responding teams. We divide them into Roles, Ceremonies/Practices and Artifacts and use Fig. 3 to highlight only those that were reported by at least one of the teams.

In the *Roles* category, we observe that 26 out of the 44 reporting teams mentioned team member roles or that they worked as a self-organizing team. Only 2 teams reported having a product owner and 10 a Scrum master. None of them mentioned the product backlog, which we feel is an important piece of the Scrum framework.

With regards to *Ceremonies/Practices*, the most often reported ones are sprints and iterations (24 teams), together with standup (12 teams) and planning (8 teams) ceremonies. As expected, this data was biased towards aspects previously practiced by students during previous coursework, which required feature planning over several iterations. We also observed a number of other practices that were seldom and inconsistently used within teams.

When it came to artifacts, we found that 27 teams used taskboards, making them and team organization the most prevalent practices. The open coding process allowed us to go into more detail and identify common trends within the student responses. An example of this is shown in Table 4, which presents some of the open coding topics discovered. We divided them into acquired knowledge and good practices.

We observed that 12 teams explicitly mentioned the importance of teamwork, which was also the subject of one organized workshop. Several aspects were identified to be important such as *"we all agreed that in the end we learned how to be a team"* (T16), *"teamwork makes the dream work"* (T33), or in more detail *"we saw how to work*

Table 5. Mentor feedback of team progress in four key areas. Scores recorded on a 1 (very poor) to 5 (excellent) scale, together with the standard deviation (σ).

Progress area	Mean score	σ
Project management	3.43	0.82
Software development	4	0.75
Communication	3.87	0.99
Team work	3.87	0.99

in a team, similar to a working place (responsibilities, targets, deadlines)" (T9) [13]. Many teams also identified the importance of communication: *"we communicated a lot throughout all the development stages"* (T32), *"The project represented a valuable exercise in improving communication"* (T45). Learning and adaptability were also highlighted by several teams: *"learn by listen to team mates opinions"*, (T6), *"We have learned to make constructive reviews and learn from the feedback we receive"*, (T11), *"adapt to others' needs"* (T15) and *"adapt to several ways of problem solving"* (T38). Finally, task management was also identified as an important practice: *"During the implementation of our software solution, we were taught that ... task management is crucial"* (T27).

RQ3.2: *How Did Mentors Evaluate the Adoption of Agile Practices?* We synthesized the feedback from the mentor questionnaire into Tables 3 and 5. We focus the present section on the evaluation of Agile practices. A generic discussion regarding the mentors' feedback is available within our precursor work [13]. We linked the challenges most often reported by mentors with the four Agile values as presented in our answer to *RQ1.1*. First of all, we observed that none of the challenges were linked to Agile value V3 (*Customer collaboration over contract negotiation*). The reason can be explained by perusing Fig. 3, which shows that only two teams discussed the *Product Owner* role. In the remaining teams, this role was jointly assumed, as the teams themselves settled on the project topic and jointly carried out task planning and allocation. Likewise, while the lack of technical knowledge represented an important hurdle for many teams, it could not be directly linked with any of the four Agile values and therefore remained unassigned.

We observed most of the encountered challenges to be linked with V1 (*Individuals and interactions over processes and tools*). As detailed in our precursor work [13] as well as the answers to the previous research questions, most challenges were linked to team communication and motivation. We note that out of the four challenges most often reported by mentors, two were linked with the V1 Agile value, and two with the V4 value (*Responding to change over following a plan*). We note the existence of agreement between the evaluations by mentors and the students themselves regarding the most prevalent issues.

With regards to progress, Table 5 shows the mentors' evaluation within four key areas critical for successful project completion. In all areas, we note the value of the standard deviation $\sigma \approx 1$, which illustrates differences between the mentors' perception. We also note that all mentors evaluated that progress had taken place, as progress in all key areas was evaluated with at least 2 points.

5 Threats to Validity

We designed, organized and carried out our study according to well-known best practices [14]. Surveys were sent to all student teams and guiding mentors after the course was completed and the evaluation had taken place. The paper's first author was responsible for coordinating the course. Both co-authors are experienced in project management and software engineering, both in academia as well as industry. The major steps carried out included setting up the questionnaire structure and collection methodology, processing free-text responses using open coding, analyzing and interpreting the results and putting them into the proper context.

We addressed **internal threats** by involving researchers with experience in teaching, software engineering and the transformative effects of adopting Agile methodologies. Student and mentor questionnaires were validated before being handed out. Open coding work was carried out in pairs, with the third researcher assuming a validation role and ensuring that consensus was reached regarding assigned labels and their interpretation. In addition, we revisited and validated the labelling process presented in the precursor study [13].

The most important **external threats** identified related to the context in which the case studies took place, namely course curricula, requirements, team size and organization as well as the means and the moment of reporting. We identified and used relevant related work to establish our study's methodology, including questionnaire structure and contents as well as the key areas our research was focused on. One of the authors had no involvement with the course's structure or activities, and their input was used to control bias. When compared to the precursor study [13], we focused on those soft-skills aspects relevant for the adoption of Agile methodologies. We confirmed that our results were in line with those from existing literature [1,5,16].

6 Related Work

A significant number of contributions can be found in the literature referring to teaching Agile methodology in academic courses. Without the claim of covering all these papers, we refer, in a chronological order, to some recent and notable studies addressing this topic.

A holistic approach to introduce agile practices into student curricula was proposed by Kropp [10], in which they highlight the importance of applied activities that must supplement theoretical lectures. The study is constructed as an experience report based on introducing Agile practices into software engineering courses at the Zurich University of Applied Studies. Buffardi [3] published another experience report of student software engineering projects, in which Agile practices were combined with lean startup practices. Highlighting the benefits of collaboration between students and clients, the study also mentioned that the approach might have limitations, especially when finding active mentors.

Extending Project Based Learning with Agile practices was reported by Heberle [7], based on their eight years of experience with such courses. The study describes the course design (including a Scrum workshop), grading methodology, students and industry perception. The eight years experience of this course provides evidence on the impact in the local industry, but also in international educational collaborations. Masood [11] addressed challenges that appeared when introducing Agile practices into student projects, showing a great similarity with challenges faced by our students. The study makes some recommendations for students and educators that can help improve these kind of projects. In [9], Ju presents a systematic approach to introduce eXtreme Programming processes in project based courses. Their conclusion, based on team observation and surveys, states that the overhead for project management does not affect learning outcomes.

Compared to existing approaches, we consider that our approach brings an important contribution to the body of knowledge addressing Agile practices in student projects. The distinctive feature of our study consists in concentrating on student perception regarding course outcomes, for which we used open coding to interpret students survey, addressing different aspects of their learning process. We also emphasize the three essential ingredients that were considered in the design of this course: importance of soft skills in Agile methodology, providing dedicated workshops throughout the semester and the participation of experienced mentors from local software companies.

7 Conclusions and Future Work

The present work represents a detailed follow-up of our initial investigation regarding how students perceived the importance and impact that soft skills have on the development of complex software projects [13]. We extended our work to specifically cover the adoption and impact of Agile methodologies, as they appeared to be prevalent in the student feedback gathered during our initial study.

We analyzed student and mentor feedback gathered in the form of free-text answers to corresponding questionnaires and took into account the results of the final project evaluation. These were carried out during live sessions where student teams presented their work in front of an experienced faculty committee. Like in the case of our initial evaluation [13] we employed open-coding in order to tag and classify the feedback of course participants; when compared with our initial investigation, we examined both student and mentor feedback in relation to the adoption of an Agile working process and benefits tangible to its adopters. We observed that many teams were challenged by the technical prowess required to lead their project towards a successful conclusion, as team members had varying levels of expertise with the required tools and frameworks. Several teams organized internal "workshops" where these issues were resolved using communication and teamwork; however, we also noticed instances where team members remained dissatisfied with the level of motivation and involvement in their teams.

Our initial investigation [13] already covered project planning, the working process and the alignment between student and mentor evaluation. As such, we devised three new research questions focused on the main subject of the present evaluation. The first two were focused on the adoption and evaluation of an Agile mindset, while the last one targeted the evaluation of the main challenges faced by students. We dedicated Sect. 4 to a detailed discussion of the results. We observed that most teams incorporated Agile ideas or methods into their working process; we also discovered instances where students claimed Agile adoption that was contradicted by their own detailed reporting.

As future work, we aim to support student teams regarding the adoption of an Agile mindset in a more focused way. We also aim to incentivise teams to foster continuous collaboration and motivation at team level. In addition, extending our investigation to cover several consecutive academic years remains one of our important interests; this is especially true since course activities were moved fully online for the 2020–2021 academic year as a result of the pandemic-related measures. In this context, we aim to investigate what impact the fully online work environment has on soft skill development and teamwork, as well as carry out a comparison between offline and online course organization.

References

1. Ahmed, F., Capretz, L.F., Bouktif, S., Campbell, P.: Soft skills and software development: a reflection from software industry. J. Inf. Process. Manag. **4**(3), 171–191 (2013). https://doi.org/10.4156/ijipm.vol4.issue3.17
2. Beck, K., Beedle, M., van Bennekum, A.O.: Agile manifesto (2001). https://agilemanifesto.org
3. Buffardi, K., Robb, C., Rahn, D.: Learning agile with tech startup software engineering projects. In: Proceedings of the 2017 ACM Conference on Innovation and Technology in Computer Science Education, ITiCSE 2017, pp. 28–33. ACM (2017)
4. Corbin, J., Strauss, A.: Basics of Qualitative Research. Techniques and Procedures for Developing Grounded Theory. 4th edn. SAGE Publications (2014)
5. Delgado, D., Velasco, A., Aponte, J., Marcus, A.: Evolving a project-based software engineering course: a case study. In: 2017 IEEE 30th CSEE&T, pp. 77–86 (2017). https://doi.org/10.1109/CSEET.2017.22
6. Glaser, B., Strauss, A.: The Discovery of Grounded Theory: Strategies for Qualitative Research. Sociology Press, Mill Valley (1967)
7. Heberle, A., Neumann, R., Stengel, I., Regier, S.: Teaching agile principles and software engineering concepts through real-life projects. In: 2018 IEEE Global Engineering Education Conference (EDUCON), pp. 1723–1728 (2018). https://doi.org/10.1109/EDUCON.2018.8363442
8. Iacob, C., Faily, S.: Exploring the gap between the student expectations and the reality of teamwork in undergraduate software engineering group projects. J. Syst. Softw. **157**, 110393 (2019). https://doi.org/10.1016/j.jss.2019.110393
9. Ju, A., Hemani, A., Dimitriadis, Y., Fox, A.: What agile processes should we use in software engineering course projects? In: Proceedings of the 51st ACM Technical Symposium on Computer Science Education, pp. 643–649. ACM (2020). https://doi.org/10.1145/3328778.3366864
10. Kropp, M., Meier, A.: Teaching agile software development at university level: values, management, and craftsmanship, pp. 179–188, May 2013. https://doi.org/10.1109/CSEET.2013.6595249
11. Masood, Z., Hoda, R., Blincoe, K.: Adapting agile practices in university contexts. J. Syst. Softw. **144**, 501–510 (2018)
12. Motogna, S., Suciu, D.M., Molnar, A.J.: Replication data set, January 2021. https://doi.org/10.6084/m9.figshare.13636445
13. Motogna., S., Suciu., D., Molnar., A.: Investigating student insight in software engineering team projects. In: Proceedings of the 16th International Conference on Evaluation of Novel Approaches to Software Engineering - ENASE, pp. 362–371. INSTICC, SciTePress (2021). https://doi.org/10.5220/0010478803620371

14. Runeson, P., Host, M., Rainer, A., Regnell, B.: Case Study Research in Software Engineering: Guidelines and Examples, 1st edn. Wiley Publishing, Hoboken (2012)
15. Solingen, R., Basili Vic, C.G., Rombach, D.: Goal Question Metric Approach. Encyclopedia of Software Engineering, Wiley, Hoboken (2002)
16. Ville, I., Daniels, M.: Searching for global employability: can students capitalize on enabling learning environments? ACM Trans. Comput. Educ. **19**(2), 1–29 (2019). https://doi.org/10.1145/3277568

Systems and Software Quality

Ontology-Based Natural Language Processing for Process Compliance Management

Muhammad Atif Javed[1(✉)], Faiz Ul Muram[2], and Samina Kanwal[3]

[1] RISE Research Institutes of Sweden, Västerås, Sweden
muhammad.atif.javed@ri.se
[2] Linnaeus University, Växjö, Sweden
faiz.ulmuram@lnu.se
[3] National University of Sciences and Technology, Islamabad, Pakistan

Abstract. Process compliance with relevant regulations and de-facto standards is a mandatory requirement for certifying critical systems. However, it is often carried out manually, and therefore perceived as complex and labour-intensive. Ontology-based Natural Language Processing (NLP) provides an efficient support for compliance management with critical software system engineering standards. This, however, has not been considered in the literature. Accordingly, the approach presented in this paper focuses on ontology-based NLP for compliance management of software engineering processes with standard documents. In the developed ontology, the process concerns, such as stakeholders, tasks and work products are captured for better interpretation. The rules are created for extracting and structuring information, in which both syntactic features (captured using NLP tasks) and semantic features (captured using ontology) are encoded. During the planning phase, we supported the generation of requirements, process models and compliance mappings in Eclipse Process Framework (EPF) Composer. In the context of reverse compliance, the gaps with standard documents are detected, potential measures for their resolution are provided, and adaptions are made after the process engineer approval. The applicability of the proposed approach is demonstrated by processing ECSS-E-ST-40C, a space software engineering standard, generating models and mappings, as well as reverse compliance management of extended process model.

Keywords: Process · Ontology · Rules · Natural language processing · Standards · Compliance management · SPEM 2.0 · EPF composer

1 Introduction

The idea with the compliance is to ensure that business processes, operations and practices are inline with the relevant regulations [10, 11]. Often, the standards describe the criteria that needs to be satisfied during the certification. The examples of standards include DO-178C [28] for software in airborne systems, CENELEC standards (e.g., EN 50126 [6]) for railway systems, ECSS (e.g., ECSS-E-ST-40C [7]) for space projects and applications, and ISO 26262 [12] for functional safety in the automotive domain. Compliance with the relevant standards is a mandatory requirement for getting the

R. Ali et al. (Eds.): ENASE 2021, CCIS 1556, pp. 309–327, 2022.
https://doi.org/10.1007/978-3-030-96648-5_14

approval or acceptance from the certification body. However, the standard documents written in natural language are usually manually processed for achieving compliance. In addition to the extraction of standard requirements and process, there is a need to provide the reference among them. The normative process models embedded in the standards typically include planning of units of work such as activities and tasks, which are expected to be executed during the development; work products taken as input or produced as output; involved roles, and a set of methods to be used. Process compliance is perceived as complex and labour-intensive task due to the manual effort required for extracting, modelling process knowledge, and managing traceability [17,18].

There exist several efforts on process extraction from textual descriptions and generation of OMG's Business Process Model and Notation (BPMN) models [1,8]. This paper builds on our previous work in which we targeted the information extraction from critical system software engineering standards using Natural Language Processing (NLP), generation of requirements, OMG's Software & Systems Process Engineering Metamodel (SPEM) compliant processes, their compliance mappings, as well as reverse compliance management of extended processes [25]. In the absence of ontology, the extraction just focuses on lexical and/or syntactic text information. The usage of ontology is promising in improving the information extraction performance. From the NLP perspective, it is used to further incorporate semantic features in the rule or machine-learning-based systems to enable extraction based on meaning. In the literature, the ontologies are proposed for different phases of software development life cycle [2,9]. The ontology developed in this paper is inline with the space software engineering processes. To date, however, the published studies have not considered the ontology-based NLP for compliance management of development processes with critical system software engineering standard documents. In this paper, the ontology-based NLP is carried out in a similar manner to the research works in construction domain by Zhou and El-Gohary [33] and Xu and Cai [31].

This paper extends our previous work on process compliance management [25] in the following ways: 1) we provided more details on NLP tasks and rule-based matching, and 2) an ontology is developed and used for capturing and structuring process knowledge; it improved the information extraction performance. The created rules are based on the syntactic features captured using NLP tasks and the semantic features captured using ontology. During the planning phase, the OMG's SPEM compliant process models, requirements, as well as compliance mappings are generated in its reference implementation, more specifically the Eclipse Process Framework (EPF) Composer[1] is utilised. In the method content part of EPF plugins, the requirements and reusable content elements, such as roles, tasks and work products are generated in a structured way. The reusable content elements are organized in the process structure with the consideration of phase, activity and milestone elements. The reverse compliance of pre-existing or extended process models is also supported. Specifically, the gaps with standard documents are detected and possible options for their resolution are informed. However, they are executed after the approval from process engineer. The applicability of the proposed approach is demonstrated by extracting text from space system software engineering standard documents, its structuring, generating requirements, process models

[1] https://www.eclipse.org/epf/

and compliance mappings in EPF Composer, as well as reverse compliance management for a selected process model.

The rest of this paper is organized as follows: Sect. 2 provides background information on process engineering and NLP. Section 3 presents the ontology-based NLP approach for extracting requirements and processes embedded in the standard documents, their structuring and mappings, generation, as well as reverse compliance management. Section 4 demonstrates the effectiveness of proposed approach for ECSS-E-ST-40C standard. Section 5 presents related work. Section 6 concludes the paper and presents future research directions.

2 Background

2.1 Process Engineering

SPEM 2.0 [26] is the Object Management Group (OMG) standard, which not only provides the support for creating libraries of reusable method content, but also supports the development and management of processes for performing projects. The combination of method content and process enables the configuration of process framework customized for a specific project's needs, and enactment of a process in real development projects. The conceptual framework of SPEM 2.0 comprises of method content, processes, configuration, and enactment. *Method Content* provides support for the definitions of reusable content elements, i.e., *Task Definitions* that specify the unit of work being performed by *Role(s) Definitions*, and may consume *Work Product Definitions* as input and produce/generate as output. *Work Product Definitions* can be a type of outcome, deliverable, or artefact. The *Category* can be used to group together any number of content elements, such as discipline, role set, domain, and tool category. *Guidance* is defined at the intersection of method content and process because it provides support for both. Specifically, it describes additional information of work, such as guideline, practice, template, example, etc.

Process takes the content elements and relate them into workflows and/or breakdown structures, and adapt them to a specific project context. The main element of process is an *Activity* that defines basic units of work within a Process as well as a Process itself. Activity Kinds are used to distinguish specific levels of the breakdown structure, such as Phase, Iteration and Process. A *Phase* represents a significant period in a project and normally ends with major milestones, or a set of deliverables, whereas *Iteration* indicates a set of nested Activities that are repeated more than once. There are two process kinds: (1) process pattern (referred as capability pattern in EPF Composer) describes reusable clusters of activities for a certain area of application/interest; and (2) *Delivery Process* describes a complete end-to-end life-cycle of a specific project. Table 1 shows the main elements for defining the process.

EPF Composer is an open-source process engineering framework, based on the conceptual framework of SPEM. It is evolved from Eclipse Galileo 3.5.2 to Eclipse Neon 4.6.3 [13,14] after 11 years. It is possible to launch the EPF Composer as a standalone application, but also in the Eclipse integrated development environment (IDE). EPF Composer is not just used to model standards and development process, but also

Table 1. Process modelling elements in EPF composer.

Task	Role	Artifact	Deliverable	Outcome	Discipline	Domain	Role Set	Tool Category
Guideline	**Practice**	**Example**	**Activity**	**Capability Pattern**	**Delivery Process**	**Iteration**	**Phase**	**Milestone**

show that process comply with standards [21,22]. EPF Composer provides the authoring capabilities to define method content and process, and browsing perspective to publish the content in the form of websites. A method library is a repository of method elements and comprised of a set of *Method Plugins* and *Configurations*. The *Method Plugins* are containers of process related information, while a *Configuration* is a selection of logical sub-sets of library content to be shown in the browsing perspective. To model the standards requirements, the guidance kinds *Practice* can be customized with an icon in a separate plugin let us say *Customized_Icon*. The *Standards_Requirements* plugin captures the requirements listed in the standards and has the variability relationship *Extends* with the previously mentioned plugin (i.e., inherits the content of the base element). The *Process_Lifecycle* plugin defines the process life cycle, whereas the mapping between standard requirements and process life cycle is provided in *Mapping_Requirements* plugin [21,22].

2.2 NLP

During the past years, NLP is effectively used to automate the interpretation of textual documents. NLP enables a computer to understand, create, and analyse texts. It has been applied in several application areas including speech recognition, machine translation, information retrieval and extraction. NLP applications are supported by text processing tasks, such as *tokenization* (broken down of a sentence into meaningful segments, called tokens), *Part-of-Speech (PoS)* tagging (assigning word types, e.g., noun, adjective, and verb to individual tokens), *morphology* (mapping deviations, e.g., "ion", "ing" and inflected forms, e.g., "plural" to the base form of a word), and *dependency parsing* (determining relations among linguistic units to the semantic level).

Typically, the NLP utilises rule or machine learning-based techniques. The rule-based techniques focus on pattern matching rules for text processing. After processing input texts as sequence of tokens, human effort is often required for defining patterns over the tokens text, and finally the patterns are encoded as pattern-matching rules. The machine learning algorithms such as Naïve Bayes (NB), Hidden Markov Models (HMM), Support Vector Machines (SVM), and Conditional Random Fields (CRF) are used to learn the extraction of patterns from training text. This requires human involvement for preparing a large training set. The usage of NLP significantly reduces effort by a human in document processing and information extraction. It also provides the means for ensuring a more objective and consistent interpretation of regulatory documents [31].

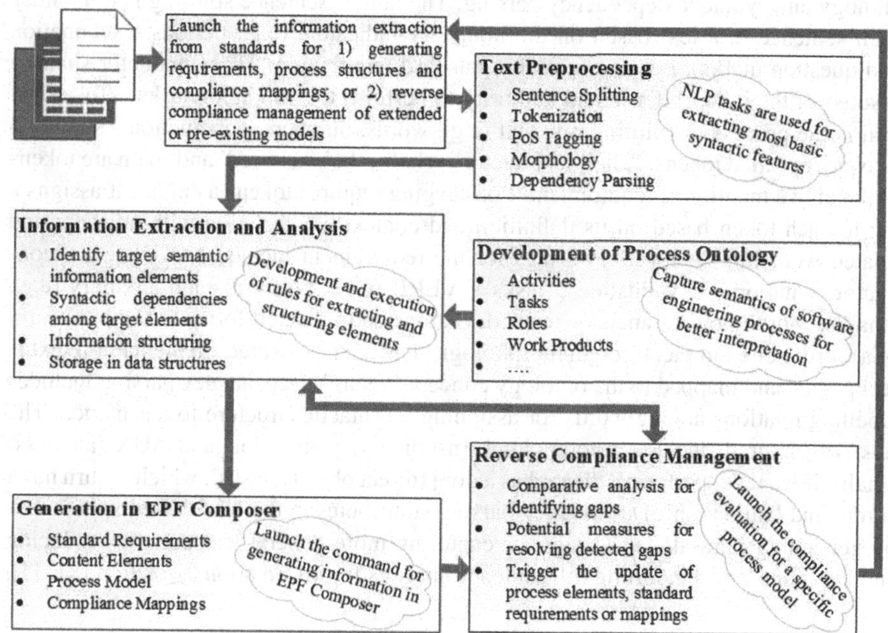

Fig. 1. An overview of the proposed approach for process compliance management

3 Process Compliance Management

Typically, the critical computer-based systems are subject to certification for which compliance is a mandatory requirement. It deals with adherence to the relevant regulations. Compliance is often a manual act/process, which is complex and labour-intensive endeavour. This section describes our proposed approach to facilitate process compliance with standard documents. Its overview is shown in Fig. 1. We used the common text preprocessing tasks to extract the most basic syntactic features, such as tokens, PoS tags, word-based forms, and syntactic dependency relation between tokens (see Sect. 3.1). An ontology is developed for the better interpretation of process elements, such as roles, tasks, work products, phases and activities (see Sect. 3.2). Both syntactic and semantic features are embedded in the rules developed for information extraction and analysis (see Sect. 3.3). Information is structured and stored. The requirements, process and compliance mappings during planning phase can be generated in EPF Composer (see Sect. 3.4). Furthermore, the reverse compliance management of extended or preexisting process models is supported during execution phase. In this context, the compliance gaps and resolution measures are determined and informed, but the changes, such as new elements are added in an automatic manner, after the approval from process engineer (see Sect. 3.5).

3.1 Text Preprocessing

Preprocessing aims to prepare the unprocessed text for further processing. In this paper, the NLP tasks used for the text preprocessing include tokenization, PoS tagging, morphology and syntactic dependency parsing. The aim of sentence splitting is to identify each sentence in a text based on the boundary indicators (e.g., periods, exclamation and question marks). Let us consider a standard requirement "The conductor shall be assured of the independence and authority to perform the validation tasks". Tokenization is the process of splitting raw text (e.g., words, numbers, punctuations, symbols) into pieces called tokens. 'The', 'conductor', 'shall', 'be', 'assured' and so on are tokens in the above mentioned requirement. PoS tagging requires tokens as input. It assigns a tag to each token based on its definition and context, i.e., relation with adjacent and related word in a sentence. PoS tags for the requirement include NOUN (e.g., 'conductor', 'authority', 'validation', 'tasks'), VERB (e.g., 'perform') and auxiliary (e.g., 'shall'). Morphological analysis maps deviations and inflected forms to the base form of a word. For example, through morphological analysis, 'assured' in the natural text is recognized and mapped to the ontology concept 'assure'. Dependency parsing includes labelling relations among words for assigning a syntactic structure to a sentence. The links of 'assured' include a noun chunk (nsubjpass) 'conductor' and AUX (auxpass) 'shall'. If we take 'perform', then it has a dobj (direct object) 'tasks', which in turn has a compound 'validation'. Dependency parsing contributes in the NLP-based approaches by generating phrasal/clausal tags for capturing more general text patterns, reducing enumerations, and supporting full sentence analysis for information extraction [31,33].

3.2 Ontology Development

For the development of an ontology, the words or phrases are defined with their corresponding categories or groups to prepare application-specific (semantics) features. The ontology helps in better interpretation of extracted information, particularly the names and assigned labels of all ontology concepts provide a basis for feature semantics. The relationships between super- and subconcepts not only provide support for hierarchical structuring, but also facilitate the pattern definition for rule-based matching. Figure 2 presents a partial view of the ontology developed inline with the space software engineering processes. It has three main categories in the schema: 'process', 'stakeholders', and 'work products'. The process super concept includes 'units of work' that are being performed throughout the project life cycle. Under the units of work, nine process phases (subcategories) are defined, such as 'requirements', 'architectural engineering', 'design and implementation', 'validation', and 'software delivery' and 'acceptance', etc. The process phases are decomposed into activities (subconcepts), which in-turn are decomposed into tasks related requirements. For example, the 'design and implementation' concept (process phase) is categorised into three subconcepts (activities): 'design software items', 'coding and testing', and 'integration'. The design software items subconcept is further categorised into different groups, such as 'develop design', 'interface design', etc.

The work product super concept is categorised into 'deliverable', 'outcome', and 'model' subconcepts. The deliverable represents a valuable output from a process that

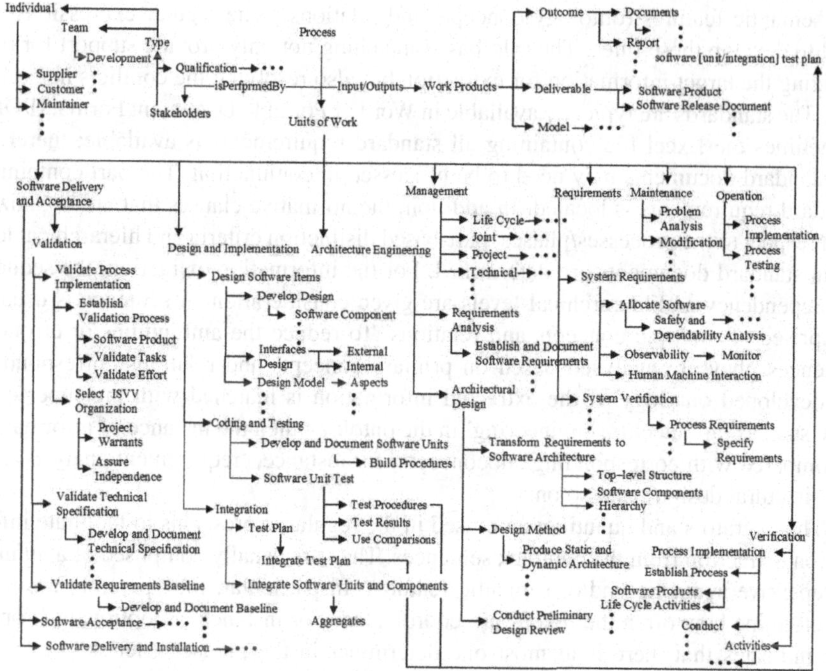

Fig. 2. Partial view of the developed ontology.

aggregates other documents or models to be delivered to a customer, or other stakeholders. For example, 'software product' and 'software release document' for installation of software in the target platform. Similarly, the outcome is further categorised into 'documents' and 'reports'. The non-hierarchical relationships between concepts are also identified and modelled to describe the semantic links between the concepts, such as units of work may require the work product(s) as input and produce them as output/outcome. For instance, the 'integrate test plan' and 'test procedures' sub-concepts are linked with 'software [unit/integration] test plan' (SUITP) subconcept under document. The model or artefact is also categorised into logical model, computational model, data model, functional model and failure model, etc. The role/stakeholder defines actor who is involved in the project and responsible for performing a defined work unit. The 'stakeholder' super concept is categorised into two groups: 'type' and 'qualification' subconcepts. In some standards skill term is used instead of qualification. The type subconcept is further subcategorised into 'individual role' (e.g., customer, supplier, designer, maintainer, etc.) and 'team role' for which many roles work together on the same phase/activity, such as design team, development team, etc. The qualification subconcept is categorised into three groups: 'certification' (e.g., degree in aerospace engineering), 'training' and 'work experience'.

3.3 Rule-Based Matching

Information Extraction. To carry out the information extraction and analysis, matching rules are defined based on the syntactic features (e.g., POS tags, phrasal tags, etc.)

and semantic features (ontology concepts and relations). The regular expressions are used to develop these rules. The rule-based matching not only provide support for recognizing the target information for extraction but also resolving the conflicts in extraction. The standards are typically available in Word or Portable Document Format (PDF). Sometimes the Excel file containing all standard requirements is available; therefore the standard documents may need to be processed in conjunction. The part containing standard requirements is located. In addition, the normative clauses that are organized with respect to the processes/phases, part-based distinction criteria and hierarchical levels in standard documents are determined. For the information extraction, the sequential dependency and hierarchical levels are given consideration. A sentence is usually comprised of multiple concepts and relations. To reduce the ambiguities or errors in sentences, they are analysed based on primary concepts and relations correspond to the developed ontology. If the extracted information is matched with the super concept, such as 'architecture engineering' in the ontology then the instance of information is compared with corresponding subconcepts, for instance, 'requirement analysis' and 'architectural design', and so on.

The operators and quantifiers are used in the regular expressions to facilitate information extraction from the complex sentences. They are usually composed of a number of repetitive syntactic and/or semantic features. In particular, the operators are used to determine how often the tokens are coordinated. For instance, an optional (?) operator indicates that there is at most one determiner in the phrase, asterisk (∗) operator indicates zero or more occurrences, negation (!) indicates not or no, and plus (+) operator shows that there must be at-least one determiner in the phrase. The deontic operator indicator is also used in the matching rules. It indicates the obligation, permission, or prohibition requirement types [3]. Let us consider a requirement, "the customer shall derive system requirements allocated to software from an analysis of the specific intended use of the system ... ". In this requirement, the text 'derive system requirements' corresponds to the 'system requirements' concept from the ontology and 'allocated to software' corresponds to the instance of concept 'allocate software'. The text 'shall' in requirement indicates the obligation.

The requirements sentences and associated information, for instance, the expected output (outcome), optional prerequisites (inputs), and identifiers are retrieved. The expected output of verification of software products requirement, such as "Software verification plan - verification process identification [DJF, SVerP; PDR]" is interpreted as the output is part of the DJF (Design Justification File), contained in the SVerP (Software Verification Plan) separated by comma and requested for the PDR (Preliminary Design Review) that is separated by semicolon. The standard documents may contain introductory material, scope, note, examples, and other supporting information, which are marked as a "NOTE" or "EXAMPLE" [7]. This information is only for providing instructions in understanding, for interpretation or clarification of the associated requirement or table, therefore this text is not considered as a requirement. The information is further followed in the normative and informative parts of the standard when necessary, for instance, to extract additional details of the prerequisites and work products (i.e., objectives, template and structure of the documents to be produced), roles responsible for them (e.g., customer, supplier), and applicability based on the certain tailoring criteria (criticality category).

Structuring Format. During the planning phase, we supported the transformation of extracted information into requirements, process models as well as compliance mappings for providing convincing justification about compliance. In particular, the rules and ontology (concepts and relations) are used for structuring and mapping extracted text to requirements and SPEM 2.0 compliant processes. The information extracted from the standard documents is connected according to the semantic features that are captured in the ontology and mapped into requirements i.e., guidance kinds *Practice* under the MethodContent/ContentPackages. The requirements statements in standard are not only mapped to the requirements, but also the tasks are created for them under ContentPackages of the process plugin. The clause, part-based distinction criteria and hierarchical levels in the standards are mapped as nested requirements (i.e., a requirement inside another requirement). This corresponds to the ontology concepts.

The extracted text concerning examples and note are mapped to the guidance kinds i.e., example and guideline in SPEM that are linked to the corresponding process task. The extracted information related to inputs or prerequisites are mapped to the work products and linked to the corresponding task using mandatoryInput or optionalInput relationship. Similarly, the expected outputs or deliverable are mapped to the work products as outcome, deliverable or model/artefact according to the subconcepts. They are linked with task using output relationship. Typically, a task is assigned to a specific role, who is responsible for the execution of work, if extracted text contained the stakeholder information then an individual role (e.g., supplier, requirements manager or designer) is created for the corresponding task. However, a group of roles (i.e., text corresponding to team concept) is mapped to RoleSet under content category in EPF Composer. A new task is created for each piece of information or standard requirement. The clause is mapped to a process component in SPEM corresponding to top-level concept, whereas hierarchical levels are mapped to phases and activities based on super- and subconcepts. The mapping is focused on the Work Breakdown Structure of processes in EPF Composer. The activities are subsequently populated by applying tasks from the method content.

3.4 Generation of Requirements, Process and Mappings

In this subsection, we present our algorithmic solution for the generation of standard requirements, SPEM 2.0 compliant processes, as well as compliance mappings in EPF Composer. The requirements and process elements are generated in a structured way. In particular, the specified mappings focus on the Method Content elements and Work Breakdown Structure of process model (decomposed linked elements, such as phases, activities etc.) in EPF Composer, as described in the previous subsection. It might be noted that the EPF Composer is based on the Unified Method Architecture (UMA), which defines library as a root container. Method plugins are divided into two primary categories: method content and processes. Algorithm 1 shows the skeleton of our transformation. It starts by creating a MethodLibrary in EPF Composer and then MethodPlugin; four plugins are generated. In the Requirements plugin, the ContentPackage is created for the main clause, i.e., top-level concept. Then, the contentElement guidance kinds Practice (used for specifying requirement) is generated under ContentPackage. The subPractices, i.e., nested requirements are generated for all those instances of

Algorithm 1. Generation of Requirements, Process and Mappings.

```
Input: Extracted and Structured Information of Standard Documents
Output: Information Generation in EPF Composer
while ExtractedInformation != null do
    if MethodLibrary = null then
        Create MethodLibrary()
        Create MethodPlugin()
        ...
        for Requirements MethodPlugin do
            Transform
            (ContentPackage ← MainClause = TopLevelConcept);
            for all RequirementConcepts in ExtractedInformation() do
                (Practice ← superConcept) & (subPractice ← subConcept);
            end for
        end for
        ...
        for Process MethodPlugin do
            Transform
            (ProcessComponent & ContentPackage ← MainClause
            = TopLevelConcept);
            for all Concepts in ExtractedInformation() do
                //breakdownElements Activity, Phase in Processes
                (Phase ← superConcept) & (Activity ← subConcept);
                //generating contentElements
                (Task ← LowLevelConcept);
            end for
            for Input & Prerequisite in ExtractedInformation() do
                (WorkProduct ← Input & Prerequisite);
                //Link WorkProduct to Task as optional/mandatoryInput
            end for
            for Stakeholder in ExtractedInformation() do
                (Role ← Stakeholder);
                //Link Role to Task as responsibleFor
            end for
        end for
        ...
        for MappingRequirements MethodPlugin do
            Practice.activityReferences;
            //Link Practice to BreakdownElements Activity or Phase
            subPractice.contentReferences; //Link subPractice to Task
        end for
        ...
    end if
end while
```

extracted information which corresponds to the subconcepts. In the Process plugin, the ContentPackage and ProcessComponent are generated for the main clauses. The contentElements, such as tasks, roles, work products are generated under ContentPackage.

A delivery process in EPF Composer is contained in the metamodel class ProcessComponent. It is automatically created each time a delivery process or capability pattern is created. After that, the BreakdownElements (Phases, Activities, and Milestones) are created for extractedInfomation matched to super- and subconcepts. For each activity, corresponding tasks are assigned as TaskDescriptors. The phases and activities are linked with the corresponding requirements (Practices) by using 'activityReferences', whereas the tasks are linked with subrequirements (subPractices) through 'contentReferences' in MappingRequirements plugin. After the generation, the engineers can extend by providing additional information to the process description like its version, authors or team profiles required for the execution of the process. They may also dedicate their time for the manual production of portions of expected outputs/deliverables that require human intervention.

3.5 Reverse Compliance of Process with Standard Documents

The reverse compliance of updated and extended process is required during the execution phase to detect inconsistencies, e.g., in work products. To carry out the reverse compliance, the EPF Composer model needs to be processed in conjunction with the extracted and structured information of standard documents. This not just gives the possibility to verify the reverse compliance of extended model, but also the previously existing process with the standard documents. It is noteworthy that the standards may not present all the information, such as used tools and roles. On the other hand, the customer or technical requirements and additional content elements are specified in process models. We focus on the comparative analysis for identifying gaps and measures for their resolution instead of the generation or replacement of extended or previously existing process models. In particular, the analysis is performed to identify the missing elements; for them, the potential candidates in process model are checked. The similarity assessment of missing and potential candidate elements is carried out based on their fields, such as name, description, roles and work products. The elements are added in an automatic manner after the approval from process engineer. Furthermore, the reverse compliance verification results include the list of elements containing sufficient and insufficient information (i.e., detected fallacies); appropriate recommendations to resolve the particular deviations are although provided, but they strictly require manual effort for resolving them [22].

4 Case Study

The ECSS Applicability Requirement Matrix (EARM) [5] is Microsoft Excel file exported from the ECSS DOORS database containing all requirements with their unique identifier, expected outputs, source reference, recommendations, permissions and informative text (notes) of the respective ECSS standard. The ECSS EARM file can be used for projects tailoring. A portion of the particular file that concerns ECSS-E-ST-40C standard is shown in Fig. 3. ECSS-E-ST-40C standard [7] is one of the series of European Cooperation for Space Standardization (ECSS) standards, which focuses on software that is the part of space system product. This standard covers all aspects of space software engineering processes including requirements, design, verification, validation, and operation, etc. The normative clause (clause 5) of this standard defines the requirements for engineering software for space systems, applicable to any space projects producing computer software. In this case study, we limit our attention to clause 5.6 *software validation process* of ECSS-E-ST-40C standard, which consists of three phases: validation process implementation, validation activities with respect to the technical specification, and validation activities with respect to the requirements baseline [7], which may contain various activities. Each phase or activity in turn consists of one or more tasks, and each task is associated with one or more outputs, which are given in the *expected output* section.

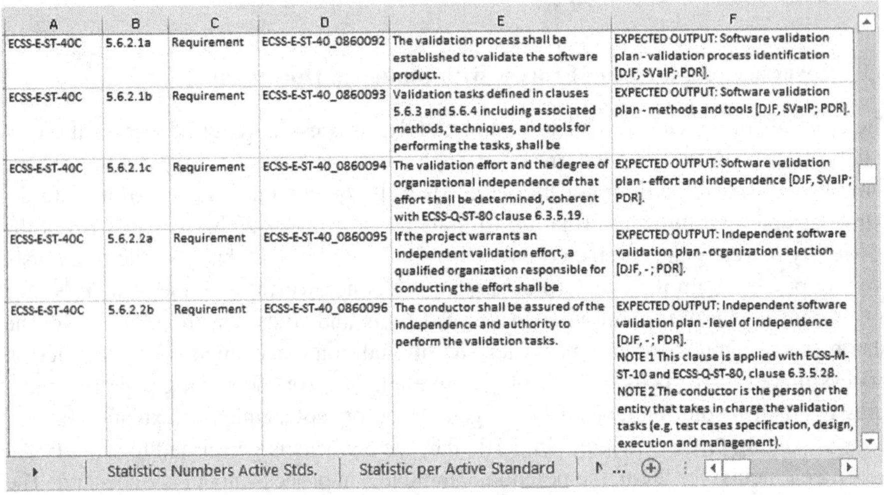

A	B	C	D	E	F
ECSS-E-ST-40C	5.6.2.1a	Requirement	ECSS-E-ST-40_0860092	The validation process shall be established to validate the software product.	EXPECTED OUTPUT: Software validation plan - validation process identification [DJF, SValP; PDR].
ECSS-E-ST-40C	5.6.2.1b	Requirement	ECSS-E-ST-40_0860093	Validation tasks defined in clauses 5.6.3 and 5.6.4 including associated methods, techniques, and tools for performing the tasks, shall be	EXPECTED OUTPUT: Software validation plan - methods and tools [DJF, SValP; PDR].
ECSS-E-ST-40C	5.6.2.1c	Requirement	ECSS-E-ST-40_0860094	The validation effort and the degree of organizational independence of that effort shall be determined, coherent with ECSS-Q-ST-80 clause 6.3.5.19.	EXPECTED OUTPUT: Software validation plan - effort and independence [DJF, SValP; PDR].
ECSS-E-ST-40C	5.6.2.2a	Requirement	ECSS-E-ST-40_0860095	If the project warrants an independent validation effort, a qualified organization responsible for conducting the effort shall be	EXPECTED OUTPUT: Independent software validation plan - organization selection [DJF, - ; PDR].
ECSS-E-ST-40C	5.6.2.2b	Requirement	ECSS-E-ST-40_0860096	The conductor shall be assured of the independence and authority to perform the validation tasks.	EXPECTED OUTPUT: Independent software validation plan - level of independence [DJF, - ; PDR]. NOTE 1 This clause is applied with ECSS-M-ST-10 and ECSS-Q-ST-80, clause 6.3.5.28. NOTE 2 The conductor is the person or the entity that takes in charge the validation tasks (e.g. test cases specification, design, execution and management).

Statistics Numbers Active Stds. | Statistic per Active Standard | ...

Fig. 3. Portion of the ECSS EARM.

The preprocessing of standard text is carried out (e.g., sentence splitting, tokenization, PoS tagging, morphology and dependency parsing) for identifying syntactic features as described in Sect. 3.1. In our previous work [25], the requirements related to the tasks are identified by a hierarchical number, made up of four distinct digits of the clause (e.g., 5.6.2.1), followed by a letter (e.g., a, b or c) to further distinguish them. For instance, a requirement "The conductor shall be assured of the independence and authority to perform the validation tasks" has an identifier "5.6.2.2b". In circumstances when several outputs are expected from a task, they are distinguished by a letter (e.g., *a or b*) and the destination file of the output is indicated in brackets. The expected output of '5.6.2.2b' requirement is 'Independent software validation plan - level of independence [DJF, –; PDR]', as shown in Fig. 3. This means that the output is the part of DJF, and requested for the review PDR that is separated by semicolon. In addition to the numbering for organisation into hierarchical levels, the subsection names are extracted from the word document for giving titles to the process component and phases. In this case, the clause 5.6 "Software validation process" is extracted from the standard document and mapped to the ConentPackage and ProcessComponent of EPF Composer. In this paper, the EARM file is used for extracting the target information elements, for example, requirement description, expected outputs, and notes are automatically retrieved. In case of ontology-based information extraction, the structuring can be supported without extracting numbering sequences and the need for locating names of process component and phases in the word version of standard can be excluded. However, there is still a need for locating text in the word version of ECSS-E-ST-40C standard for obtaining additional details, such as document content at milestone (e.g., PDR/SWRR). In this paper, the ontology and rule based matching is carried out for identification and extraction of target information elements, and their organisation into hierarchical levels as described in Sect. 3.3. By considering the ontology concepts and relations, the mapping of subconcepts supports in determining the top-level concepts and structuring in process component, phases and activities in an automated way. The names given to the process component, phases and activities are retrieved from the ontology.

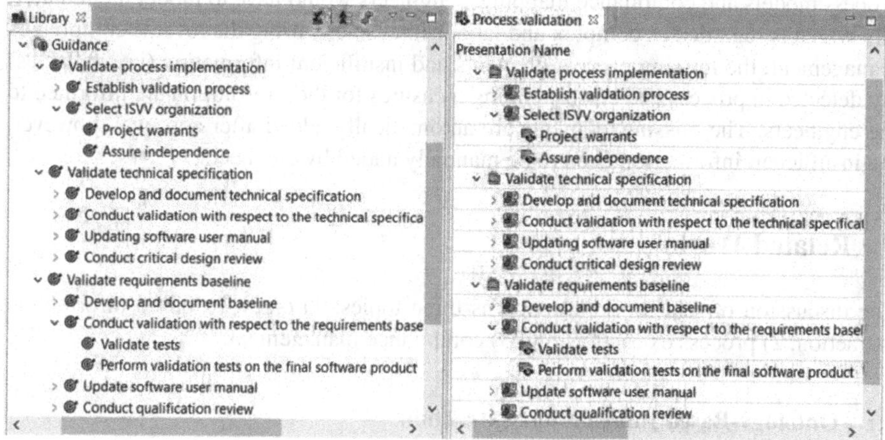

Fig. 4. Generated requirements and process model

The requirements, process model and compliance mappings are automatically generated in EPF Composer. In particular, a method library and four method plugins are generated: (1) CustomizedIcon plugin; (2) Requirements plugin; (3) Process plugin and (4) MappingRequirements plugin. Figure 4 shows the generated requirements and the process model compliant to the SPEM 2.0. The super concepts of ontology under the validation are generated as high-level requirements i.e., Practices in EPF Composer (e.g., Validate process implementation, Validate technical specification, and Validate requirements baseline), whereas the next hierarchy level under these subconcepts is regarded as subrequirements (e.g., Establish validation process, and Select ISVV organization). Finally, the requirements that have outputs and matched with low level concepts are created as subsubrequirements (e.g., Project warrants and Assure independence). In the Process plugin, the content elements are generated under ContentPackage, such as tasks (e.g., Project warrants and Validate tests), work products (e.g., Software validation plan as outcome, and Software user manual as deliverable), roles (e.g., conductor and supplier), and notes as guidelines. The work products, responsible roles and guidelines are linked to the corresponding task. The ProcessComponent i.e., DeliveryProcess is created for the standard clause (i.e., top-level concept) in EPF Composer. Similar to the nested requirements, a Work Breakdown Structure of a process is generated (i.e., phases and activities). For each activity corresponding tasks are associated as TaskDescriptors.

In the MappingRequirements plugin, high-level requirements are associated to phases, all subrequirements are associated to activities and subsubrequirements are associated to tasks. The content elements such as tasks, work products, roles, which are the part of process are linked to the corresponding standard requirements through contentReferences; whereas the phases and activities in process are linked to the requirements through activityReferences. The generated requirements and process can evolve during the life cycle. In the absence of ontology-based NLP approach for automatic extraction of information from standard documents and generation of requirements, process models and compliance mappings, engineers would have to model them manually which is regarded as complex and labour-intensive. During the reverse compliance management, the missing process elements and insufficient information (i.e., fallacies) are detected in process and corresponding measures for their resolution are informed to the engineers. The missing elements are automatically added after approval; however, the insufficient information need to be manually added by engineers.

5 Related Work

The discussion of related work concerns three topics: 1) ontology-based information extraction, 2) process extraction, and 3) compliance management.

5.1 Ontology-Based Information Extraction

Anquetil et al. [2] defined an ontology for software maintenance that is divided into five subontologies: 1) the concepts of software system ontology include software system, users, and documentation; 2) the computer science skills ontology contains concepts such as computer science technologies, modelling and programming languages; 3) the concepts of modification process ontology include modification request and maintenance activity; 4) the concepts of organisational unit and directive are part of the organisational structure ontology; and 5) the application domain ontology associates domain concepts with the tasks to be performed. Post-mortem analysis is applied for eliciting maintenance knowledge. However, the authors have not considered the information extraction using NLP. Zhou and El-Gohary [33] integrated domain-specific preprocessing techniques, a deeper domain ontology, and sequential dependency based/cascaded extraction methods for automatic extraction from building energy conservation codes. Similarly, the research in Xu and Cai [31] used the ontology and rule-based NLP to automate the interpretation of textual regulations on underground utility infrastructure. The authors incorporated both syntactic and semantic features in the extraction rules.

The ontology developed in this paper concerns space system software engineering processes and is in accordance with the ECSS-E-ST-40C standard. Similar to the works by Zhou and El-Gohary [33] and Xu and Cai [31], in this paper, the ontology based information extraction is carried out.

5.2 Process Extraction

The research in Friedrich et al. [8] focused on the generation of BPMN process model from natural language text. In particular, they utilised existing syntax parsing and semantic analysis mechanisms in combination with anaphora resolution. The sound and complete models, often with elements such as lanes or data sources are generated. van der Aa et al. [1] extracted declarative process models from textual descriptions. The authors extended existing NLP techniques for identifying activities and their inter-relations from textual constraint descriptions. Based on the extracted components, the declarative constraints are generated that aims at capturing the logic defined in the textual description. Yanuarifiani et al. [32] proposed a methodology for mapping the requirements ontology to BPMN elements and generating the BPMN XML file. The requirements ontology consists of three classes: action, position and object. Qian et al. [27] proposed a hierarchical neural network to extract process models from process texts. They focused on the coarse-to-fine grained learning mechanism, training multi-grained tasks in coarse-to-fine grained order, to apply the high-level knowledge for the low-level tasks. The published studies primiarily focused on the extraction from textual descriptions and generation of BPMN model elements. Both SPEM and BPMN are OMG specifications. SPEM 2.0 provides additional information structures needed for the processes modelled with UML 2.0 activities or BPMN to describe an actual development process [26]. We targeted the ontology-based NLP of standard documents for automatic generation of requirements, a broad set of SPEM-based process elements including tasks, roles, work products, phases and activities, as well as compliance mappings. The requirements, process and mappings are generated in EPF Composer.

5.3 Compliance Management

Sànchez-Ferreres et al. [29] used existing NLP techniques for aligning a textual description and a process model. They converted both inputs (text and BPMN) into an identical representation of feature vectors and compared them by means of standard distance metrics. Winter et al. [30] also exploited the NLP to enable assessment of compliance between a set of paragraphs from a regulatory document and BPMN models. Delicado et al. [4] introduced an online platform called NLP4BPM that converts a textual description into a BPMN model and vice versa. The platform also computes the alignment between two BPMN models and a textual description with a BPMN model. The presented interface adapted or modified techniques appeared in the last years [8,20,29].

Governatori et al. [11] exploited the SemanticWeb technologies and languages, such as LegalRuleML, to manually model a legal document. The authors annotated the representation of norms and the BPMN process tasks with the LegalRuleML semantic model to perform compliance checking using Regorous–a business process regulatory compliance checker. Ardila et al. [3] presented the transformation of SPEM 2.0-compatible requirements and process models into input models of Regorous to perform compliance checking. However, not only standards information is manually extracted but also requirements and process models are manually modelled in EPF Composer. Jiang et al. [19] proposed a consistency and compliance checker framework that analyses the consistency of a set of regulations itself and also verifies the process compliance with a set of interrelated regulations. However, the translation of natural language regulations into a formal model is manually performed. In this paper, we used the rules in which both syntactic and semantic features are encoded for information extraction from standard documents. The extracted information is stored and used for comparison with the process model; specifically, for identifying gaps and their corresponding resolution measures during reverse compliance management.

6 Conclusion and Future Work

This paper leverages the ontology-based NLP for process compliance management with standard documents. An ontology is developed to facilitate the better interpretation of software system engineering processes. Rules are defined using regular expressions for information extraction in which both syntactic features captured using NLP tasks (POS tags, phrasal tags, etc.) and semantic features (ontology concepts and relations) are encoded. The extracted information such as requirements are mapped to their semantics via ontology. The ontology not just supports the information extraction, but also its structuring for which a broad set of SPEM-based process elements are considered, such as tasks, roles, work products and phases. At the planning phase, we supported the generation of requirements, processes and mappings in EPF Composer. However, to carry out the reverse compliance management of pre-existing or extended process model, the gaps with extracted information are detected and potential resolution measures are informed; missing elements are added after the approval from process engineer. The applicability of the proposed approach is demonstrated for the ECSS-E-ST-40C compliant space system software engineering standard.

This work is limited to the extraction and compliance management with software engineering processes embedded in a space standard. However, we need to conduct further detailed evaluations for stabilisation of information extraction from other standards. In the future, we also aim to consider the extraction of process models from digital twins [15,23]. Furthermore, we plan to leverage the NLP for transforming assurance (safety and security) cases [16,24] from free text or tabular to the graphical Goal Structuring Notation (GSN) format. Another direction for future work is to use the NLP for assessment and change management of process- and product-based assurance argument fragments.

Acknowledgment. This work is partially supported by FiC project funded by SSF (Swedish Foundation for Strategic Research). The first author has also participated during the tenure of an ERCIM "Alain Bensoussan" Fellowship Programme.

References

1. Van der Aa, H., Ciccio, C.D., Leopold, H., Reijers, H.A.: Extracting declarative process models from natural language. In: 31st International Conference on Advanced Information Systems Engineering, CAiSE 2019, pp. 365–382. Rome, Italy (2019). https://doi.org/10.1007/978-3-030-21290-2_23
2. Anquetil, N., De Oliveira, K.M., De Sousa, K.D., Dias, M.G.B.: Software maintenance seen as a knowledge management issue. Inf. Softw. Technol. **49**(5), 515–529 (2007). https://doi.org/10.1016/j.infsof.2006.07.007
3. Ardila, J.P.C., Gallina, B., Muram, F.U.: Transforming SPEM 2.0-compatible process models into models checkable for compliance. In: International Conference on Software Process Improvement and Capability Determination, SPICE 2018, Tessaloniki, Greece, pp. 233–247 (2018). https://doi.org/10.1007/978-3-030-00623-5_16
4. Delicado, L., Sànchez-Ferreres, J., Carmona, J., Padró, L.: NLP4BPM - natural language processing tools for business process management. In: 15th International Conference on Business Process Management, BPM 2017 Demo Track, Barcelona, Spain (2017)
5. ECSS: European Cooperation for Space Standardization, ECSS Applicability Requirement Matrix (EARM) (2019). https://ecss.nl/standards/downloads/earm/
6. European Commitee for Electrotechnical Standardization (CENELEC): EN 50126: Railway applications - The specification and demonstration of Reliability, Availability, Maintainability and Safety (RAMS), Part 1 Basic requirements and generic process (1999)
7. European Cooperation for Space Standardization (ECSS): ECSS-EST-40C, Space Engineering Software (2009). http://wwwis.win.tue.nl/2R690/doc/ECSS-E-ST-40C(6March2009).pdf
8. Friedrich, F., Mendling, J., Puhlmann, F.: Process model generation from natural language text. In: 23rd International Conference on Advanced Information Systems Engineering, CAiSE 2011, pp. 482–496. London, UK (2011). https://doi.org/10.1007/978-3-642-21640-4_36
9. Gašević, D., Kaviani, N., Milanović, M.: Ontologies and Software Engineering. In: Staab, S., Studer, R. (eds.) Handbook on Ontologies. IHIS, pp. 593–615. Springer, Heidelberg (2009). https://doi.org/10.1007/978-3-540-92673-3_27
10. Governatori, G.: Representing business contracts in RuleML. Int. J. Coop. Inf. Syst. **14**(2–3), 181–216 (2005). https://doi.org/10.1142/S0218843005001092
11. Governatori, G., Hashmi, M., Lam, H., Villata, S., Palmirani, M.: Semantic business process regulatory compliance checking using legalruleml. In: Knowledge Engineering and Knowledge Management - 20th International Conference, EKAW 2016, vol. 10024, pp. 746–761. Bologna, Italy (2016). https://doi.org/10.1007/978-3-319-49004-5_48
12. International Organization for Standardization (ISO): ISO 26262: 2018-Road vehicles-Functional safety. International Standard (2018)
13. Javed, M.A., Gallina, B.: Safety-oriented process line engineering via seamless integration between EPF composer and BVR tool. In: 22nd International Systems and Software Product Line Conference - Volume 2, SPLC 2018, pp. 23–28. Gothenburg, Sweden (2018). https://doi.org/10.1145/3236405.3236406
14. Javed, M.A., Gallina, B., Carlsson, A.: Towards variant management and change impact analysis in safety-oriented process-product lines. In: 34th ACM/SIGAPP Symposium on Applied Computing, SAC 2019, pp. 2372–2375. Limassol, Cyprus (2019). https://doi.org/10.1145/3297280.3297634
15. Javed, M.A., Muram, F.U., Fattouh, A., Punnekkat, S.: Enforcing geofences for managing automated transportation risks in production sites. In: Dependable Computing - EDCC 2020 Workshops - AI4RAILS, DREAMS, DSOGRI, SERENE 2020, Munich, Germany. Communications in Computer and Information Science, vol. 1279, pp. 113–126 (2020). https://doi.org/10.1007/978-3-030-58462-7_10

16. Javed, M.A., Muram, F.U., Hansson, H., Punnekkat, S., Thane, H.: Towards dynamic safety assurance for industry 4.0. J. Syst. Archit. **114**, 101914 (2021). https://doi.org/10.1016/j.sysarc.2020.101914
17. Javed, M.A., Muram, F.U., Zdun, U.: On-demand automated traceability maintenance and evolution. In: 17th International Conference on New Opportunities for Software Reuse, ICSR 2018, vol. 10826, pp. 111–120. Madrid, Spain (2018). https://doi.org/10.1007/978-3-319-90421-4_7
18. Javed, M.A., Zdun, U.: The supportive effect of traceability links in change impact analysis for evolving architectures – two controlled experiments. In: Schaefer, I., Stamelos, I. (eds.) ICSR 2015. LNCS, vol. 8919, pp. 139–155. Springer, Cham (2014). https://doi.org/10.1007/978-3-319-14130-5_10
19. Jiang, J., Aldewereld, H., Dignum, V., Wang, S., Baida, Z.: Regulatory compliance of business processes. AI Soc. **30**(3), 393–402 (2014). https://doi.org/10.1007/s00146-014-0536-9
20. Leopold, H., Mendling, J., Polyvyanyy, A.: Supporting process model validation through natural language generation. IEEE Trans. Softw. Eng. **40**(8), 818–840 (2014)
21. Muram, F.U., Gallina, B., Kanwal, S.: A tool-supported model-based method for facilitating the EN50129-compliant safety approval process. In: Reliability, Safety, and Security of Railway Systems. Modelling, Analysis, Verification, and Certification (RSSRail) - Third International Conference, pp. 125–141. Lille, France (2019). https://doi.org/10.1007/978-3-030-18744-6_8
22. Muram, F.U., Gallina, B., Rodriguez, L.G.: Preventing omission of key evidence fallacy in process-based argumentations. In: 11th International Conference on the Quality of Information and Communications Technology (QUATIC), Coimbra, Portugal, pp. 65–73 (2018). https://doi.org/10.1109/QUATIC.2018.00019
23. Muram, F.U., Javed, M.A.: Drone-based risk management of autonomous systems using contracts and blockchain. In: 28th IEEE International Conference on Software Analysis, Evolution and Reengineering, SANER 2021, Honolulu, HI, USA, pp. 679–688. IEEE (2021). https://doi.org/10.1109/SANER50967.2021.00086
24. Muram, F.U., Javed, M.A., Hansson, H., Punnekkat, S.: Dynamic reconfiguration of safety-critical production systems. In: 25th IEEE Pacific Rim International Symposium on Dependable Computing, PRDC 2020, pp. 120–129. Perth, Australia (2020). https://doi.org/10.1109/PRDC50213.2020.00023
25. Muram, F.U., Javed, M.A., Kanwal, S.: Facilitating the compliance of process models with critical system engineering standards using natural language processing. In: 16th International Conference on Evaluation of Novel Approaches to Software Engineering, ENASE 2021, Online Streaming, pp. 306–313 (2021). https://doi.org/10.5220/0010455903060313
26. Object Management Group (OMG): Software & Systems Process Engineering Metamodel Specification (SPEM), Version 2.0 (2008). http://www.omg.org/spec/SPEM/2.0/
27. Qian, C., et al.: An approach for process model extraction by multi-grained text classification. In: 32nd International Conference on Advanced Information Systems Engineering, CAiSE 2020, pp. 268–282. Grenoble, France (2020). https://doi.org/10.1007/978-3-030-49435-3_17
28. Radio Technical Commission for Aeronautics (RTCA): DO-178C: Software Considerations in Airborne Systems and Equipment Certification, RTCA (European Organisation for Civil Aviation Equipment (EUROCAE) ED-12C) (2011)
29. Sànchez-Ferreres, J., Carmona, J., Padró, L.: Aligning textual and graphical descriptions of processes through ILP techniques. In: 29th International Conference on Advanced Information Systems Engineering, CAiSE 2017, pp. 413–427. Essen, Germany (2017). https://doi.org/10.1007/978-3-319-59536-8_26

30. Winter, K., van der Aa, H., Rinderle-Ma, S., Weidlich, M.: Assessing the compliance of business process models with regulatory documents. In: 39th International Conference on Conceptual Modeling, ER 2020, vol. 12400, pp. 189–203. Vienna, Austria (2020). https://doi.org/10.1007/978-3-030-62522-1_14
31. Xu, X., Cai, H.: Ontology and rule-based natural language processing approach for interpreting textual regulations on underground utility infrastructure. Adv. Eng. Inform. **48**, 101288 (2021). https://doi.org/10.1016/j.aei.2021.101288
32. Yanuarifiani, A.P., Chua, F., Chan, G.: Automating business process model generation from ontology-based requirements. In: 8th International Conference on Software and Computer Applications, ICSCA 2019, pp. 205–209. Penang, Malaysia (2019). https://doi.org/10.1145/3316615.3316683
33. Zhou, P., El-Gohary, N.: Ontology-based automated information extraction from building energy conservation codes. Autom. Constr. **74**, 103–117 (2017). https://doi.org/10.1016/j.autcon.2016.09.004

UI-Test: A Model-Based Framework for Visual UI Testing– Qualitative and Quantitative Evaluation

Bryan Alba(✉), Maria Fernanda Granda(✉), and Otto Parra(✉)

Computer Science Department, Universidad de Cuenca, Av. 12 de Abril s/n, Cuenca, Ecuador
{bryan.albas,fernanda.granda,otto.parra}@ucuenca.edu.ec

Abstract. During the testing stage in the software development life cycle, developers can take advantage of combining the requirements specification with the testing specification. This will allow the specification of the tests to require less manual effort, since, they can be defined or generated automatically from the requirements specification. The requirements specification will thus be based on a more structured language, gaining in quality and reducing ambiguity, inconsistency, and inaccuracy. In this research work, the UI-Test model-based methodological framework and its tool support are proposed. Both of these can generate evidence based on the specification of agile user stories that are used in the validation of the functional requirements that must be included in the final version of the user interfaces of the developed software. Our proposal makes use of two model transformations to obtain the test scripts from user stories that will be applied in the process using SikuliX for automated visual UI testing. The results of the empirical evaluation of the effectiveness and user experience of the framework and its tool support suggest that the UI-Test tool can benefit testers by confirming that the actions proposed in the user stories can be run on the UIs.

Keywords: UI-Test · Visual UI testing · User stories · Test scripts · Model-based testing · Testing framework

1 Introduction

In the field of Software Engineering, agile software development methodologies have gained momentum because of their benefits to software developers in the software development life cycle (SDLC) [1]. In this context, organizations are increasingly deploying agile methodologies in their software development projects in order to efficiently produce higher quality software in a shorter period of time. This methodology enables a software developer to be more flexible and responsive to changing environments and customer demands. However, it has been pointed out that agile methods largely ignore issues of designing the user interface (UI). To some extent this is understandable: agile processes are highly iterative and incremental, while traditional approaches to user interface design have been big-bang with heavy reliance on upfront design [2].

R. Ali et al. (Eds.): ENASE 2021, CCIS 1556, pp. 328–355, 2022.
https://doi.org/10.1007/978-3-030-96648-5_15

The Agile Model-Driven Development (AMDD) method, which combine Model-driven Development (MDD) and Agile Development [3] has many benefits for developing suitable solutions by means of a better understanding of the requirements [4]. In the agile method there is no requirements freezing, they are obtained using a face-to-face conversation with the stakeholders, and the solutions change over time based on the requirements [5]. In this context, developers have a problem: how to test the software to seek evidence that the requirements specified by the stakeholders are satisfied by the software. Our proposal considers visual testing for both user interface types: Graphical User Interface (GUI) and Web User Interfaces (WUI) and it checks if the requirements previously defined in the software development life cycle have been included in the implemented software product. However, designing and executing test cases is very time-consuming and error-prone when done manually and frequent changes in the requirements reduce the reusability of these manually written test cases.

In the software development life cycle, there are several available techniques for requirements testing when the software engineers require them. In our research work, we use the requirements specification obtained from the stakeholders in order to describe user stories [2]. We then derive a task-based test model using ConcurTaskTree (CTT) [6] by applying a parsing process to the user stories to describe test scenarios with abstract test cases. The next step generates concrete test cases by means of a semiautomatic process in test scenarios. At this point the test cases are transformed into test script by applying model transformations and SikuliX language[1], which is a standardized test language for UI-based testing.

Two research approaches were used to evaluate the proposed UI-Test tool: a qualitative evaluation to measure the user experience quality of the proposal with seventeen subjects, and a quantitative evaluation to measure the effectiveness of the test cases generated by the tool.

The contributions of this paper are: (1) an extension of the UI-Test, a model-based testing framework described in [7] and its tool support, (2) an empirical evaluation of the framework which was applied in order to assess effectiveness and user experience in two scenarios: using (i) GUI and (ii) WUI, described in this paper.

The rest of this paper is structured in 5 sections. Section 2 presents the background of related topics and also introduces related works. Section 3 includes the description of the UI-Test framework and the tool support implemented to test the proposed approach. In Sects. 4 and 5, the empirical evaluations are described. Section 6 contains a discussion of the results. Section 7 summarizes the threats to validity and Sect. 8 includes our conclusions and our plans for future work.

2 Background and Related Work

Within Agile methods, user stories are mostly used as primary requirements artefacts and units of functionality of a software project [8]. Typically, a user story includes three components (Fig. 1): (1) a short description of the user story used for planning (Who?), (2) conversations about the user story to discover the details (What?), and (3) acceptance criteria (Why?) [6].

[1] http://sikulix.com/.

Component	Describes
As a [user/stakeholder]	Who?
I want to [requirement]	What?
So that [motivation]	Why?

Fig. 1. A user story template.

ConcurTaskTree belongs to the family of hierarchical task analysis notations, the most common approach to task analysis [6]. Using ConcurTaskTree as the task modelling notation has some advantages [10]: (i) the models are at a level of abstraction familiar to user interface designers/developers; (ii) testing will follow the anticipated use of the system; and, (iii) the cost incurred in developing the oracle is much reduced.

UIs are composed of graphical objects called widgets, such as buttons, text fields, menus, etc. Users interact with these widgets (e.g. press a button) to produce an action that modifies the state of the system [8]. This type of user interface is used in this research work for UI testing. Regarding the types of faults that can occur in an UI, we consider the classification presented by Lliet Lelli et al. [9], which considers two groups: user interface faults and user interaction faults.

According to the related literature, there are three generations of automated GUI-testing [9]: the first generation relies on GUI coordinates but is not used in practice due to unfeasible maintenance costs caused by fragility to GUI change. Second generation tools instead operate against the system's GUI architecture, libraries or application programming interfaces. Whilst this approach is successfully used in practice, it does not verify the GUI's appearance and it is restricted to specific GUI technologies, programming languages and platforms. The third generation, referred to as Visual GUI Testing (VGT), is an emerging technique in industrial practice with properties that mitigate the challenges experienced with previous techniques.

Visual UI Testing is an emerging technique in industrial practice and uses tools with image recognition capabilities to interact with the bitmap layer of a system, i.e. what is shown to the user on the computer monitor. SikuliX, JAutomate, etc. are some examples of tools that apply this type of testing. In this research work we use SikuliX [7], a standardized test language for visual UI-based testing (VGT) on GUI and WUIs. Alégroth et al. [10], in their study related with challenges, problems and limitations (CPL) of VGT in practice, their main conclusion is still that VGT is a valuable and cost effective technique with equal or even better defect-finding ability than manual testing.

In the following paragraphs, we describe several works reported by the related literature in the automated testing field.

In the context of the generation of test cases from agile user stories, Rane [11] developed a tool to derive test cases from natural language requirements automatically by creating UML activity diagrams. However, their work requires the Test Scenario Description and Dictionary to execute the test case generation process. The authors developed a tool that uses NLP (natural language processing) techniques to generate functional test cases from the free-form test scenario description automatically.

Elghondakly et al. [12] proposed a requirement based testing approach for automated test generation for Waterfall and Agile models. This proposed system parses functional and non-functional requirements to generate test paths and test cases. The paper proposes the generation of test cases from Agile user stories but does not discuss any implementation aspects such as the techniques for parsing, or the format of the user stories that are parsed. This implementation does not follow a model-based approach.

Finsterwalder, M. [13], reports how he uses automated acceptance tests for interactive graphical applications. However, according to the author, it is difficult to automate tests that involve GUI intensive interactions. To test the application in its entirety, tests should actually exercise the GUI of the application and verify that the results are correct. In extreme programming (XP), the customer writes down small user stories to capture the requirements and specifies acceptance tests. These tests are implemented and run frequently during the development process.

Tao, C. et al. [14] propose a novel approach to mobile application testing based on natural language scripting. A Java-based test script generation approach is developed to support executable test script generation based on the given natural language-based mobile app test operation script. According to the authors, a unified automation infrastructure is not offered with the existing test tools. In order to deal with the massive multiple mobile test running, there is a lack of well-defined mobile test scripting methods, so that test automation central control is needed to support behaviour-based testing or scenario-based testing at multiple levels.

Ramler et al. [15], describe the introduction of Model-based Testing (MBT) for automated GUI testing in three industry projects from different companies. Each of the projects already had automated tests for the GUI but they were considered insufficient to cover the huge number of possible scenarios in which a user can interact with the system under test (SUT). MBT was introduced to complement the existing tests and to increase the coverage with end-to-end testing via the GUI.

Kamal [16] presents a test-case generation model to build a testing suite for webpages using their HTML file. The proposed model has two branches. The first one focuses on generating test cases for each web-element individually based on its type. The other branch focuses on generating test cases based on different paths between web-elements in the same webpage.

Coppola et al. [17] provide a detailed and fine-grained taxonomy of the modifications performed on the production code of Android apps, which may trigger the necessity for maintenance of test suites. The authors believe that the fragility issue – a problem that has already been explored extensively in the field of web applications – can seriously hinder large-scale use of automated testing for Android apps.

Silva et al. [18] describe an effort to develop tool support enabling the use of task models as oracles for model-based testing of user interfaces. The subject of interest in their research is the test oracle that will be used as a measure of the implementation quality.

Our contribution is a model-based framework to apply visual UI testing with the aim of checking if all the user story requirements of a software system are included in the final version (UI) of the developed software product. For this we use a task model, a parsing process and transformations using Java and SikuliX language.

Table 1 Summarizes the related work included in this section.

Table 1. The related work: a summary

Paper	Proposal	Pros	Cons
[11]	Generation of test cases from user stories	Automation by creating UML activity diagrams	Requires the dictionary and description of the test scenario to run the process
[12]	Requirements-based approach to automated test generation for waterfall and agile models. Generation of test cases from user stories	This proposed system analyses the functional and non-functional requirements to generate test routes and test cases	Does not discuss any implementation aspects such as analysis techniques or the format of the user stories being analysed. Does not follow a model-based approach
[13]	Automated acceptance testing for interactive graphics applications	Requirements capture through user stories. Acceptance tests are specified. The client gains confidence in the functionality of the developed application	To fully test the application, the tests should exercise the application GUI and verify that the results are correct
[14]	Natural language scripting based mobile app testing.	Executable tests based on the natural language based mobile app test operation script	There is a lack of a well-defined mobile test script method to deal with the mass execution of multiple mobile tests
[15]	Test-Based Models (MBT) for Automated GUIs	MBT was introduced to supplement existing testing and to increase coverage with end-to-end testing via the GUI	Automated tests are considered insufficient to cover the large number of possible scenarios
[17]	Check the status of Android Widget-based GUI Testing considering fragility of test suites	The authors aim at validating and extending the taxonomy through the application of more rigorous procedures based on grounded theory	Automated GUI testing comes with a high cost in term of deployment and maintenance, and the rapid evolution of Android GUIs may exacerbate those costs for developers
[18]	Develop tool support enabling the use of task models as oracles for model-based testing of user interfaces	They have shown in their research work that task models, despite limitations, can be used to generate oracles economically in an interactive systems model based testing context	They have found limitations to generate the test oracles directly from task models

3 UI-Test Framework: Our Proposal and Tool Support

This section describes the proposed approach (Fig. 2) in two stages: test derivation and visual testing. To demonstrate and discuss the suitability of the approach, we applied it on the Microsoft Notepad application. This application was selected because this is a common and well-known application for readers, which facilitates the explanation of the approach. We implemented a tool support using the Eclipse[2] platform and Java programming language. This tool support can be used in three platforms: Microsoft Windows, Linux, MacOS because the Java Virtual machine is available in each platform.

3.1 Test Derivation

In this first test derivation stage, we defined six steps:

Step 1. We need the requirements specification obtained from the stakeholders by some method (e.g., requirements specification using natural language, using case analysis, using the Quality Attribute Workshop – QAW, or global analysis) [19]. The modeller/requirements engineer then writes the user stories based on the requirements. In this case, we consider only the functional requirements because this type of requirement mainly involves actions on UI.

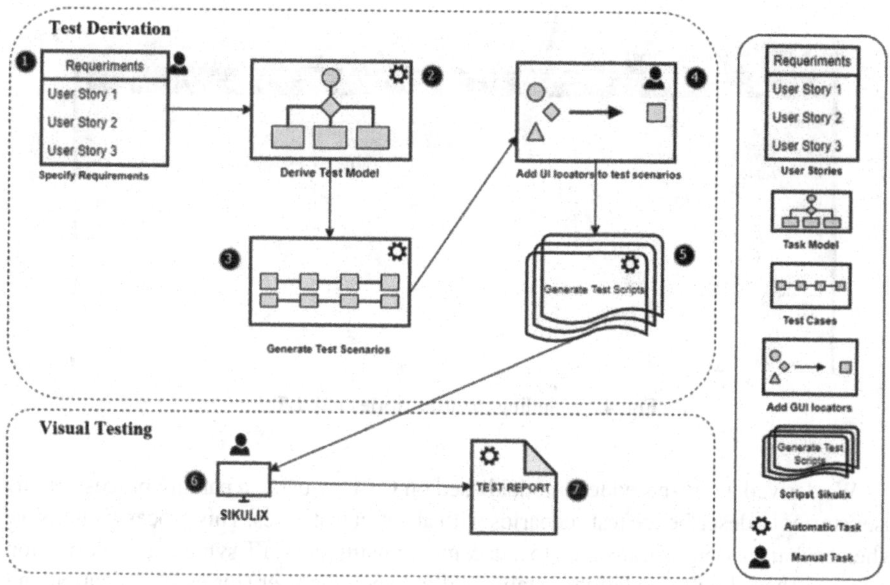

Fig. 2. The approach proposed.

[2] www.eclipse.org.

User stories follow a standard predefined format [8] to capture three aspects of a requirement: (1) who wants the functionality; and (2) what functionality the end users or stakeholders want the system to provide. The user stories are written according to the template (Fig. 1) and then they are stored in a text file. An excerpt of the user stories defined for Notepad application is shown in Fig. 3.

In this version of the tool support, the user stories are included in UI-Test by "copy and paste". In this context, we check all user stories in order to confirm that each user story is written according to the aforementioned template (Fig. 4).

Step 2. In the second step, we use the previously inserted user stories in the tool support as a basis for the test model derivation (i.e. task model). As mentioned in the previous section, we use CTT to represent the task model by means of an XML file to describe the tasks included in the model following the syntax defined in CTT. Figure 5 shows an excerpt from a CTT file describing a task.

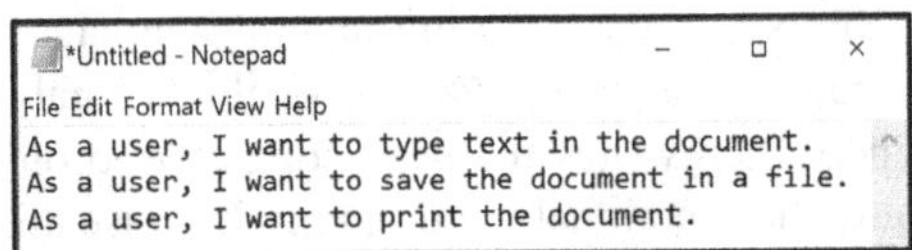

Fig. 3. An excerpt of the user stories defined in Notepad.

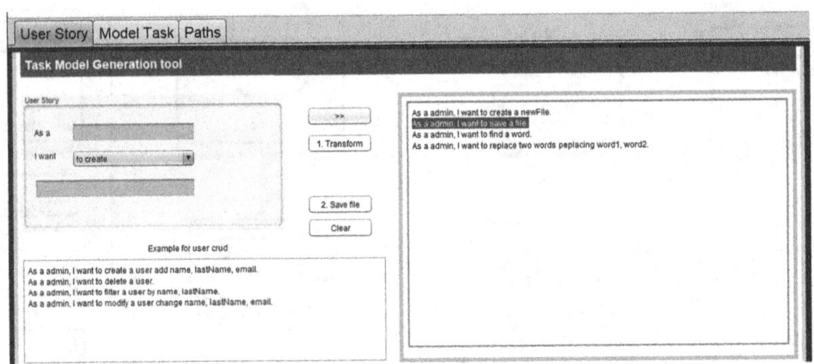

Fig. 4. Including the user stories in UI-Test.

We derived a task-based test model based on CTT by using a parsing process on the user stories to describe the test scenarios with abstract test cases. This process is iterative when each user story is translated to a task model using the CTT syntax. This derivation process is based on the relations established between the user stories specification and the syntax of the task model. It is possible to associate the user story concepts with the task model syntax and some of the keywords made available by an application (e.g. Notepad, Calculator, etc.). These keywords are associated with the main menu and its options in an application (e.g. File, Edit, Format, etc.) and these keywords describe the

```xml
<?xml version="1.0" encoding="UTF-8" standalone="no"?>
<TaskModel xmlns="http://giove.isti.cnr.it/ctt" xmlns:coop="http://giove.isti.cnr.it/cttcoop" NameTaskModelID="root">
<Task Category="abstraction" Frequency=" " Identifier="root" Iterative="false" Optional="false" PartOfCooperation="false">
<Name>name</Name>
<Type>None</Type>
<SubTask>
<Task Category="abstraction" Frequency=" " Identifier="createnewFile." Iterative="false" Optional="false" PartOfCooperation="false">
<Name>name</Name>
<TemporalOperator name="SequentialEnablingInfo"/>
<Parent name="root"/>
<SiblingRight name="savefile."/>
<SubTask>
<Task Category="interaction" Frequency=" " Identifier="selectcreatenewFile." Iterative="false" Optional="false" PartOfCooperation="false">
<Name>name</Name>
<TemporalOperator name="SequentialEnablingInfo"/>
<Parent name="createnewFile."/>
<SiblingRight name="processcreatenewFile."/>
</Task>
```

Fig. 5. An extract from a CTT tree describing a task.

steps required to do an action. For instance, the sequence of commands "Format" and "Font" permits changes to the text font, font style and size of the text in a document using a text editor.

The result obtained in this step obtains a tree containing the information of each node of the task model. Each node of the tree is defined by three fields: (a) the task to be done ("Save a Document"); (b) if each node has children, the reference to each child; (c) the relationship with other nodes of the tree. The relationships are created by default as interleaving (|||), since tasks can be performed in any order. However, the tester can change them by editing the CTT model.

Step 3. Test scenarios are obtained in this step, which is based on the definition of different paths obtained as a result of applying two basic operations in the CTT tree: enumerating (to traverse the tree) and searching (to find a specific node).

In order to generate test scenarios, we need to traverse the tree. In the example (see Fig. 6) on Notepad, a first scenario can be obtained when the tree is traversed from the root node (Managing Document in Notepad), and then the left node is visited (Open Document). Other test scenarios can be obtained when we start in the root node and then visit the central node (Edit Document). Considering this last node as the root of the subtree, then the next node to visit is "Save Document", the next is "File name:" and the last node is "Save". In this traverse, we need to consider the relationship between nodes in order to define the next node to visit. The relationship is shown by the temporal operations defined in the ConcurTaskTree [20].

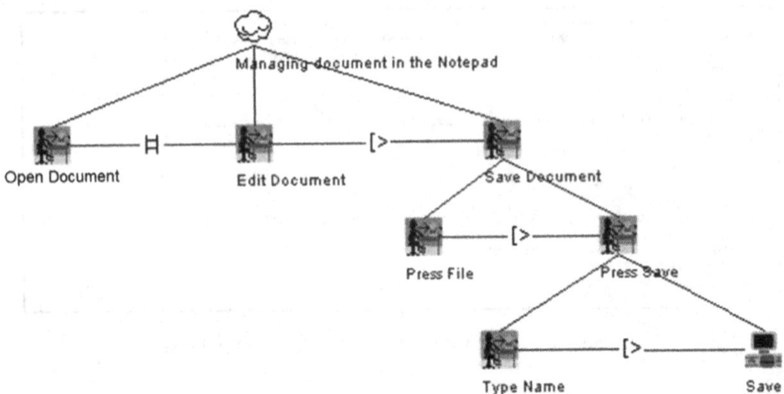

Fig. 6. An extract of CTT tree describing a task of the Notepad example.

Step 4. Now, it is required to complete the test scripts generated in the previous step by using locators for selecting the target widgets. In this case, the locators are referred to as (i) path to an image file or (ii) just plain text (e.g., file name in Fig. 7, right side), which can be used as a parameter of the widget (UI element image).

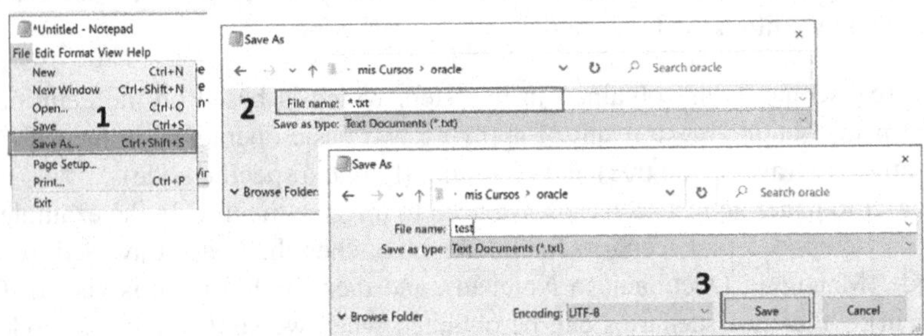

Fig. 7. Sequence of steps in Notepad to save a document

In this work we include widgets for input data or to do an action, except widgets such as the scroll bar and sliders. Table 2 gives some examples of widgets used in Windows/Web applications.

An application typically contains some elements (widgets) such as buttons, text fields, links, etc. in its user interface, which allow the user to perform some previously defined action in the application, a type of interaction between the user and the application. Each of these elements has a specific locator, which identifies it from other elements in the UI. During visual UI testing, these elements are used to locate a certain position defined by the test case. In order to automate the test script generation and execution, it is necessary to identify these locators to include respective UI elements of the user interface during the execution of the test. The value of the required variables must be entered by the tester (e.g. filename of a file, text to search, etc.) using the tool support (see Fig. 8).

Table 2. Examples of widgets

GUI widget	Action	WUI widget	Action
Save	Save a file/image	☰	Activate a menu
test	Enter a text	↻	Reload a web page
☐ Unpublished work · Mendeley Web cat	Checkbox	Copy link	A hyperlink/button

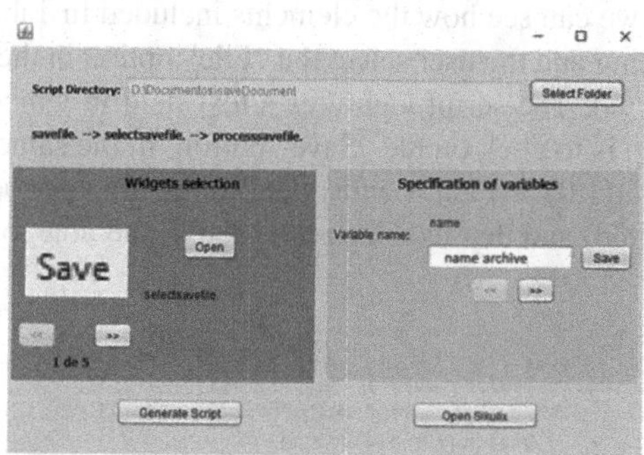

Fig. 8. Interface for specifying variables in the tool.

Step 5. Test scripts are generated in this step. The generation process is based on relations established between the user story specification (see Column 1 in Table 3) and UI widgets (see Column 2 in Table 3) and SikuliX code (see Column 3 in Table 3). It is possible to associate the UI concepts with the UI-Test framework syntax and some of the keywords made available in the menus and the user interface of the Notepad application (see Table 3).

Table 3. Elements and functions of SikuliX to save a file in Notepad (adapted from [7]).

Task Type from User Story	UI element	Generated Code
Start the application		Screen s=new Screen();
select/order/filter an option in the application	Button	s.click($locator)
	Element	
Edit a field text in the application	Text field	s.type($locator,"text");

3.2 Visual UI Testing

In this second stage, called visual UI testing, we define two steps which are described below:

Step 6. The elements and functions of SikuliX and the code to apply UI-based testing in an application (e.g. Notepad) in order to evaluate our proposal is written and shown in Fig. 9. We can use the Eclipse editor or any text editor to check this source code.

Firstly, SikuliX finds a text field button and writes "Notepad" and clicking "Enter". The process to do an action in the application is then started. In the excerpt of the source code shown in Fig. 9, we can see how the elements included in Table 3 are used. When the application is running and the user select the "File" option in the Notepad menu, the "Save" option is selected. The script identifies a text field in which the user types the file name. The last step is to click on the "Save" button. In the same figure, we can also see the sentence "s.wait(1.0)" which is equivalent to the time period to wait to load the application (e.g. Notepad) and that its interface is active and able to execute the tests on its elements.

```
public class Notepad {
    public static void main(String[] args) {
        Screen s = new Screen();
        s.click("file.png");// click file button
        s.click("save.png");// click save button
        s.find("textFiel.png"); // identify textFiel
        s.wait(1.0);// wait for 1 second to show results
        s.type("nameFile"); // write name file
        s.click("saveButton.png");
    }
}
```

Fig. 9. An excerpt from a source code to apply UI-based testing in Notepad.

Step 7. Once the script is completely filled in, the tests are run and the test results are displayed. In this test we select the "File" option, then click on the "Save" option to save a file in Notepad running in Microsoft Windows 10. We need to type the file name and then click on the "Save" button" to save the file on the hard disk of the computer. At the end, the test returned one result as expected and so the generated test suite could not find any faults (Fig. 10).

On the other hand, if the UI locator (image/text) cannot be found, SikuliX will stop the script by raising an Exception FindFailed, so that the test found a fault (Fig. 11).

There are several reasons why the exception will be triggered: (a) a UI locator of the interface is disabled, (b) the image of a UI locator included in the interface was not assigned correctly by the tester, or (c) the value of a variable has not been assigned. In all these cases, the tester needs to analyse the results to verify (i.e. detect test inconsistencies and problems) and validate (i.e., ensure that the customer requirements are correctly captured) the requirements specification.

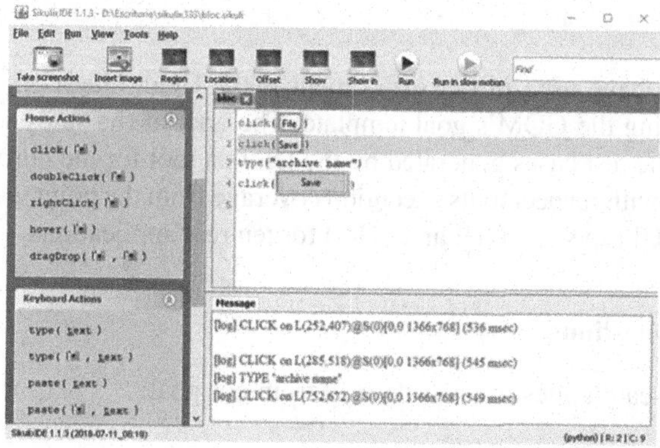

Fig. 10. Script text written in SikuliX to run the “Save” option in Notepad.

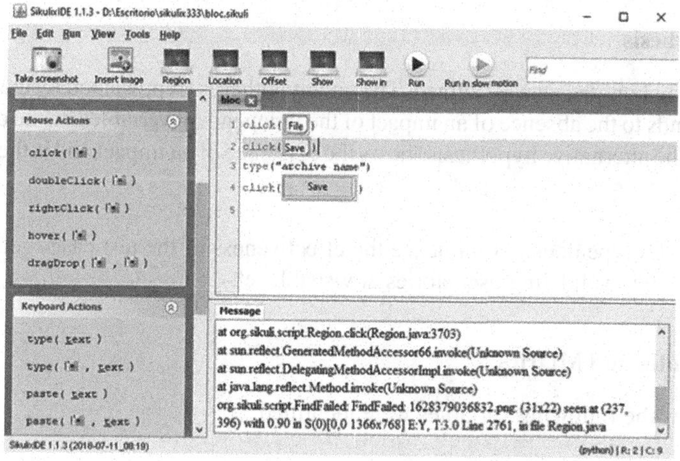

Fig. 11. Exception FindFailed when the test failed in SikuliX.

4 Quantitative Evaluation

Since the evaluation was motivated by the need to assess the effectiveness of the proposed framework for visual UI testing we conducted two evaluations, one qualitative and one quantitative. This first evaluation was a quasi-experiment carried out in June 2021. This section describes the goal of the study and the research questions, variables and metrics used, the analysed applications, and the experimental settings of the quantitative evaluation.

4.1 Goal

The approach we have used in our experiment is the Goal, Question, Metric (GQM) methodology. Using the GQM's goal template. The goal of the study is to analyse the effectiveness of the test cases generated by the UI-Test tool for the purpose of carrying out an evaluation with respect to its execution coverage from the point view of the testers in the context of UI type (i.e. GUI and WUI) for ten real applications.

4.2 Research Questions

The following research question was derived from our goal:

- **RQ1**: How does the UI type influence the effectiveness of the test cases generated by UI-Test tool when testing user stories at the visual level?

4.3 Hypothesis

The following hypothesis was defined. The null hypotheses (represented by the subscript 0) corresponds to the absence of an impact of the independent variables on the dependent variables. The alternative hypothesis shows the existence of an impact and is the expected result.

- $\mathbf{H_{10}}$: The UI type does not influence the effectiveness of the test cases generated by UI-Test tool in validating user stories at visual level.

4.4 Variables and Metrics

In this study, the following variables were identified:

a) **Independent Variables**
   - **Selected UI Type.** We considered two types of UI:

   – Windows-based UI (GUI): these applications can only be accessed from the system in which it is installed and has a graphical user interface.
   – Web-based UI (WUI): a web application that can be accessed from any system through the Internet browser.

b) **Dependent Variables and Metrics**
   The following dependent variable was considered and was expected to be influenced to some extent by the independent variable. In this study the effectiveness of the test cases generated by UI-Test tool when validating user stories in application UI is measured by:

- **Test Execution Coverage (TEC) Percentage.** This is also called the executed tests and is the percentage of passed/executed tests out of the total number of tests. The advantage of this metric is that it gives an overview of the testing progress by counting the number of passed and failed tests.

$$TEC = \frac{number\ of\ test\ cases\ run}{Total\ number\ of\ tests\ to\ be\ run} x100\% \tag{1}$$

4.5 Analysed Applications

Ten popular applications were used for this first study, which contains a variety of input widgets that can be tested at the UI level, including buttons, text fields, icons, menus, check boxes, and hyperlinks. We selected 5 applications with GUIs and 5 with WUIs (See Table 4).

Table 4. Widgets types of the selected applications.

Application	UI type	Button	Text field	Icon	Menu	Radio Button	Check Box	Hyper Link
App1: Eclipse is an open source platform with a set of programming tools.	GUI	✓	✓	✓	✓			✓
App2: Microsoft Word is an office suite.	GUI	✓	✓	✓	✓	✓	✓	✓
App3: Microsoft Excel is a spread-sheet.	GUI	✓	✓	✓	✓	✓	✓	✓
App4: Windows Calendar is a personal calendar application.	GUI	✓	✓	✓	✓			✓
App5: Windows Mail is an news-group and email client	GUI	✓	✓	✓	✓		✓	✓
App6: Youtube[a] is a website dedicated to sharing videos.	WUI	✓	✓	✓	✓			✓
App7: Google Translator[b] is a free service that translates words, phrases and web pages into more than 100 languages.	WUI	✓	✓	✓	✓			✓
App8: Netflix[c] is a streaming service.	WUI	✓	✓	✓	✓			✓
App9: Facebook[d] is a social network.	WUI	✓	✓	✓	✓			✓
App10: Instagram[e] allows users to edit and upload photos and videos.	WUI	✓	✓	✓	✓			✓

[a] https://www.youtube.com
[b] https://translate.google.com/
[c] https://www.netflix.com/
[d] https://www.facebook.com
[e] https://www.instagram.com/

4.6 Experimental Procedure

This section describes the details of the experimental setup including the applications used, instrumentation, data collection, and analysis. Figure 12 summarizes the experimental process, which involved the following eight steps:

Choose the Applications. The selected applications are described in Sect. 4.5. These applications are of different sizes and domains (e.g. email, social network, translator service, etc.). The applications are real cases and were selected because they contained the UI widgets required for using the UI-test tool.

Write the User Stories. For this phase we did a reverse process to what should be done normally. We select real applications already implemented and write user stories that describe how they work. 187 user stories were then randomly selected for our 10 selected applications. For each user story, a syntax analysis was performed by using the UI-Test parser to ensure that the user story was valid and could be used in the testing process. The reader is referred to URL (https://xurl.es/5un0l) for a more detailed information.

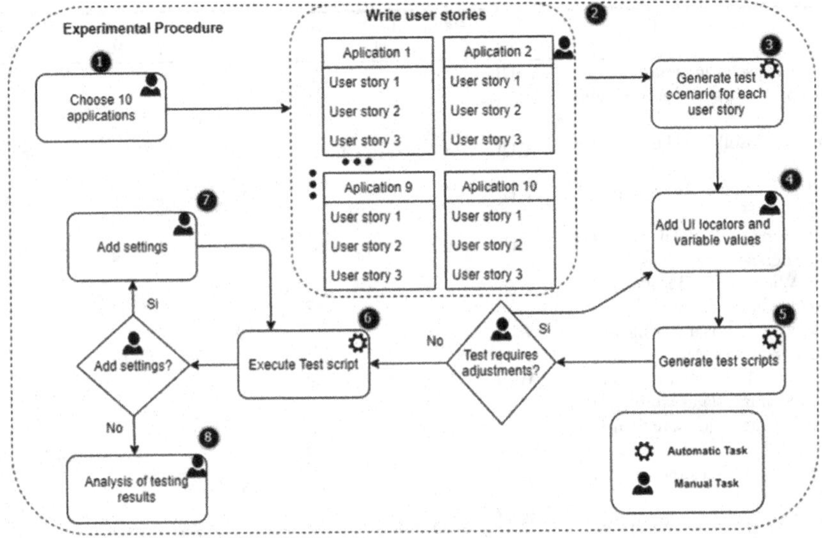

Fig. 12. Experimental procedure for measuring effectiveness of the UI-Test using 10 UIs.

Generate Test Scenarios. Each user story is transformed into an executable test script by using the respective UI-Test module (see Step 1 in Sect. 3.1).

Add UI Locators and Variable Values to Test Scripts. The values were specified manually for each test scenario.

Execute Test Scripts on Applications and Collect Data. Each test script was executed using the SikuliX tool. The status of the test scripts (i.e. passing/failing/not executable) were manually registered.

Analysis of Testing Results. Finally, the value of execution coverage of the UI-Test test scripts is calculated from the information recorded in the previous stage. These results are given in the next Section.

4.7 Analysis and Interpretation of Results

This section describes the analysis and interpretation of the results related to our response variable for RQ1. The Statistical analysis was carried out on the Statistical Package for Social Sciences (SPSS).

Since the first research question (RQ1) was aimed at evaluating the execution coverage of the UI-Test tests, we compared the number of tests that could be executed by UI type (i.e. GUI and WUI) in the different selected applications. Table 5 shows the number of the user stories used with the tool (column 2), and the rate and percentage of the execution coverage (columns 3 and 4) of the tests generated for each application.

Shapiro-Wilk tests were performed to evaluate the samples normality. We used this test as our numerical means of assessing normality because it is more appropriate for small sample sizes (<50 samples).

Table 5. Results of the coverage of the test script generated by UI-Test.

Software application	Selected user stories	Execution coverage	
		Rate	Percentage
App1	13	0.8	80%
App2	12	0.6	60%
App3	12	0.6	60%
App4	19	0.8	80%
App5	24	0.9	90%
App6	24	0.8	80%
App7	24	0.6	60%
App8	11	0.6	60%
App9	24	0.8	80%
App10	24	0.4	40%
Total	*187*		

Since all Sig. values for the Shapiro-Wilk tests were 0.201 for GUI and 0.314 for WUI (see Table 6). As these variables follow a normal distribution (>0.05), we considered both UI types as independent groups. The T-Student test was used to test the first null hypothesis (H10). Figure 13 shows the box-plot containing the execution coverage per UI type and Table 7 shows the mean and standard deviation.

Table 6. Tests of Normality for Execution Coverage metric.

	UI Type	Shapiro-Wilk		
		Statistic	df	Sig
Coverage	GUI	,852	5	,201
	WUI	,881	5	,314

Table 8 shows the results of the T-student test. We did not find a statistically significant difference between the execution coverage of GUIs (M = 0,74; DE = 0,13416) and WUIs (M = 0,64; DE = 0,16733) t(8) = 1,043, p = 0,328, d = 0.000659 and therefore accepted the null hypothesis H_{10}. In other words, with 95% confidence we can say that the median value of the rate of execution coverage is similar for both types of UI; $p = 0.728 > 0.05$.

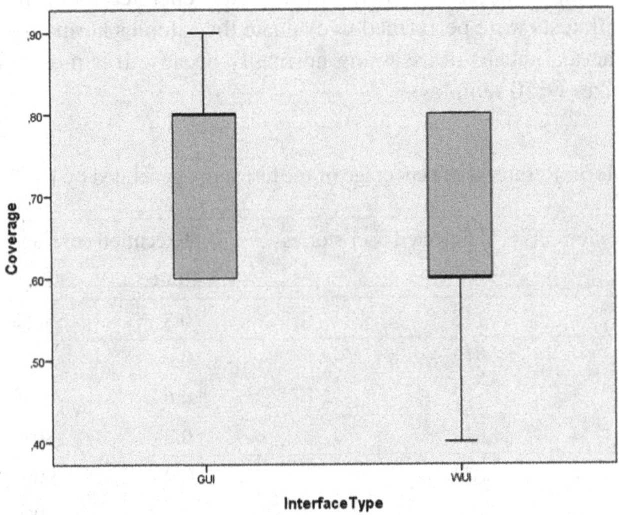

Fig. 13. Box-plot for execution coverage by UI type

Table 7. Group statistics for execution coverage

	UI Type	N	Mean	Std. Deviation	Std. Error Mean
Execution	GUI	5	.7400	.13416	.06000
Coverage	WUI	5	.6400	.16733	.07483

5 Qualitative Evaluation

Due to the COVID-19 pandemic, this study was conducted fully online. In this section, we present the design used for running a quasi-experiment.

Table 8. Hypothesis H01 test summary.

Independent Samples Test										
		Levene's Test for Equality of Variances		t-test for Equality of Means						
		F	Sig	t	df	Sig. (2-tailed)	Mean Difference	Std. Error Difference	95% Confidence Interval of the Difference	
									Lower	Upper
Execution	Equal variances assumed	.130	.728	1.043	8	.328	.10000	.09592	−.12118	.32118
Coverage	Equal variances not assumed			1.043	7.639	.329	.10000	.09592	−.12302	.32302

5.1 Goal

The goal of the study was to analyse the test suite generated by the UI-Test tool for the purpose of evaluating the perceived user experience of the tool from the point view of the academy in the context of UI testing activities.

5.2 Research Questions

From the above goal, the following research question was derived:

- **RQ2**: How was the user experience affected during testing tasks in UIs?

5.3 Hypothesis

The following hypothesis was defined.

- $\mathbf{H_{20}}$: The UI-test tool does not influence the participants' user experience.

5.4 Variables and Metrics

In this study, the following variables were identified:

a) **Independent Variables.**

  - **Selected GUI type**. As in the quantitative study, the independent variable was the type of application interface (i) GUI and (ii) WUI.

b) **Dependent Variables and Metrics.**
The following dependent variable was considered and was expected to be influenced to some extent by the independent variable.

User Experience. The short version of the questionnaire (UEQ-S) [21] was used for this variable. The questionnaire addresses two aspects in general, which are pragmatic quality aspects, i.e. they describe interaction qualities that are related to the tasks or objectives that the user intends to achieve when using the software product (in our case the UI-test), and hedonic quality aspects, i.e. they are not related to tasks and objectives, but rather describe aspects related to pleasure or fun while using the product.

5.5 Participants

The experiment involved 17 volunteer subjects (14 men and 3 women), who accepted an invitation to participate in the study. The participants ranged in age from 21 to 28 years old. Prior knowledge and experience in requirements eliciting and software testing were strict requirements, so that this competence was requested during registration for participation in the event.

5.6 Study Context

The study was carried out as part of an online course. An invitation was sent to Computer Science undergraduate students at the Universidad de Cuenca (Ecuador). The duration of the course was one hour. Although the course counted had 26 attendees, only 17 participated in the study (S1-S17 in Table 9).

5.7 Experimental Design

A between-subjects (or between-groups) study design was selected for the experiment, in which different people test each condition, so that each person is only exposed to a single type of UI.

5.8 Instrumentation

Questionnaire: We implement a web-based survey using Google Forms, which was composed of three sets of questions regarding:

- **Demographic Data:** Gender, range of age, educational background, and domain expertise.
- **User Experience (UE):** The shortened version of the questionnaire is made up of 8 pairs of opposite properties that the product (i.e. UI-test) may have [21]. The UEQ considers aspects of pragmatic and hedonic quality. For each of the adjectives, we used a 7-point Likert scale to measure the quality aspects, considering that the values 1, 2 and 3 corresponded to the adjective on the left, and the values 5, 6 and 7 to the adjective on the right. 4 meant a neutral value.
- **Tool Feedback:** A post-questionnaire that included an open question on how the tool could be improved.

UI Testing Tasks: The participants had to derivate and execute the test scripts in two UI: App1 (Windows notepad) which is a text editor included in Microsoft Windows operating systems, and App2 (i.e. Google translator). Following the testing task proposed in Sect. 3, each App has three user stories associated to be used with the UI-test tool. Each test scenario generated by the tool validates widgets in the corresponding application UI. After running the test scenarios with SikuliX, the tool displays the list of actions in the output windows that the test scenario executes. When the action could not be executed, the tool displays the exception in the output window. The participants then have to decide whether the test case passed, failed or had some other problem that did not allow it to run. Different defects such as incorrect appearance of widgets or incorrect state of widgets were injected into the test scenarios.

To carry out the study, we provided the participants with the following material: (i) a virtual machine for VirtualBox[3] with all the software required for the study, (ii) an installation and user guide, (iii) an example with four user stories to be used during the training phase, (iii) an instructional video, and (iv) a set of three user stories for each system used as App1 and App2.

5.9 Procedure

The procedure is shown in Fig. 14 and its 8 main stages are explained below.

Training Session: The details of the study were explained in the first session (15 min), a demonstration video was shown to the participants. As the UI-Test was a new tool for the participants, we gave training for about 30 min including instructions to configure the virtual machine and the execution of the tool testing process using a test App (i.e. user CRUD). We also ensured all the participants had uniform knowledge (e.g., someone could have been lost in the sequence of steps performed), so they were asked to reproduce the UI testing tasks in their own computers and to report their results or any problems that occurred.

[3] https://www.virtualbox.org/.

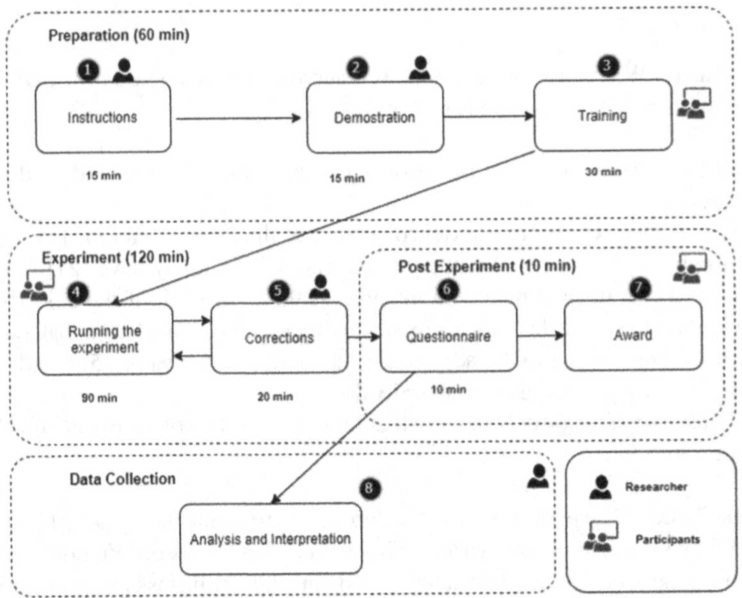

Fig. 14. Experimental procedure for measuring user experience.

Experimental Session: This stage takes about 120 min and its activities can be seen in the Experimental Session in Fig. 14. First, the details of the experiment were explained (10 min). Then, the participants were randomly divided into two groups (i.e. GUI and WUI groups) and the resources (e.g., user stories, description of the application) required for this session was delivered (20 min). All the participants derived the test models and test scripts of each application and executed them (see Subsect. 5.8 for more details regarding the testing tasks) (40 min). It is important to highlight that they were able to submit their results at any time within this stage. The corrections that had to be made were then indicated so that the test cases not executed could be carried out (20 min).

Post-experiment: After finishing the UI testing activity, the participants were asked to complete a brief demographic questionnaire (10 min), and give information on the UI-Test user experience and feedback for improving the tool (see Subsect. 5.8 for further details of the questionnaires). After processing all the participants' submissions, we rewarded the participants who completed all the activities.

Data Collection. The user experience values were calculated from the information recorded in this experiment. The results are given in the next Section.

5.10 Analysis and Interpretation of Results

This section describes the analysis and interpretation of the results related to our response variable for RQ2. As in the quantitative study, the statistical analysis was performed on SPSS software.

Since the second research question RQ2 was aimed at evaluating the user experience quality of the UI-Test, we compared the results of the questionnaire for UI type (i.e. GUI and WUI) in the different applications. Table 9 shows the value of this metric.

Table 9. User experience values collected by the questionnaire.

Subject ID	UI type	User experience		
		Pragmatic quality	Hedonic quality	Overall
S1	GUI	1.00	−0.50	0.25
S2	GUI	1.25	1.25	1.25
S3	GUI	2.00	3.00	2.50
S4	GUI	1.75	0.50	1.13
S5	GUI	0.50	2.50	1.50
S6	GUI	2.50	1.75	2.13
S7	GUI	3.00	3.00	3.00
S8	GUI	2.75	2.75	2.75
S9	WUI	2.50	0.75	1.63
S10	WUI	0.25	0.00	0.13
S11	WUI	1.25	1.25	1.25
S12	WUI	2.25	2.00	2.13
S13	WUI	1.00	1.00	1.00
S14	WUI	1.00	1.00	1.00
S15	WUI	0.25	0.00	0.13
S16	WUI	2.00	1.75	1.88
S17	WUI	1.00	1.25	1.13

The consistency of the pragmatic quality and hedonic quality scales was reasonably good. For GUI, the corresponding Cronbach Alpha values were 0.87 (pragmatic quality) and 0.77 (hedonic quality), and for WUI were 0.84 (pragmatic quality) and 0.65 (hedonic quality).

Shapiro-Wilk tests were performed to evaluate the samples normality. We used this test as our numerical means of assessing normality because it is more appropriate for small sample sizes (<50 samples).

Since all Sig. values for the Shapiro-Wilk tests were 0.767 for GUI and 0.471 for WUI (see Table 10), these variables follow a normal distribution (>0.05), so that we considered both GUI types as independent groups. The T-Student test was then used to test the second null hypothesis (H20).

Table 10. Tests of normality.

	UI type	Shapiro-Wilk		
		Statistic	df	Sig
User experience quality overall	GUI	.956	8	.767
	WUI	.929	9	.471

Figure 15 shows the box-plot containing the user experience values per UI type and Table 11 shows the means and standard deviation.

Table 12 shows the results of the T-student test, in which we did not find any statistically significant difference between the user experience of GUI (M = 1.81; DE = 0.94) and WUI (M = 1.14; DE = 0.69) t(15) = 1.69, p = 0.112, g = 0.820825.

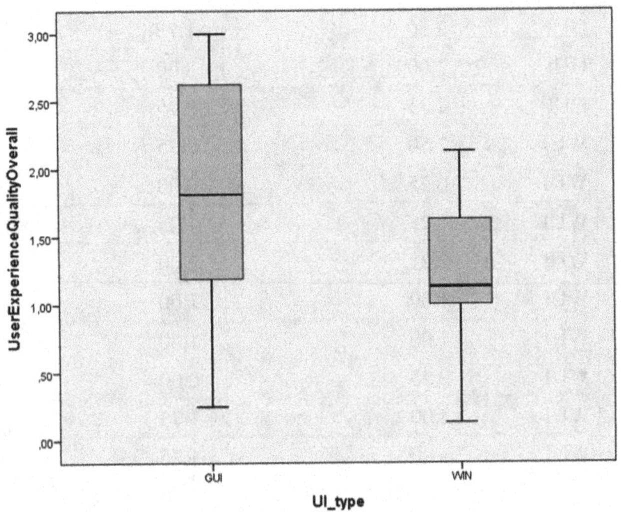

Fig. 15. Box-plot for user experience by GUI type

Therefore, we accepted the null hypotheses H_{20}. In other words, with 95% confidence we can say that the media value of the user experience quality is similar for both types of UI.

Table 11. Group statistics for user experience metric.

	UI_type	N	Mean	Std. Deviation	Std. Error Mean
User experience quality overall	GUI	8	1.8138	.93989	.33230
	WUI	9	1.1422	.69456	.23152

Table 12. Hypothesis H_{20} test summary.

Independent samples test										
		Levene's Test for Equality of Variances		t-test for Equality of Means						
		F	Sig	t	df	Sig. (2-tailed)	Mean Difference	Std. Error Difference	95% Confidence Interval of the Difference	
									Lower	Upper
User experience quality overall	Equal variances assumed	1.618	.223	1.689	15	.112	.67153	.39760	−.17594	1.51899
	Equal variances not assumed			1.658	12.805	.122	.67153	.40500	−.20478	1.54784

6 Discussion

The main results of the effectiveness of UI-Test test cases (RQ1) and the User Experience Quality (RQ2) are the following: although the GUI have a slightly better value than the WUI, we can confirm that the UI type does not influence the analysed variables.

Most of generated test scripts (>60%) allowed to find inconsistencies between the requirements that were elicited (i.e. user story) with they that were actually implemented as widgets for both types of UI (i.e. GUI and WUI). These results suggest that user stories show potential to be used as source for generating test scripts and using them in Visual UI testing with the UI-test tool.

However, it was also found that there are issues that require manual intervention by the tester to be resolved and make the test scripts executable, as explained in Table 13.

From these results, while preliminary, suggest the necessity of doing more research with more applications and user stories that allow evaluating the scalability of the framework and proposed tool support.

In addition, we applied the user experience questionnaire (UEQ) to measure the subjective impression of users towards the user experience of the framework and tool. From these results, we can see a good overall evaluation (1,81 for GUI; 1,14 for WUI). However, a better value was achieved in the pragmatic than hedonic aspects, which indicates that it possible improve in how the product (i.e. framework and tool support) catches the user's attention and interest. That is, making it more interesting and stimulating for users.

These positive results were reinforced by the qualitative feedback obtained during the post-study. Some participants considered that UI-Test was useful and interesting, since it allowed them to perform early testing tasks. However, some consider it necessary to improve the ease of use of the tool, especially when adding UI locators and variable values to test scripts.

Table 13. Some issues found in test scripts that prevented their execution.

Issue	Description	Possible solution
ISSUES FOUND IN BOTH TYPES OF UIs: GUI AND WUI		
Incorrect appearance of widgets	It is not possible to click on a button/icon since it is not recognized	Capture the widget image again
Incorrect data type or format in a text field	A text field accept a data type different from the one entered	Change the value of the variable
Incorrect state of widgets	It is not possible to click on a button/icon since it is not activated/visible	Specify previous actions to get the button to activate/visible
ISSUES FOUND IN WUIs		
Missing widget	Delay in loading the web page	Add a wait time to click on the widget
Missing widget	Need to use scrolling before clicking on the widget	Add scroll command with SikuliX code
ISSUES FOUND IN GUIs		
Missing widget	It is required to manipulate several menus and submenus to access the widget	Add the actions required to access the widget through the menus and submenus

7 Threats to Validity

There are several threats that potentially affect the validity of our experiments including threats to internal validity, threats to external validity, and threats to construct validity.

Internal Validity. This validity is related to subjects and measurements in the experiment that could affect the observed variables. As the subjects in our experiment might have had different prior knowledge of the tools before the experiment, we tried to minimize this threat by training them to homogenize their knowledge and experience. We also identified experiment settings as a possible threat; which we mitigated by performing the experiment in similar conditions for each participant (i.e., material, testing tasks). For example, the settings of the required tools (i.e., UI-Test, Concur Task Tree and SikuliX) were predefined on the virtual machine to simplify the software installation. However, even though we notified the participants one week before the experiment, 9 subjects did not download the virtual machine and thus did not participate in the experiment.

External Validity. This issue is about the generalization of our results; possible threats could be the selection of subjects and selected applications. With respect to the participants (i.e. final-year computer science students) as experimental subjects, several authors suggest that the results can be generalized to industrial practitioners [22]. However, one of the major limitations of this study was that there were few participants, so, further empirical research is needed to confirm the results. With respect to the selected applications, this threat was reduced by using ten real applications of different sizes (see Sect. 4.5), domains (e.g. social network, services, mail) that contained the different UI widgets required for this study.

Construct Validity. Threats to construct validity refer to the suitability of our evaluation metrics and selected instruments. However, we used well-known metrics to measure the execution coverage of the test scripts generated by the UI-Test. Regarding to User Experience quality, participants filled it out in their native language (i.e. Spanish). Also, we used an inter-item correlation analysis to evaluate its construct validity (see Subsect. 5.10). We therefore believe there is little threat to the construct validity.

8 Conclusion and Future Work

This paper proposes a model-based framework toward generating executable test cases for UIs to assure that the functionality specified in the requirements specification is performed through the different UI actions of the application. Also, in this research work, two research approaches were used to evaluate the framework and proposed the UI-Test tool. First, through a quantitative evaluation, we measured the effectiveness of the test scripts generated by the tool. Second, using a qualitative evaluation, the subjective impression of users towards the user experience of the framework and tool was measured.

The test script effectiveness was calculated based on the execution coverage of the test cases generated (i.e. the rate of number of tests executed) for both types of UI (i.e. GUI and WUI). From the results, the effectiveness of the tests was not affected by the UI type. These results suggest that the UI-Test tool can benefit testers by validating that the actions proposed in the user stories can be run on the application UI.

Regarding to user experience quality, we found that most of our participants agreed in considering the UI-Test tool as good quality for user experience. As one of the major limitations of this study was that there were few participants, further empirical research is needed to identify features of test scripts that would lead to improved effectiveness. We also intend to replicate this experiment on a wide variety of subjects and applications to confirm the results.

This automatic test case generation framework will help to reduce the effort needed, improving the quality test cases and the coverage of the requirements by the test cases generated from user stories. This research work can be applied in development projects using Agile methodologies for testing their software products.

Acknowledgments. This work has been supported by the Dirección de Investigación de la Universidad de Cuenca (DIUC) – Ecuador.

References

1. Al-Saqqa, S., Sawalha, S., Abdelnabi, H.: Agile software development: methodologies and trends. Int. J. Interact. Mob. Technol. **14**(11), 246–270 (2020)

2. Cohn, M.: User Stories Applied for Agile Software Development. Pearson Education Inc., Boston (2004)
3. Alfraihi, H., Lano, K., Kolahdouz-Rahimi, S., Sharbaf, M., Haughton, H.: The impact of integrating agile software development and model-driven development: a comparative case study. In: Khendek, Ferhat, Gotzhein, Reinhard (eds.) SAM 2018. LNCS, vol. 11150, pp. 229–245. Springer, Cham (2018). https://doi.org/10.1007/978-3-030-01042-3_14
4. Grangel, R., Campos, C.: 'Agile model-driven methodology to implement corporate social responsibility. Comput. Ind. Eng. **127**, 116–128 (2019)
5. De Lucia, A., Qusef, A.: Requirements engineering in agile software development. J. Emerg. Technol. Web Intell. **2**(3), 212–220 (2010)
6. Mori, G., Paternò, F., Santoro, C.: CTTE: support for developing and analyzing task models for interactive system design. IEEE Trans. Softw. Eng. **28**(8), 797–813 (2002)
7. Granda, M., Parra, O., Alba-Sarango, B.: Towards a model-driven testing framework for GUI test cases generation from user stories. In: Proceedings of the 16th International Conference on Evaluation of Novel Approaches to Soft. Engineering (ENASE 2021), pp. 453–460 (2021)
8. Wautelet, Y., Heng, S., Kolp, M., Mirbel, I.: Unifying and extending user story models. In: Jarke, M., et al. (eds.) CAiSE 2014. LNCS, vol. 8484, pp. 211–225. Springer, Cham (2014). https://doi.org/10.1007/978-3-319-07881-6_15
9. Lelli, V., Blouin, A., Baudry, B.: Classifying and qualifying GUI defects. In: 2015 IEEE 8th International Conference on Software Testing, Verification and Validation, ICST 2015 - Proceedings (2015)
10. Alégroth, E., Feldt, R., Ryrholm, L.: Visual GUI testing in practice: challenges, problems and limitations. Empir. Softw. Eng. **20**(3), 694–744 (2015)
11. Rane, P.P., Martin, T.L., Harrison, S.R., Abbott, A.L.: Automatic generation of test cases for agile using natural language processing (2017)
12. Elghondakly, R., Moussa, S., Badr, N.: 'Waterfall and agile requirements-based model for automated test cases generation. In: ICICIS, pp. 607–612 (2015)
13. Finsterwalder, M.: Automating acceptance tests for GUI applications in an extreme programming environment. In: XP, pp. 114–117 (2001)
14. Tao, C., Gao, J., Wang, T.: An approach to mobile application testing based on natural language scripting. In: SEKE 2017, vol. 1, pp. 260–265 (2017)
15. Ramler, R., Klammer, C., Wetzlmaier, T.: Lessons learned from making the transition to model-based GUI testing. In: A-TEST, pp. 22–27 (2019)
16. Medhat Kamal, M., Darwish, S.M., Elfatatry, A.: Enhancing the automation of GUI testing. In: ICSIE 2019, no. 1, pp. 66–70 (2019)
17. Coppola, R., Morisio, M., Torchiano, M.: Maintenance of android widget-based GUI testing: a taxonomy of test case modification causes. In: Proceedings of 2018 IEEE 11th International Conference Software Testing, Verification Validation Working ICSTW 2018, pp. 151–158 (2018)
18. Silva, J., Campos, J., Paiva, A.: Model-based user interface testing with spec explorer and ConcurTaskTrees. Electron. Notes Theoret. Comput. Sci. **208**, 77–93 (2008)
19. Bass, L., Bergey, J., Clements, P., Merson, P., Ozkaya, I., Sangwan, R.: A comparison of requirements specification methods from a software architecture perspective, Technical report C. ESC-TR-2006-013 (2006)
20. Brüning, J., Forbrig, P.: TTMS: a task tree based workflow management system. In: Halpin, T., et al. (eds.) BPMDS/EMMSAD -2011. LNBIP, vol. 81, pp. 186–200. Springer, Heidelberg (2011). https://doi.org/10.1007/978-3-642-21759-3_14

21. Schrepp, M., Hinderks, A., Thomaschewski, J.: Design and evaluation of a short version of the user experience questionnaire (UEQ-S). Int. J. Interact. Multimed. Artif. Intell. **4**(6), 103 (2017)
22. Runeson, P.: Using students as experiment subjects–an analysis on graduate and freshmen student data. In: 7th International Conference on Empirical Assessment & Evaluation in Software Engineering, pp. 95–102 (2003)

Author Index

Al Mahmud, Abdullah 29
Alba, Bryan 328
Alkubaisy, Duaa 67
Al-Obeidallah, Mohammed Ghazi 67
Aloui, Nadia 112
Andrianjaka, Rapatsalahy Miary 156
Ayed, Nourchène Elleuch Ben 112

Borchert, Angela 88
Borredà, Carles 213

Chua, Caslon 29
Cox, Karl 67

Dewam, Agrim 132
Dioşan, Laura 3
Dobrean, Dragoş 3

Gambo, Ishaya 183
García S., Alberto 213
Gonzalez-Ibea, Daniel 213
Granda, Maria Fernanda 328
Grundy, John 44, 241

Hajarisena, Razafimahatratra 156
Heisel, Maritta 88

Ibanez, Victoria 213
Iñiguez-Jarrín, Carlos 213

Javed, Muhammad Atif 309
Jim, Aria YukFan 44

Kanij, Tanjila 44, 241
Kanwal, Samina 309
Kapur, Ritu 132
Khalajzadeh, Hourieh 44, 241
Khlif, Wiem 112
Krämer, Nicole 88

Lopez, Oscar Pastor 213

Madugalla, Anuradha 241
Martin-Rodilla, Patricia 265
McIntosh, Jennifer 241
Mihaela, Ilie 156
Molnar, Arthur-Jozsef 288
Motogna, Simona 288
Mouratidis, Haralambos 67
Mueller, Ingo 241
Mühlhäuser, Max 88
Muram, Faiz Ul 309

Obie, Humphrey O. 241

Parapar, Javier 265
Parra, Otto 328
Pérez-Román, Estela 213
Piot-Perez-Abadin, Paloma 265
Piras, Luca 67

Raft, Razafindrakoto Nicolas 156
Rao, Poojith U. 132
Razanakolona, Livaniaina 156

Shim, Hyun 44
Sodhi, Balwinder 132
Sorin, Ilie 156
Suciu, Dan Mircea 288

Talón, Manuel 213
Taveter, Kuldar 183
Terol, Javier 213
Thomas, Mahatody 156

Wainakh, Aidmar 88
Wang, Jue 44
Wijaya, Lionel Richie 44

Xu, Rongbin 44

Yalamu, Philemon 29

Printed in the United States
by Baker & Taylor Publisher Services